T0305754

The Competitiveness of Nations 1

Navigating the US–China Trade War
and the COVID-19 Global Pandemic

The Competitiveness of Nations: Theory and Practice

Series Editors: Dong-sung Cho *(The Institute for Industrial Policy Studies, South Korea and Seoul National University, South Korea)*
Hwy-chang Moon *(The Institute for Policy & Strategy on National Competitiveness, South Korea and Seoul National University, South Korea)*

Published:

The Competitiveness of Nations 1: Navigating the US–China Trade War and the COVID-19 Global Pandemic
by Dong-sung Cho and Hwy-chang Moon

The Competitiveness of Nations: Theory and Practice

The Competitiveness of Nations 1
Navigating the US–China Trade War and the COVID-19 Global Pandemic

Dong-sung Cho
The Institute for Industrial Policy Studies, South Korea
Seoul National University, South Korea

Hwy-chang Moon
The Institute for Policy & Strategy on National Competitiveness, South Korea
Seoul National University, South Korea

NEW JERSEY · LONDON · SINGAPORE · BEIJING · SHANGHAI · HONG KONG · TAIPEI · CHENNAI · TOKYO

Published by

World Scientific Publishing Co. Pte. Ltd.

5 Toh Tuck Link, Singapore 596224

USA office: 27 Warren Street, Suite 401-402, Hackensack, NJ 07601

UK office: 57 Shelton Street, Covent Garden, London WC2H 9HE

Library of Congress Cataloging-in-Publication Data

Names: Cho, Tong-sŏng, author. | Mun, Hwi-chʻang, author.

Title: The competitiveness of nations. 1, Navigating the US-China trade war and the COVID-19 global pandemic / Dong-sung Cho, The Institute for Industrial Policy Studies, South Korea Seoul National University, South Korea, Hwy-chang Moon, The Institute for Policy & Strategy on National Competitiveness, South Korea Seoul National University, South Korea.

Description: New Jersey : World Scientific, [2022] | Series: The competitiveness of nations: theory and practice | Includes bibliographical references and index.

Identifiers: LCCN 2021052473 | ISBN 9789811261138 (hardcover) | ISBN 9789811261145 (ebook) | ISBN 9789811261152 (ebook other)

Subjects: LCSH: Competition, International.

Classification: LCC HF1414 .C56 2022 | DDC 338.6/048--dc23/eng/20211228

LC record available at https://lccn.loc.gov/2021052473

British Library Cataloguing-in-Publication Data

A catalogue record for this book is available from the British Library.

For any available supplementary material, please visit
https://www.worldscientific.com/worldscibooks/10.1142/12989#t=suppl

Desk Editors: Aanand Jayaraman/Yulin Jiang

Typeset by Stallion Press
Email: enquiries@stallionpress.com

Printed in Singapore

About the Authors

Dong-sung Cho is Professor Emeritus and former Dean of the College of Business Administration at Seoul National University. After he received a DBA degree from Harvard Business School in 1976, he worked at Boston Consulting Group in Tokyo and Gulf Oil Corporation in Pittsburgh before joining Seoul National University. He has been a visiting professor at Harvard Business School, University of Michigan, Boston University, Duke University, INSEAD, Helsinki School of Economics (currently Aalto University), University of Sydney, the University of Tokyo, and Peking University. He spent a year as Research Fellow at the Institute for Strategy and Competitiveness, HBS. He has published research articles and monographs on the Mechanism-Based View, the semiconductor industry, the general trading company, and national competitiveness. He is a frequent speaker at international conferences such as Davos Forum, World Knowledge Forum, and QS Conference. He is Chairman of the Board of Inspection, Supreme Prosecutors' Office in the Republic of Korea and Honorary Consul General of Finland in Korea. He served as the President of Incheon National University from 2016 to 2020. He is the Second President of Hanseatic League of Universities which is a society of 120+ universities around the world. He is also on the top in the list of "Representative Management Gurus" in Korea.

Hwy-chang Moon (Ph.D. from University of Washington) is Professor Emeritus and former Dean in the Graduate School of International Studies at Seoul National University. Professor Moon is currently the Chairperson of the Institute for Policy and Strategy on National Competitiveness

(IPSNC) in Seoul, Korea, a consultant to United Nations Conference on Trade and Development (UNCTAD), and an Honorary Ambassador of Foreign Investment Promotion for South Korea. He has been frequently invited to deliver lectures at several universities including Stockholm University and Helsinki School of Economics (currently Aalto University) in Europe, Keio University and Beijing Normal University in Asia, and The State University of New York at Stony Brook and Stanford University in the US. He has conducted many consulting/research projects for multinational companies (e.g., Samsung Electronics), international organizations (e.g., UNCTAD), and governments (e.g., Korea, Malaysia, Dubai, Azerbaijan, Guangdong Province of China, and India). For interviews and debates, he has been invited by international newspapers and media, including New York Times, NHK World TV, and Reuters. He has published numerous articles and books, including *The Strategy for Korea's Economic Success* (2016, Oxford University Press) and *The Art of Strategy: Sun Tzu, Michael Porter, and Beyond* (2018, Cambridge University Press).

About the Contributors

Pınar Büyükbalcı is an Associate Professor at Yıldız Technical University — Department of Business Administration, Istanbul. Her research spans entrepreneurship (international entrepreneurship, entrepreneurial ecosystems, subsidiary level entrepreneurship), innovation strategies, and multinational network structure. She has active affiliations with several NGOs, business associations, and Science Parks in Turkey to support ongoing entrepreneurship projects. She is a Fulbright Scholar, British Academy fellow and a member of the Academy of International Business. She also acts as the board member and vice president of two research centers at Yildiz Technical University.

Minji Hong, Eunwon Shim, and Jungbin Yun are researchers at the Institute for Policy and Strategy on National Competitiveness (IPSNC) in Seoul, Korea. IPSNC conducts global competitiveness research, particularly by integrating different perspectives from East and West, to help the government and business leaders around the world gain a better understanding of national and corporate competitiveness.

Vimala Asty F. T. Jaya is a Policy Analyst at the Bureau for Foreign Technical Cooperation, Ministry of State Secretariat of the Republic of Indonesia. Her main roles are to manage, implement, and evaluate Indonesia's South–South Cooperation programs and to provide policy analysis and recommendation on Indonesia's development cooperation. She has a Master of Arts in International Development Policy from Seoul National University (SNU) — Korea and a Bachelor of Economics from

Bogor Agricultural University. Her research interests are development cooperation, international relations, and international development economics.

Evodio Kaltenecker (orcid.org/0000-0002-6431-5007) holds a BA in engineering from the Military Institute of Engineering (Brazil), a master's degree in Industrial Engineering from the Federal University of Rio de Janeiro (Brazil), an MBA from the Harvard Business School (USA), and a Ph.D. from the University of Sao Paulo (USP, Brazil). He occupied several senior positions at multinational companies and currently holds the positions of international faculty both at the Tecnologico de Monterrey (Mexico). Additionally, he has taught in MBA and Executive MBA programs in several universities around the world, such as MCI and Vienna University of Economics and Business (Austria), Stellenbosch University (South Africa), Fundacao Dom Cabral (Brazil), Trinity Business School Ireland), and BBS Business School (Angola), to name a few. He is also a research fellow at the Emerging Markets Institute at the Cornell University and is a member of Mexico's National Research System. He can be contacted at kaltenecker@tec.mx.

Damir Kušen is Croatia's first Ambassador to the Republic of Korea. Previously, he served as Ambassador to Australia and New Zealand, to Finland and Estonia, as Deputy Ambassador in Washington, DC, and as diplomat in London. He held various high-level positions at the Croatian Ministry of Foreign Affairs. Ambassador Kušen holds a PhD in Mediterranean Studies from King's College London, as well as an MA in Diplomacy from Westminster University, a BA in Psychology from Zagreb University, and has completed an Executive Education Program at Harvard University's John F. Kennedy School of Government. Ambassador Kušen is a regular speaker on international affairs, business, competitiveness, technology, and innovation at numerous international conferences and seminars, as well as guest lecturer at various universities in the US, Croatia, Finland, Australia, New Zealand, and the Republic of Korea. He was also an Elected Member of the Canberra Innovation Network — Advisory Group, and an Honorary Member of the Graduate Union of the University of Melbourne.

Tae-Shin Kwon has been Vice Chairman and CEO of the Federation of Korean Industries or the FKI since 2017. Mr. Kwon has served as

President of the Korea Economic Research Institute since 2014. He has built most of his career in the Korean government. From 2011 to 2013, he was Vice Chairman of the Presidential Council on National Competitiveness. From 2009 to 2010, he served as the Minister of Government Policy Coordination. From 2006 to 2008, he served as Ambassador, Permanent Representative of Korea to the OECD, in Paris, right after he worked for the Ministry of Finance and Economy as Vice Minister from 2005 to 2006. In 2004, Mr. Kwon was appointed as Secretary to the President for Economic Policy. Mr. Kwon was appointed as Deputy Minister for International Affairs of the Ministry of Finance and Economy right after his service as Director-General for International Finance of the Ministry in 2003. He has worked for the Korean government over 35 years since he joined the Ministry of Finance and Economy in 1977. Mr. Kwon received a BA degree from Seoul National University (1972), an MA degree in Economics from Vanderbilt University (1982), and an MBA degree from CASS Business School, UK (2001).

Kirankumar S. Momaya (momaya@iitb.ac.in) earned his PhD from the University of Toronto and is currently a Professor of Competitiveness at Indian Institute of Technology Bombay, Mumbai, India. He has been working on practices related to competitiveness since the start of his PhD research related to competitiveness in the early 1990s. He has guided several PhDs on competitiveness or related topics of international business (IB), management of technology and innovation (MoT), and Strategy. He has undertaken consulting or research projects for several international companies or organizations (including ministries in India and Japan). He serves on Board of Directors of IAMOT, USA and SINE, the Business Incubator of IIT Bombay that has nurtured more than 150 start-ups. He is a rare academic to have published popular articles in each of the leading journals of management in India (e.g., *IIMB Management Review*, *Vikalpa*, *JFSM*) and leading competitiveness or related journals of Europe or North America or Asia. He has authored or edited (singly or jointly) four books and published more than 60 articles in refereed national and international journals, and many articles for leaders in industry. He can be reached at momaya@iitb.ac.in.

Miguel A. Montoya (orcid.org/0000-0002-5545-6334) has a B.A. in Economics, a master's degree and a Ph.D. in Applied Economics at the Universidad Autonoma de Barcelona, Spain. Currently, he is Professor in the Tecnologico de Monterrey. He is a Regular Member in the Mexican Academy of Sciences, also he is part of the National Council for Technology and Science, Academy of International Business, and Academy of Management, among others. He has published articles in academic journals and book chapters and he has participated in different academic conferences. Dr. Montoya teaches courses of International Economics and International Business at Tecnologico de Monterrey and, as a visitor professor, at Moore School of Business (University of South Carolina, USA), ESAN (Peru), Universidad de San Francisco de Quito (Ecuador), Instituto Ortega y Gasset (Spain), Burdeaux School of Business, and Montpellier Business School (France). His areas of interest are multinational companies (multimexicanas) and business for BoP.

Jeongmin Seo and Aejung Kwon are researchers at the Institute for Policy and Strategy on National Competitiveness (IPSNC) in Seoul, Korea. IPSNC conducts global competitiveness research, particularly by integrating different perspectives from East and West, to help the government and business leaders around the world gain a better understanding of national and corporate competitiveness.

Miranda Tahalele is a Faculty Member at Department of International Relations - Faculty of Humanities, Bina Nusantara (BINUS) University, Jakarta-Indonesia. She holds a Ph.D. in Anthropology (Development Studies) from the Australian National University (ANU), an MA in Peace Studies (Conflict Resolution) from the University of Bradford, UK, and a Bachelor of International Relations from Parahyangan Catholic University, Indonesia. She has previously worked as a development practitioner with UNDP, the Search for Common Ground (SFCG), and the Centre for East Indonesian Affairs (CEIA), and as a development cooperation consultant for the Ministry of National Development Planning (BAPPENAS) and the Ministry of Women Empowerment and Child Protection (MOWE-CP) of the Government of Indonesia.

Francisco J. Valderrey (orcid.org/0000-0002-7160-8836) completed a BA at the University of Houston, Texas, a master's degree in International Management from Thunderbird, Arizona, and a Ph.D. in Administration and Marketing from the University of Valencia, Spain. Francisco Valderrey occupied several positions at multinational enterprises and was a co-founder of a technology company in California. Eventually, he joined

Tecnologico de Monterrey, first as a professor and finally as a degree program director for international business in Mexico. Presently he is a full-time research professor at Campus León. He has also been teaching international business courses at universities in Europe and Asia. He has co-authored two books in marketing. His research focuses primarily on The New Silk Road and China's Latin America presence, with different publications. Other lines of research include multiculturalism and digital business transformation. He is a member of Mexico's National Research System. He can be contacted at francisco.valderrey@tec.mx.

Christoph A. von Arb is President and Founder of Swiss-based International Initiatives Inc. — TRIPLEYE, a private consulting firm with a focus on Education, Research, and Innovation at the interface between industry, academia, and government and he serves as Executive Vice President of Strategic Development and International Outreach at Franklin University, Switzerland. In the late 1990s, he negotiated Switzerland's participation in the EU-Research Framework Programs. From 2002 to 2008, Dr. von Arb was Consul General and Director of the world's first Digital Science Consulate — swissnex — in Boston, a novel concept of Diplomacy based on public–private partnership, which he initiated while he was Head of International Affairs in the Ministry of Science. Dr. von Arb is assisting start-ups, acts as an advisor of university presidents, and serves on various boards of R&D organizations. He received his PhD in Plant Molecular Biology in 1984 from the University of Berne.

Wenyan Yin (Ph.D.) is Assistant Professor at Seoul School of Integrated Sciences and Technologies (aSSIST) and Lecturer in the Graduate School of International Studies at Seoul National University. She also serves as Consultant to UNCTAD of the United Nations. She has published a number of articles including those in the journals indexed by SSCI, A&HCI, and SCOPUS. Her research areas are global value chain, foreign direct investment, international business strategy, and national competitiveness. She has also conducted many research projects related to the international competitiveness and foreign direct investment for firms and governments.

Feihu Zheng is currently Associate Professor in the international economics department of Business School, Beijing Normal University

(BNU). He is also the executive director of the International Industrial Cooperation and Innovation Center of BNU and was a visiting scholar for Haas, UC Berkeley in 2012. His research interests include family firm governance, open innovation, and MNC outsourcing. His research articles were published in *Journal of Knowledge Management, Technology Analysis & Strategic Management, World Economy, Nankai Economy Studies*, etc. His recent academic books include *Super-Ownership Advantages and Risk Governance of Firm's International Investment* (2019) and *Super-Ownership Advantages and Study of OBOR Investment Strategy* (2017).

Acknowledgments

We would like to extend thanks to Korea Trade-Investment Promotion Agency (KOTRA) for their continuous support. It was through their extensive global network that we were able to reach out and collect survey data from more than sixty economies. We would especially like to thank our research team who spent countless hours gathering information and working on this manuscript. Special thanks to Dr. Wenyan Yin, who has made enormous contributions in terms of providing feedback for improvements and organizing this project from the beginning to the end. Minji Hong also offered crucial assistance in organizing and editing the manuscript as well as helping with the timely completion of this project. Additionally, Jeongmin Seo, Aejung Kwon, Jungbin Yun, and Eunwon Shim all provided valuable inputs for the chapters on special topics. We would like to further extend our thanks to Stephen Ranger for his valuable comments and editing which helped to improve the manuscript. We also offer our appreciation to all the authors of the invited chapters for the country-level case studies. For the publication of this book, we are particularly grateful to John Stuart, Yulin Jiang, Aanand Jayaraman, and other colleagues at World Scientific who recognized the value of this book and provided many insightful suggestions.

Contents

Introduction

Free trade, global value chain, and offshoring are no longer new economic concepts. The rapid globalization throughout the 1990s and 2000s has allowed countries around the world to take comparative advantage and maximize their profits by producing goods at the lowest cost. This trend has been challenged in recent years most notably by the COVID-19 global pandemic as well as the rise in protectionism that has disrupted globalization. In response, some commentators have begun to forecast a trend of "deglobalization" as they have recognized the "fragility of global supply chains" in the wake of the pandemic (Bloomberg, 2020). With growing uncertainty on which country will have to bear the cost of the pandemic, the reliance on other countries has not been appreciated in recent times. Instead, it is "becoming a source of fear" as many have argued (Bloomberg, 2020).

The pandemic has disrupted not just the physical supply chains but also the trust among countries. As a result, some countries have moved to establish barriers among themselves, while others have sought to move their production facilities inward, which has led to new interest in establishing a self-reliant economy. This will be a development that could threaten the old trend of economic integration.

Given this context, it is worth paying attention to the current trend of globalization by revisiting the sources of national competitiveness and the impact of internationalization on national competitiveness. This book discusses the theoretical background of national competitiveness as well as its policy implications. Overall, it seeks to discover a sustainable strategy for countries to gain international competitiveness.

Volatility, Uncertainty, Complexity, and Ambiguity

The term volatility, uncertainty, complexity, and ambiguity (VUCA) that is used to describe unstable geopolitical conditions after the Cold War has now been stretched to describe a rapidly changing business environment (Murugan *et al.*, 2020). The term VUCA is pretty self-explanatory, which refers to a situation where there is not much information about the issue which creates a high level of uncertainty. The COVID-19 pandemic is prominent example of VUCA as many businesses are struggling to adopt a new strategy to cope with the instability and uncertainty derived from it (Fenews, 2021). The surge of an unexpected number of cases each day marks the "volatility"; the lack of information on the nature and treatment of COVID-19 indicates the "uncertainty"; the unclear understanding of transmission routes and exact symptoms represents the "complexity"; the fact that there is no definite "best strategy" for the successful containment of the virus highlights very much the "ambiguity" of the issue (Murugan *et al.*, 2020).

In the face of the VUCA situation amid the COVID-19 pandemic, many countries have been pursuing more nationalist policies toward their economy. As these countries are facing uncertainty amidst the prolonged crisis, what has been understood as economically effective strategies such as offshoring or establishing global value chains are no longer considered to be "safe" options. Indeed, the spread of the pandemic accelerated the disruption of an already chaotic trade order — due to the growing trade war between the US and China — as the COVID-19 pandemic brought back an "everyman-for-himself" mentality (Riecke, 2020).

Prior to the COVID-19 pandemic — before the fragility of economic integration was revealed — the opportunities derived from economic integration were believed to exceed the costs (or risks), and therefore the trend of globalization was sustained. However, the situation with the pandemic has exposed the fragility of globalization. Some even claimed that "we have perhaps gone too far in globalization" (Business Standard, 2020). For instance, many European companies had to bear the cost of the disruption of the supply chain when the supply of critical components for pharmaceutical products was delayed as the operation of key production units were shut down in China, India, and Latin American countries (Raconteur, 2020). As the fragility unfolded and many witnessed the incapacity to maintain the production facility when the global value chain was disrupted, countries began to reevaluate the costs and opportunities of globalization.

Economic Nationalism

Economic nationalism aligns with the current context of deglobalization; some countries are prioritizing the national interest over the economic benefit by rather intervening in the free economies and practicing protectionism. The following examples outline the practice of nationalist policies around the world.

Protectionist measures

In 2018, US President Trump raised tariffs to 25 percent on $200 billion worth of Chinese goods; in response, China imposed tariffs on $110 billion worth of US products (Amadeo, 2021). This dispute between the US and China accelerated the already slowing globalization (CNN, 2019). In fact, President Biden has not moved far away from this protectionist approach as he extended Trump's protectionist policies such as the imposition of tariffs on metal imports, and issued the "Buy American" executive order to incentivize American citizens to purchase domestic electric cars (Vox, 2021).

As the US has been imposing restrictions on the access of Chinese technology firms to the international market (the US itself makes up a large part of the global economy), President Xi Jinping has responded with a new strategy, "domestic circulation," which prioritizes domestic consumption over overseas investments (*Wall Street Journal*, 2020). Both approaches and measures taken by the US and China are clear representations of the deglobalization — or the slowbalization — trend that has been taking place in recent years.

Self-reliant economy

Derived from the idea to create a self-reliant (or self-sufficient) economy, many countries are putting efforts to strengthen their domestic economies to make them less vulnerable to external factors such as global pandemics. In this context, China recently announced its plan to boost the reconstruction of its economic structure: from the export-oriented (and trade-dependent) economy to a domestic consumption-driven economy (The News Lens, 2020). Although this is not the first time for China to strengthen its domestic economy, the COVID-19 pandemic, as well as tensions with the US, certainly did accelerate the pace of shift to an economy driven by domestic consumption. At the same time, China is seeking opportunities to establish a self-sufficient technology base by injecting massive investment to "support the rollout of everything from wireless networks to massive data centers" (The News Lens, 2020).

Reshoring

Throughout the pandemic, many politicians have raised concerns about globalization, more specifically that of outsourcing: Germany's Chancellor Angela Merkel echoed this by asking "how can we withstand a crisis like this if we don't even have local production of face masks, surgical gloves, and pharmaceutical inputs?" (Norberg, 2021). This worry about the lack of production facilities for medical supplies links with the concern of producing agricultural and manufacturing products which may have fueled the trend of deglobalization (Norberg, 2021). The idea of "resource nationalization[1]" has arisen to allow constant access to the resources so that the production lines in countries will not be vulnerable to the difficulties in other places (Jstor Daily, 2021). Hence, the notion of international cooperation seemed to have faded away during the course of the pandemic. In this respect, it triggered a new trend of reshoring the production facilities of necessity products such as medical supplies — as mentioned previously — perhaps, this is the trend that is not just limited to necessity goods.

Significance of Internationalization on Sustainable National Development

Many countries are currently striving for a strategy to enhance domestic competitiveness over an international one. However, the significance of gaining international competitiveness by strengthening overall national competitiveness should not be undermined. This book argues both domestic and international competitiveness are crucial for countries to gain national competitiveness; thus, it shows that it is not the best decision to prioritize the domestic economy while neglecting the international dimension of the economy.

---

[1] Resource nationalization "includes encouraging vertical integration in industries, investing in strategic stockpiling and even reimposing export quotas, tariffs and stronger licensing" (Jstor Daily, 2021).

Limitations of economic nationalism

Although COVID-19 may have induced many countries to realize the fragility of global value chains, a number of cases also depict the weakness of a self-reliant strategy. The trade war between the US and China as well as that between Japan and Korea are examples that display the limitations of economic nationalism. The former was triggered by the US imposition of tariffs on Chinese products in order to reduce the trade deficit and retain (manufacturing) job positions in the US (Brookings, 2020). However, this only imposed a negative spillover on both countries as the trade tension between the two countries "resulted in a sharp decline in bilateral trade, higher prices for consumers, and trade diversion effects[2]" (UNCTAD, 2019). Similarly, the trade dispute between Japan and South Korea was initiated in 2018 as Japanese firms refused to comply with Korea's Supreme Court order to compensate Koreans who had been used as forced labor by Japan during World War II (BBC, 2019). In response to the rejection by Japanese firms to provide compensation, consumers in Korea announced a boycott of Japanese products; in 2019, Japan announced the removal of Korea's "favored trade partner status" along with the imposition of export restrictions (BBC, 2019). Thus, by examining these two cases, it is reasonable to conclude that economic nationalism (or protectionism) often comes with the spillover of economic loss. Although protectionist policies may buffer the damage on the domestic economy in the short run, it is always significant to evaluate the long-term consequence on economic growth.

In the end, globalization allows countries to enjoy a comparative advantage by specializing in the productions while producing at the best efficiency. Although globalization presents social costs, such as uneven development (McMillan and Rodrik, 2011) or risks like vulnerability to external factors, on the whole it provides economic efficiency. Hence, when it comes to the discussion of whether the pandemic triggers the reverse of globalization or deglobalization, it becomes highly uncertain whether the advantage of establishing a self-sufficient economy is great enough to give up the opportunities to produce the best efficiency.

---

[2]The trade diversion effect refers to a situation where trade is diverted "from a more efficient exporter toward a less efficient one by the formation of a free trade agreement"; in the context of the US–China trade war, there has been an increase in "imports from countries not directly involved in the trade war" (UNCTAD, 2019; UNESCWA, 2021).

Thus, this book identifies the discrepancy between the theories of national competitiveness and the policies implemented in reality that could affect national competitiveness. This book aims to discover sustainable development strategies to enhance national competitiveness. To this end, this book is composed of three parts and fifteen chapters.

The first part of the book introduces the theoretical framework and reports the key research findings of national competitiveness. It is composed of five chapters: "Extant Literature on National Competitiveness and Major Issues," "Highlights of IPS National Competitiveness Research 2021," "Conceptual Framework and Analytical Methodologies," "Application of MASI: The Case of Republic of Korea," and "Snapshot of Top 30 Economies." The first one "Extant Literature on National Competitiveness and Major Issues" points out the limitations of traditional models and the necessity to extend the model to better evaluate national competitiveness. "Highlights" introduces the key rankings of IPS National Competitiveness Research 2021, including overall rankings, intra-group rankings, simulation rankings based on cost and differentiation strategy, and the changing pattern compared to the previous year. Following this, "Conceptual Framework and Analytical Methodologies" presents the methodology for evaluating and analyzing the national competitiveness while "Application of MASI: The Case of Republic of Korea" shows the case study of Republic of Korea (hereafter Korea) by applying the methodology introduced previously. Finally, "Snapshot of Top 30 Economies" analyzes various (social, political, and economic) factors that have positively or negatively influenced national competitiveness.

The second part of this book deals with the two critical issues impacting upon the world — "Current Issues in China and their Implications for China's Competitiveness" and "Building Resilient Global Value Chains in the Post Pandemic Era: A Conceptual Framework and Case Studies of Singapore and Vietnam." The former analyzes the three major issues in China: the US-China trade war, the Belt and Road Initiative (BRI), and the national security law in Hong Kong SAR (hereafter Hong Kong). Throughout the discussion on each topic, the authors raise crucial implications for China. Following this, "Building Resilient Global Value Chains in the Post-Pandemic Era: A Conceptual Framework and Case Studies of Singapore and Vietnam," stresses the growing trend of protectionism among many countries during the COVID-19 pandemic in particular; this chapter establishes the conclusion that despite various challenges of globalization, firms need to continually pursue globalization during and after the pandemic, by reconfiguring their GVCs to build more resilient ones. Specifically, this chapter suggests four strategies to achieve this goal. Moreover, the authors introduced two exemplary countries, Vietnam and Singapore that have achieved economic success by adopting open door policies, and how they have taken actions to move up their respective position when hosting the value chain activities of MNCs.

The third part is composed of eight chapters on various cases by invited authors. These can be further categorized into four topics: digitalization, the role of government, business ecosystem and innovation, and cooperation with other institutions. Two chapters addressing "digitalization" include Chapter 8 that highlights the role of digital ventures in leading to the transformation of the digital economy in Turkey and Chapter 9 that signals the need for incorporating digital innovations in mental health treatment in Croatia. Another two chapters are focused on the role of government in influencing national competitiveness. Chapter 10 discusses the significance of political factors in evaluating the national competitiveness of Mexico and Brazil. For its part, Chapter 11 establishes three key conditions required to enhance national competitiveness in Korea. The following two chapters emphasize the significance of business ecosystem and innovation. Chapter 12 addresses the significant role of start-ups (and emerging technologies) in enhancing India's national competitiveness while Chapter 13 pinpoints China's economic policies to adopt open innovation as a key component of its economic success. The last two chapters emphasize the cooperation with other institutions by addressing the specific example of South–South Cooperation (SSC) policy in Chapter 14 and the key role of higher education to establish a connection between innovators (or scholars) and the market in creating market value in Chapter 15.

References

Amadeo, K. 2021. President Donald Trump's economic plans and policies. The balance. https://www.thebalance.com/donald-trump-economic-plan-3994106. Accessed May 7, 2021.

BBC. 2019. South Korea and Japan's feud explained. https://www.bbc.com/news/world-asia-49330531.

Bloomberg. 2020. How the coronavirus is accelerating deglobalization. https://www.bloomberg.com/news/newsletters/2020-02-29/why-deglobalization-is-accelerating-bloomberg-new-economy.

Brookings. 2020. More pain than gain: how the US–China trade war hurt America. https://www.brookings.edu/blog/order-from-chaos/2020/08/07/more-pain-than-gain-how-the-us-china-trade-war-hurt-america/#.

Business Standard. 2020. Indians must replace imported products, become 'vocal for local': PM Modi. https://www.business-standard.com/article/current-affairs/indians-must-replace-imported-articles-become-vocal-for-local-pm-modi-120122700242_1.html.

CNBC. 2019. The escalating dispute between Tokyo and Seoul is already affecting businesses. https://www.cnbc.com/2019/07/31/japan-korea-trade-dispute-can-hurt-businesses-and-the-global-economy.html.

CNN. 2019. America-first trade policy is crushing the global economy. https://edition.cnn.com/2019/09/01/perspectives/trade-protectionism-us-trump/index.html.

Deseret News. 2021. Who will get the third Pfizer shot first? https://www.deseret.com/coronavirus/2021/5/6/22420758/third-pfizer-covid-shot-eligibility.

Fenews. 2021. Volatility, uncertainty, complexity and ambiguity, how to plan for the world of the future. https://www.fenews.co.uk/fevoices/66344-volatility-uncertainty-complexity-and-ambiguity-how-to-plan-for-the-world-of-the-future.

Irwin, D. A. 2020. The pandemic adds momentum to the deglobalization trend. Peterson Institute for International Economics. https://www.piie.com/blogs/realtime-economic-issues-watch/pandemic-adds-momentum-deglobalization-trend.

Jstor Daily. 2021. Semiconductor shortages end an era of globalization. https://daily.jstor.org/semiconductor-shortages-end-an-era-of-globalization/.

McMillan, M. S. and D. Rodrik. 2011. Globalization, structural change and productivity growth. National Bureau of Economic Research. https://www.nber.org/papers/w17143.

Murugan, S., S. Rajavel., A. K. Aggarwal., and A. Singh. 2020. Volatility, uncertainty, complexity and ambiguity (VUCA) in context of the COVID-19 pandemic: challenges and way forward. *International Journal of Health Systems and Implementation Research* 4(2): 10–16.

Norberg, J. 2021. Covid-19 and the danger of self-sufficiency: how Europe's pandemic resilience was helped by an open economy. European Centre for International Political Economy. https://ecipe.org/publications/covid-19-and-self-sufficiency/.

OECD. 2020. Investment screening in times of COVID-19 and beyond. https://www.oecd.org/coronavirus/policy-responses/investment-screening-in-times-of-covid-19-and-beyond-aa60af47/.

Raconteur. 2020. Could reshoring help manufacturers survive COVID? https://www.raconteur.net/supply-chain/reshoring-manufacturing-covid/.

Riecke, T. 2020. Covid-19 causes a new wave of economic nationalism. Mercator Institute for China Studies. https://merics.org/en/analysis/covid-19-causes-new-wave-economic-nationalism.

The News Lens. 2020. Covid-19 is accelerating China's economic self-reliance. https://international.thenewslens.com/article/137204.

Wall Street Journal. 2020. China's Xi speeds up inward economic shift. https://www.wsj.com/articles/chinas-xi-speeds-up-inward-economic-shift-11597224602.

UNCTAD. 2019. Trade war leaves both US and China worse off. https://unctad.org/news/trade-war-leaves-both-us-and-china-worse.

UNESCWA Trade diversion. https://www.unescwa.org/trade-diversion. Accessed May 11, 2021.

Vox. 2021. Biden's America First hangover. https://www.vox.com/policy-and-politics/22408089/biden-trump-america-first-policy-immigration-vaccines.

Part I

IPS National Competitiveness Research 2021

The first part of this book[1] introduces the theoretical framework of national competitiveness and reports its key research findings. It is composed of five chapters: "Extant Literature on National Competitiveness and Major Issues," "Highlights of IPS National Competitiveness Research 2021," "Conceptual Framework and Analytical Methodologies," "Application of MASI: The Case of Republic of Korea," and "Snapshot of Top 30 Economies."

The chapter, "Extant Literature on National Competitiveness and Major Issues" points out the limitations of the traditional measurements for national competitiveness (e.g., single diamond model), addressing the need to extend the existing models to better evaluate national competitiveness. The following chapter, "Highlights of National Competitiveness Research," introduces the key rankings of IPS National Competitiveness Research 2021, including overall rankings, intra-group rankings, simulation rankings based on cost and differentiation strategy. It also highlights the year-over-year changing patterns and shows a categorization of 62 economies from advancers, ordinaries, and laggers, which facilitates the readers to grasp the overall picture of each economy's competitiveness index through the relative comparison. Following this, "Conceptual Framework and Analytical Methodologies" presents the methodology for

---

[1] This book is authored by Dong-sung Cho and Hwy-chang Moon, except for the chapters in Parts II and III where the chapter authors are specified.

evaluating and analyzing the national competitiveness through the comparison of methodologies of other two renowned institutions, the Institute for Management Development (IMD) and the World's Economic Forum (WEF), which also release the annual competitiveness rankings and reports. The chapter "Application of MASI: The Case of Republic of Korea" demonstrates the application of the previously introduced methodologies for measuring national competitiveness with Korea's case study. This chapter discusses the strengths, as well as the weaknesses, of Korea, thus it suggests in which area Korea should further strengthen to gain overall national competitiveness. Finally, "Snapshot of Top 30 Economies" verifies the validity of the 2021 National Competitiveness Rankings by analyzing various (social, political, and economic) issues that may influence positively or negatively each economy's national competitiveness.

Chapter 1

Extant Literature on National Competitiveness and Major Issues*

Definition of National Competitiveness

Competitiveness is, in fact, an intricate term. National competitiveness has been conceptualized and measured in many ways (Berger, 2008; Fainshmidt *et al.*, 2016). Preceding studies have utilized national export performance (Grein and Craig, 1996), national productivity (Scott, 1985; Porter, 1990; Moon *et al.*, 1998), firm-level foreign sales (Rugman *et al.*, 2012), and industry-level performance (Sakakibara and Porter, 2001; Pajunen and Airo, 2013) to measure national competitiveness. However, despite the diverse approaches adopted by the previous studies, many tend to solely focus on productivity as the primary indicator of national competitiveness (Fainshmidt *et al.*, 2016).

From the perspective of productivity, the most popular definition of competitiveness at the national level can be found in the Report of the President's Commission on Competitiveness, written for the Reagan administration in 1984:

> A nation's competitiveness is the degree to which it can, under free and fair market conditions, produce goods and services that meet the test of international markets while simultaneously expanding the real incomes of its citizens. Competitiveness at the national level is based on superior productivity performance.

---

*This chapter is abstracted and extended from Cho and Moon (2013).

Such views have been echoed by other scholars. For example, Porter (1990, p. 6) maintained that the only meaningful concept of competitiveness at the national level is national productivity. Krugman (1994) stated that competitiveness would turn out to be an odd way of saying productivity and would have nothing to do with international competition. However, competitiveness and productivity are conceptually different (Moon, 2010). A nation can sometimes enhance its competitiveness by simply altering strategies (e.g., protectionism or currency devaluation), without any increase in productivity.

Productivity refers to the internal capability of an organization, while competitiveness refers to the relative position of an organization against its competitors. These two important concepts are often confused and used interchangeably. The relative competitive position in the international market, not just the absolute amount of productivity, is the critical element for a nation's competitiveness. Another important point in defining a nation's competitiveness is that it is more meaningful to compare nations with similar comparative advantages competing in similar industries (Cho and Moon, 1998). Therefore, a nation's competitiveness can now be defined as a nation's relative competitive position in the international market among nations in a similar situation. In this regard, our study — IPS National Competitiveness Research — measures rankings among similar nations (or intra-group rankings) as well as overall rankings among all economies for evaluation.

Krugman (1994), however, argued that making decisions purely based on competitiveness poses three dangers. First, it could result in increasing government expenditure on enhancing national competitiveness. Second, it could trigger protectionism and trade wars. Finally, it could lead to undesirable public policies. By pointing out these three perils, Krugman warned that an obsession with competitiveness could be dangerous. Contrary to this, other scholars such as Thurow (1992) argued this is not always wrong or dangerous. They argued a passion for building a world-class economy in generating a high living standard for citizens is what all countries should seek to achieve. In doing so, benchmarking is not to declare economic warfare on foreign competitors but to emulate them and elevate a country's standards of performance. Therefore, despite all these threats, we need to develop a theory to explain what competitiveness is because it is essential to every nation.

Traditional Model and Limitations

Research on national competitiveness began in the early 1980s, but the theoretical background is based on many important concepts of works from traditional economists and trade theories that were previously proposed.

Mercantilism viewed trade as a zero-sum game in which a trade surplus of one country is offset by a trade deficit of another country. The essence of mercantilism was well explained by Thomas Mun (1571–1641), who was director of the British East India Company and a principal mercantile theorist. To accumulate national wealth, Mun advised the government to encourage domestic production, prohibiting imports, and subsidize exports. A tax policy is often utilized to achieve the mercantilist goals by lowering taxes for exports and imposing high tariffs on imports.

Adam Smith, however, criticized the view of trade as a zero-sum game. In contrast, he viewed trade as a positive-sum game in which all trading partners can benefit. Smith argued that there are advantages of specialization by regions and nations. In this respect, Smith showed how each nation would be far better off economically by concentrating on what it could do best rather than following the mercantilist doctrine of national self-sufficiency.

There was a problem with Adam Smith's theory of absolute advantage. According to Smith, a superior country might gain no benefits from international trade. In contrast, according to David Ricardo, the superior country should specialize in production where it has the least absolute disadvantage, which came to be known as the theory of comparative advantage. One important implication of this theory is that even if a country did not have an absolute advantage in any good, this country and other countries would still benefit from international trade. This theory is thus very useful in explaining the reasons why trade may happen and how trade increases the welfare of the trading partners. However, this model is incomplete, and one of the critical limitations is that it does not satisfactorily explain why the differences in productivity levels between countries exist.

Heckscher and Ohlin (HO) explained that comparative advantage arises from differences in factor endowments. The HO model highlights that a country will have a comparative advantage in some productions, and therefore will export these goods at which that country is relatively well endowed to produce. The logic is that the more abundant a factor is, the lower its cost. The HO model is referred to as the neoclassical theory of international trade, and it contains several appealing elements; it is simple, logical, commonly understood, and appears to be virtually self-evident.

Leontief (1953), however, found a paradoxical result. He expected that the United States (US) as the most capital-abundant country in the world, should export capital-intensive goods and import labor-intensive goods; but in reality, the US imports goods that required more capital per worker than its export goods. This finding was the opposite of what the HO model predicted and later became well known as the Leontief Paradox. Many economists, including Leontief, have attempted to explain this.

Vernon's (1966) product cycle is one of the typical attempts to explain the Leontief Paradox. Vernon argued that many manufactured goods go through a product cycle of introduction, growth, maturity, and decline. Thus, comparative advantages of these goods shift over time from one country to another. The product cycle model is useful in reconciling the Leontief Paradox. Suppose the US has a comparative advantage in new manufactured products. The production method of these new products may be quite labor-intensive because investment in fixed capital is not likely to occur at this stage. Thus, US exports tend to be labor-intensive. When the product becomes standardized, producers become familiar with efficient engineering and receives market feedback. A large amount of fixed capital can now be invested; the production process may thus be quite capital-intensive. The Leontief Paradox can be reconciled because US exports in the introducing stage where the production is labor-intensive and imports in the maturing stage where the production is capital-intensive.

We have discussed traditional trade theories, which are all still relevant. They remain useful in understanding many of today's industrial and trade policies. For example, the theory of comparative advantage is a basic guideline for many countries when they consider industrial and trade policies. Even mercantilism, a popular theory before Adam Smith's absolute advantage theory, seems to gain popularity among many leading developed and developing countries. Still, no single theory is sufficient to explain the current flows of international trade because today's world is more complicated than before.

Traditional trade theorists argue that national competitiveness is a function of capital, labor, and natural resources. However, many developed countries, such as Western European countries and Japan, have prospered without abundant natural resources, and many resource-rich countries like Latin American countries are not as developed. On a similar note, developed countries usually have expensive labor cost while less developed countries have cheaper costs. Thus, it is fair to say that the reality is almost the opposite of what traditional theorists have predicted.

As Porter (1990) mentions in his book, the traditional model whose origins date back to Adam Smith and David Ricardo and that is embedded in classical economics, is at best incomplete and at worst incorrect. Other economists see national competitiveness as a macroeconomic or financial phenomenon. They suggest that cheap currencies and balanced budgets enhance competitiveness. Despite this, there are many cases where nations have prospered despite appreciating currencies and budget deficits.

Since the 1980s, the argument that competitiveness is driven by government policies or influenced by different types of management practices was favored by many scholars. But, once again, the counter-examples to this were discovered as some countries succeeded without direct government intervention in which the government's role has been only modest. Moreover, different industries require different approaches to management, which calls for a new national competitiveness model.

Porter's (1990) Diamond Model and Limitations

There are two prerequisites for a good competitiveness theory. One is that the theory should be comprehensive enough to capture more than one variable, such as natural resources or labor, to explain the ever-increasing complexity of the real world. The other is that the theory should be dynamic enough to explain the changing nature of national competitiveness; this condition has not been effectively fulfilled by the classical theories such as absolute advantage and comparative advantage principles. Porter's Diamond Model satisfies both of these conditions. The model consists of four comprehensive variables: factor conditions, demand conditions, related and supporting industries, and firm strategy, structure, and rivalry. In addition, Porter demonstrated that the Diamond Model is dynamic by arguing that national prosperity is created, not inherited. This implies that national competitiveness does not grow out of resource endowments or currency value, as traditional models suggest, but it can be created by strategic choices based on the four determinants of the Diamond Model (see Figure 1).

Factor conditions: The nation's strong position in factors of production, such as skilled labor or infrastructure, is necessary to compete in a given

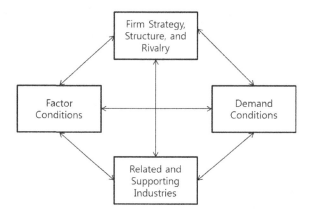

Figure 1. The Diamond Model.

Source: Porter (1990).

industry. Basic factors, such as a pool of labor or a local raw-material source, do not necessarily place the nation in an advantageous setting in knowledge-intensive industries, as firms can access them easily through globalization or overcome such shortages via technology development. In the sophisticated industries that form the backbone of any advanced economy, a nation does not inherit, but instead creates, the most important factors of production — such as skilled human resources or a scientific base. These specialized and created factors are scarce and more difficult for foreign firms to imitate.

Demand conditions stress the nature of home-market demand for the industry's product or service. Nations gain competitive advantages in industries where the home demand gives the firms a clearer or earlier picture of emerging buyer needs, and therefore the demanding buyers pressure companies to innovate faster than their foreign rivals. In this factor, the size of home demand proves far less significant than the sophistication or quality of home demand.

Related and supporting industries represent the presence or absence in the nation of supplier industries and other related industries that are internationally competitive. A far more significant factor than mere access to components and machinery is the advantage derived from home-based related and supporting industries, which provide innovation — an advantage based on close working relationships. Suppliers and end-users located near each other can take advantage of short lines of communication, a quick and constant flow of information, and an ongoing exchange of ideas and innovations.

Firm strategy, structure, and rivalry: This factor refers to the nation's governance conditions related to how companies are created, organized, and managed, as well as the nature of domestic rivalry. No one managerial system is universally accepted. Competitiveness in a specific industry results from a convergence of the management practices and organizational modes favored in the country and the sources of competitive advantages in the industry. Porter particularly emphasized the presence of strong local rivals as a powerful stimulus to the creation and persistence of competitive advantage. Domestic rivalry creates pressure on companies to innovate and constantly upgrade the sources of competitive advantage.

Since the introduction of the Diamond Model in 1990, it has been widely used in analyzing the strength of a single, or a few countries to suggest ways to pursue further development (Fainshmidt *et al.*, 2016). For example, this model was used in the analysis of New Zealand (Crocombe *et al.*, 1991), Turkey (Oz, 2002), the United Kingdom (UK) (Porter and Ketels, 2003), Ireland (Clancy *et al.*, 2001), Mexico (Hodgetts, 1993), and China (Karjula, 2013). Results from many of the studies have confirmed the validity of Porter's idea on the competitive advantage of nations and the strengths of major industries (Kharub and Sharma, 2017). Nonetheless, Porter's Diamond Model is not free from criticism.

Grant (1991) argued that most of the existing studies adopted a case approach, much in line with Porter's original approach, although such an approach may lack accuracy and generalizability. Rigorous examinations of the Diamond Model have been rare, and there have been few empirical attempts that support a broad assortment assortment of national outcomes (Fainshmidt *et al.*, 2016). For example, Greign and Craig (1996) found a positive relationship between factor conditions and GDP per capita, but no similar support from the other three diamond factors. However, these criticisms are mainly about the limitations of the quantification and operational problems of the Diamond Model, rather than the problem of the model itself.

Regarding the criticism on the conceptual framework, many scholars have argued that although Porter's single diamond includes several important variables, it is not comprehensive enough to be used in explaining the increasingly complex economies of today. The following section will discuss the main limitations of a Single Diamond Model and the extended models proposed by latter scholars.

Extended Models

Some international business scholars have criticized that the Diamond Model mainly focuses on home country factors for the sources of national competitiveness, and ignores the role of multinational activities and influences on the competitiveness enhancement. The single diamond is not so relevant in small economies because their domestic variables are very limited (Rugman, 1991) and its geographical constituency has to be established on a very different criteria (Dunning, 1993). In the era of globalization, international factors must be considered to appropriately assess a nation's competitiveness. To solve this problem, the Double Diamond Model (Rugman and D'Cruz, 1993) and the Generalized Double Diamond Model (Moon *et al.*, 1998) have been proposed (see Figure 2).

The Double Diamond Model, developed by Rugman and D'Cruz (1991), suggests that managers build upon both domestic and foreign diamonds to become globally competitive in terms of survival, profitability, and growth. While Rugman and D'Cruz's North American diamond framework fits well for Canada and New Zealand, it does not carry over

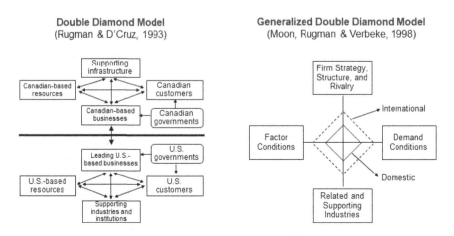

Figure 2.   Double Diamond Model and Generalized Double Diamond Model.

to other small nations relying on integration with other (foreign) countries for access to international resources, such as Korea and Singapore. Thus, Moon *et al.* (1995, 1998) adapted the double diamond framework to a generalized double diamond, which works well for analyzing small economies.

Furthermore, the Single Diamond Model does not distinguish human factors from physical factors. Porter duly explains the sources of national competitiveness possessed by the economies of advanced nations but is limited in its applicability when explaining the levels and dynamic changes of economies in less developed or developing countries. For this matter, Cho (1994) proposed the Nine-factor Model by incorporating the role of human factors, which was not explicit in Porter's Diamond Model (see Figure 3). In this model, the human factors include workers, politicians and bureaucrats, entrepreneurs, and professionals; physical factors include endowed resources, domestic demand, related and supporting industries, and other business environments. An external factor, chance, was added to these eight internal factors to make a new paradigm, the

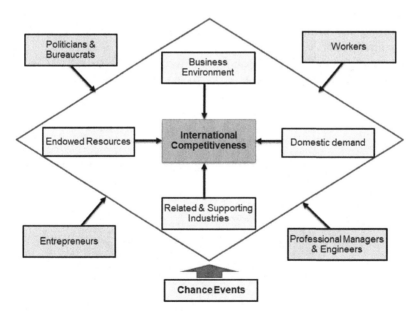

Figure 3. Nine-factor Model.

Source: Cho (1994).

Nine-factor Model. The human factors in the Nine-factor Model drive the national economy forward by creating, motivating, and controlling the four physical factors in Porter's Diamond Model. Human factors mobilize the physical factors, and the countries combine and arrange the physical factors with the aim of obtaining international competitiveness. The role of human factors is particularly important in developing countries because physical factors are not sufficiently developed at this stage.

These two models, double diamond and nine factor, are meaningful as they extended the scope and sources of national competitiveness. However, they need to be incorporated into a single framework in order to analyze and explain national competitiveness more thoroughly. The IPS report incorporates both of these extensions into a single framework or IPS model (see Figure 4), which analyzes national competitiveness by physical factors and human factors in terms of the domestic and international context. This model thus is very useful in explaining the development pattern and sources of competitiveness for large and small countries as well as both developed and developing economies. Cho *et al.* (2009) have empirically tested the explanatory power of the IPS model. The results showed that the IPS model is more comprehensive than the Generalized Double Diamond and Nine-factor Models in explaining the country-specific advantage of nations with heterogeneous attributes.

In addition to the above-extended models, theoretical extensions have been largely absent to date, as Porter's original model continues

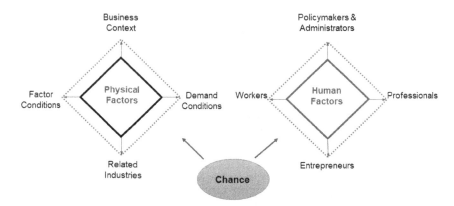

Figure 4.   IPS model.

to be criticized for its overly home country orientation and oversight of the direct influences of national institutions (Fainshmidt *et al.*, 2016). More recently, Fainshmidt *et al.* (2016), suggested two additional variables including multinational firm and governance quality, to enhance the explaining power of Porter's Diamond Model. However, such an attempt overlapped with the above-mentioned extended models, such as Moon *et al.* (1998), Cho, (1994), and the IPS model (2013). Therefore, to the best of our knowledge, the IPS model is the most comprehensive model among the extended models of Porter's single diamond, and this further provides the legitimacy of adopting the IPS model in the analysis and evaluation of national competitiveness in our research.

References

Berger, T. 2008. Concepts on national competitiveness. *Journal of International Business and Economy* 9(1): 3–17.

Cho, D. S. 1994. A dynamic approach to international competitiveness: The case of Korea. *Journal of Far Eastern Business* 1(1): 17–36.

Cho, D. S. and H. C. Moon. 1998. A nation's international competitiveness in different stages of economic development. *Advances in Competitiveness Research* 6(1): 5–19.

Cho, D. S. and H. C. Moon. 2013. *From Adam Smith to Michael Porter: Evolution of Competitiveness Theory* (extended edition). Singapore: World Scientific Publishing.

Cho, D. S., H. C. Moon, and M. Y. Kim. 2009. Does one size fit all? A dual double diamond approach to country-specific advantages. *Asian Business & Management* 8(1): 83–102.

Clancy, P., E. O'Malley, L. O'Connell, and C. van Egeraat. 2001. Industry clusters in Ireland: An application of Porter's model of national competitive advantage to three sectors. *European Planning Studies* 9(1): 7–28.

Crocombe, F. T., M. J. Enright, and M. E. Porter. 1991. *Upgrading New Zealand's Competitive Advantage.* Auckland: Oxford University Press.

Dunning, J. H. 1993. Internationalizing Porter's diamond. *Management International Review* 33(2): 7–15.

Fainshmidt, S., A. Smith, and W. Q. Judge. 2016. National competitiveness and Porter's diamond model: The role of MNE penetration and governance quality. *Global Strategy Journal* 6: 81–104.

Grant, R. M. 1991. Porter's competitive advantage of nations: An assessment. *Strategic Management Journal* 12(7): 535–548.

Grein, A. F. and C. S. Craig. 1996. Economic performance over time: Does Porter's diamond hold at the national level? *International Executive* 38(3): 303–322.

Hodgetts, R. M. 1993. Porter's diamond framework in a Mexican context. *Management International Review* 33: 41–54.

Karjula, H. 2013. Finnish cleantech SMEs in China: Challenges and solutions. https://www.utupub.fi/handle/10024/90767. Accessed March 4, 2021.

Kharub, M. and R. Sharma. 2017. Comparative analyses of competitive advantage using Porter diamond model: The case of MSMEs in Himachal Pradesh. *Competitiveness Review* 27(2): 132–160.

Krugman, P. R. 1994. Competitiveness: A dangerous obsession. *Foreign Affairs* 73(2): 28–44.

Leontief, W. 1953. Domestic production and foreign trade: The American capital position re-examined. *Proceedings of the American Philosophical Society* 97: 331–349.

Moon, H. C. 2010. *Global Business Strategy: Asian Perspective*. Singapore: World Scientific Publishing.

Moon, H. C., A. M. Rugman, and A. Verbeke. 1995. The generalized double diamond approach to international competitiveness. In Rugman, A. M., J. V. den Broeck, A. Verbeke (Eds.), *Research in Global Strategic Management, Vol. 5: Beyond the Diamond*. Greenwich, CT: JAI Press, pp. 97–114.

Moon, H. C., A. M. Rugman, and A. Verbeke. 1998. A generalized double diamond approach to the global competitiveness of Korea and Singapore. *International Business Review* 7(2): 135–150.

Öz, Ö. 2002. Assessing Porter's framework for national advantage: The case of Turkey. *Journal of Business Research* 55(6): 509–515.

Pajunen, K. and V. Airo. 2013. Country-specificity and industry performance: A configurational analysis of the European generic medicines industry. *Research in the Sociology of Organizations* 38: 255–278.

Porter, M. E. 1990. *Competitive Advantage of Nations*. Free Press: New York.

Porter, M. E. and C. H. Ketels. 2003. U.K. competitiveness: moving to the next stage. https://www.hbs.edu/ris/Publication%20Files/file14771_83b42e5a-7e88-49be-9d33-2fc7585a87d9.pdf. Accessed March 4, 2021.

Rugman, A. M. 1991. Diamond in the rough. *Business Quarterly* 55(3): 61–64.

Rugman, A. M. and J. R. D'Cruz. 1991. *Fast Forward: Improving Canada's International Competitiveness*. Toronto: Kodak Canada Inc.

Rugman, A. M., C. H. Oh, and D. S. K. Lim. 2012. The regional and global competitiveness of multinational firms. *Journal of the Academy of Marketing Science* 40(2): 218–235.

Sakakibara, M. and M. E. Porter. 2001. Competing at home to win abroad: Evidence from Japanese industry. *Review of Economics and Statistics* 83(2): 310–322.

Scott, B. R. 1985. U.S. competitiveness: Concepts, performance, and implications. In B. R. Scott and G. Lodge, editors, *U.S. Competitiveness in the World Economy*. Boston, MA: Harvard Business School Press, pp. 13–69.

Thurow, L. C. 1992. *Head to Head: The Coming Economic Battle among Japan, Europe, and America*. New York: Morrow.

Vernon, R. 1966. International investments and international trade in the product cycle. *Quarterly Journal of Economics* 80: 190–207.

Chapter 2

Highlights of IPS National Competitiveness Research 2021

Overall Rankings

This section presents only the highlights of national rankings.[1] For more information about specific rankings of factor and sub-factor levels, please refer to the Appendix and visit the website (https://www.ipsncr.org/). The top three countries in the IPS National Competitiveness Research 2021 are Denmark (1), Canada (2), and Netherlands (3) (see Table 1). Compared to the previous year, Canada stepped one place down while Denmark stepped one place up, switching rankings with each other this year. Denmark showed high competitiveness in most of the eight factors of evaluation, particularly, in demand conditions. And as a low-debt country, Denmark had room to provide stimulus packages in the time of crisis. The strong performance of Canada was due to its high competitiveness in Factor Conditions (2), Entrepreneurs (5), and Professionals (6). The Canadian government's support measures on household income have boosted consumption which played an important role for Canada to quickly escape from the economic recession. The Netherlands on the other hand benefited from Brexit, which contributed to its improvement in the overall rankings. After Brexit, many companies in the UK relocated to the Netherlands, which is known to have an attractive business context (4).

---

[1]This chapter is abstracted and extended from IPSNC (2020).

Table 1.   Overall Rankings.

Rank	Country/Region	Index	Rank	Country/Region	Index
1	Denmark	61.82	32	Vietnam	39.29
2	Canada	61.80	33	Philippines	39.16
3	Netherlands	61.79	34	Chile	39.09
4	Sweden	61.51	35	Greece	38.39
5	Singapore	61.19	36	Indonesia	38.15
6	Switzerland	59.83	37	Panama	38.13
7	Australia	59.83	38	Russia	38.08
8	United States	59.63	39	Hungary	37.82
9	Finland	59.57	40	Colombia	37.30
10	New Zealand	58.04	41	Jordan	37.28
11	Hong Kong SAR	57.81	42	Spain	36.41
12	Belgium	54.73	43	Dominican Republic	34.45
13	U.A.E.	53.37	44	Turkey	34.45
14	China	52.79	45	Mexico	31.87
15	Austria	52.57	46	Argentina	31.77
16	Germany	52.07	47	Nigeria	31.73
17	Israel	46.70	48	Egypt	31.57
18	Taiwan, China	46.63	49	Slovak Republic	31.50
19	United Kingdom	45.51	50	Ukraine	31.05
20	Kuwait	44.06	51	Peru	30.02
21	Saudi Arabia	44.06	52	Bangladesh	29.91
22	Japan	43.98	53	Brazil	28.81
23	France	43.84	54	Croatia	27.40
24	Republic of Korea	43.53	55	Guatemala	26.96
25	Slovenia	42.66	56	Morocco	26.18
26	Czech Republic	41.95	57	Sri Lanka	25.62
27	India	41.58	58	Pakistan	25.55
28	Poland	41.46	59	Oman	25.44
29	Italy	41.44	60	Cambodia	24.87
30	Malaysia	41.25	61	South Africa	24.79
31	Thailand	40.88	62	Kenya	19.78

Among Asian economies, Singapore ranked the highest but dropped by two places to fifth compared to the previous year. Although Singapore showed weak performance in factor conditions, it showed strength in the other six factors, including Professionals (8), Policymakers and Administrators (6), Business Context (4), and Related Industries (3). Singapore is heavily dependent on cross-border flows, which has been hit hard during the pandemic; its major demand market is likely to record low growth. The tourism and transportation sectors have been "severely affected" by the "sudden drop" in the number of travelers, especially the number of Chinese travelers, deepening the recession.

The economies in the Greater China region showed a fluctuation in their overall competitiveness ranking except for Taiwan, China (hereafter Taiwan). Among the four first-tier Newly Industrialized Economies (NIEs), Hong Kong has been affected by trade friction between China and the US; many companies even disclosed their plans to move to Singapore to avoid the current unstable economic conditions of Hong Kong where the ranking of Entrepreneur (7) went down from the previous year. Contrary to this, Korea (26) and China (14) moved two steps up in their overall competitiveness ranking, especially due to their successful containment of coronavirus. Japan (21) fell by two positions compared to the previous ranking. The second-tier NIEs which include Indonesia, Malaysia, and the Philippines showed a positive trend by securing or stepping up in global competitiveness ranking, except for Thailand that went down four places.

In Europe, in addition to Denmark and the Netherlands (3), Sweden (4), Switzerland (6), and Finland (9) were also ranked in the top 10 countries. Many other European countries, such as Finland (from 17 to 19), Germany (from 17 to 16), France (23 to 23), Poland (28 to 28), and Italy (29 to 29), either showed improvement in their rankings or maintained the same position compared to the previous year. Although many Latin American countries have generally remained at lower levels ranging from 44th to 55th, many countries such as Chile (34), Colombia (40), Peru (51), and Guatemala (55) have all showed an improvement in their overall performance.

Intra-Group Rankings

Large group

Among the 22 economies categorized in the large group, four were strong, eight were intermediate, and ten were weak. In the large-strong group,

Canada ranked number one followed by Australia, the US, and China. Saudi Arabia maintained the position in the large-intermediate group, and ranked number one in the large-intermediate group, followed by Japan and India. Saudi Arabia has drastically reorganized the industries related to foreign direct investment and has since been showing rapid growth. Mexico, however, moved down from the 43rd to the 45th. Mexico mismanaged the spillover of the pandemic on its economy, recorded high rates of crime and violence, and showed deterioration of democratic institutions and values such as the rule of law and human rights (Table 2).

Table 2.   Intra-group rankings.

Competitiveness	Size	Large (22 economies)	Medium (22 economies)	Small (18 economies)
Strong (19 economies)		Canada (2) Australia (7) United States (8) China (14)	Sweden (4) Finland (9) New Zealand (10) Germany (16) Taiwan, China (18) United Kingdom (19)	Denmark (1) Netherlands (3) Singapore (5) Switzerland (6) Hong Kong SAR (11) Belgium (12) U.A.E (13) Austria (15) Israel (17)
Intermediate (23 economies)		Saudi Arabia (21) Japan (22) India (27) Vietnam (39) Philippines (33) Indonesia (36) Russia (38) Colombia (40)	France (23) Republic of Korea (24) Poland (28) Italy (29) Malaysia (30) Thailand (31) Chile (34) Greece (35) Spain (42)	Kuwait (20) Slovenia (25) Czech Republic (26) Panama (37) Hungary (39) Jordan (41)
Weak (20 economies)		Turkey (44) Mexico (45) Argentina (46) Nigeria (47) Egypt (48) Peru (51) Bangladesh (52) Brazil (53) Pakistan (58) South Africa (61)	Ukraine (50) Guatemala (55) Morocco (56) Sri Lanka (57) Oman (59) Cambodia (60) Kenya (62)	Dominican Republic (43) Slovak Republic (49) Croatia (54)

Note: Economies in each group are listed in the order of overall competitiveness rankings, and numbers in the parentheses are their competitiveness rankings.

Medium group

The medium group consists of six strong, nine intermediate, and seven weak economies. Sweden remained in first place among the medium-strong group and all six economies of this group were also previously categorized in the medium-strong group. France was ranked in first place among the medium-intermediate group, maintaining the same position from the last year. The country which is newly incorporated in IPS National Competitiveness Research 2021 is Oman. It secured the middle place in the medium-weak group, while Ukraine took the top position in this group.

Small group

The small group consists of nine strong, six intermediate, and three weak economies. The small-strong group includes two Asian economies and six European countries. Kuwait moved down from small-strong to small-intermediate group, while most of the other economies in the small-interme-diate group maintained their positions. Kuwait is very vulnerable to changes in business environment. About 90 percent of the Kuwait government's rev-enues come from oil, and trade restrictions inside and outside made the Kuwaiti economy shrink.

Advancer, Ordinary, and Lagger (AOL)

As Table 3 shows, 62 economies are divided into three tiers — Advancer, Ordinary, and Lagger (AOL) — according to the results of the quartile analysis. Among the 62 economies, those showed that improvements of two or more steps (compared to the previous year) in the overall ranking are categorized as Advancers; those with two or more steps down in the competitiveness ranking are labeled as the Lagger group; the rest are categorized as the Ordinary group. As a result, 19 economies have been classified as Advancer, and twenty have been identified as the Lagger group, while the other twenty-three are in the Ordinary group, showing no significant changes in their overall competitiveness ranking. About 60 percent of the 62 economies are classified either in Lagger or Advancer group, with a larger number of economies in the Lagger group.

Table 3.   Advancers, Ordinaries, and Laggers (AOL).

Competitiveness	Size	Large	Medium	Small
Strong	Advancer	Australia (+3) China (+2)	Finland (+2)	Netherlands (+4) Austria (+2)
	Ordinary	Canada (−1) United States (−2)	Sweden (+1) Germany (−1) Taiwan, China (0) UK (+1)	Denmark (+1) U.A.E (−1) Belgium (+1)
	Lagger		New Zealand (−2)	Singapore (−2) Switzerland (−2) Hong Kong SAR (−2) Israel (−3)
Intermediate	Advancer	Saudi Arabia (+4) Philippines (+2) Indonesia (+1)	Republic of Korea (+2) Chile (+5) Greece (+3)	Czech Republic (+5) Panama (+5) Jordan (+3)
	Ordinary	Japan (−1) Vietnam (0) Colombia (+1)	France (0) Poland (0) Italy (0) Malaysia (0)	Kuwait (−1)
	Lagger	India (−3) Russia (−4)	Thailand (−4) Spain (−6)	Slovenia (−3) Hungary (−6)
Weak	Advancer	Bangladesh (+4)		Dominican Republic (+6) Croatia (+3)
	Ordinary	Egypt (0) Peru (0) Brazil (−1) Pakistan (+1)	Ukraine (0) Guatemala (−1) Cambodia (+1) Kenya (0)	
	Lagger	Turkey (−4) Mexico (−2) Argentina (−2) Nigeria (−2) South Africa (−3)	Morocco (−3) Sri Lanka (−2)	Slovak Republic (−2)

Note: The economies in each cell are listed in the order of overall competitiveness rankings and the numbers in the parentheses represent the change of competitiveness rankings compared to the previous year.

Strong group

Countries that showed strength in manufacturing were among the advancer countries; Netherlands, Austria, Finland, Australia, and China. On the other hand, Switzerland, Israel, and New Zealand fell into the Lagger group along with Hong Kong and Singapore. The nine remaining economies in the Ordinary group were in Asia, America, Europe, and the Middle East. Here we see that fourteen economies were grouped into either Advancer or Ordinary groups.

Intermediate group

Among the 23 countries in the intermediate group, nine countries were classified as Advancers. Eight countries including Kuwait, France, Poland, Italy, Malaysia, Japan, Vietnam, and Columbia were classified in the Ordinary group. The remaining six countries were in the Lagger group. Therefore, unlike the strong group with a larger number of countries categorized in the Ordinary group, about 40 percent of countries in the intermediate group were classified as Advancers.

Weak group

Among 19 countries in the weak group, 40 percent of them were categorized into Laggers, about 15 percent as Advancers, and more than 40 percent as the Ordinary group. Turkey and Mexico moved to a weak group from an intermediate group this year.

Simulation

In this simulation, economies can have one of two choices: cost and differentiation strategy. The combination of these strategic options will result in various scenarios, as summarized in Table 4 which shows the results of five scenarios. For example, assuming that other economies do not use any strategy, the Netherland's current ranking of third will fall to sixteenth with a cost strategy, but it can rise to first by adopting a differentiation strategy. However, if all other economies adopt an optimal strategy, which is the one with a higher competitiveness index between cost and differentiation strategy, the Netherland's ranking will fall to 27th with a cost strategy and rise to third with a differentiation strategy. Therefore, in both cases, the differentiation strategy will be the optimal strategy for the Netherlands to enhance its national competitiveness.

Table 4 also highlights the importance of implementing appropriate strategies in order to remain competitive amidst increasing economic uncertainty. For example, the Netherland's ranking at third may fall to 16th if it chooses the cost strategy instead of the optimal strategy which is differentiation. The simulation table thus is a useful guide for understanding the current competitive positions of economies and help them choose their future strategic direction.

There is a notable finding in Table 4. The numbers in Column 3 (NS–CS) and Column 5 (OS–CS) show that the rankings of most of the 62 economies are much lower than those in Column 4 (NS–DS) and Column 6 (OS–DS). This comparison implies that a differentiation strategy is better than a cost strategy for all of the economies except for Pakistan, Oman, and Cambodia.

Introduction of the Text Information Analysis (TIA) Method

Our research has so far used traditional methods to collect hard and soft data for evaluating national competitiveness. Despite their strengths and complementarity, these two types have their own shortcomings. For hard data, despite its strengths in objectivity toward measuring competitiveness, there is usually a time lag when reflecting the recent development status of economies. To overcome this shortcoming, we collected additional data using a survey instrument. However, it should be noted that a survey alone is an inadequate complement because there are risks associated with validity and reliability, resulting from the high level of subjectivity involved with the data. This can lead to the data being biased particularly when the response rate is low. To address this problem, we used content analysis of text information (TIA) to complement the limitations of both hard and soft data.

In recent times, big data analytics has become increasingly important in both academic and business fields (Chen *et al.*, 2012). Big data is defined by Goes (2014) as "massive amounts of observational data, of different types, supporting different types of decisions" and consists of three common features: volume, velocity, and variety (Kwon *et al.*, 2014). Yet, one of the main challenges for this approach is data acquisition

Table 4.   Results of five scenarios.

Strategy of all economies except for one's own	NS			OS	
Strategy of one's own	NS	CS	DS	CS	DS
Scenario	Scenario 1	Scenario 2	Scenario 3	Scenario 4	Scenario 5
Denmark	1	16	1	28	1
Canada	2	12	1	18	9
Netherlands	3	16	1	27	3
Sweden	4	16	1	26	2
Singapore	5	16	1	25	6
Switzerland	6	19	1	32	4
Australia	7	12	1	18	10
United States	8	19	1	34	8
Finland	9	16	1	27	5
New Zealand	10	16	1	21	12
Hong Kong SAR	11	16	1	27	7
Belgium	12	24	1	38	11
U.A.E.	13	16	10	26	16
China	14	16	10	22	15
Austria	15	27	1	42	13
Germany	16	31	6	44	14
Israel	17	42	17	51	24
Taiwan, China	18	31	12	44	18
United Kingdom	19	42	17	47	20
Kuwait	20	20	19	34	30
Saudi Arabia	21	22	17	35	21
Japan	22	41	17	47	23
France	23	42	17	51	22
Republic of Korea	24	41	12	47	17
Slovenia	25	42	17	51	28
Czech Republic	26	42	19	47	31
India	27	35	17	45	26
Poland	28	42	17	47	27

(*Continued*)

Table 4.   (*Continued*)

Strategy of all economies except for one's own	NS			OS	
Strategy of one's own	NS	CS	DS	CS	DS
Scenario	Scenario 1	Scenario 2	Scenario 3	Scenario 4	Scenario 5
Italy	29	42	15	50	19
Malaysia	30	34	19	45	29
Thailand	31	39	17	46	25
Vietnam	32	39	20	46	34
Philippines	33	41	20	47	32
Chile	34	39	20	46	33
Greece	35	44	24	53	36
Indonesia	36	39	20	47	35
Panama	37	41	24	47	38
Russia	38	32	30	44	43
Hungary	39	44	26	53	39
Colombia	40	42	24	50	37
Jordan	41	42	27	51	42
Spain	42	52	27	57	41
Dominican Republic	43	47	30	56	44
Turkey	44	50	26	56	40
Mexico	45	50	40	57	47
Argentina	46	49	43	56	49
Nigeria	47	53	32	60	45
Egypt	48	48	43	56	50
Slovak Republic	49	56	40	61	46
Ukraine	50	52	43	57	48
Peru	51	45	45	56	53
Bangladesh	52	46	43	56	51
Brazil	53	53	45	60	55
Croatia	54	61	45	61	52
Guatemala	55	53	51	59	57
Morocco	56	61	45	61	54

(*Continued*)

Table 4. (*Continued*)

Strategy of all economies except for one's own	NS			OS	
Strategy of one's own	NS	CS	DS	CS	DS
Scenario	Scenario 1	Scenario 2	Scenario 3	Scenario 4	Scenario 5
Sri Lanka	57	56	53	61	59
Pakistan	58	53	54	58	61
Oman	59	54	61	61	62
Cambodia	60	53	60	60	61
South Africa	61	62	45	62	56
Kenya	62	62	62	62	62

Note: NS: no strategy, CS: cost strategy, DS: differentiation strategy, OS: optimal strategy.

(Labrinidis and Jagadish, 2012). As not all of the data will be pertinent, researchers or decision makers have to place great effort in defining the filters so that the data collection will provide useful information. To this end, the credibility of the data source is crucial with downstream analysis. Another challenge is that the information collected is not in a format ready for analysis (Labrinidis and Jagadish, 2012). To address this, a process for information extraction is necessary so that the required information can be taken out from the underlying sources and allows for them to be expressed in a structured form suitable for analysis (Labrinidis and Jagadish, 2012). Moreover, as Shah *et al.* (2012) have pointed out, good data will not guarantee a good decision. In order to use of the information more effectively, firms need to make a good decision, often called "big judgement."

Given the two challenges mentioned above, we have introduced a new framework as shown in Figure 1, which seeks to collect more reliable text information and to analyze the text more reliably. This framework comprises of two variables — information reliability and analysis reliability. The degree of *information reliability* can be measured as high or low and is greatly influenced by the information source. On the other hand, *analysis reliability* refers to the degree of processing the text for extracting and translating the necessary information for reliable analysis, and this dimension can also be measured as high or low. Despite the variety of the data format, our research focuses on text data from sources with high reliability. These texts

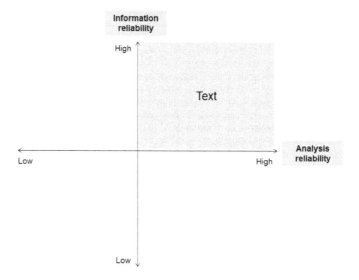

Figure 1.   Text information analysis (TIA) model.

are filtered by our researchers to extract useful information that will be suitable for analyzing national competitiveness (the upper-right shaded area).

In order to compile a collection of articles on the most recent developments among economies from around the world, searches were conducted through Google using the keywords of "(nation name), competitiveness, 2020–2021." Based on the relevance to the research objective, we selected articles published in English by established and reputable media sources. Regarding the sample size, there is no commonly accepted level for qualitative studies, and the optimal sample often depends on the purpose of the study, research questions, and richness of data (Elo *et al.*, 2014). However, Guthrie *et al.* (2004) suggested that the saturation of data could indicate that the data reached an optimal sample size. According to Morse *et al.* (2002), saturated data ensures the replication in content categories, which can help verify and ensure comprehension and completeness. In our study, the top 100 articles listed in Google search are considered as the optimal sample size. These articles often refer to the last six months, thereby covering a recent period which is missed when using both hard and soft data.

For the variable of analysis reliability, we used the technique of content analysis to extract the useful information. Content analysis is broadly defined by Shapiro and Markoff (1997) as "any methodological measurement applied to text (or other symbolic materials) for social science purposes." There are several advantages to this approach (Krippendorff, 1980; Duriau *et al.*, 2007; Short and Palmer, 2008). First, it is unobtrusive and useful when dealing with a large volume of data. Second, it is a powerful technique for data reduction by compressing many words of text into a few content categories. Third, it can be used to extract both manifest and latent content.

For data coding with content analysis, there are three approaches: human scored system, individual word count system, and computerized systems using artificial intelligence (Short and Palmer, 2008). Among the three methods, we selected the human scored system as this approach has particular strength in capturing the latent content in the given text. We scored the articles based upon the level of positive reporting on the economy covered in the piece. Using a scale ranging from −5 to +5, if the article delivers a more positive reporting, it will be given a higher score toward +5 and vice versa. Data coding was conducted by one trained coder, and then checked by two experienced researchers. For the 2021 report, we coded economies that displayed changes in rankings by more than five places compared to the previous year while economies that maintained their position were assessed by using only hard and soft data. The coded economies and results are shown in Table 5. By adding the adjusted scores to the overall competitiveness index for these coded economies, our competitiveness rankings are strengthened to better reflect both the most recent advancements and attain the desired level of objectivity.

Table 5.   Coded economies and results of coding.

Rank	Country/Region	Adjusted score
2	Canada	1.33
3	Netherlands	0.14
11	Hong Kong SAR	−1.22
17	Israel	3.05
23	France	−0.37
24	Republic of Korea	−3.03
27	India	1.03
29	Italy	−2.39
34	Chile	−1.46

References

Chen, H., Chiang, R. H. L., and Storey, V. C. 2012. Business intelligence and analysis: From big data to big impact. *MIS Quarterly*, 36(4): 1165–1188.

Duriau, V. J., Reger, R. K., and Pfarrer, M. D. 2007. A content analysis of the content analysis literature in organization studies: Research themes, data sources, and methodological refinements. *Organizational Research Methods*, 10(1): 5–34.

Elo, S., Kääriäinen, M., Kanste, O., Pölkki, T., Utriainen, K., and Kyngäs, H. 2014. Qualitative content analysis: A focus on trustworthiness. *Sage Open*, January–March: 1–10.

Goes, P. B. 2014. Big data and IS research. *MIS Quarterly*, 38: iii–viii.

Guthrie, J., Yongvanich, K., and Ricceri, F. 2004. Using content analysis as a research method to inquire into intellectual capital reporting. *Journal of Intellectual Capital*, 5: 282–293.

Institute for Policy and Strategy and National Competitiveness (IPSNC). 2020. *IPS National Competitiveness Research 2019–2020*. Seoul: IPSNC.

Krippendorff, K. 1980. *Content Analysis: An Introduction to its Methodology*. London: Sage Publication.

Kwon, O., Lee, N., and Shin, B. 2014. Data quality management, data usage experience and acquisition intention of big data analytics. *International Journal of Information Management*, 34(3): 387–394.

Labrinidis, A. and Jagadish, H. V. 2012. Challenges and opportunities with big data. *Proceedings of the VLDB Endowment*, 5(12): 2032–2033

Morse, J. M., Barrett, M., Mayan, M., Olson, K., and Spiers, J. 2002. Verification strategies for establishing reliability and validity in qualitative research. *International Journal of Qualitative Methods*, 1(2): 1–19.

Shah, S., Horne, A., and Capellá, J. 2012. Good data won't guarantee good decisions. *Harvard Business Review*, 90(4): 23–25.

Shapiro, G. and Markoff, G. 1997. Methods for drawing statistical inferences from text and transcripts. In Roberts, C. W. (Ed.), *Text Analysis for the Social Sciences*. Mahwah, NJ: Lawrence Erlbaum Associates, pp. 9–31.

Short, J. C. and Palmer, T. B. 2008. The application of DICTION to content analysis research in strategic management. *Organizational Research Methods*, 11(4): 727–752.

Chapter 3

Conceptual Framework and Analytical Methodologies*

The Theoretical Evolution of National Competitiveness

Porter (1990) developed a comprehensive approach to analyze national competitiveness entitled the Diamond Model. It was then extended by other scholars into two directions. One is the Double Diamond Model (Moon *et al.*, 1998; Rugman, 1991) and the other is the 9-Factor Model (Cho, 1994). Later on, a new comprehensive model was introduced by integrating the two models into one framework (Cho *et al.*, 2008, 2009; IPS, 2006). This new model was labeled as the IPS Model (IPS, 2008), which forms the underlying analytical framework for the IPS National Competitiveness Research.

While there are several reports on national competitiveness, many have been unsatisfactory in their methodologies and findings. Further discussion on these limitations can be found in Cho and Moon (2000, 2013). It is very important to note here that rankings for national competitiveness are unreliable if they are not based on rigorous models and effective methodologies. Policymakers, who often become sensitive to the results of national competitiveness reports, may then pursue distorted policies based on misleading outcomes. In order to solve this problem, therefore, the theoretical and methodological problems evident in the existing reports were corrected in this study. And hopefully, policymakers and business leaders will derive useful implications from this research.

---

*This chapter is abstracted and extended from IPSNC (2020).

Critical Review of Existing Reports

The International Institute for Management Development (IMD) and the World Economic Forum (WEF) are world-renowned institutions publishing national competitiveness reports. These two reports often make big headlines around the world; however, a careful examination of their methodologies reveals some notable problems.

Theoretical background

The two reports provide different explanations for how to define competitiveness. The IMD describes competitiveness as "the ability of a nation to create and maintain an environment that sustains more value creation for its enterprises and more prosperity for its people" (IMD, 2014: 502). By contrast, the WEF sees competitiveness as "the set of institutions, policies, and factors that determine the level of productivity of a country" (WEF, 2019: 13). While their definitions of competitiveness are different, both institutes adopted very similar factors for competitiveness in their early reports (see Cho and Moon [2013] for details). Regarding the evaluation model, the IMD added "location attractiveness" to its original model in 1999 and introduced a completely new one in 2001, which consisted of four variables: economic performance, government efficiency, business efficiency, and infrastructure. Alongside this, there were changes in the index. The IMD formerly used a single index until 2002 but introduced customized rankings according to population size in 2003, and two more rankings based on GDP per capita and geographic region in 2004. However, careful observation will notice immediately that this model and index are not as rigorous as Porter's Diamond Model.

The WEF, on the other hand, used eight variables until 2000, but since then the number of variables has been changed. In addition, the WEF showed frequent index changes from Current Competitiveness Index (CCI) to Microeconomic Competitiveness Index (MICI) and Business Competitiveness Index (BCI) until 2007. Furthermore, the WEF launched a new index, the Global Competitiveness Index (GCI) in 2005 as part of an attempt to integrate the two separate indices (Growth Competitiveness Index and BCI) into a single index. More recently, the GCI 4.0 introduced in 2018, provides a series of factors and attributes that drive productivity, growth, and human development in the era of the Fourth Industrial Revolution (WEF, 2019: 7). There are major differences between this research and the other reports which are illustrated in Table 1.

Table 1. Comparison of the three competitiveness reports.

Report	IMD World Competitiveness Yearbook (2020)	WEF Global Competitiveness Report (2019)	IPS National Competitiveness Research (2020–2021)
Sponsoring institute	International Institute for Management Development	World Economic Forum	IPSNC
Location	Lausanne (Switzerland)	Geneva (Switzerland)	Seoul (Korea) & Sorengo (Switzerland)
Year started	1989	1996	2001
Theoretical base	No particular theory	No particular theory	IPS model
Main factors	A collection of 4 factors • Economic performance • Government efficiency • Business efficiency • Infrastructure	A collection of 12 factors • Institutions • Infrastructure • ICT adoption • Macroeconomic stability • Health • Skills • Product market • Labor market • Financial system • Market size • Business dynamism • Innovation capability	A collection of 8 factors Four Physical factors • Factor conditions • Demand conditions • Related industries • Business context Four Human factors • Workers • Policymakers & administrators • Entrepreneurs • Professionals
Criteria	255 (Computed in the rankings)	103	98
Data base	Hard data: 163 Soft data: 92	Hard data 56 Soft data: 47	Hard data 57 Soft data: 41

(Continued)

Table 1.   (*Continued*)

Report	IMD World Competitiveness Yearbook (2020)	WEF Global Competitiveness Report (2019)	IPS National Competitiveness Research (2020–2021)
Weights	Hard data: 2/3 Soft data: 1/3	The same weight for factors, sub-factors, and criteria	Different weights for different strategies
Partner institutes	Global network of 56 partner institutes	Local partner institutes	KOTRA offices abroad Partner scholars
Number of countries/ regions	63	141	62
Strengths	• The first and largest survey on national competitiveness • A collection of multiple variables for competitiveness	• Similar to IMD, but more effective in elaborating the variables • Ongoing efforts to improve the study	• Strong theoretical basis with minimum multi-colinearity • Useful information of intra-group rankings • A series of analytical tools for policy implementation
Weaknesses	• Weak theoretical basis • Lack of consistency among partner institutions conducting the surveys	• In general, similar to IMD, but more emphasis on soft data • Lack of consistency among partner institutions conducting the surveys	• Improved weighting method, but still controversial

Note: WEF published Global Competitiveness Report Special Edition 2020 and did not report its ranking. In this report WEF suggested priorities for policymakers to consider in their decision-making process and overcome the COVID-19 pandemic.

Methodology

Although the IMD and WEF reports originally employed eight variables, which were almost identical, they produced different results. This was because they applied different weights to the same variables. The IMD report contains both hard data (that is, statistical indicators published by organizations) and soft data (that is, survey results compiled from people like executives). As soft data can be volatile to the changes in the environment, hard data accounts for two-thirds of the factors in determining the overall ranking, while survey data accounts for one-third of the overall ranking.

The WEF report, on the other hand, applies different weights to a range of groups at various stages of development, as shown in Table 2. In the 2006–2007 Report, the WEF classified countries by the level of GDP per capita. Countries with a GDP per capita smaller than US$2,000 are in the factor-driven stage (Stage 1); countries with a GDP per capita between US$3,000 and US$8,999 are in the efficiency-driven stage (Stage 2); countries with a GDP per capita larger than US$17,000 are in the innovation-driven stage (Stage 3). In addition, countries between two of the three stages are regarded as "in transition" (WEF, 2006: 12). However, in the 2007–2008 Report, when determining the stages of development, another criterion was added: the share of exports of mineral goods in total exports (goods and services). All countries whose exports are more than 70 percent of mineral products are categorized in the factor-driven group, regardless of whether they are in Stage 2 or 3. The recent WEF report since 2018, however, gives the same weight to the scores of the components of sub-factors and factors.

Table 2. Weights of the three main pillars at each development stage.

Sub-index	Factor-driven stage (%)	Efficiency-driven stage (%)	Innovation-driven stage (%)
Basic requirements	60	40	20
Efficiency enhancers	35	50	50
Innovation and sophistication factors	5	10	30

Source: Global Competitiveness Report 2017–2018 (WEF, 2017).

Policy implications

Both reports rank countries by their overall national competitiveness. For example, in the WEF Global Competitiveness Report 2019, Singapore ranked number one, while the Philippines ranked 64th among one hundred and forty-one countries measured. However, more critical questions arise: What are the useful implications from these findings? Will such knowledge help the Philippines change its policy to enhance its competitiveness? Does this mean that the country has to invest large amounts of money and effort toward developing technologies in the hope that someday it might catch up with Singapore?

On the other hand, we argue that a nation's competitiveness is more relevant when compared among nations endowed with similar comparative advantages competing in similar industries rather than among those with different comparative advantages. For example, it is not very meaningful to say that Korea is less competitive than the US. By contrast, it is more relevant to say that Korea is more (or less) competitive than Taiwan because these two are very similar in terms of comparative advantages. Therefore, in order to derive useful policy implications, we need to consider rankings in groups of similar countries (Intra-Group Ranking), as well as overall rankings for all countries around the world (World Ranking). Based on the principles of theory, methodology, and policy implications mentioned above, the IPS National Competitiveness Research (the IPS research) reports both intra-group rankings and overall (or world) rankings.

IPS National Competitiveness Research

By correcting the problems evident among existing studies, the IPS research pursues four different approaches. First, the competitiveness of 62 economies is measured by using the IPS Model. Second, the competitiveness of these economies is analyzed within the economy group. Third, the structure of national competitiveness is demonstrated through strategy simulation, followed by the Optimal Strategic (OS) Mix and the Term-Priority (TP) Matrix. Figure 1 illustrates the MASI methodology of the IPS research.

Measuring national competitiveness

There are two conditions necessary for a good competitiveness theory. One is to be comprehensive enough to capture the most important

Figure 1.   The MASI methodology.

variables in order to explain the complexity of the real world. The other is to be dynamic enough to explain the changing nature of national competitiveness. Porter's (1990) Diamond Model satisfies both of these aspects by incorporating four competitiveness variables: Factor Conditions, Demand Conditions, Related & Supporting Industries, and Firm Strategy, Structure & Rivalry. Notably, Porter has demonstrated that the Diamond Model is dynamic by arguing that national prosperity is created, rather than inherited. This implies that national competitiveness does not grow out of resource endowments or currency value, as traditional models suggest, but that it can be created by a combination of strategic choices along with the four determinants of the Diamond Model (see Figure 1 of Chapter 2).

Despite its advantages, Porter's Diamond Model is not free from criticism. Specifically, it is limited to application in the international context. The model is not that relevant for small economies because their domestic variables are very limited (Rugman, 1991) while their geographical constituency requires different criteria (Dunning, 1993). In the era of globalization, international factors must be considered in order to accurately assess a nation's competitiveness. To address this problem, the Double Diamond Model (Rugman and D'Cruz, 1993) and the Generalized Double Diamond Model (Moon *et al.,* 1998) have been proposed.

Another issue is that the Single Diamond Model does not distinguish human factors from physical factors. In reality, the roles of different groups of people are important for economies at different levels of economic development. For this matter, Cho (1994) proposed the 9-Factor Model by incorporating the role of human factors, which are not well reflected in Porter's Diamond Model. Human factors in the 9-Factor Model drive the national economy forward by creating, motivating, and controlling the four physical factors in Porter's Diamond Model. The related literature in this regard is well documented in Cho and Moon (2000, 2013).

These two models, the Double Diamond and 9-Factor, are meaningful since they extend the scope and source of national competitiveness. The IPS research incorporates both of these extensions into the IPS Model, which analyzes national competitiveness by assessing physical and human factors in terms of domestic and international contexts (see Figure 4 of Chapter 2).

Appendix 2 shows the 98 criteria used in IPS NCR 2019–2020 for measuring national competitiveness. Among these 57 criteria are hard data, and the other 41 criteria are soft data. The hard data were collected through various statistical sources published by international and government organizations. The soft data were collected by our partner institution Korea Trade-Investment Promotion Agency (KOTRA) which has more than one hundred offices abroad as well as our partner scholars for a number of other economies.

Analyzing national competitiveness

Table 3 illustrates a 3 × 3 matrix of economy groups and Table 4 shows economies (in competitiveness order) for each of the nine groups. By considering the size and competitive structure simultaneously, we can now more realistically compare and contrast the relative positions of economies.

Table 3.   Typology of economy groups.

Competitiveness \ Size	Large	Medium	Small
Strong	Large–Strong	Medium–Strong	Small–Strong
Intermediate	Large–Intermediate	Medium–Intermediate	Small–Intermediate
Weak	Large–Weak	Medium–Weak	Small–Weak

Table 4.   Economy groups: Results.

Competitiveness \ Size	Large	Medium	Small
Strong	Canada (2)	Sweden (4)	Denmark (1)
	Australia (7)	Finland (9)	Netherlands (3)
	United States (8)	New Zealand (10)	Singapore (5)
	China (14)	Germany (16)	Switzerland (6)
		Taiwan, China (18)	Hong Kong SAR (11)
			Belgium (12)
		United Kingdom (19)	U.A.E. (13)
			Austria (15)
			Israel (17)
Intermediate	Saudi Arabia (21)	France (23)	Kuwait (20)
	Japan (22)	Republic of Korea (24)	Slovenia (25)
	India (27)	Poland (28)	Czech Republic (26)
	Vietnam (32)	Italy (29)	Panama (37)
	Philippines (33)	Malaysia (30)	Hungary (39)
	Indonesia (36)	Thailand (31)	Jordan (41)
	Russia (38)	Chile (34)	
	Colombia (40)	Greece (35)	
		Spain (42)	
Weak	Turkey (44)	Ukraine (50)	Dominican Republic (43)
	Mexico (45)	Guatemala (55)	Slovak Republic (49)
	Argentina (46)	Morocco (56)	Croatia (54)
	Nigeria (47)	Sri Lanka (57)	
	Egypt (48)	Oman (59)	
	Peru (51)	Cambodia (60)	
	Bangladesh (52)	Kenya (62)	
	Brazil (53)		
	Pakistan (58)		
	South Africa (61)		

Note: Economies in each group are listed in the order of National Competitiveness Rankings, and the numbers in parentheses stand for the national competitiveness rankings.

Simulation

When economies want to enhance their competitiveness to provide a higher standard of living and a better environment for doing business, two generic strategies, cost and differentiation, can be applied at the national level (Porter *et al.*, 2000). The cost strategy aims to achieve "low cost and high efficiency," utilizing mainly cheap workers and natural resources. By contrast, the differentiation strategy emphasizes "high cost but high value added," and focuses more on Demand Conditions and Professionals. The differences are illustrated in Figure 2.

We give different weights to the competitiveness variables for different strategies, as shown in Table 5. To derive appropriate weights for the competitiveness variables in our research, we use the analytic hierarchy process (AHP), which is a popular multi-criteria decision-making tool in the related literature (Sureshchandar and Leisten, 2006). For cost strategy, equal weight (50 percent) is given to physical and human factors. However, factors and sub-factors are given different weights. For differentiation strategy, equal weight (50 percent) is given to physical and human factors, but more weight is given to Demand Conditions and Professionals. The following simulations and their results suggest sophisticated but practical scenarios for policy makers.

All countries with the same strategy

This simulation focuses on the changes in the score of the No Strategy Index (NSI) when cost and differentiation strategies are applied.

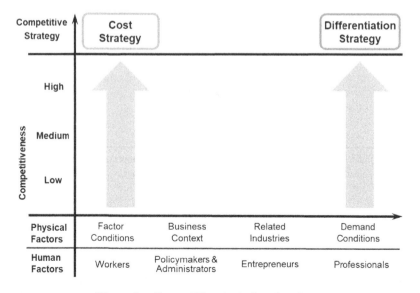

Figure 2.   Competitive strategies of nations.

Table 5. Weights for cost strategy and differentiation strategy.

Main Factors	Weights		Sub-factors	Weights	
	C	D		C	D
Physical Factors					
Factor conditions	32/120	4/120	Energy resources	3/4	1/4
			Other resources	1/4	3/4
Business context	16/120	8/120	Structure	3/4	1/4
			Strategy	1/4	3/4
Related industries	8/120	16/120	Industrial infrastructure	3/4	1/4
			Coordination and synergy	1/4	3/4
Demand conditions	4/120	32/120	Demand size	3/4	1/4
			Demand quality	1/4	3/4
Human Factors					
Workers	32/120	4/120	Quantity of labor force	3/4	1/4
			Quality of labor force	1/4	3/4
Policymakers & administrators	16/120	8/120	Policymakers	3/4	1/4
			Administrators	1/4	3/4
Entrepreneurs	8/120	16/120	Personal competence	3/4	1/4
			Social context	1/4	3/4
Professionals	4/120	32/120	Personal competence	3/4	1/4
			Social context	1/4	3/4

Note: C: Cost Strategy; D: Differentiation Strategy.

The two strategies — cost and differentiation strategies — are given to all economies, respectively. Thus, this is ideally a controlled simulation. Figure 3 shows the results of changes in the absolute index for each strategy. It shows that an economy with higher competitiveness should pursue a differentiation strategy rather than a cost strategy. The indices of the three strategies are calculated to determine the relationship of the changes in the competitiveness index (CSI–NSI, DSI–NSI) with the size

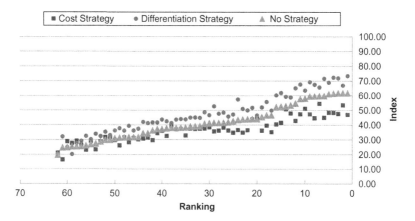

Figure 3.   Changing indices with different strategies.

Note: The rankings and indices are based on the IPS National Competitiveness Research 2021.

of an economy or its competitiveness (NSI). The results are shown in Table 6.

Some important implications are derived from this analysis. First, the cost strategy is more suitable for larger economies with lower competitiveness (Model 1). Second, regardless of an economy's size, the differentiation strategy is more appropriate for stronger economies that have higher competitiveness (Model 2). This reveals that an economy should carefully choose between cost and differentiation strategies as the best approach to enhance its competitiveness, according to an accurate assessment of its current position.

More realistic stories

The previous simulation assumes that all economies will adopt the same strategy, which is far from reality. Therefore, the following section introduces more realistic scenarios. In general, economies have a choice among two strategies: best or worst. The best strategy refers to the one that produces the highest performance between cost and differentiation strategies, and the worst strategy is the one which leads to the lowest performance between the two strategies. An optimal strategy represents the situation where all economies choose the best approach in a competitive environment. Figure 4 illustrates the strategic choices where no strategy is the base and the starting point. The rankings that result from the choice of a cost

Table 6. Multiple linear regression model between the changes in variables.

	CSI–NSI (Model 1)	DSI–NSI (Model 2)
Size	0.076	−0.026
(P-value)	(0.003)	(0.217)
Competitiveness (NSI)	−0.289	0.275
(P-value)	(0.000)	(0.000)
Constant	6.061	−6.072
(P-value)	(0.000)	(0.000)
N (observations)	62	62
R^2	0.549	0.592
Adjust R^2	0.534	0.578
Residual Std. Error	2.918 (df = 59)	2.459 (df = 59)
F statistic	35.980 (df = 2; 59)	42.797 (df = 2; 59)
(P-value)	(0.000)	(0.000)

Note: (1) CSI: Cost Strategy Index; DSI: Differentiation Strategy Index; NSI: No Strategy Index; CSI–NSI: Cost Strategy Index–No Strategy Index; DSI–NSI: Differentiation Strategy Index–No Strategy Index. (2) If a *P*-value of an independent variable is smaller than 0.01, the variable is significant in these models.

strategy under no strategy and optimal strategy basis are shown on the left side. The rankings that come from choosing a differentiation strategy under the two bases are listed on the right side. Table 7 contrasts the different indices of the best strategy and the worst strategy. For example, Jordan ranks forty-second with the best strategy, while falling to fifty-first with the worst strategy. The difference in Korea's case is even more remarkable. It ranks seventeenth with the best strategy but falls to forty-seventh with the worst strategy. Therefore, choosing the right strategy is more crucial for Korea than for Jordan.

Implementation

Optimal strategic mix (Macro level)

Once the strategic implications are clarified, a series of concrete strategies across different stages of economic development should be followed to guarantee further success. To this end, the optimal strategic mix by the stage of economic development is illustrated in Table 8.

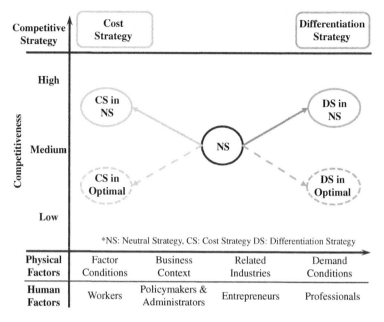

Figure 4.   **Changing rankings with different strategy simulation.**

The strategic capabilities of countries should be focused on the accomplishment of solutions listed in the next stage. In doing so, the eight factors comprising of national competitiveness may have different weight schemes according to the country's current status of economic development. In the early stage of national competitiveness development, the viable strategy should be the cost strategy with a focus on Factor Conditions and Workers. As countries move into higher stages of national economic development, the strategy should gradually move from a cost to a differentiation strategy. In the final stage, countries should employ a differentiation strategy to enhance national competitiveness with an emphasis on Demand Conditions and Professionals.

Term-priority matrix (Micro level)

The term-priority matrix is a policy tool to improve weak criteria. The detailed methodology is as follows. First, the 98 criteria are classified into strong (criteria in which an economy displays relative strengths), medium

Table 7. Strategy simulation under optimal strategy basis.

Region	BSR	BSI	WSR	WSI	Region	BSR	BSI	WSR	WSI
Denmark	1	73.4	28	47.03	Philippines	32	45.1	47	37.23
Sweden	2	72.32	26	48.36	Chile	33	45.02	46	37.64
Netherlands	3	71.92	27	47.64	Vietnam	34	44.84	46	37.53
Switzerland	4	71.63	32	45.03	Indonesia	35	44.07	47	37.36
Finland	5	69.21	27	47.36	Greece	36	43.79	53	32.96
Singapore	6	68.91	25	48.4	Colombia	37	43.69	50	35.96
Hong Kong SAR	7	67.64	27	47.38	Panama	38	43.64	47	37.04
United States	8	67.5	34	44.73	Hungary	39	42.47	53	32.64
Canada	9	66.94	18	53.49	Turkey	40	42.01	56	30.86
Australia	10	65.67	18	54.51	Spain	41	41.75	57	29.74
Belgium	11	65.04	38	42.86	Jordan	42	41.37	51	34.5
New Zealand	12	63.53	21	51.19	Russia	43	41.73	44	39.47
Austria	13	61.88	42	41.58	Dominican Republic	44	41.26	56	31.59
Germany	14	60.21	44	40.46	Nigeria	45	39.37	60	28.27
China	15	59.25	22	50.79	Slovak Republic	46	37.79	61	26.13
U.A.E.	16	58.78	26	47.9	Mexico	47	37.43	57	30.21
Republic of Korea	17	57.35	47	36.61	Ukraine	48	36.22	57	29.74
Taiwan, China	18	55.68	44	39.68	Argentina	49	36.21	56	31.16
Italy	19	52.68	50	35.68	Egypt	50	36.13	56	31.65

(Continued)

Table 7.   (*Continued*)

Region	BSR	BSI	WSR	WSI	Region	BSR	BSI	WSR	WSI
United Kingdom	20	51.97	47	36.27	Bangladesh	51	35.35	56	31.77
Saudi Arabia	21	51.68	35	43.89	Croatia	52	33.89	61	23.25
France	22	50.96	51	34.86	Peru	53	33.11	56	31.94
Japan	23	49.95	47	36.49	Morocco	54	32.51	61	23.04
Israel	24	49.81	51	35.21	Brazil	55	32.36	60	28.72
Thailand	25	48.6	46	37.63	South Africa	56	32.11	62	16.5
India	26	48.37	45	38.28	Guatemala	57	30.23	59	29.1
Poland	27	47.68	47	36.24	Pakistan	58	29.25	61	27.69
Slovenia	28	47.14	51	34.82	Sri Lanka	59	29.19	61	26.45
Malaysia	29	46.63	45	38.47	Cambodia	60	28.86	61	24.98
Kuwait	30	46.5	34	44.52	Oman	61	27.7	62	20.12
Czech Republic	31	45.81	47	36.34	Kenya	62	21.13	62	20.41

Note: BSR: Best Strategy Ranking, BSI: Best Strategy Index, WSR: Worst Strategy Ranking, WSI: Worst Strategy Index

Table 8. Optimal strategic mix for different stages of economic development.

Stage / Factor	Developing	Transitional	Developed
Physical factors			
Factor conditions	Resource-based	Manufacturing-based	Knowledge-based
Business context	Protectionism	Efficiency	Competition
Related industries	Physical infrastructure (Roads & Ports)	Industrial cluster	Regional integration
Demand conditions	Quantity	Quality	Sophistication
Human factors			
Workers	Cheap	Motivated	Skilled
Policymakers & administrators	Facilitation	Support & regulation	Advice
Entrepreneurs	Risk taking	Efficiency developing	Value creating
Professionals	Operational	Managerial	Strategic

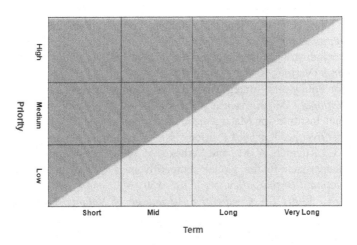

Figure 5.   The term-priority matrix.

(criteria in which an economy ranks in moderate positions), and weak categories (criteria in which an economy shows relative weaknesses). Secondly, the sub-factors with weak criteria are categorized into 12 groups by terms (or time span) and priorities of policies. The degree of priority

(*Y*-axis) is determined by the correlation between the sub-factors and GDP per capita. The upper-left triangle represents the more important and effective policies while the lower-right triangle shows the less important ones (see Figure 5).

References

Cho, D. S. 1994. A dynamic approach to international competitiveness: The case of Korea. *Journal of Far Eastern Business*, 1(1): 17–36.

Cho, D. S. and Moon, H. C. 2000. *From Adam Smith to Michael Porter: Evolution of Competitiveness Theory*. Singapore: World Scientific.

Cho, D. S. and Moon, H. C. 2013. *International Review of National Competitiveness: A Detailed Analysis of Sources and Rankings*. Cheltenham, UK and Northampton, MA: Edward Elgar Publishing Limited.

Cho, D. S., Moon, H. C., and Kim, M. Y. 2008. Characterizing international competitiveness in international business research: A MASI approach to national competitiveness. *Research in International Business and Finance*, 22(2): 175–192.

Cho, D. S., Moon, H. C., and Kim, M. Y. 2009. Does one size fit all? A dual double diamond approach to country-specific advantages. *Asian Business and Management*, 8(1): 83–102.

Dunning, John H. 1993. Internationalizing Porter's diamond. *Management International Review*, 33(2): 7–15.

Institute for Industrial Policy Studies (IPS). 2006. *IPS National Competitiveness Research* (Various Issues). Seoul: IPS.

Institute for Policy and Strategy and National Competitiveness (IPSNC). 2020. *IPS National Competitiveness Research 2019–2020*. Seoul: IPSNC.

International Institute for Management Development (IMD). 2014. *The World Competitiveness Yearbook* (Various Issues). Lausanne, Switzerland: IMD.

Moon, H. C., Rugman, A. M., and Verbeke, A. 1998. A generalized double diamond approach to the global competitiveness of Korea and Singapore. *International Business Review*, 7: 135–150.

Porter, M. E. 1990. *The Competitive Advantage of Nations*. New York: Free Press.

Porter, M. E., Takeuchi, H., and Sakakibara, M. 2000. *Can Japan Compete?* Cambridge, MA: Perseus Publishing.

Rugman, A. M. 1991. Diamond in the rough. *Business Quarterly*, 55(3): 61–64.

Rugman, A. M and D'Cruz, R. J. 1993. The "double diamond" model of international competitiveness: The Canadian experience. *Management International Review*, 33(2): 17–39.

World Economic Forum (WEF). 2019. *The Global Competitiveness Report* (Various Issues). Geneva, Switzerland: WEF.

Chapter 4

Application of MASI: The Case of Republic of Korea

This section[1] examines the case example of Korea for the application of a series of analytical tools (MASI) (Cho and Moon, 2013) introduced in the previous section.

Measurement

In 2021, Korea ranked 24th out of 62 economies, rising by two steps from 2020. Korea's competitiveness structure at specific factor levels is shown in Figure 1. Korea belonged to the low-level group in Factor Conditions (53) and Workers (50). The ranks of Korea in Business Context (32) and Policymakers & Administrators (23) which showed medium-level competitiveness, were stable without any significant changes compared to 2020. In the other four factors including Demand Conditions (11), Related Industries (16), Entrepreneurs (20), and Professionals (19), Korea was classified as a high-level country.

Analysis

Korea was categorized in the medium–intermediate group. It can then be compared with the six medium-strong countries in order to analyze its relative strengths and weaknesses. Figure 2 shows that Korea was

---

[1] This chapter is abstracted and extended from IPSNC (2020).

49

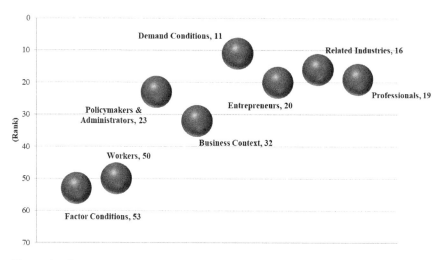

Figure 1.   Structure of Korea's national competitiveness (factor level).

Note: The numbers are the national competitiveness rankings of each factor.

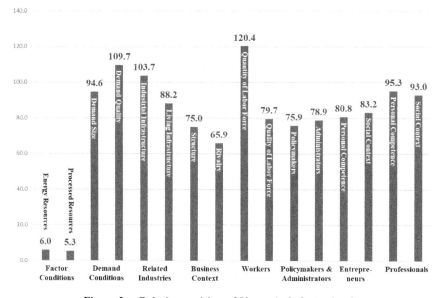

Figure 2.   Relative position of Korea (sub-factor level).

weaker than the medium-strong countries in most of the sub-factors. Korea was particularly weak in Quality of Labor Force under Workers and the sub-factors under Factor Conditions, Business Context,

Policymakers & Administrators, and Entrepreneurs, where Korea was less than 85 percent of the average level among the six medium-strong countries. In addition, for Demand Size, Living Infrastructure, and Social Context of Professionals, Korea was 85–95 percent of the average level among the six medium-strong countries. However, with respect to Demand Quality, Industrial Infrastructure, and Quantity of Labor Force, Korea had similar or higher competitiveness than the average among the six medium-strong countries.

Simulation

Korea ranked 24th in the overall national competitiveness rankings, such as the no strategy ranking. If Korea pursues a cost strategy, it will drop to 41st place. On the other hand, if Korea applies a differentiation strategy, it will move up to the 12th place, which is higher than its current ranking (24) by 12 places. Korea has a competitive structure with relatively high scores on Demand Conditions and Related Industries in the physical factors and Entrepreneurs and Professionals in the human factors. Therefore, Korea should pursue a differentiation strategy for further enhancement of its national competitiveness.

Implementation

Optimal strategic mix (Macro level)

The key strategic variables are listed in Table 1 to indicate the different stages of economic development. In the far-right column of the table, specific strategic implementations are suggested. For example, in the case of Factor Conditions, Korea's deficiency in natural resources can be overcome through internationalization such as imports or investment in foreign mining industries. Korea's manufacturing-based economy can be upgraded to a knowledge-based economy by creating higher value-added products. The strategic guidelines of this table are illustrated for Korea after an in-depth analysis of its competitiveness. A similar illustration can be made for other countries based on the competitiveness data included in this National Competitiveness Research report.

Table 1.   Development stages and policy implementations: A case of Korea.

Factors	Stages			Strategies for enhancing competitiveness
	Developing	Transitional	Developed	
Physical Factors				
Factor conditions	Resource-based	Manufacturing-based	Knowledge-based	• Overcome problems through internationalization • Create high value-added products by applying high technology and design to the production processes
Business context	Protectionism	Efficiency	Competition	• Enhance corporate competences such as management techniques and labor-management relations • Attract investment and establish a system to encourage competition by opening up the domestic market
Related industries	Physical infrastructure (Roads & Ports)	Industrial cluster	Regional integration	• Develop R&D competence by strengthening academic-industrial cooperation and increasing R&D expenditures • Create synergies of technology, human resources, and services through regional integration
Demand conditions	Quantity	Quality	Sophistication	• Enlarge the market size by exporting and investing abroad • Pay more attention to the sophistication of the market

Human Factors

Workers	Cheap	Motivated	Skilled	• Establish mutually beneficial labor-management relations and improve worker motivation • Improve skill level of the workforce by establishing a lifetime education and training system
Policymakers & administrators	Facilitation	Support & regulation	Advice	• Enhance the stability and efficiency of the political system • Regulate critical issues such as environment, health and safety as an adviser; reduce other regulations and unnecessary intervention
Entrepreneurs	Risk taking	Efficiency developing	Value creating	• Improve the market mechanism for enhancing a creative mindset among entrepreneurs • Reduce direct support for start-up firms
Professionals	Operational	Managerial	Strategic	• Enhance tertiary education and open the skilled labor market • Create a social context for professionals

Term-priority matrix (*Micro level*)

Identification of weak criteria

The weak criteria that need to be improved are summarized in Figure 3. If a rank of a certain criterion is lower than that of the sub-factor, we categorize it as the weak area of Korea. Two sub-factors under demand conditions do not have weak criteria and will be excluded from the term-priority matrix. Moreover, we excluded the uncontrollable variables such as natural resources under factor conditions. Accordingly, 38 criteria under 13 sub-factors, or about 39 percent of the total 98 criteria, are classified as Korea's weak area.

- Factor Conditions

Energy Resources (56): Korea ranked 56th in this sub-factor due to its small land size (58) and poor endowment of natural resources. Korea had low competitiveness in oil reserves (50) and natural gas reserves per capita (46). And it was placed in the medium-level group in coal reserves per capita (30) and freshwater resources per capita (39).

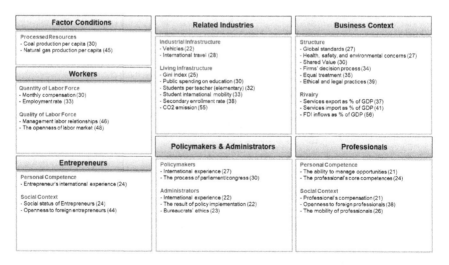

Figure 3.   Criteria for public policy formulation.

Note: Two sub-factors under Demand Conditions do not have weak criteria and thus are not included for policy formulation.

Processed Resources (48): Except for natural gas production (45) and coal production per capita (30) in which Korea was classified in the low-level group, Korea had medium-level competitiveness in meat production (26) per capita, wood production per capita (32), and oil production (38).

- Demand Conditions

Demand Size (14): Korea showed high competitiveness in GDP (12), export of goods and services (8), and import of goods and services (10), while it showed relatively weak performance in GDP per capita (22), which leads it to be classified in the medium-level group.

Demand Quality (6): Korea's strength in this sub-factor was derived from its superior position in consumer sophistication on design (8) and new technology (3); Korea also showed strong performance in consumer sophistication on quality (12), health and environmental issues (16), and intellectual property rights (19).

- Related Industries

Industrial Infrastructure (8): Korea showed the best performance in Industrial Infrastructure among the whole sub-factors. The country was categorized in the medium-level group with vehicles (22) and international travel (28). However, Korea displayed remarkably high-level competitiveness in transportation, such as international maritime (11), communication infrastructure such as internet users (4), and technology infrastructures such as R&D expenditures as a percentage of GDP (2) and patents granted (3).

Living Infrastructure (20): In education, such as public spending on education (30), students per teacher (32), and student mobility (33), Korea was classified in the medium-level group, performing relatively weak. Instead, it showed high-level competitiveness in tertiary enrollment rate (4), medical services (2), personal security (14), social safety net (19), and leisure, sports, and culture facilities (18). However, it demonstrated relative weakness or very low-level competitiveness in the Gini index (25) and CO_2 emissions (55).

- Business Context

Structure (26): Korea showed high-level competitiveness in some criteria measuring business strategy and governance among firms, particularly in unique brands (10). However, Korea showed relatively weak performance in most of the other criteria, such as ethical value (24) and firms' decision structure (23), shared value (30), equal treatment (35), and health, safety, and environmental concerns (27), where the country belonged to the medium-level group.

Rivalry (35): While Korea had high-level competitiveness in outward foreign direct investment (FDI) as a percentage of GDP (15) in investment openness, it recorded low-level competitiveness in inward FDI (56). For trade openness, Korea showed medium-level competitiveness in goods exports (25) and imports (28) openness but had relatively weak positions in services exports (41) and imports (37) as a percentage of GDP. In regard to portfolio openness, Korea had medium-level competitiveness in terms of both financial inflows (27) and outflows (23) as a percentage of GDP.

- Workers

Quantity of Labor Force (39): Korea showed high-level competitiveness in the number of labor force (20) and medium-level competitiveness in working hours (14). It performed relatively weak in the criteria of employment rate (33) and monthly compensation for manufacturing workers (30), in which the country was categorized as the medium-level group and the low-level group, respectively.

Quality of Labor Force (39): Korea ranked high in literacy rate (7) and education (16). In attitude and motivation (27), the competitiveness of Korea was medium-level. However, the country showed low-level competitiveness in the openness of the labor market (48) and the relationship between managers and workers (46).

- Policymakers & Administrations

Policymakers (26): Korea showed high-level competitiveness in the education level of policymakers (15). And the country was classified in the medium-level group in the process of parliament/congress (30), the results of legislation (24), policymakers' ethics (24), and international experience (27).

Administrators (20): Similar to the sub-factor for Policymakers, Korea displayed high-level competitiveness in the education level of administrators (17) and the process of government (19). However, it showed only medium-level competitiveness in criteria of international experience (22), the result of policy implementation (22), and bureaucrats' ethics (23).

- Entrepreneurs

Personal Competence (21): Korea showed an exceptionally strong standing in entrepreneur's competence (1), and also established high-level competitiveness in the areas of the process of decision making (19), the result for decision making (20), and education level (20). And Korea was classified in the medium-level country in international experience (24), in which the ranking of the country was slightly lower than in that of the other criteria for this sub-factor.

Social Context (21): Korea had high-level competitiveness in new business (5), availability of entrepreneurs (15), and support for the social system (15). However, the country should make some improvements in entrepreneurs' social status (24) and openness to foreign entrepreneurs (44), where it was classified in the medium-level group and the low-level group, respectively.

- Professionals

Personal Competence (18): Korea displayed high rankings in most criteria under this sub-factor, including the professional's decision making (17), education level (18), and international experience (19). And the country was classified in the medium-level group in these two criteria: the professional's core competences (24) and the ability to manage opportunities (21).

Social Context (18): Except for the criterion of openness to foreign professionals (38) where Korea showed low-level competitiveness, the country displayed high and medium level performance in the other four criteria: availability of professionals (11), social status of professionals (18), and professional's compensation (21), and the mobility of professionals (26).

Constructing a Term-Priority Matrix

The 13 sub-factors listed in Figure 3 are organized into a 4 × 3 matrix in order to provide an overview for policy suggestions as shown in Table 2. The sub-factors in the short term (Term 1) in the order of correlation are Administrations, Policymakers, and Rivalry. The sub-factors under the

Table 2.   Correlation with GDP per capita (2020–2021).

Priority	Term 1		Term 2		Term 3		Term 4	
	Sub-factor	r.	Sub-factor	r.	Sub-factor	r.	Sub-factor	r.
High	Administrators	0.907	Industrial infrastructure	0.914	Personal competence (E)	0.899	Living infrastructure	0.826
Medium	Policymakers	0.758	Social context (E)	0.823	Structure	0.763	Quality of labor force	0.554
Low	Rivalry	0.562	Processed resources	0.400	Social context (P)	0.671	Quantity of labor force	−0.625
					Personal competence (P)	0.654		

Note: All correlation coefficients are significant at 1 percent.

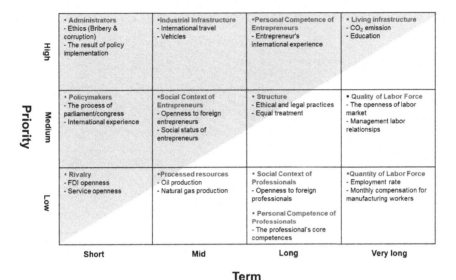

Figure 4. Term-Priority Matrix: The case of Korea.

midterm (Term 2) are Industrial Infrastructure, Social Context of Entrepreneurs, and Produced Resources. The sub-factors in the long term (Term 3) are Personal Competence of Entrepreneurs, Structure, and Social Context and Personal Competence of Professionals. The sub-factors in the very long term (Term 4) are Living Infrastructure, Quality of Labor Force, and Quantity of Labor Force. Therefore, it would be more effective for the Korean government to pay strategic attention to the areas in the upper-left hand corner in Figure 4.

References

Cho, D. S. and H. C. Moon. 2013. *From Adam Smith to Michael Porter: Evolution of competitiveness theory* (extended edition). Singapore: World Scientific Publishing.

Institute for Policy and Strategy and National Competitiveness (IPSNC). 2020. *IPS National Competitiveness Research 2019–2020*. Seoul: IPSNC.

Chapter 5

Snapshot of Top 30 Economies*

#1. Denmark (+1)

With public debt at around 33 percent of GDP (as of 2019), a figure much lower than the OECD average; Denmark had room to finance support for its businesses. Denmark's GDP contracted by −3.3 percent in 2020, which is smaller than the average contraction among EU countries, −6.1 percent. Exports of services dropped, while exports of goods held up slightly better, mainly thanks to record-high sales of pharmaceutical products. Denmark shows a relatively fast pace of economic recovery as mobility data and consumption covered by credit card transactions have returned to to 2019 levels by June 2020. In addition, international travel restrictions gave a boost to domestic tourism which partially offset the losses.

#2. Canada (−1)

The scale of Canada's GDP loss was −5.4 percent in 2020, which is larger than the world's average scale of loss, −3.3 percent. The export sector was damaged due to the reliance on US exports (the US accounts for 73.5 percent of total Canadian exports in 2020). Additionally, Canadian crude oil exports plunged as North American fuel demand dropped due to measures taken to control the COVID-19 pandemic (oil revenue accounts

---

*Figure in parenthesis is the positional change from the previous edition of National Competitiveness 2019–2020.

for about 10 percent of Canada's GDP and 20 percent of merchandise exports). However, economic activity picked up following the start of de-confinement in May 2020. Monthly GDP troughed at 18 percent below pre-crisis levels in April; by July, the gap was only around 6 percent. Activity in some sectors, including retail and wholesale trade, is already back to pre-crisis levels. The large injection of support to household income has played an important role, but income increases have also outstripped consumption and the household saving rate has risen substantially.

#3. Netherlands (+4)

The scale of GDP loss (−3.8 percent) in the Netherlands was smaller than the EU average (−6.1 percent). Although the infection rate proliferated in the Netherlands from September towards the end of 2020, the COVID-19 situation in the Netherlands remained relatively stable over half of the year of 2020 (until August). In other areas, the Netherlands is benefitting from companies exiting the UK due to Brexit. According to the Netherlands Foreign Investment Agency (NFIA), 140 companies have made the move from the UK to the Netherlands since the Brexit referendum in 2016 and another 420 internationally operating firms that have their European base in the UK are discussing possible plans to move to the Netherlands. Digital connectivity in the Netherlands has always ranked amongst the best in the world, which has facilitated the seamless transition to home-working (the Netherlands has one of the highest internet user penetration rates in the EU at 96 percent).

#4. Sweden (+1)

Due to the government's herd immunity approach to the COVID-19 pandemic, Sweden only went through mild lockdown measures. Despite the mass disruption brought about by the pandemic, the damage to the Swedish economy was limited. It recorded a GDP growth rate of −2.8 percent in 2020 while its contraction was a lot smaller than the average among EU countries, −6.1 percent. On top of this, the Swedish economy expanded at a far superior rate (increased by 0.1 percent) than many of its European counterparts over the first three months of 2020 following the government's decision not to impose a full lockdown. The household consumption remained resilient: the level of consumption in May was close to the December 2019 level. For the whole year, private consumption expanded by 6.3 percent in the third quarter in 2020 and fell just by 0.8 percent in the fourth quarter of 2020. Consumer confidence is recovering since the summer of 2020 (domestic tourism during the summer months supported by private consumption and card transactions have increased since the end of June, including for non-grocery goods). On the external front, exports of goods and services increased 4.5 percent on a seasonally-adjusted quarterly basis in the fourth quarter, which was below the third quarter's 14.9 percent expansion.

#5. Singapore (−2)

Ever since the outbreak of the COVID-19 pandemic, Singapore managed to keep the infection rate under control. However, Singapore recorded a GDP growth rate of −5.4 percent in 2020, which is lower than the world's average GDP growth rate, −3.3 percent. This is mainly due to Singapore's high dependency on both trade and cross-border flows of people. Foreigners without permanent residence make up roughly 30 percent of Singapore's population. In the first six months of 2020, Singapore's foreign workforce shrank by 75,700. The foreign direct investment (FDI) flows into Singapore fell by 37 percent (Singapore's fall in FDI was steeper than that for ASEAN as a whole, where FDI fell by 31 percent). The escalation of the trade conflict between the US and China disrupted the trade flows of Singapore's open economy; bilateral trade between the US and China indirectly contributes to 1.1 percent of Singapore's GDP. Singapore is a very open economy and it depends not only on what happens domestically, but also on how the whole global economy changes. And until the virus is contained globally, it will be very difficult to say how Singapore alone can recover.

#6. Switzerland (−2)

Switzerland's lockdown triggered a large decline in GDP in the second quarter of 2020, albeit to a lesser extent than in many other European countries. Switzerland experienced dramatic decline in both imports and exports (Switzerland exports of goods and services as a percentage of GDP is 66.13 percent). The tourism sector was largely damaged due to lockdown measures, for example only 8 percent of hotels in eastern Switzerland remained open. Furthermore it is the world's biggest gold refining center and a major transit hub. A collapse in shipments to China and India, whose vast jewelry markets were partially shut down by the COVID-19 pandemic, drove Swiss exports of gold in 2020 to the lowest point since at least 2012. China, once the biggest buyer, received no gold at all from Switzerland for the third straight month in December of 2020. The value of Swiss watch exports declined by almost 22 percent in 2020 compared to 2019, and accommodation and food services recorded a 54.2 percent drop in economic output.

#7. Australia (+3)

The Australian economy has been hit by the pandemic less severely than many other countries. The export sector remained resilient as 75 percent of its goods exports are to East Asia, a region that is growing faster than Europe or the US and which, in most cases, has handled the pandemic well. However, Australia is weathering diplomatic and trade tensions following sanctions imposed by China on several export products. Specifically, seven categories of products barley, sugar, lobster, wine, timber, coal, and copper ore and concentrate have been refused by Chinese customs since 6 November 2020. Nevertheless, the overall contraction in exports has been mitigated by the continued strong performance of certain mineral commodity exports. Iron ore, Australia's top export and a critical ingredient for China's massive steel sector, have been spared from any crossfire due to the importance of iron ore in overall export values to Mainland China (around 60 percent of China's iron ore imports originates from Australian mines). Consequently, total Australian exports of goods to China actually increased in 2020. Furthermore, due to the high percentage of domestic tourism revenue to the total tourism revenue (international and domestic tourism accounts for 26 percent and 74 percent respectively), Australia was able to escape the worst situation.

#8. United States (−2)

The US GDP growth rate in 2020 was −3.5 percent, which is slightly lower than the world's average GDP growth rate of −3.3 percent. Throughout the year, spending on most services remained weak. After the country entered an emergency in March 2020, most states issued "stay-at-home" orders, and the peak of social distancing behavior took place in the first half of April (during this period, mobility inflow decreased by about 35 percent). By late April 2020, even after several states announced partial reopening, nationally, mobility inflow has only recovered to the level 20 percent lower than the typical inflow observed in January 2020. As a result, consumer spending, which accounts for more than two-thirds of the economy, plunged by 3.9 percent in 2020, the worst performance since 1932. The COVID-19 crisis has damaged the nation's industrial production (i.e., output in the manufacturing, mining, and utility sectors). The manufacturing sector employs nearly 13 million workers. And as the unemployment rate surged, the number of people filing for weekly unemployment claims remained over four times as high as they were before the pandemic, the unemployment rate peaked in April 2020 at 14.8 percent before declining to a still-elevated level in December 2020 at 6.7 percent. The US also recorded a 49 percent drop in FDI, falling to an estimated US$134 billion. The sharp decline took place in wholesale trade, financial services, and manufacturing. Plus, cross-border M&A sales of US assets to foreign investors in 2020 fell by 41 percent, mostly in the primary sector.

#9. Finland (+2)

The GDP contraction in Finland was −2.9 percent, which is a lot smaller than the EU average contraction of −6.1 percent in 2020. The Finnish economy has undergone one of the mildest of all eurozone contractions in the first half of 2020 as the restrictive measures imposed were relatively lenient (Google mobility data indicates that Finland has seen just a modest drop from the peak in activity in early October), which was in line with a relatively small number of infections. Finland took the top spot for digital skills so that it was well-prepared for a shift in working practices in the wake of the COVID-19 pandemic. Before the outbreak, 14.1 percent of Finland's workforce already reported working from home, compared with just 3.6 percent in the US. Despite the Eurozone crisis, the Finnish industry fared better than expected: production in the electrical and electronics industry has remained on the rise and the industrial manufacturing of machinery and equipment has performed better than the European reference group. The manufacturing sector, in particular, has shown good resilience: the turnover of companies in the electronics and electrotechnical industry (telecommunications equipment, electrical equipment, and medical technology) grew by approximately 6 percent; the turnover of information technology companies (IT services and software) grew by 5 percent in 2020. Finally, Finnish exports in the food and beverage sector increased by 7 percent year-on-year in 2020.

#10. New Zealand (−2)

New Zealand has reported only a handful of new cases. As a result, the pace of recovery for its domestic economy was relatively fast (electronic card spending bounced back quickly from a sharp fall in April and remains robust). However, international tourism, which represented 20 percent of total exports in New Zealand (as of 2019), has been constrained to nil as the border remains closed to foreign non-residents, although this impact was partially offset by the increase in domestic tourism. This generated a direct contribution of 5.5 percent to GDP and the indirect value added of industries supporting tourism generated an additional 3.8 percent of GDP. Beyond this, the supply chain disruption in China had some effects on New Zealand as China is one of its top trading partners, accounting for about 28 percent of New Zealand's total exports. Amid the COVID-19 pandemic, New Zealand's exports have taken a major hit since the epidemic, with everything from timber to meat and fruit facing delays and cancellations. For example, from January to October 2020, food service consumption also dropped 21 percent, compared to 2019. Furthermore, factory closures in China have left New Zealand outlets short of vacuums, televisions, and iPhones.

#11. Hong Kong SAR (−2)

Hong Kong's GDP growth rate in 2020 was −6.1 percent, which is lower than the world's average, −3.3 percent. Economic activity in Hong Kong weakened significantly since 2019 as rising trade tensions between the US and China and heightened uncertainty took a toll on exports and investment while private consumption and visitor arrivals have declined due to the demonstrations throughout the summer of 2019 and this negative trend continued throughout the year of 2020. The same dynamics are visible in the fund flows. For example, the foreign currency deposits at banks operating in Singapore have nearly doubled since July; economists see this as a signal that money has started to flow out of Hong Kong and into

Singapore. According to the American Chamber of Commerce in Singapore survey, 23 percent of companies with offices in Hong Kong, were thinking of leaving to escape the ongoing turmoil related to the demonstrations. Hong Kong lost its title as the world's freest economy to Singapore for the first time since 1995 in a global survey, due to social unrest and uncertainties that have rattled its reputation as a global financial hub. Hong Kong's overall economic freedom score fell primarily due to a decline in its marks for investment freedom, according to the 2020 Index of Economic Freedom published by the Heritage Foundation.

#12. Belgium (+1)

Belgium recorded a GDP growth rate of −6.4 percent in 2020, which is slightly lower than the average GDP contraction of EU countries, −6.1 percent. On the demand side, household consumption was almost 10 percent below its pre-crisis level at the end of 2020 due to the stringent lockdown measures. However, the other components of demand are lagging far less behind. It is particularly noteworthy that after a strong rebound of 20 percent in the third quarter, productive investment continued its recovery in the fourth quarter (+4.6 percent), so that by the end of 2020, it only lags 3.6 percent behind its pre-crisis level. Alongside this, the employment level remained resilient despite lockdown. After having lost 50,000 jobs during the first and second quarters of the last year, the labor market has regained jobs: more than 7,000 in the third and more than 20,000 in the fourth, mainly in the scientific, technical, and administrative support professions (+11,600 jobs in Q4) and the healthcare sector (+6,500 jobs).

#13. United Arab Emirates (−1)

The GDP contraction in the United Arab Emirates (UAE) was −5.9 percent in 2020, which is smaller than the average contraction among Gulf Cooperation Council (GCC) countries (−7.6 percent). The UAE has been largely successful in containing the spread of the virus as its vaccination rate is the world's second-highest after Israel. However, as the region has had one of the strictest lockdowns in the world, such travel restrictions and strict lockdown measures have had a serious impact on tourism, businesses, and the supply chain of businesses in the UAE (the travel and tourism sector has a total contribution of around 12 percent of GDP). Emirates Airlines, hotels, and other tourism-related businesses have experienced significant material losses. In particular, the drop in 82 percent of scheduled departure flights from the UAE was particularly damaging. The impact of low oil prices due to OPEC+ oil production cuts, lower oil prices, and reduced global oil demand is another key reason for the decline in the UAE economy (the UAE is the world's eighth largest oil producer).

#14. China (+2)

The coronavirus outbreak seems largely under control in China, and thus it was able to record a positive GDP growth rate of 2.3 percent in 2020. China is expected to be the only major economy to have grown in 2020. Exports rose 3.6 percent over the full year; exports have boomed on the back of pent-up demand for masks and other COVID-19-related materials: medical appliances (+41 percent), textiles (+29 percent; for personal protective equipment (PPE[1]), and home appliances accounting for +24 percent). Booming sales of fridges, toasters, and microwaves to households across the locked-down world have helped propel China's manufacturing engine back to life. The highest export value item, automated machinery, and parts grew by 11 percent from a year ago. This is a good result bearing in mind that some Chinese technology companies were banned from selling their products to major markets, in particular, the US.

#15. Austria (+2)

Austria's GDP contracted by 6.6 percent in 2020. Nevertheless, private consumption has proven remarkably resilient, thanks to the very favorable labor market situation, with unemployment registering at the 5 percent mark (the unemployment rate stood at 5.7 percent, which is 1.3 percent above the pre-pandemic level). Inflation has also recently slowed down to below 2 percent, supporting household purchasing power. Investment activity has proven rather robust despite the weaker export performance.

---

[1] Includes protective clothing, helmets, goggles, or other garments or equipment designed to protect the wearer's body from injuries or infection.

Austria's government took quick, decisive measures to combat the spread of COVID-19, closing much of the retail sector and mandating a strict stay-at-home policy in March 2020. As a result of the success in reducing infection rates, Austria was one of the first Western countries to reopen their economy in stages beginning in April 2020. Moreover, Austria's agricultural exports managed growth of 4 percent in the first six months of 2020 by comparison with the same period in 2019, with imports rising by 1 percent (the agricultural sector employs 3.5 percent of the active population and represents 1.1 percent of GDP). Simultaneously, Austria's trading relationships in the agricultural sector have become more international than ever before: The proportion of trade with European third countries (including Russia) has risen and exports to the US and Asia have continued to follow an upward trend.

#16. Germany (−1)

Germany's economy shrank by 4.9 percent in 2020; this is a smaller contraction than many countries in the eurozone. Germany is benefiting from a marked rebound as exports to China, Germany's second-largest trading partner, increased by 15.4 percent in June compared with the same month a year earlier. However, the manufacturing sector saw a strong reduction in its activity due to limited demand from both the internal and external markets. Production in Germany's key automotive industry was rebounding in June, but this remains about 20 percent below production levels in February — before the virus struck. Compared with February 2020 (the month before restrictions were imposed), manufacturing production in October 2020 was 4.9 percent lower with production in the automotive industry recording a decrease of 6 percent. Furthermore, the COVID-19 pandemic had a strong impact on all of the services sub-sectors, with tourism being particularly affected due to a significant decline in the number of international tourists. The restaurant industry was also hit hard, with the overall turnover from March to August 2020 being 40.5 percent lower than the same period a year earlier.

#17. Israel (−3)

Israel's economic performance was one of the weakest among developed countries. Private consumption fell by 9.4 percent (due to its stringent lockdown), which is a greater decline than the fall of 3.9 percent in the US, 4.9 percent in South Korea, and 6.4 percent in Japan. Even in France, which suffered greatly from the pandemic and lockdowns, the decline in private consumption was smaller, at 7.1 percent. On top of this, the fall in employment in Israel was almost the steepest among the OECD countries. By April, Israel's unemployment rate jumped from 4 percent (before the outbreak) to 24.4 percent. Although Israel had the fastest rollout of vaccinations in the world (54 percent of the population is vaccinated as of March 2021), the country went through a series of stringent lockdowns before it launched the vaccination campaign in December 2020. The first lockdown ran from late March until early May; the second lockdown began in September and lasted for three weeks (Israel was the first country in the world to announce the second national coronavirus lockdown; Israel instituted its third national lockdown in late December, which lasted for 6 weeks. The economy has been devastated by these lockdowns and many young Israelis have lost their jobs. To add to the difficulties, Prime Minister Benjamin Netanyahu is on trial for fraud, breach of trust, and accepting bribes for his role in a series of scandals, and there have been demonstrations staged weekly for many months demanding his resignation. As a result, there have been several elections held in Israel without a clear winner.

#18. Taiwan, China (–)

Taiwan's economy recorded a GDP growth of 2.98 percent in 2020, outpacing China's growth rate of 2.3 percent. Taiwan is one of the few economies to record positive growth amid the COVID-19 pandemic. Taiwan's domestic demand has held up better than many other economies — thanks to the early containment of the pandemic — as Taiwan has been able to maintain most of its domestic economic activities without implementing any lockdown measures. Although the uncertainty surrounding US–China relations poses great challenges to Taiwan's economic prospects, goods exports grew by 4.9 percent in 2020 compared to a year ago. Exports of electronic components registered especially high growth (technology products account for more than half of Taiwan's total exports) due to the fact that the restriction on people's activities and business interactions as well as the increase in remote work and online learning boosted the demand for 5G communication applications, high-performance computing devices, electronic components, video component, and other information communications technology-related products. Taiwan Semiconductor Manufacturing Company (TSMC) has been another major contributor to export growth as there were many surging orders from Huawei before the US ban on such sales in September 2020.

#19. United Kingdom (+1)

Over the first half of the year, the economic impact on the UK was the second worst (after Spain) among all OECD countries. The GDP contraction of the UK in 2020 (−9.9 percent) exceeded the contraction of its neighboring countries (the Netherlands, Denmark, and Belgium). Brexit adds further uncertainty to Britain's economic outlook. On the positive side, the UK technology sector has been showing solid growth: investment into the UK tech sector hit US$15bn in 2020 — US$200m higher than the previous record set in 2019 (this puts the UK in third place globally behind only the US and China). It is also notable that deep-tech investments into research and development (R&D)-intensive companies rose by 17 percent, the highest growth rate globally. Nearly two-thirds (63 percent) of the investment (US$9.4bn) into UK tech came from abroad, which shows Britain's tech sector is solidifying its position as one of the world's top tech hubs. Furthermore, the lockdown imposed in the UK amid the second wave of the COVID-19 pandemic was less stringent than the first one. Hence, the impact of the lockdown on economic activity has been lower in autumn 2020 than in spring 2020. The employment level in the UK has remained resilient despite the stringent measures taken amid the COVID-19 pandemic: the unemployment rate fell to 5 percent in the three months between November (2020) and January (2021), down from 5.1 percent in the previous three-month period in 2020. This is much lower than the average unemployment rate of EU countries, 7.3 percent during the same period (between November and January).

#20. Kuwait (−1)

Kuwait's GDP contracted by 8.1 percent in 2020, which is a larger contraction than the average among GCC countries (−7.6 percent).

The pandemic came as a double whammy to Kuwait's economy–with global lockdowns creating an almost overnight drop in demand and oil prices and local lockdowns impacting economic activity. The global COVID-19 pandemic has substantially reduced external demand for Kuwaiti exports while domestic lockdown measures adversely affected non-oil GDP. Public spending and the plunge in oil revenues will lead to a fiscal deficit of 7.3 percent of GDP as about 90 percent of the Kuwaiti government's revenues are derived from oil. The restriction measures on movement have drastically reduced the usage of automobiles, industrial activity, shipping, and transportation and this impact was immediately felt with Kuwait's oil and gas demand. The lack of physical demand for crude oil saw prices collapse quickly. LNG prices, which were already under pressure from weak fundamentals have also fallen further as working from home has caused a sharp decline in Kuwait's electricity usage.

#21. Saudi Arabia (+4)

Saudi Arabia recorded a GDP growth rate of −4.1 percent in 2020, which is far less than the average GDP decline of GCC countries of −7.6 percent. The oil prices have been hit hard by the spread of COVID-19 around the world, as the pandemic disrupted supply chains. However, the non-oil sector remained strong (+1.6 percent in Q1; −8.2 percent in Q2; −2.1 percent in Q3) despite the major decline in the oil sector (−4.6 percent in Q1; −5.3 percent in Q2; −8.2 percent in Q3) which had partially offset the economic loss. Saudi Arabia has also had room to provide fiscal support as its debt to GDP for 2019 was at 24 percent, the second-lowest in the G20. Saudi Arabia's FDI increased by 12 percent in the first half of 2020 compared with the same period last year; FDI to Saudi Arabia is estimated at US$4.7 billion in 2020, a rise of 4 percent compared to a year earlier. Saudi Arabia has revamped over half of the 400 foreign direct investment (FDI) regulations. As a result, Saudi Arabia ranked 62nd out of 190 economies in the World Bank's 2020 Doing Business Report, up by 30 places from a year earlier. Moreover, Saudi Arabia is in the process of diversifying its economy through the "Vision 2030" program by investing in the tourism and entertainment sectors. This should strengthen the non-oil sector of the economy, and therefore a revival in growth is expected as the economy diversifies.

#22. Japan (−1)

As Japan's large trading partners were recovering rapidly towards the end of 2020, its exports have started to pick up since the second half of 2020. However, Japan has shown a larger contraction in its economy compared to its neighboring countries, South Korea and China. Japan was the first major country to slide into a recession as of Q1 of 2020 since the country had already posted negative GDP growth figures in late 2019 before the outbreak of the COVID-19 pandemic. As a result, consumer spending was already weakening in late 2019. Ongoing difficulties in bringing COVID-19 infections under control further held back the recovery of domestic demand. The country's exports in 2020 plunged by 11.1 percent as the pandemic battered global demand for industrial products such as cars (Japan's car exports plummeted by 20 percent). The declines in automobiles and parts manufacturing were significant, reflecting factory suspensions and weak consumer demand due to the pandemic. Major car manufacturers in Japan have begun implementing planned output cuts at their domestic assembly plants: Toyota Motor, the country's biggest carmaker, in late March of 2020 announced its first-ever major suspension of domestic production lines. In March 2020, Japan announced the postponement of the Tokyo 2020 Olympics by a year.

#23. France (0)

The French economy contracted by 8.2 percent in 2020, which is larger than the average contraction of EU countries (−6.1 percent). The spread of the COVID-19 pandemic has affected the whole production capability of the country coupled with a slowdown in global demand, and concerns regarding the availability of raw materials; the manufacturing and other industries in the country have temporarily shut down their industrial operations. The French lockdown was stringently enforced until May, with non-essential shops closed, and was only gradually lifted over the second quarter, with cafes and restaurants being allowed to open in June. The massive decline in the number of international travelers and tourists visiting France resulted in international visitors spending dropping by a staggering 82 percent (travel & tourism accounts for 8.5 percent of the French economy). Contrary to this, France remained a popular destination for foreign investment despite the pandemic. France recorded 1,215 new foreign direct investment projects in 2020; this was 17 percent less than the 1,468 new projects the year before; the drop was smaller than feared after the pandemic forced the economy into a near standstill last spring. The number of jobs created or preserved as a direct result of these investments: 34,567 in total, of which 29,809 were new jobs (the number of jobs created or preserved was 13 percent less than in 2019, but represented a 14 percent rise compared to 2018).

#24. Republic of Korea (+2)

Effective measures to contain the spread of the COVID-19 pandemic have limited the estimated fall in GDP to just by 1 percent in 2020, the smallest decline among the OECD countries. The government has introduced massive policy support (spending 15 percent of GDP) to minimize the loss. Exports of goods began to improve in the second half as key export markets started to recover. In the third quarter exports to the US rebounded by 10.1 percent, with similar or stronger growth to Taiwan, Germany, and Canada. In the fourth quarter, exports returned to growth with key partners in South and Southeast Asia such as India, Vietnam, Malaysia, Indonesia, and Thailand. The sales of IT products boosted overall growth. Notably, some areas, such as non-memory chips, OLED, COVID-19 test kits, and eco-friendly automobiles have posted a record-high performance for 2020. Semiconductor exports were exceptionally strong as overseas sales of semiconductors surged 30 percent from a year earlier. Other major items such as mobile devices, displays, and computers also soared 39.8 percent, 28.0 percent, and 14.7 percent year-on-year. Exports in the second half of 2020 came to a US$272.2 billion surplus. This helped trim the losses of the first half when exports had plunged more than 10 percent.

#25. Slovenia (−3)

Slovenia recorded a GDP growth of −5.5 percent in 2020, which is higher than the average GDP growth rate of EU countries (−6.1 percent). In the first quarter of 2020, the economy was already contracting by 2.4 percent year-on-year, one of the steepest falls in the region. In the second quarter, as the country felt the full effect of the crisis, the contraction reached almost 13 percent year-on-year as lockdown measures resulted in a significant drop in domestic demand. Furthermore, as the economy is highly integrated into EU value chains (Slovenia exports goods and services as a percentage of GDP is 85.38 percent), the outlook remains highly uncertain. Exports of goods dropped by 12 percent year-on-year in the first half of 2020 mostly due to the weak performance of Slovenia's main trading partners (the neighboring countries). Slovenian exports to the EU have plummeted by 30 percent since March, especially automotive and capital goods exports to Italy, France, and Germany. The tourism sector has also received considerable damage from the COVID-19 pandemic and tourism revenue accounts for about 8.4 percent of the total GDP. The number of foreign tourists decreased by as much as 74 percent, and overnight stays by 71 percent.

#26. Czech Republic (+5)

The economic contraction in the Czech Republic (−5.6 percent) was less severe than the average contraction of the EU countries (−6.1 percent). The Czech Republic benefited from a relatively strong starting economic position going into the crisis, with unemployment at 1.8 percent in February 2020, strong wage growth (2019: 6.4 percent), high household savings (1Q20: 13.5 percent of gross disposable income), and low debt levels overall. The fiscal balance posted annual surpluses from 2016 to 2019 and total public debt fell from a peak of 45 percent of GDP in 2013 to just 31 percent in 2019. Therefore, although we expect fiscal deficits of approximately −6 percent of GDP in 2020 and 2021, respectively, and a rise of public debt, the figure of the fiscal deficit would still be fairly low as compared to peers. Alongside this, the unemployment rate remained resilient: the unemployment rate increased to 2.9 percent in October 2020, from 2.0 percent a year before, but remained the lowest in the European Union (EU). Moreover, despite the downfall of the FDI inflow in 2020 due to the disruption of the manufacturing industry, the country remained the second-largest recipient of FDI inflows in Central Europe. In the Global Innovation Index (GII), the Czech Republic ranked 24th out of 131 economies in 2020, outperforming the average of European countries in five out of seven GII pillars.

#27. India (−3)

India's GDP fell by 8 percent in 2020, far exceeding the world's average contraction of −3.3 percent. As of June 2021, India is the second-worst affected country by the COVID-19 pandemic in terms of overall case numbers (India recorded 20 million cases as of May 2021). India is susceptible to a rapid spread of the virus, due among other things to high population density in combination with health care services that are less abundant than in many developed countries. As of September 2020, approximately 21 million salaried jobs in the country have since been lost. According to a survey by Local Circles, within the first eight months after the pandemic began, 78 percent of Indian startups and SMEs had reduced their workforces to supply chain disruptions, lockdowns, and economic losses. The credit information company Experian in October 2020 estimated that 43 percent of Indian consumers witnessed a decline in their household income due to the impact caused by the pandemic. In March 2021, India imposed a nationwide lockdown that remained in effect until May. The lockdown in India was one of the most stringent in the world: except for some essential services and activities, the rest of India's US$2.9 trillion economies remained closed during the lockdown period. For the Indian economy, private consumption and investment are the two biggest engines for growth. However, during the first quarter of 2020, private consumption declined by 27 percent, while investments by private businesses fell by 47 percent.

#28. Poland (0)

The economic contraction of Poland in 2020 (−2.7 percent) was a lot smaller compared to the average contraction of EU countries (−6.1 percent). The Polish economy was strong when the COVID-19 pandemic hit (the country performed well during the 2014−2019 period, with the real GDP growth rate generally exceeding 3 percent, driven by private consumption). Poland has the second-lowest unemployment rate compared to other EU member states. Despite the impact of the pandemic, Poland has actually increased its number of FDI projects from 145 to 165 when comparing January–April in 2020 to the same period in 2019. Only a few countries, including Poland, managed to increase the inflow of foreign direct investment projects in the first four months of 2020. Real estate projects continue to make up the bulk of FDI into Poland, but it was renewable energy investments that drove the growth compared to a year earlier (foreign investors announced 16 new projects in the renewables sector in the January to April period). While the unemployment rate has been structurally low (just above 3 percent), more than one in four employees in Poland have temporary contracts, twice the EU average. The industrial sector in Poland accounts for 17 percent of Poland's GDP according to 2019 data. Amongst the industrial sectors, the automotive sector has been the worst-hit domestic sector amid the COVID-19 pandemic, with passenger car production down 99 percent on an annual basis after the first wave of the pandemic. Furthermore, the tourism sector has been largely damaged as the number of tourists fell by 54.3 percent in the first half of 2020 compared to the previous year.

#29. Italy (0)

Italy's GDP decline in 2020 (−8.9 percent) was sharper than the average decline of EU countries (−6.1 percent). Italy entered the crisis with a very high public debt, the second-highest in the Eurozone. The weak public balances imply that the government has to strike a difficult balance between supporting the economy and preserving debt sustainability. On the other hand, there is one sector that has grown despite the impact of the COVID-19 pandemic, food and beverage (Italy is one of the main agricultural players in the EU, being the biggest European producer of rice, fruits, vegetables, and wine; the agricultural sector represents 1.9 percent of Italian GDP). The turnover of the food and beverage sector grew by 3.1 percent in Italy. The food and beverage industry have accelerated production to respond to the growing demand of end consumers, who have returned to the kitchen and are forced to eat at home due to lockdown measures. Many food and beverage companies in Italy are increasing their production capacity and investing in new automation equipment to allow for more flexible production and to keep up with potential demand variation during the coming years. However, the Italian economy showed weak performance overall as industrial production shrank by 31 percent compared to the same quarter in 2019 and car sales by 57 percent. Alongside this, international tourism is expected to remain muted, which is very troublesome for the economy as it contributes to 13 percent of GDP).

#30. Malaysia (0)

Malaysia's GDP contracted by 5.6 percent in 2020, which is larger than the world's average contraction of 3.3 percent. Malaysia has continued to perform strongly in recent years thanks to strong global demand for electronics, increased demand for commodities, such as oil and gas (Malaysia is a major outsourcing destination for components manufacturing, after China and India). Despite the unprecedented nature of the pandemic, Malaysia's external trade performed fairly well with exports rebounding in the second half of 2020 as rubber products, electrical and electronics (E&E) products, as well as palm oil and palm oil-based agriculture products registered strong export expansion. Malaysia recorded a significant year-over-year expansion in shipments to major trading partners China (46.8 percent) and the US (27.6 percent). Exports of machinery and appliances also grew by 29 percent year-over-year as of June 2020. Meanwhile, imports fell by 5.6 percent year-over-year for that month, leaving the country with its largest trade surplus on record at RM20.9bn (US$4.9bn); Malaysia's trade surplus widened by 26.9 percent in 2020, the largest trade surplus ever recorded thus far, while total trade amounted to RM1.8 trillion, down 3.6 percent year-on-year. However, despite the strong performance of exports, the foreign investment inflows to Malaysia fell by 68 percent in 2020, the worst rate in Southeast Asia (FDI in Southeast Asia decreased by 31 percent on average). Experts say a key contributor to the dismal performance (or decrease in investor confidence) is growing political risk and the policy implications as populism around the world takes precedence. Despite the strong performance of the trading sector, Malaysia is estimated to have lost more than MYR 100 billion (USD 24.61 billion) this year due to the coronavirus pandemic (Malaysia is the second-most favorite tourist destination in Asia after Thailand; its tourism revenue account for 5.7 percent of GDP).

References

Aburumman, A. A. 2020. COVID-19 impact and survival strategy in business tourism market: the example of the UAE MICE industry. *Ideas*. https://ideas.repec.org/a/pal/palcom/v7y2020i1d10.1057_s41599-020-00630-8.html.

Aljazeera. 2020. Tens of thousands rally in Israel calling on Netanyahu to resign. https://www.aljazeera.com/news/2020/10/10/tens-of-thousands-rally-in-israel-calling-on-netanyahu-to-resign.

Alshammari, H. 2021. Spending efficiency program saves $106bn in four years. *Arab News*. https://www.arabnews.com/node/1852691/business-economy.

Argaam. 2021. FDI inflows to Saudi Arabia rise 4% to $4.7 bln in 2020: UNCTAD. https://www.argaam.com/en/article/articledetail/id/1438403.

Argaam. 2021. Saudi Arabia revamped over 200 regulations to drive up FDI, says investment minister. Arab News. https://www.arabnews.com/node/1799461/business-economy.

Argus. 2020. Manufacturing slowdown intensifies in Japan. https://www.argusmedia.com/news/2095607-manufacturing-slowdown-intensifies-in-japan.

Astone, P. 2020. Renewables power Poland FDI surge amid pandemic. FDI Intelligence. https://www.fdiintelligence.com/article/77865.

Augustine, B. D. 2021. How Gulf countries are recovering from the economic slump. GulfNews.https://gulfnews.com/special-reports/how-gulf-countries-are-recovering-from-the-economic-slump-1.1615454572962.

Austria. 2020. Agricultural exports from Austria are defying the coronavirus. https://www.advantageaustria.org/id/news/20201103_Agrarexporte_aus_Oesterreich.en.html.

Bauer, L., K. Broady., W. Edelberg., and J. O'Donnell. 2020. Ten facts about Covid-19 and the U.S. economy. Brookings. https://www.brookings.edu/research/ten-facts-about-covid-19-and-the-u-s-economy/.

BBC. 2020. Coronavirus: Israel to impose three-week national lockdown. https://www.bbc.com/news/world-middle-east-54134869.

BBC. 2021. Japan's economy shrinks 4.8% in 2020 due to Covid. https://www.bbc.com/news/business-56066065.

Bernama. 2021. Malaysia's trade surplus rises 26.9% to RM184.8 billion — DOSM. The Edge Market. https://www.theedgemarkets.com/article/malaysias-total-trade-shrinks-36-yoy-rm18-trillion-tandem-softer-global-demand-due-covid19.

Biehl, F. 2021. Austria: Walking a tightrope. ING. https://think.ing.com/articles/austria-walking-a-tightrope/.

BNP Paribas. 2020. Strong capacity to rebound. https://economic-research.bnpparibas.com/html/en-US/Strong-capacity-rebound-7/23/2020,39227. Accessed March 1, 2021.

Buchholz, K. 2020. Japanese household consumption hits rock bottom. Statista. https://www.statista.com/chart/22481/japanese-household-consumption/.

Budget Direct Australian Tourism Statistics. 2020. https://www.budgetdirect.com.au/travel-insurance/research/tourism-statistics.html. Accessed March 1, 2021.

Business Standard. 2021. UK jobs market shows further resilience in Feb even during lockdown. https://www.business-standard.com/article/international/uk-jobs-market-shows-further-resilience-in-feb-even-during-lockdown-121032301114_1.html. Accessed May 3, 2021.

Canadian Press. 2020. Crude-by-rail exports fall to four-year low as economic slump frees pipeline space. City News. https://ottawa.citynews.ca/national-business/crude-by-rail-exports-fall-to-four-year-low-as-economic-slump-frees-pipeline-space-2583424.

Charef, K. and J. Proutat. 2020. Sweden. BNP Paribas. https://economic-research.bnpparibas.com/html/en-US/hard-economy-12/17/2020,40647.

Chiang, M. 2020. Taiwan's economic challenges beyond COVID-19. East Asia Forum. https://www.eastasiaforum.org/2020/10/09/taiwans-economic-challenges-beyond-covid-19/.

China-CEE. 2020. Czech Republic economy briefing: The Czech Economy in 2020: Slump & Recovery. https://china-cee.eu/2020/12/27/czech-republic-economy-briefing-the-czech-economy-in-2020-slump-recovery/.

China-CEE. 2021. Poland economy briefing: Impact of the pandemic on the Polish economy in 2020. https://china-cee.eu/2021/01/27/poland-economy-briefing-impact-of-the-pandemic-on-the-polish-economy-in-2020/.

Choudhury, S. R. 2021. India reports more than 357,000 new Covid cases as total crosses 20 million. CNBC. https://www.cnbc.com/2021/05/04/india-covid-crisis-total-reported-cases-cross-20-million.html.

Coface. 2021. Czechia (Czech Republic). https://www.coface.com/Economic-Studies-and-Country-Risks/Czechia-Czech-Republic. Accessed March 1, 2021.

Cohen, K. 2020. Tokyo 2020 Olympics officially postponed until 2021. ESPN. https://www.espn.com/olympics/story/_/id/28946033/tokyo-olympics-officially-postponed-2021.

Cook, C. 2020. Coronavirus: Supply disruptions for New Zealand importers and exporters. RNZ. https://www.rnz.co.nz/news/business/410810/coronavirus-supply-disruptions-for-new-zealand-importers-and-exporters.

Coljin, B. 2020. Finland in 2021: Strong Covid-19 report card provides no guarantees. ING. https://think.ing.com/articles/finland-strong-corona-report-card-provides-no-guarantees-for-2021-recovery/.

Corporate Services. 2020. China's Security Law pushes Hong Kong firms to Singapore. https://www.corporateservices.com/chinas-hong-kong-security-law-singapore-relocation/.

D'Andrea & Partners. 2020. The impact of COVID-19 on the UAE economy. https://www.dandreapartners.com/the-impact-of-covid-19-on-the-uae-economy/.

Derekduck. PPE Protective Clothing. https://www.derekduck.com/page/238#. Accessed March 1, 2021.

Destatis. 2020. Production in October 2020: +3.2% on the previous month. https://www.destatis.de/EN/Press/2020/12/PE20_483_421.html.

DW. Germany. Trade and production surges after coronavirus. https://www.dw.com/en/germany-trade-and-production-surges-after-coronavirus/a-54484400. Accessed March 1, 2021.

EBRD. Country Assessment: Slovenia. file:///C:/Users/13U70P/Downloads/ transition-report-202021-slovenia%20(1).pdf. Accessed March 1, 2021.

Edwards, J. 2020. The cost of Covid: Australia's economic prospects in a wounded world. Lowy Institute. https://www.lowyinstitute.org/publications/ costs-covid-australia-economic-prospects-wounded-world.

Erken, H., R. Hayat. and Ji. K. 2020. Coronavirus: The economic impact of COVID-19 on India. Rabobank. https://economics.rabobank.com/publications/ 2020/march/coronavirus-economic-impact-covid-19-on-india/.

Euler Hermes. Deep recession ahead. https://www.eulerhermes.com/en_global/ economic-research/country-reports/Kuwait.html. Accessed March 1, 2021.

Euler Hermes. External challenges, strong domestic fundamentals. https://www. eulerhermes.com/en_global/economic-research/country-reports/Austria. html. Accessed March 1, 2021.

Euler Hermes. Strong fundamentals help to mitigate the impact of Covid-19. https://www.eulerhermes.com/en_global/economic-research/country-reports/Czech-Republic.html. Accessed March 1, 2021.

Eurostat. 2021. Euro area unemployment at 8.1%. https://ec.europa.eu/eurostat/ documents/portlet_file_entry/2995521/3-04032021-AP-EN.pdf/cb6e5dd6-56c2-2196-16b7-baf811b84a4f. Accessed May 3, 2021.

Fitch Ratings. 2020. Fitch affirms Czech Republic at 'AA-'; Outlook Stable. https://www.fitchratings.com/research/sovereigns/fitch-affirms-czech-republic-at-aa-outlook-stable-24-07-2020.

FMT Reporters. 2021. UN Report: Malaysia's FDI drops by 68% to just US$2.5bil in 2020. FMT. https://www.freemalaysiatoday.com/category/ nation/2021/01/25/malaysias-fdi-drops-by-68-to-just-us2-5bil/.

General Authority of Statistics. Gross domestic product third quarter 2020. https:// www.stats.gov.sa/sites/default/files/Gross%20Domestic%20Product%20Third%20Quarter%202020%20EN_0.pdf. Accessed March 1, 2021.

Gillen, N. 2021. Study finds Tokyo 2020 with no spectators would result in economic loss of up to $23 billion. inside the games. https://www.insidethe-games.biz/articles/1103338/tokyo-2020-no-spectators-economic-loss#.

Gulf News. 2021. Why UAE economy is positioned for strong post-COVID transformation? GR. https://www.globalreinsurance.com/why-uae-economy-is-positioned-for-strong-post-covid-transformation/1436379.article.

Fairless, T. 2020. Germany expects V-shaped economic rebound from coronavirus. Wall Street Journal. https://www.wsj.com/articles/germany-expects-v-shaped-economic-rebound-from-coronavirus-11598973469.

Falk, G., J. A. Cater., I. A. Nicchitta., E. C. Nyhof., and P. D. Romero. 2021. Unemployment Rates During the COVID-19 Pandemic: In Brief. Congressional Research Service. https://fas.org/sgp/crs/misc/R46554.pdf.

Focus, F. 2020. How Covid hit New Zealand seafood exports to China. Tridge. https://www.tridge.com/news/how-covid-hit-nz-seafood-exports-to-china.

Focus Economics. Investment in Sweden. https://www.focus-economics.com/country-indicator/sweden/investment. Accessed March 1, 2021.

Global Business Outlook. 2020. Key sectors to drive Saudi Arabia's Vision 2030 strategy. https://www.globalbusinessoutlook.com/key-sectors-to-drive-saudi-arabias-vision-2030-strategy/.

Global Monitor. 2020. Kuwait Oil and Gas Market Report with COVID-19 impact analysis. EIN Presswire. https://www.einnews.com/pr_news/529157455/kuwait-oil-and-gas-market-report-with-covid-19-impact-analysis.

Goh, G. 2021. Singapore's FDI flows were down 37% in 2020. The Business Times. https://www.businesstimes.com.sg/government-economy/singapores-fdi-flows-were-down-37-in-2020.

Gronholt-Pedersen, J. and S. Jacobsen. 2020. Boom in Denmark's economy may be replaced by 10% contraction, central bank says. Reuters. https://www.reuters.com/article/us-health-coronavirus-denmark-cenbank/boom-in-denmarks-economy-may-be-replaced-by-10-contraction-central-bank-says-idINKBN21J4TG.

Hall, M. 2020. How China is moving beyond Australia for its iron ore hunger. Mining Technology. https://www.mining-technology.com/features/how-china-is-moving-beyond-australia-for-its-iron-ore-hunger/. Accessed March 1, 2021.

Halon, E. 2020. Israeli unemployment exceeds one million: 24.4% of workforce. The Jerusalem Post. https://www.jpost.com/breaking-news/the-number-of-unemployed-in-israel-tops-1-million-for-the-first-time-623151.

Hertzberg, E. 2020. Exports to China plunge after Canada arrests Huawei CFO. Aljazeera. https://www.aljazeera.com/economy/2020/2/5/exports-to-china-plunge-after-canada-arrests-huawei-cfo.

Hincks, J. 2020. How Israel became the first rich country to go into a second nationwide coronavirus lockdown. Times. https://time.com/5889096/israel-second-lockdown-covid-19/.

Hobson, P. 2021. Swiss gold exports fell to record low in 2020 as pandemic upended trade. Reuters. https://www.reuters.com/article/swiss-trade-gold-idINKBN29X1HQ.

Holton, K. and M. Chambers. 2020. Britain resists COVID lockdown as Europe counts cost. Reuters. https://www.reuters.com/article/uk-health-coronavirus-idUSKBN27E1QR

Hong, J., R. Chang., and K. Varley. 2021. The best and worst places to be as variants outrace vaccinations. Bloomberg. https://www.bloomberg.com/graphics/covid-resilience-ranking/. Accessed March 1, 2021.

Hospitality Net. 2020. WTTC Says France Looks Set To Lose €48 Billion From Missing Tourists And Visitors Due To Pandemic. https://www.hospitalitynet.org/news/4100385.html.

ICAEW. 2020. Emerging from COVID-19: A Kuwait perspective. https://www.icaew.com/insights/viewpoints-on-the-news/2020/nov-2020/emerging-from-covid-19-a-kuwait-perspective.

I Feel Slovenia. 2021. 2020: A tourist year marked by the Covid-19 pandemic. https://www.slovenia.info/en/press-centre/press-releases/15084-2020-a-tourist-year-marked-by-the-covid-19-pandemic.

IMF. 2019. IMF Executive Board Concludes 2019 Article IV Consultation Discussions with People's Republic of China–Hong Kong Special Administrative Region. https://www.imf.org/en/News/Articles/2019/12/26/pr19485-hksar-imf-executive-board-concludes-2019-article-iv-consultation-discussions.

IMF. 2021. Real GDP growth. https://www.imf.org/external/datamapper/NGDP_RPCH@WEO/OEMDC/ADVEC/WEOWORLD/JPN/SAU/ISR.

ING. 2021. China: a good year ahead for exports. Hellenic Shipping News. https://www.hellenicshippingnews.com/china-a-good-year-ahead-for-exports/.

Kapoor, R. and R. Biswas. 2020. Assessing the economic impact of escalating Australia-China trade frictions. IHS Markit. https://ihsmarkit.com/research-analysis/assessing-the-economic-impact-escalating-australiachina-trade-frictions-Nov2020.html.

Khanna, V. 2021. Covid-19's impact to still weigh on Singapore's economy in 2021. The Straitstimes. https://www.straitstimes.com/opinion/virus-impact-to-still-weigh-on-economy-0

Kyodo News. 2021. Japan exports rebound in Dec. from pandemic, 1st rise in 25 months. https://english.kyodonews.net/news/2021/01/ee92c5bc42bb-update1-japans-2020-exports-fall-11-largest-drop-in-11-yrs-due-to-pandemic.html.

Ledent, P. 2021a. Belgium: The abnormal cycle. ING. https://think.ing.com/articles/belgium-the-abnormal-cycle/.

Ledent, P. 2021b. Belgian economic forecasts. ING. https://www.ing.be/en/retail/my-news/economy/Focus-Belgian-economy.

Lee, Y. N. 2021. Asia's top-performing economy in 2020 could grow even faster this year. CNBC. https://www.cnbc.com/2021/02/23/taiwan-asias-top-performing-economy-in-2020-could-grow-faster-in-2021.html.

Liu, S. 2020. Taiwan faces a changed economic outlook in Asia following COVID-19. Brookings. https://www.brookings.edu/blog/order-from-chaos/2020/06/29/taiwan-faces-a-changed-economic-outlook-in-asia-following-covid-19/.

Malaysia External Trade Development Corporation. 2020. Trade Performance 2020. Matrade. https://www.matrade.gov.my/en/malaysia-trade-performance/181-malaysian-exporters/trade-performance-2020#. Accessed May 6, 2021.

Manlangit, M. 2020. Amid COVID-19, Singapore Safeguards Citizens' Jobs at the Expense of Foreign Workers. The Diplomat. https://thediplomat.com/2020/11/amid-covid-19-singapore-safeguards-citizens-jobs-at-the-expense-of-foreign-workers/.

Meredith, S. 2020. Sweden's economy actually grew in the first quarter after it opted against a full virus lockdown. CNBC. https://www.cnbc.com/2020/05/29/coronavirus-swedens-gdp-actually-grew-in-the-first-quarter.html.

Ministry of Business, Innovation & Employment. 2020. Tourism and the economy. https://www.mbie.govt.nz/immigration-and-tourism/tourism-research-and-data/tourism-data-releases/tourism-and-the-economy/. Accessed March 1, 2021.

Mutikani, L. 2021. COVID-19 savages U.S. economy, 2020 performance worst in 74 years. Reuters. https://www.reuters.com/article/us-usa-economy-idUSKBN29X0I8.

News Wires. 2021. Israel eases Covid-19 restrictions 6 weeks after lockdown. France 24. https://www.france24.com/en/middle-east/20210207-israel-lifts-first-restrictions-6-weeks-after-lockdown.

Nijland, J. 2020. 2020 – the year of CLASSIC Dutch resilience and robustness. Invest in Holland. https://investinholland.com/news/2020-the-year-of-classic-dutch-resilience-and-robustness/.

Nikkei Staff Writers. 2020. Japan business sentiment dives to 11-year low on coronavirus hit. Nikkei Asia. https://asia.nikkei.com/Economy/Japan-business-sentiment-dives-to-11-year-low-on-coronavirus-hit.

Nordea. The economic context of Slovenia. https://www.nordeatrade.com/dk/explore-new-market/slovenia/economical-context. Accessed March 1, 2021.

Nordea. The economic context of Malaysia. https://www.nordeatrade.com/en/explore-new-market/malaysia/economical-context. Accessed March 1, 2021.

Nordea. The economic context of Poland. https://www.nordeatrade.com/en/explore-new-market/poland/economical-context. Accessed March 1, 2021.

Nordea. 2020. The Danish economy's recovery. https://insights.nordea.com/en/economics/danish-economic-outlook-sep2020/.

Nordea. The economic context of Italy. https://www.nordeatrade.com/dk/explore-new-market/italy/economical-context. Accessed March 1, 2021.

Nordea. 2021. The economic context of Switzerland. https://www.nordeatrade.com/no/explore-new-market/switzerland/economical-context. Accessed March 1, 2021.

Nordea. The economic context of Germany. https://www.nordeatrade.com/dk/explore-new-market/germany/economical-context. Accessed March 1, 2021.

Nordea. The economic context of Austria. https://www.nordeatrade.com/fi/explore-new-market/austria/economical-context. Accessed March 1, 2021.

Nordea. 2021. Foreign direct investment (FDI) in Saudi Arabia. https://www.nordeatrade.com/en/explore-new-market/saudi-arabia/investment. Accessed March 1, 2021.

Nordea. 2021. The economic context of the United Arab Emirates. https://www.nordeatrade.com/en/explore-new-market/united-arab-emirates/economical-context. Accessed March 1, 2021.

OECD. 2020. Slovenia. https://www.oecd-ilibrary.org/urban-rural-and-regional-development/oecd-tourism-trends-and-policies-2020_93f6c6fb-en.

OECD. 2020. Slovenia Economic Snapshot. https://www.oecd.org/economy/slovenia-economic-snapshot/.

OECD. 2020. Denmark economic snapshot. https://www.oecd.org/economy/denmark-economic-snapshot/.

OECD. 2020. Sweden economic snapshot. https://www.oecd.org/economy/sweden-economic-snapshot.

OECD. 2020. Switzerland economic SNAPSHOT. https://www.oecd.org/economy/switzerland-economic-snapshot/.

OECD. 2020. Australia economic SNAPSHOT. https://www.oecd.org/economy/australia-economic-snapshot/.

OECD. 2020. New Zealand economic Snapshot. https://www.oecd.org/economy/new-zealand-economic-snapshot/.

OECD. 2020. Korea economic SNAPSHOT. https://www.oecd.org/economy/korea-economic-snapshot/.

OECD. 2020. Japan Economic Snapshot. https://www.oecd.org/economy/japan-economic-snapshot/.

OECD. 2020. United States Economic Snapshot. https://www.oecd.org/economy/united-states-economic-snapshot/.

Office for National Statistics. 2021. Coronavirus: how people and businesses have adapted to lockdowns. https://www.ons.gov.uk/economy/economicoutputandproductivity/output/articles/coronavirushowpeopleandbusinesseshaveadaptedtolockdowns/2021-03-19

Oh, C. 2021. Korean exports rebound in Dec in double digits, helping to trim 2020 losses. Pulse. https://pulsenews.co.kr/view.php?year=2021&no=5340.

O'Collins, Paul. 2020. Why the UK tech sector is proving so resilient to Covid-19. UKRI. https://www.innovateukedge.ukri.org/blog/Why-UK-tech-sector-proving-so-resilient-Covid-19.

Oxford Business Group. 2020. Malaysian exports rise despite Covid-19, but will it last? https://oxfordbusinessgroup.com/news/malaysian-exports-rise-despite-covid-19-will-it-last.

Pandey, P. C. 2021. India's Path to 10.8 Million Covid-19 Cases: Socio-Economic Impact and State Response. Mei@75. https://www.mei.edu/publications/indias-path-108-million-covid-19-cases-socio-economic-impact-and-state-response.

Pan, T. and K. Liu. 2021. Taiwan posts 2.98% GDP growth in 2020. Focus Taiwan. https://focustaiwan.tw/business/202101290018.

Paul, M. 2020. Malaysia unveils 10-year tourism plan after USD 25 billion loss in 2020. TD. https://www.traveldailymedia.com/malaysia-unveils-10-year-tourism-plan-after-usd-25-billion-loss-in-2020/.

Pharmaceutical Technology. 2021. How Finland's pandemic response is securing new investment opportunities. https://www.pharmaceutical-technology.com/

sponsored/how-finlands-pandemic-response-is-securing-new-investment-opportunities/. Accessed March 1, 2020.

Qiu, S. and G. Crossley. 2021. China's export growth beats expectations on resilient global demand. Reuters. https://www.reuters.com/world/china/chinas-export-growth-beats-expectations-resilient-global-demand-2021-01-14/.

Research and Markets. 2020. Impact of COVID-19 on the French Economy. https://www.researchandmarkets.com/reports/5013562/impact-of-covid-19-on-the-french-economy.

Reuters. 2020. Coronavirus impact: French economy shrank by record 13.8% in Q2, better than feared. The Economic Times. https://economictimes.indiatimes.com/news/international/business/coronavirus-impact-french-economy-shrank-by-record-13-8-in-q2-better-than-feared/articleshow/77278092.cms?from=mdr.

Reuters Staff. 2020. China's exports, imports seen expanding at faster pace in November: Reuters poll. Reuters. https://www.reuters.com/article/us-china-economy-trade-poll-idUSKBN28E0K6.

Reuters Staff. 2020. Timeline: Tension between China and Australia over commodities trade. Reuters. https://www.reuters.com/article/us-australia-trade-china-commodities-tim-idUSKBN287099.

Rhee, C. and K. Utsunomiya. 2020. Transcript of April 2020 Asia and Pacific Department Press Briefing. IMF. https://www.imf.org/en/News/Articles/2020/04/16/tr041520-transcript-of-april-2020-asia-and-pacific-department-press-briefing.

Roh, J. 2021. South Korea exports post sharpest expansion in 26 months in December, but slide 5.4% year-on-year in 2020. Reuters. https://www.reuters.com/article/us-southkorea-economy-trade-idUSKBN2961WZ.

Rosen, B., R. Waitzberg., and A. Israeli. 2021. Israel's rapid rollout of vaccinations for COVID-19. *Israel Journal of Health Policy Research*. https://doi.org/10.1186/s13584-021-00440-6.

Roy, E. A. 2020. New Zealand economy faces 'serious impact' from coronavirus outbreak. *The Guardian*. https://www.theguardian.com/world/2020/feb/27/new-zealand-economy-faces-serious-impact-from-coronavirus-outbreak.

Rushe, D. 2021. US economy shrank by 3.5% in 2020, the worst year since second world war. *The Guardian*. https://www.theguardian.com/business/2021/jan/28/us-economy-shrank-2020-worst-year-since-second-world-war.

Saadi, D. 2020. IMF raises its forecast of Gulf economies contraction to 7.6% for 2020. *S&P Global*. https://www.spglobal.com/platts/en/market-insights/latest-news/oil/063020-imf-raises-its-forecast-of-gulf-economies-contraction-to-76-for-2020.

Sakpal, P. 2020. Malaysia macro update — It's downtime. *ING*. https://think.ing.com/articles/malaysia-macro-update-its-the-downtime/.

Santander. Poland: Economic and Political Outline. https://santandertrade.com/en/portal/analyse-markets/poland/economic-political-outline. Accessed May 3, 2021.

Sella, A. and R. Fuller. 2020. Lessons from Italy: The impact of COVID-19 on the food and beverage industry. *Duff & Phelps*. https://www.duffandphelps.com/insights/publications/valuation/italy-impact-of-covid-19-on-food-beverage-industry.

Sfakianakis, J. 2019. 2020 to be a year of resilience and performance. *Arab News*. https://www.arabnews.com/node/1597151.

Shiao, V. 2018. US, China trade war to impact Singapore's economy in three ways: Chan Chun Sing in Parliament. *The Business Times*. https://www.businesstimes.com.sg/government-economy/us-china-trade-war-to-impact-singapore%E2%80%99s-economy-in-three-ways-chan-chun-sing-in

Shukla, S. 2020. 43% Indian consumers record decline in household income: Experian Global. *The Economic Times*. https://economictimes.indiatimes.com/news/economy/indicators/43-indian-consumers-record-decline-in-household-income-experian-global/articleshow/78658994.cms?from=mdr.

Singh, K. 2020. COVID-19 has pushed the Indian economy into a Tailspin. But there's a way out. *The Wire*. https://thewire.in/economy/covid-19-india-economic-recovery.

Sipalan, J. 2021. Malaysia says FDI inflows dropped 56% in 2020 to $3.4 bln. Reuters. https://www.reuters.com/article/malaysia-economy-investment-idINL3N2L014I.

Skelton, S. K. 2021. One-fifth of all UK tech investment went to just 10 scaleup firms in 2020. *Computer Weekly*. com. https://www.computerweekly.com/news/252497962/One-fifth-of-all-UK-tech-investment-went-to-just-10-scaleup-firms-in-2020#.

Smyth, J. 2020. New Zealand's 'go hard and early' Covid policy reaps economic rewards. *Financial Times*. https://www.ft.com/content/b8c4ab58-99db-4af2-9449-5fd70a9235ce.

Stangarone, T. 2021. The Impact of COVID-19 on South Korean Trade in 2020. *The Diplomat*. https://thediplomat.com/2021/02/the-impact-of-covid-19-on-south-korean-trade-in-2020/.

Strachan, R. 2020. The state of play: FDI in the Czech Republic. *Investment Monitor*. https://investmentmonitor.ai/manufacturing/the-state-of-play-fdi-in-the-czech-republic.

Strachan, R. 2020. The state of play: FDI in Poland. *Investment Monitor*. https://investmentmonitor.ai/poland/the-state-of-play-fdi-in-poland.

SWI. 2020. Pandemic could cost Swiss tourism sector CHF6 billion. https://www.swissinfo.ch/eng/covid-19_pandemic-could-cost-swiss-tourism-sector-chf6-billion/45656158.

SWI. 2021. Pandemic leads to historic drop in Swiss foreign trade. https://www. swissinfo.ch/eng/pandemic-leads-to-historic-drop-in-swiss-foreign-trade/46325736#.

Technology Industries of Finland 2021. Economic Outlook. https://teknologiateollisuus.fi/sites/default/files/inline-files/T_Talousn%C3%A4kym%C3%A4t_1-2021-ENG-01.pdf.

Teoh, S. 2021. Foreign direct investments into Malaysia plunge, experts cite growing political risk. *The Straitstimes*. https://www.straitstimes.com/asia/se-asia/foreign-direct-investments-into-malaysia-plunge-experts-cite-growing-political-risk.

The Canadian Press Staff. 2020. Merchandise trade deficit more than doubles in April as exports plunge. *CTV News*. https://www.ctvnews.ca/business/merchandise-trade-deficit-more-than-doubles-in-april-as-exports-plunge-1.4968966.

The Economist. 2020. Oil price plunge to leave lasting damage on Canadian economy. http://country.eiu.com/article.aspx?articleid=769264060&Country=Canada&topic=Economy&subtopic=Rec_6.

The First News. 2020. Foreign direct investments grew in Poland despite crisis — daily. https://www.thefirstnews.com/article/foreign-direct-investments-grew-in-poland-despite-crisis--daily-13460.

The Local. 2021. 'Second best year in a decade' — France remains popular to foreign investors despite Covid. https://www.thelocal.fr/20210304/second-best-year-in-a-decade-france-remains-popular-to-foreign-investors-despite-covid/.

The National. 2020. Saudi Arabia's economy to rebound after Covid-induced contraction. https://www.thenationalnews.com/business/saudi-arabia-s-economy-to-rebound-after-covid-induced-contraction-1.1088371.

The Straitstimes. 2020. Singapore overtakes Hong Kong as world's freest economy. https://www.straitstimes.com/business/economy/singapore-overtakes-hong-kong-as-worlds-freest-economy.

The World Bank. 2020. Polish Economy to Shrink in 2020 due to Pandemic: Then It May Start a Moderate Recovery. https://www.worldbank.org/en/news/press-release/2020/10/07/polish-economy-to-shrink-in-2020-due-to-pandemic-then-it-may-start-moderate-recovery.

Tourism New Zealand. 2020. About the tourism industry. https://www.tourismnewzealand.com/about/about-the-tourism-industry/#.

TUC. 2020. Impact of Covid-19 and Brexit for the UK economy. https://www.tuc.org.uk/research-analysis/reports/impact-covid-19-and-brexit-uk-economy.

UNCTAD. 2021. Global foreign direct investment fell by 42% in 2020, outlook remains weak. https://unctad.org/news/global-foreign-direct-investment-fell-42-2020-outlook-remains-weak#.

U.S. Department of State 2019. 2019 Investment Climate Statements: Netherlands. ecoi.net. https://www.ecoi.net/de/dokument/2031895.html.

U.S. Department of State 2020. Custom Report Excerpt: Netherlands. https:// www.state.gov/report/custom/34d05c4d96/.

U.S. Department of State 2020. 2020 Investment Climate Statements: Austria. https://www.state.gov/reports/2020-investment-climate-statements/austria/.

Vindobona. 2021. Austrian Foreign Trade: Covid-19 Pandemic Takes its Toll. https://www.vindobona.org/article/austrian-foreign-trade-covid-19-pandemic-takes-its-toll.

Wijffelaars, M. 2020. COVID-19 has a devastating impact on Italy's economy. Rabobank. https://economics.rabobank.com/publications/2020/july/covid-19-devastating-impact-on-italy-economy/.

WITS. *Slovenia Trade Statistics.* https://wits.worldbank.org/CountryProfile/en/ SVN. Accessed March 1, 2021.

WITS. *Switzerland Trade Statistics: Exports, Imports, Products, Tariffs, GDP and related Development Indicator.* https://wits.worldbank.org/CountryProfile/en/ CHE#:~:text=Switzerland%20exports%20of%20goods%20and,percentage %20of%20GDP%20is%2053.90%25. Accessed March 1, 2020.

Worldometer. 2021. Netherlands. https://www.worldometers.info/coronavirus/ country/netherlands/. Accessed March 1, 2021.

Workman, D. Canada's Top Trading Partners. *World's Top Exports.* https://www. worldstopexports.com/canadas-top-import-partners/. Accessed March 1, 2021.

Workman, D. Germany's Top Trading Partners. https://www.worldstopexports. com/germanys-top-import-partners/. Accessed March 1, 2021.

Xiong, C., S. Hu., M. Yang., W. Luo., and L., Zhang. 2020. Mobile device data reveal the dynamics in a positive relationship between human mobility and COVID-19 infections. *Pnas.* https://www.pnas.org/content/117/44/27087.

Yonhap. 2021. S. Korea's exports fall 5.4% in 2020 on COVID-19 fallout. *The Korea Herald.* http://www.koreaherald.com/view.php?ud=20210101000037.

Zabezhinsky, A. 2021. Israeli economy's 2020 performance not what it seems. *Globes.* https://en.globes.co.il/en/article-israeli-economys-2020-performance-not-what-it-seems-1001361306.

Part II

Special Topics: Introduction

This part discusses two key global issues; "Current Issues in China and their Implications for China's Competitiveness" and "Building Resilient Global Value Chains in the Pandemic Era: A Conceptual Framework and Case Studies of Singapore and Vietnam." The first chapter for Part II analyzes the three major issues in China including the US–China trade war, the Belt and Road Initiative (BRI), and the national security law in Hong Kong. Throughout the analysis, it provides practical implications for China, suggesting the strategies for China to increase the sustainability of the BRI, successfully manage the current dispute with the US, and address the issues with the Hong Kong protesters with the minimum economic cost. In the end, this chapter highlights a similarity of all three issues which is that the political and business interests need to be more sufficiently distinguished. Therefore, this chapter concludes that politics and the economy should always be addressed from separate contexts.

The next chapter summarizes the growing trend of protectionism among many countries amid the COVID-19 pandemic. However, this chapter points out that, indeed, many multinational corporations (MNCs) have chosen to strengthen the global value chains which are against the popular belief (or trend) that businesses would seek to re-shore their operations. This chapter argues that firms need to further pursue globalization despite the current temporary threat on the value chain; it provides the strategies to build more sustainable or resilient Global Value Chains (GVCs). In discussing this idea, this chapter addresses the examples of two countries, Vietnam and Singapore that have achieved remarkable economic success by adopting open-door policies and taking advantage of access to international resources.

Chapter 6

Current Issues in China and Their Implications for China's Competitiveness

Hwy-chang Moon, Minji Hong, Eunwon Shim, and Jungbin Yun

Abstract

The remarkable economic development of China in recent decades presents a threat to the traditional status of global hegemony. Along with the rising question of whether China will become the next new leader on the global stage, this chapter discusses the three key issues in China: the US–China trade war, the Belt and Road Initiative (BRI), and the national security law in Hong Kong. Throughout the discussion on these three major issues, we highlight the importance of distinguishing the national and business interests. Firstly, the US–China conflict will be largely alleviated when both countries distinguish the national and business interests. Similarly, the BRI will be more sustainable once the Chinese government successfully addresses the business and state interests separately. Lastly, establishing a clear boundary between politics and economy will effectively resolve the tension between the Hong Kong protesters and the central government of China. Although this chapter discusses the current issues in China, the findings from these issues are not only limited to China's situation. Perhaps, the majority of conflicts in the contemporary world will be — at least partially although it is not fully — mitigated when the politics and economy are distinguished as this chapter argues.

Keywords: The US–China trade war, the investment war, the Belt and Road Initiative (BRI), national security law, Hong Kong protest

Introduction

As the Chinese economy has risen to a dominant position in the world over the past twenty years, the decisions made by China have always drawn close interest. Hence, it is worth paying attention to the current issues that it is confronted with. To start with, the tensions between the US and China have been escalating over the past few years. As China has been expanding its influence around the world, it has come to challenge the long unquestioned dominant position of the US. The conflict between the two countries is often understood as a political issue or a hegemonic rivalry, however, the economic aspects of this issue should not be underestimated. Throughout this chapter, we attempt to correct the misled interpretations on three economic issues. In this respect, this chapter includes three sections: The US–China trade war, the Belt and Road Initiative (BRI), and the national security law of Hong Kong. In each section, we analyze the issue from various perspectives including social, political, and economic ones.

For the US–China trade war, we discuss the multiple dimensions to view it from the perspectives of trade, technology, and investment. The second section discusses the BRI issue by analyzing the connection between it and the ongoing US–China trade war to grasp a deeper understanding of the direction that China is pursuing. As a policy recommendation, we suggest an approach to make the current BRI more sustainable, which is to establish an industry cluster along with infrastructure investments. The last section discusses the national security law in Hong Kong as well as its economic impact on both Mainland China and Hong Kong. Throughout this analysis, we attempt to discover the central government's rationale to enact the law in Hong Kong despite the economic cost. This section suggests a reasonable middle ground between the Hong Kong protesters and the Chinese government, which is to distinguish politics and the economy. In conclusion, we provide the economic implications for China, which are not just limited to this case. Throughout the analysis, we have grasped a rich understanding: all three issues in China will be largely alleviated once the political and economic objectives are distinguished.

The US–China Trade War

Background

According to the data released by the International Monetary Fund (2020), the US and China ranked first and second, accounting for about 25 and 18 percent of global GDP respectively. The noticeable interaction between the two countries began in the late 1970s as the volume of trading goods between them has grown rapidly. Much of this was due to the economic reforms launched at the time by the Chinese leader Deng Xiaoping (Guo, 2018). China then joined the World Trade Organization (WTO) in 2001 and received the most favored nation (MFN) status. Lipton (The Atlantic, 2018) points out that this was a key moment that has laid the foundation for the current trade war.

As China has become the world's second-largest economy, its rapid economic growth has been viewed by the US government as a threat to its current economic and geopolitical dominance. This became very much a prominent issue of concern following the election of Donald Trump in 2016 whose administration adopted stronger protectionist policies. After his inauguration, Trump imposed economic sanctions on China with tariffs and regulations on technologies. While the conflict between the two countries appears to be a trade war at first glance, it is a complex issue that goes beyond trade and this will be addressed in the following part.

Analysis

Trade issue

The international trade deficit of the US has widened in recent years (Bureau of Economic, 2019). This trade deficit in goods with China reached up to US$419 billion in 2018, which accounts for about a half of the US total international trade deficit (*New York Times*, 2019). This aggravating bilateral deficit resulted in the adoption of protectionist measures by President Trump who eventually triggered a trade war with China to address the problem. Beginning on July 6, 2018, the US imposed tariffs on US$34 billion worth of Chinese goods. In response, China imposed higher tariffs on US products, a 25 percent tariff on US$34 billion worth of US goods. Thus, the opening shots began in this trade war.

The trade war between the US and China pinpoints one significant fact: the damage on the Chinese economy in the trade war far exceeds that on the US economy due to the big difference in the scale of imports in each country. While US exports to China only account for US$125 billion worth of goods, the US imports US$436 billion worth of goods from China (United States Census, 2021a). In other words, US imports are about four times greater than what China imports, which means that China has to bear four times higher tariffs than the US has to endure. Moreover, the largest export items from China to the US include computers, cell phones, apparels, toys, games, and sporting goods, which are elastic products that can be easily substituted by exports from other countries such as Indonesia, Malaysia, or South Korea (United States Census, 2021b, 2021c).

On the contrary, China's largest imports from the US include commercial aircraft, soybeans, automobiles, and semiconductors, which are not easy for China to substitute the trading partners (United States Census, 2021b). Nevertheless, China has not stepped back. In reflecting this tough stance, the Chinese state news publication *The Global Times* (環球時報, *Huánqiú Shíbào*), sharply criticized US policies by stating, "the trade war would be the biggest political joke in economic history" (*Global Times*, 2019b). It also emphasized that this is a war by the (Chinese) people to resist the US, insisting "China is a big and booming market, not one the US can easily give up [so that] China's economic prospects should and must be in Chinese people's own hands" (*Global Times*, 2019a).

Hegemonic issue

When discussing the US–China trade conflict, it is important to consider the nature of this hegemonic competition. Let us take a look at the changes in China's hegemonic position since the death of Mao Zedong in 1976. After a brief power struggle, Deng Xiaoping emerged to take power in China. He led his country on the path to economic reform by adopting the open-door policies to build what he termed as a "moderately prosperous society (小康社會, *xiǎokāng shèhuì*)," which is actually an idea that originated from Confucius. This refers to "a society composed of a functional middle-class" (People's Daily Online, 2020). In December 1979, Deng introduced this idea of *Xiaokang* that was rooted in what he described as the four modernization principles. Quoting an old Chinese proverb, "it doesn't matter whether a cat is black or white; if it catches mice well, it is a good cat," Deng prioritized economic development by adopting some capitalistic measures alongside communist principles or as it would be known "socialism with Chinese characteristics." As a result, in late 1978, the US aerospace company Boeing announced the sale of its 747 aircraft to various airlines in China while Coca-Cola revealed its plan to open a production plant in Shanghai (Macro Polo, 2019). From 1979, the economic reform policies helped accelerate the development of a market economy, opening it up to foreign trade. In terms of diplomatic strategy, however, Deng summarized his approach as "not to show oneself while improving one's skills and waiting for the right time," which is known as "韜光養晦 (*tāoguāngyǎnghuì*)" in Chinese. Simply, this strategy is about China hiding its time until it has obtained sufficient economic and political power.

After thirty years of reforms, China was ranked second place in GDP for the first time in 2010 when it overtook Japan (*New York Times*, 2010). In 2012, President Xi Jinping unveiled the ambitious "Chinese Dream (中國夢, *Zhōngguó Mèng*)," which would become the hallmark of his administration. Simply, it stresses the goal to achieve "the great rejuvenation of the Chinese nation" and is composed of "Two 100s." The first is the material goal of China to become a moderately prosperous society by 2021, the 100th anniversary of the Communist Party of China. The second is the modernization goal of China to become a fully developed nation by 2049, the 100th anniversary of the People's Republic of China. The Chinese Dream includes four specific goals: Strong China (economically, politically, diplomatically, scientifically, and militarily); Civilized China (equity and fairness, rich culture, and high morals); Harmonious China (amity among social classes); and Beautiful China (healthy environment and low pollution) (*New York Times*, 2013). Specifically, this includes doubling the 2010 GDP per capita (US$10,000 per person) by 2021 and completing urbanization of 70 percent of China's population (roughly one billion people) by 2030. The "modernization" aims to solidify China's position as a world leader in scientific and technological development as well as in business innovation (*New York Times*, 2013).

In 2015, Chinese Premier Li Keqiang and his cabinet issued the national strategic plan entitled "Made in China 2025 (MIC 2025, 中國製造2025, *Zhōngguózhìzào* 2025)." It set out the approach to further develop the manufacturing sector of China and aims to transform China into a global superpower by 2050, overtaking the US in sectors it currently dominates, such as semiconductors, robotics, aerospace, clean-energy cars, and artificial intelligence. China plans to upgrade its manufacturing capabilities in these industries by transforming its large labor force into a technology-intensive powerhouse. In this attempt, several Chinese companies are now leading their respective sectors, such as Baidu, Huawei, Alibaba, Xiaomi, and SMIC. The goals of MIC 2025 include increasing the domestic content of core materials by 40 percent in 2020 and 70 percent by 2025. However, since 2018, due to the trade war with the US and a backlash from European countries, MIC 2025 is becoming less of a priority for the central government. In June 2018, the Trump administration imposed higher tariffs on Chinese goods, especially manufacturing goods included in the MIC 2025 plan (Reuters, 2018b). As a result, China seemed to be easing its high-tech industrial development push, MIC 2025, while initiating a conversation with the US to reduce the tensions over trade. However, to pursue technological indigenization, the Chinese government is investing heavily in high technologies (Reuters, 2018b).

Technology issue

Huawei is a Chinese multinational technology company, mainly producing telecommunications equipment, consumer electronics, and semiconductors. It is well-known for its rapid growth: for example, it overtook Apple in 2018 and became the second-largest manufacturer of smartphones in the world, behind Samsung Electronics (*The Guardian*, 2018a). In July 2020, Huawei surpassed both Samsung and Apple, recording the largest number of phones shipped (CNN, 2020b). However, despite this notable success and recognition around the world, some governments have been seeking to restrict Huawei's access to their markets due to its recipient of undue state support and fears over its connection with the People's Liberation Army. This has provoked cybersecurity concerns that Huawei's infrastructure equipment may enable surveillance by the Chinese government (*Wall Street Journal*, 2019). As a result, with the development of 5G wireless networks around the world, there have been calls from the US and its allies to not do any kind of business with Huawei or other Chinese telecommunications companies such as ZTE (*New York Times*, 2020a). As well as this, Huawei has also been accused of assisting the state authorities in the surveillance and mass detention of the Uyghur minority population in Xinjiang (*The Times*, 2019). For instance, Huawei has tested facial recognition software that could be used to send automated "Uyghur alarms" to state authorities when it identifies members of the oppressed minority group (*Washington Post*, 2020).

In the past, Huawei has been accused of stealing the router technology of Cisco[1] (Network World, 2003). Upon discovering this, Cisco sued Huawei for "source copying," which has deepened the conflict between the two countries over technology issues. In 2012, after investigating Huawei's activities, the Intelligence Committee of the US Congress reported that Huawei and ZTE threatened the country's intellectual property rights and that this could potentially invade consumer privacy (*Wall Street Journal*, 2012). It was also reported that these two firms were involved in transactions with Iran and are thus vulnerable to the political interests of the Communist Party of China, which raises further security concerns. This security issue then led to one of the most significant diplomatic incidents between the two countries.

On December 1, 2018, Meng Wanzhou, the chief financial officer of Huawei and daughter of the company's founder, was arrested in Vancouver on an allegation of violating the US sanctions against Iran[2] by selling telecom equipment through Huawei's subsidiary, Skycom. Meng fought against extradition to the US while under house arrest in Vancouver. As a retaliation to this — although China has refused this claim — China had detained two Canadians, Michael Kovrig and Michael Spavor for "spying on national secrets" (BBC, 2020b). Moreover, in 2020, the US issued a new rule prohibiting any foreign semiconductor company from selling semiconductor chips that were produced using US software or technology to Huawei (*Wall Street Journal*, 2020b). Another consequence of the rising tensions has been efforts by the US to deny popular Chinese social media platforms like TikTok and WeChat access to the US market.

Investment issue

On April 18, 2017, President Trump signed the "Buy American and Hire American Executive Order," which seeks to increase the wages and

---

[1]Cisco is an American technology company for networking hardware, software, telecommunication equipment, and other high-technology services and products (RepTrak, 2021).
[2]The Iran Sanctions Act (ISA) prohibits any person or firm from providing Iran with any goods, services, technology, information, or support that would allow Iran to maintain or expand its domestic production (CRS, 2009).

employment rates in the US (to protect domestic workers) by tightening immigration regulations. This policy gained popularity, especially among the middle and lower classes in the US. As part of his "America First" strategy, Trump emphasized creating manufacturing jobs and increasing the number of factories in the US. Following this, in 2018, Trump signed the "Foreign Investment Risk Review Modernization Act (FIRRMA)," which granted the Committee on Foreign Investment in the United States (CFIUS) greater authority over particular types of FDI. This mainly raised the concern of Chinese investors in technology, real estate, and other industries which maintain and collect personal data, and joint ventures where technology companies contribute intellectual property. The US has weighed on blocking Chinese investments and companies from operating in its market insisting that they pose a threat to the country's national security (CGTN, 2020b).

During the 2016 campaign, Trump called the World Trade Organization (WTO) a "disaster." He stated that if US companies moved their manufacturing operations abroad, he would impose tariffs of 15–35 percent on their products. When Trump was informed that this would be against the rules of the WTO, he answered "even better. Then, we're going to renegotiate or we're going to pull out of the WTO" (*The Hill*, 2016). China, which labeled the US as being "addicted to quitting," has been taking a more collaborative approach under President Xi: Chinese officials have taken four seats among the 15 top UN agencies and boosted China's World Health Organization (WHO) contributions to US$2 billion. Furthermore, China has formed its own multilateral institutions such as Asia Infrastructure Investment Bank (AIIB).

Biden administration and China

Let us go over Trump's policies before we move on to discuss the Biden administration. "Make America Great Again" and "America First" were Trump's two major campaign slogans, which demonstrates his strong stance on protectionism and isolationism. As part of this effort, Trump reduced the corporate tax rate and eliminated the estate tax (*New York Times*, 2017b). Illegal immigration was also one of the main issues that Trump emphasized throughout his presidential campaign; he expressed a solid stand to pursue anti-immigration policies. For example, he announced his plan to build a wall on the border between the US and Mexico for which he famously claimed that Mexico would pay for it (*Washington Post*, 2018). During his term in office, Trump strengthened regulations on immigration policies and guest-worker visas. Finally, he prioritized bilateral relations over multinational agreements (CNN, 2016).

On January 20, 2021, Joe Biden was inaugurated as the 46th US president and it was clear from the beginning that he would be taking a very different approach. For example, Biden emphasized, "We (the US) will lead not merely by the example of our power but by the power of our example" (The White House, 2021). While the Trump administration has undermined the US soft power, Biden is willing to move away from the "America First" policies to one based more upon trust and establish relationships using soft power (Kokas, 2021). In this case, one of his first acts in office was to sign an executive order to rejoin the Paris Climate Agreement (Reuters, 2021). Throughout this, the Biden Administration is effectively reconstructing US alliances, which were weakened in the previous administration (*AP News*, 2021).

With personal income tax, Biden remains committed to his pledge from the campaign that there will be no tax increase for anybody making under US$400,000 dollars a year (*CNBC*, 2021). Meanwhile, there will be a rise in the corporate tax rate, which is mostly paid by wealthy owners of large capital, from 21 percent to 28 percent (Vox, 2020). Regarding immigration policies, Biden urged Congress with his immigration reform proposal that will enact policies to provide permanent protection for undocumented immigrants (Nikkei, 2021). Therefore, it is expected that the Biden administration will gradually ease immigration regulations, which have been strengthened under the Trump administration. Biden also halted the construction of the wall on the Mexican border (CNN, 2021).

Although Biden and Trump stand on different political lines, both of them employ a tough stance toward China. In addition, China's human rights concerns, environmental issues, and China's censorship are against Biden's democratic values and beliefs. Thus, his administration intends to strengthen its alliances to confront possible human rights violation issues in China such as its pressure on Hong Kong and repression of the Uyghur people. Biden stated (2020):

> The US on its own represents about a quarter of global GDP. When [the US] joins together with fellow democracies, [its] strength more than doubles. China can't afford to ignore more than half the global economy. That gives us substantial leverage to shape the rules of the road on

everything from the environment to labor, trade, technology, and transparency, so they continue to reflect democratic interests and values.

Biden emphasized that rebuilding alliances, especially those in Asia, will produce an effective coalition to persuade China to abide by the rules. The Biden administration is willing to offer support to those seeking to build democratic institutions while strengthening the military capabilities among the US allies to establish a new form of hegemony. Biden and his team will now seek to build on these efforts and make the US an attractive partner to its future alliances. As the US and its Asian partners have a shared interest to redefine the terms of international economic and security cooperation, they will work to encourage China to modify its current course and join the general consensus on economic policies (Foreign Policy, 2021).

How can China move forward?

Amidst the fourth industrial revolution, success in technological advancement will determine who will be at the center of the global economy. Under such circumstances, the question arises: how can China take a leading position to accomplish its goal of "the great rejuvenation of the Chinese nation?" Firstly, China should aim to become an attractive partner by magnifying its soft power. Such an approach allows a nation to promote itself as an attractive place to invest in. It is crucial that what China renders in the global economy is not antagonism but strategic cooperation, especially in regards to scientific collaboration with other countries and multinational firms.

Implications

The US–China trade war is not just a competition over the scale of trade or a matter of who is making a greater profit, but it is rather related to the investment deals each country is making. At the same time, the conflict between the two largest economies is closely linked to a hegemonic struggle, as it will determine whether China will achieve its "Chinese Dream" or the US will maintain its dominance on the global stage. Therefore, it is necessary to employ a holistic perspective to view the US–China trade war as an investment war as well as a form of hegemonic competition.

In recent years, the economic growth of China has been remarkable. It has even made positive growth in 2020 despite the COVID-19 global pandemic (*Wall Street Journal*, 2021). According to the prediction by HSBC, China will surpass the US in 2030 to become the country with the world's highest GDP. As these predictions show, the Chinese economy is full of potential. In order to maximize this opportunity, it is crucial for China to pursue the correct strategic approach. Perhaps, instead of solely focusing on the current measures on the volume of the trade with the US, China should put more effort into establishing a long-term strategy, like invigorating the BRI or pursuing more multilateral approaches. When the Chinese economy becomes stronger it will possess more capacity to handle the current problems of trade, hegemonic, and technological issues. The establishment of multinational corporations contributes to the growth of the country in its R&D and manufacturing, and it can even mitigate political issues and economic issues.

The Belt and Road Initiative

Background

China's BRI, also known as the One Belt One Road (OBOR[3]; 一带一路, *yídài yílù*), is a massive foreign investment project. The BRI was first introduced during President Xi's official visits to Kazakhstan and Indonesia in 2013 (Chatzky and McBride, 2020). The BRI intends to establish a modern silk road that will serve as an economic network to connect the countries in Asia, Africa, and Europe. The cost of the initiative to build the associated infrastructures such as the roadways, railways, gas pipelines, and ports will be funded by China. According to the Chinese government, the BRI will establish the world's longest economic corridor with massive potential in economic growth for the participating countries. The BRI will have an impact on an estimated 4.4 billion people, which is equivalent to 63 percent of the world's total population, and 29 percent of the world's GDP, US$21 trillion (CRI, 2014). The Chinese government's ultimate goal with the BRI is "to construct a unified large market and make full use of both international and domestic markets, through cultural

---

[3]The "One Belt (一带)" refers to the "Silk Road Economic Belt (the overland routes)" and the "One Road (一路)" refers to the "21st Century Maritime Silk Road (the sea routes)" (The Guardian, 2018b).

exchange and integration, to enhance mutual understanding and trust of member nations, ending up in an innovative pattern with capital inflows, talent pool, and technology database" (Koenig, 2019).

Analysis

Critical evaluation

To what extent then can the BRI benefit China? First, the BRI will open new pathways to export China's overproduction so that it can maintain its rapid economic growth (Mint, 2017). The other objective of the BRI is to increase the use of China's currency, the *renminbi*, in international transactions and consolidate its position as an international currency. In this attempt, China joined the European Bank for Reconstruction and Development in 2015 and established the Asian Infrastructure Investment Bank to invest in projects in which the *renminbi* is used in loans (Djankov and Miner, 2016). China's attempt to boost the use of the *renminbi* has been successful so far. For example, the International Monetary Fund allowed the *renminbi* to be considered as a global currency by including it in their Special Drawing Rights basket along with US Dollar, Euro, Japanese Yen, and Pound Sterling (IMF, 2016). However, there has been a controversial argument over this approach as some countries view the BRI as part of China's strategy to achieve regional dominance by establishing a China-centered trading network (Investopedia, 2020).

Furthermore, the BRI can offer a good opportunity for China to promote cooperation with other countries, and thus it is important to encourage the participation of neighboring countries into the BRI as it will boost cultural exchange and expand the trade partners of China to countries in Central Asia, West Asia, the Middle East, as well as to those in Europe (*The Guardian*, 2018b). The "21st Century Maritime Silk Road (the BRI)" is also considered to be particularly attractive for promoting international trade because of the great number of countries involved, so that the development opportunities and the market size are expected to be large. The BRI serves as a good tool for China to grow as a dominant global stakeholder (perhaps, even greater than now) and attract multinational corporations as the BRI is expected to improve the investment environment. The bottom line is that China should actively seek collaborative opportunities to create a better business environment.

Sustainability of the BRI

The participating countries of the BRI will have better access to the Chinese and other participating countries' markets. Through the investments provided by China, smaller countries will be able to strengthen their inland infrastructure. Moreover, the sharing of knowledge and technology between countries will lay a foundation for sustainable economic growth and innovation. Through the BRI, the cost of exporting goods is expected to be reduced as the infrastructure improves (Frost and Sullivan, 2017). However, regardless of the BRI's expected benefits to both China and the investment recipient countries, the initiative presents risks for the participating countries.

The biggest problem of the BRI is that there may be no clear economic benefit for the investment recipient countries. For example, Sri Lanka's Hambantota port was built and funded by the BRI to ease pressure on Sri Lanka's Colombo port and provide a place for ships that take a detour to get refueling and repairing and to handle logistics. The first country to whom Sri Lanka turned to for financial assistance in the development of the Hambantota port was India. However, the proposal was turned down because India found the proposal to be economically unprofitable. The project was also turned down by multilateral development banks (MDBs). China by contrast has seen Hambantota Port's potential due to its strategic location, only ten nautical miles north of the bustling international maritime transport route of the Indian Ocean. Hambantota Port meets the growing business demands of China because it can serve as the supply base for a large number of ships. Thus, China Exim Bank finally decided to finance the development of the Hambantota Port.

The situation soon turned sour. Due to poor management, lack of trade and economic activity, and failure to attract passing ships to dock, Hambantota Port failed to raise sufficient revenue to pay back the (construction) debt to China. For instance, the port was only able to bring in 34 ships in 2012 even though a large number of ships were passing nearby; the total loss of US$304 million was reported by the end of 2016 (*Beijing Review*, 2018). Consequently, the Sri Lanka government had to lease the port and 15,000 acres of land in the area for 99 years after negotiating with the China Merchants Port Holdings. This granted China the power to control this territory that is only a few hundred miles off the coast of India and a sea route with potential for military and trading purposes (*New York Times*, 2018).

Some analysts pointed out that over half of the projects involved in the BRI were inefficiently managed, showed cost overruns, did not create a real profit, and there had been almost no returns to investors (Ansar *et al.*, 2016). The unsuccessful results of the BRI somewhat verify that China prioritized the strategic importance of the project, rather than the economic value in its overseas infrastructure investments. For instance, China has invested in constructing power plants in Botswana and railways in Laos; unfortunately, both projects only induced unprofitable outcomes. Eventually, Botswana decided to sell its 600-megawatt power plant built by the Chinese corporation because of its technical problems and defects (Reuters, 2016). Followed by this, the IMF warned Laos that their public debt can rise to about 70% of the Laotian economy as China's Export–Import Bank loaned it US$ 800 million to build the railway (*New York Times*, 2017a).

The cases of these two countries (Sri Lanka and Laos) highlight that for BRI partner countries, it does not necessarily offer the most beneficial choices. The projects issued by the BRI are often in the best interest of China, not that of participating countries. On many occasions, the proposals issued by the BRI require political agreements that would bestow the exclusive bidding rights to Chinese enterprises (Chatzky and McBride, 2020). Looking at the case of Kenya, Chinese firms provided the main part of the standard gauge railway at $5.6 million per kilometer, which is very costly, three times higher than the international standard (BBC, 2017).

Another important aspect of the BRI is that the participation of local firms is discouraged. According to the Center for Strategic & International Studies' (CSIS) Reconnecting Asia database, 89 percent of all contractors involved in Chinese-funded projects were Chinese firms, while only 7.6 percent consisted of local firms, and only 3.4 percent of participating companies were foreign firms (Hillman, 2018). By contrast, in the programs initiated by other multilateral development banks, 29 percent of the contractors employed were Chinese firms while 40.8 percent were local, and 30.2 percent were international companies (Hillman, 2018). Eventually, the BRI-participating countries (or the Chinese loan recipient countries) will have to pay the price if they make decisions with a lack of evaluation over the profitability of the projects as it is likely that they will not be able to pay back the debts.

The US–China tension

The BRI prioritizes the mutual benefits between China and its partner countries, therefore in principle, it seeks to avoid becoming involved in the internal affairs of the participating countries. However, the recent BRI-related development projects demonstrate that China has actually become involved in the internal affairs of the partner countries. Therefore, the criticism to view the BRI as China's effort to seize new geopolitical allies and to create a global order that serves the interests of China have been unavoidable (DW, 2017).

The US is currently employing a multitude of tools to maintain its dominant position in the world, which include military supremacy, alliances, and unrivaled soft power. Yet, China's BRI could be a threat to US dominance. Firstly, its maritime projects are linked with overland projects in vital geostrategic regions, specifically Eurasia, which helps China to gain further influence in neighboring regions. This has led the US to keep an eye on the expansion of China's maritime influence in the Indo-Pacific region while questioning its massive investments in neighboring countries. Eventually, China's investments will replace US influence in this vital geostrategic area in Eurasia. China is also challenging the military force of the US. For example, China has been constructing military bases and airstrips in the islands of the South China sea to reduce the US naval presence in the area (CNN, 2020a). The military modernization program, which has gained momentum under President Xi, poses another threat to the US military force as it introduces "advanced weapons" and "structural reforms to make People's Liberation Army more effective" (East Asia Forum, 2020). Regarding this, US Army General James Dickenson also expressed concern about China's growing military force stating, "China was one of [my] highest military concerns [especially considering] its rapid development of space-based military capabilities" (TRT World, 2021).

Secondly, China has taken advantage of US entanglements in the Middle East, particularly as it became clear there was a limitation to US unilateral power in Iraq and Afghanistan. At the same time, China rose as a strong rival to the US in some key regions of Eurasia. For example, over the past few decades, China has been fostering bilateral ties with Iran, which has developed as a way to curb US influence. This mutual relationship benefits both countries as Iran can supply China with oil which helps Iran alleviate the impact of the international sanctions against it.

China has also been expanding its influence over South Asia and the Indian Ocean as it became alarmed by the US military intervention during the War on Terror in areas near China's Xinjiang Province. In response to China's effort to expand its influence, the US has worked hard to establish a strategic relationship with India. Additionally, the US is seeking to reconcile with Myanmar as well as to initiate a New Silk Road between Afghanistan, Central Asia, and South Asia to counter China as well as other competitors. However, despite these efforts, the Indian subcontinent has already been largely dominated by China. For example, China began to develop overland corridors linking Myanmar and Pakistan such as the China–Pakistan-Economic Corridor (CPEC) which is expected to connect Iran, Afghanistan, and Central Asia.

As part of the Trump administration's National Security Strategy, the US has sought to help countries in South Asia establish some autonomy from China as China was expanding its presence over the region. As a result, the Quad, a collaboration that includes the US, India, Australia, and Japan, was revived and strengthened. Yet, the US appears to be stagnated by problems closer to home, such as financial downturn and domestic political issues. By comparison, China has been strengthening its influence on Pakistan, Sri Lanka, Myanmar, and many other countries. This might eventually lead China to become a "resident power" in the region (The Diplomat, 2018).

In response, the US is promoting the Free and Open Indo-Pacific Strategy (FOIP) with Japan, which aims to connect the continents of Asia and Africa, as well as the Indian and Pacific Oceans. This will promote economic growth in this region as it encourages free trade and the development of infrastructure. To preserve regional order and the rules, the initiative also promotes security cooperation between countries of the region (Tomotaka, 2021). The ultimate goal of the FOIP is to preserve and reinforce the transparent maritime order that will prevent disputes, and in particular, prohibit any one country from dominating the Indo-Pacific maritime region (Policy Forum, 2019). In recent years, the minor and major conflicts between the US and China to secure or overtake have been prolonged.

Implications

The sustainability of the BRI is crucial to discuss. Some claim that China's BRI is a more hegemonic and political issue rather than the economic one. They believe the BRI was implemented to expand China's political influence on neighboring countries. However, for the success of the BRI, the economic problem needs to be tackled as a priority over the hegemonic or political problems. The BRI must induce a certain level of economic achievement to be successful, and more importantly to be sustainable.

One of the main disadvantages of the BRI is that it is solely focused on infrastructure development regardless of whether there is enough demand for it in the recipient countries. Simply building ports and highways in a country, where there is little to no manufacturing base will only lead to unsuccessful outcomes of the BRI. Therefore, it would be more prudent to pursue industrial development as part of such infrastructure projects, which highlights the need to examine the outcome for BRI investment projects thoroughly. Its overall objectives will only be achieved when China successfully establishes a foundation for infrastructure-clustered business in the BRI-participating countries.

The National Security Law in Hong Kong

Background

The pro-democracy movement in Hong Kong

In February 2018, Poon Hiu-wing from Hong Kong went missing during a visit to Taipei, Taiwan. Later her boyfriend Chan Tong-kai confessed to murdering her when confronted with evidence that he had traveled with her. Although the police in Hong Kong detained him, there was no way they could prosecute him as the crime had occurred out of their jurisdiction. At the same time, because of the legal complexities between Hong Kong and Taiwan, there was no way to extradite him to Taiwan either (*HRIC*, 2021). Consequently, he was only charged with a lesser crime in Hong Kong. It was on the basis of this case that the Hong Kong executive proposed an extradition bill in April 2019 to facilitate the judicial process of criminals who had committed a crime outside of Hong Kong's jurisdiction (BBC, 2019b). However, concerns arose as the extradition bill did not just include Taiwan, but also Mainland China. Regarding the proposal of the extradition bill, Professor Johannes Chan pointed out in an interview with the BBC "effectively, they (Hong Kong legislators) are imposing the People's Republic of China's criminal system onto the Hong Kong common law system" (BBC, 2020a). Thus, the policy holds the possibility and capability to erode the principle of "one country, two systems" and weaken Hong Kong's independent judicial authority, which was established with the Joint Declaration agreed between Britain and China in 1984 (*South China Morning Post*, 2019).

The first big protest, opposing the extradition bill, was organized in early June 2019, in which around one million people came out onto the streets to march (BBC, 2019b). The protests continued throughout the summer of 2019; prompting Hong Kong's Chief Executive Carrie Lam to announce the withdrawal of the extradition bill. However, this did not tame the protesters. From this point, the protesters began to call out for "five demands[4]" in an attempt to further secure democratic values in Hong Kong and strengthen its independent judiciary. The pro-democracy movement and the violent clashes between the police force and Hong Kong protesters lasted for a year until the national security law was enacted on June 30, 2020 (CNN, 2020c). Under this newly implemented law, anyone claiming for the independence of Hong Kong (considered as secession) or vandalizing public property in protests (considered as terrorism) will face a long custodial sentence (CNN, 2020c). Consequently, the key figures in the pro-democracy movement, Joshua Wong and Agnes Chow[5] received prison sentences under the national security law on December 2, 2020 (*HRIC*, 2021). The implementation of the national security law in Hong Kong marks a new era for Hong Kong as it signals the vulnerability of Hong Kong to China's intervention.

The response of the international community

As there is no doubt that Hong Kong is now under the tightened control of the central government of China, there was a surge in the number of people planning to emigrate from Hong Kong throughout 2019. For example, referring to Canada's immigration authority, the number of "visa applications from Hong Kongers jumped more than 10% [in 2019] to 8,640" (Reuters, 2020b). For Mainland China, the pressure it has been receiving

---

[4]The "five demands" — include the followings: the withdrawal of the extradition bill, correction of the expression to label protesters as riots, the release of all protestors who had received criminal charges, the establishment of a separate institution to investigate the abuse of police force in the protest, and a provision of universal suffrage in an election for chief executive (SupChina, 2019).

[5]Joshua Wong & Agnes Chow — pro-democracy activists in Hong Kong, who have been taking the leadership positions of Hong Kong's pro-democracy movement since 2012 when they were engaged in a protest against the education reform in Hong Kong calling it is "Beijing's brainwashing tool"; in 2014 they took a part in umbrella movement calling for universal suffrage in Hong Kong (Nikkei Asia, 2020).

from the international community is significant. The US had shown consistent support to Hong Kong protesters, for example, the US enacted the "Human Rights and Democracy Act" in November 2019, condemning China's suppression of protestors in the Hong Kong territory (*HRIC*, 2021). Moreover, the UK announced a new scheme for Hong Kong British National Overseas status holders to facilitate their immigration to the UK. Starting from January 2021, this new policy allows the immigration of an estimated five million Hong Kong residents to settle in the UK and obtain British citizenship (BBC, 2021; The Conversation, 2021). Alongside this, the US, UK, Australia, and Canada all signed a joint statement expressing "deep concern regarding China's proposed (national security) law" (*CNBC*, 2020). However, disregarding the growing external pressure, China has not expressed any plan to step back — the process of which will be further discussed in the following section.

Analysis

The future of Hong Kong

The two major changes Hong Kong residents will face upon the enactment of a national security law include economic and cultural integration with the Mainland. Firstly, the alignment with the Chinese economy will be an inevitable change for Hong Kong. For instance, Hong Kong Exchanges and Clearing Limited recently announced its plan to expand the stock connect programs[6], which will increase the accessibility of Mainland Chinese investors to Hong Kong-listed companies. Specifically, the expansion of the existing program allows Hong Kong investors to purchase stocks traded in the Sci-Tech Innovation Board of the Shanghai exchange market and Mainland investors to purchase the shares of Hong Kong-listed biotech companies from early 2021 (Xinhua News Agency, 2020). Furthermore, the Hong Kong monetary authority added that "the People's Bank of China had agreed to expand the currency swap[7] line between the

---

[6]Stock Connect Program — firstly introduced in 2014 connecting Shanghai and Hong Kong exchange market; later in 2016, it was expanded encompassing Shenzhen exchange markets as well creating one of the largest stock markets in the world (Goldman Sachs, 2016).

[7]Currency Swap — also known as cross-currency swap, allows an exchange the interest which would provide a more favorable interest rate for the loans (Investopedia, 2021).

two by 25% to 500 billion yuan ($75.5 billion)," intending to increase the use of the Chinese currency, the *renminbi* in Hong Kong (Nikkei Asia, 2020). Regarding the growing presence of Mainland China's capital in Hong Kong, Garcia added, "... I am pretty certain that [Hong Kong] won't be a global financial center. Hong Kong is now China's financial center, which is different" (*Financial Times*, 2020).

A number of observers predict that there will be further political interference in Hong Kong derived from the growing inflow of capital from Mainland China. For example, to ensure control over the business, the Community Party of China recently established the "party cell" system, which requires companies operating in China to include party cells in their governance structure (The Conversation, 2020). While the party cell system was designed to facilitate the understanding of foreign firms, there have been controversial arguments on this policy, whether the system facilitates or distracts the operation of foreign firms. Regarding this, the sales and marketing authority in China from one of the major US firms stated "[the party cell] ... had pushed for locating a new facility in a district where the local government was promoting investment" (Reuters, 2017). The interference of the central government and political attachment to the operating business in China has been a major concern for foreign firms as their access to the Mainland markets have been inhibited. And it is likely that this concern of foreign firms may be stretched to foreign firms operating in Hong Kong. Under these circumstances, it is uncertain whether Hong Kong will preserve its reputation as an attractive investment site or not in the future.

Perhaps, the new era that Hong Kong is facing now may already have been anticipated. Kwong (2016) claimed there are two possible approaches the central government could take to manage the growing discrepancy between Hong Kong and the Mainland: either initiating constitutional reform to allow greater autonomy or pressing Hong Kong to align closer with China's values by increasing its level of intervention. Considering the current situation, it seems like the central government is pursuing the latter option, even at the expense of economic costs in Hong Kong. One of the many reasons behind this decision is the risk of growing demands among the protesters in Hong Kong. In the extreme, China may concern that there is a possibility the Hong Kong protesters could begin to demand complete independence from China if the current "five demands" are met. Needless to say, this would have serious implications for other regions in China including Taiwan. It is therefore clear why the central government has decided to reduce the discrepancy between Hong Kong and Mainland China at this stage.

In addition to economic integration, China intends to pursue cultural integration between the cities in the Mainland and Hong Kong, which is known for its distinct local culture and identity formed around its heritage as a former British colony. Due to this unique historical background, Hong Kong contains many democratic components in its culture, which clash with the values of China's authoritarian government. In this sense, China believes the cultural "incompatibility between Hong Kong's distinctive local culture and Mainland Chinese culture" is one of the causes that have led to the long-lasting conflict between these two regions, and therefore China seeks to align Hong Kong's values and practices to those of Mainland China (The Diplomat, 2020). Hence, with the Greater Bay Area (GBA)[8] project, the central government intends to promote the development of the coastal cities of China — including Hong Kong — and also boost cultural integration among them. As a result, the democratic features in Hong Kong culture are expected to be diminished.

Economic consequences

In the short run, a brain drain may be a primary concern for Hong Kong. Referring to the data provided by the Hong Kong Public Opinion Research Institute, 70 percent of the respondents expressed that they lacked confidence in the city's future suggesting that some Hong Kong residents were considering to emigrate (Reuters, 2020a). As a greater number of countries are opening up the border to ease the immigration process for Hong Kong citizens, the threat of a brain drain from the city is growing larger. The UK is one of the countries that opened up the border for Hong Kong people, especially for those who hold the British National Overseas status, by allowing them to stay for up to five years, which is the point when they can start applying for citizenship (Reuters, 2020b). If a considerable number of the population in Hong Kong decides to settle down in other countries, the loss of a distinctive local Hong Kong culture will be accelerated.

---

[8]Greater Bay Area — is China's economic plan to link Hong Kong, Macau, and other Southern cities in Mainland China to promote economic growth in this area "by developing technology and innovation, boosting infrastructure and increasing financial links between the cities" (BBC, 2019a).

From an economic perspective, it will also be a great loss of human capital.

These recent changes in Hong Kong may also be a threat to its reputation as a global hub. For example, the US revoked its recognition of Hong Kong's special status as a way to signal that its autonomy is at risk from the newly imposed national security law. This means that Hong Kong is now subjected to higher tariffs and sanctions on trading sensitive tech products (*China Briefing News*, 2020). The removal of special status is a direct threat to Hong Kong, especially to its position as a "re-exporter" as it has long filled the role of a "second leg" between the US and China. As Hong Kong was used to reduce the tariffs imposed on Chinese exports, around 8 percent of Mainland China's exports to the US, and around 6 percent of Mainland China's imports from the US, went through Hong Kong in 2018 (Pang, 2020). However, the current role of Hong Kong as a trading bridge between China and the US is likely to be replaced by another country as Hong Kong is now subject to higher tariffs. Thus, from a larger perspective, the implementation of the national security law marks the point in which Hong Kong became involved in the ongoing US–China conflict.

The implementation of the national security law has certainly deepened the conflict between the US and China which thus has accelerated the trend among some US firms to leave the Chinese markets (including that of Hong Kong). Referring to the statistics provided by the American Chamber of Commerce, among the 250 US companies operating in Hong Kong, nearly 40 percent of respondents expressed their willingness to relocate their production facilities outside of China (DW, 2021b). For instance, the *New York Times* announced its plan to relocate its Asia bureau to Seoul in South Korea due to the growing concerns over censorship and surveillance related to the national security law (Brookings, 2020). Moreover, some of the major investment banks in Hong Kong have been diversifying possible risks by expanding their recruitment scale in Singapore, as an alternative to Hong Kong. Referring to data provided by the *Financial Times*, the recruitment scale of UBS and JP Morgan in Singapore was eight times larger than that of Hong Kong in 2020 (Chosunbiz, 2020). Considering the relatively smaller population size in Singapore, this is a significant change. The director of Michael Page indicated, that "until now, the financial companies were mainly operated in Hong Kong, however, nowadays when there is an opportunity for recruitment in Asia Pacific area, the opportunity is assigned in Singapore first"

(Chosunbiz, 2020). Furthermore, Moody and Fitch announced the downgrading of Hong Kong's credit rating from Aa2 to Aa3 and AA to AA- respectively, which explicitly hurt Hong Kong's reputation as an attractive investment site (Business Insider, 2020; Fitch Ratings, 2020). All of these factors demonstrate Hong Kong's threatened status as a global hub.

These economic costs are not limited to Hong Kong; the Mainland's economy is similarly affected. Firstly, if Hong Kong were to lose its competitiveness as a financial hub, there would then be a negative spillover effect on the Mainland China's economy. Because the Mainland's companies account for a large proportion of Hong Kong's stock exchange market, roughly 96 percent of the total Initial Public Offering (IPO) funds raised were for Mainland companies in the first quarter of 2020 (The Interpreter, 2020). Due to this great interconnection between the economies of the Mainland and Hong Kong, the deterioration of Hong Kong's competitiveness — such as a plunge of Hong Kong's IPO market by nearly 43 percent in 2019 — has a broader impact on the overall Chinese economy, not just on Hong Kong's (*CNBC*, 2019). Secondly, the national security law in Hong Kong has deteriorated the relationship between the US and China, given the support the US has expressed toward the pro-democracy protestors and the resulting backlash shown by China (Thorup, 2020). This is likely to persist throughout the Biden administration which will be an added burden for China.

Interpretation: Understanding the rationale

This section discusses our interpretation on China's rationale behind the implementation of the national security law in relation to its economic development plan and political vision toward global governance. It is crucial here to bear in mind the importance of the BRI and Hong Kong's main role in supporting the project as it requires large-scale investment. The Asian Development Bank calculated that the project required US$1.7 trillion in funding for the projects pursued in the developing countries of Asia from 2016 to 2030 (García-Herrero *et al.*, 2021; *China Daily HK*, 2019). In this respect, Hong Kong offers compelling investment options for foreign investors, thanks to its solidified position as an attractive investment site.

Hong Kong plays an important role in the GBA project. This undertaking will not only benefit Mainland China but also Hong Kong since China intends to promote the development of all major cities in the surrounding area: Shenzhen as a technology hub, Macau as a tourism and trade center,

Guangzhou as a manufacturing hub, and Hong Kong as a strengthened financial hub (BBC, 2019a). As part of the GBA project, Hong Kong will provide a credible benchmark for other Chinese cities to flourish as international hubs. As such, China wishes to align the policies and legal system among these cities to increase the mobility of people, capital, goods, and services across the regions as well as promote the development of all regions in the GBA (*China Briefing News*, 2019). This is expected to alleviate the obstacles that exist between each region's business environments.

Another key objective of the national security law for China is to promote legitimacy and internal political stability. Recently, the Chinese government has been facing challenges to its authority due to a sense of dissatisfaction among the public over the country's economic stagnation. It has been noted that China's economic growth stalled to 6.6 percent, which is a 27-year low (Rohlinger, 2019). With such questioning of the government's handling of the economy, the national security law could be interpreted as an effort to guarantee its legitimacy. With the imposition of the policy, China has demonstrated its sovereignty, clarifying that no other country has the right to intervene in Hong Kong. Reflecting this, Zhang stated "the time that the Chinese people have to please others has passed" (*The Harvard Gazette*, 2020). China is in a different position in terms of the global economy compared to decades ago and it is no longer ashamed to be an authoritarian country (*New York Times*, 2020b). The Hong Kong issue confirms that China is no longer as vulnerable to external pressure as was believed in the past.

As well as seeking to consolidate domestic control, the national security law places China in a better position to achieve its ultimate vision on global governance. The ultimate vision for China's global governance is not simply to displace the US in terms of economic power or political influence, but rather it wishes to restructure the whole system of global governance. This would be very different from the current one: in China's political ideology, there is no authority greater than the Communist Party of China whereas within the current global governance the decisions are made primarily based on international rules (Hart and Johnson, 2019). Therefore, from a larger perspective, China's attempt to tighten its control over Hong Kong is about the survival of the Communist Party of China, not just another small component of the US–China conflict. This also explains why promoting unity through integration is far more important than securing the revenues of Hong Kong. No matter how much China will have to lose, the priority for the central government will always be on political stability.

Evaluation: Cost and opportunity for Hong Kong

The national security law has both positive and negative effects on Hong Kong. On the negative side, it is a clear threat to civil liberties. As the national security law prohibits any act of secession, subversion, terrorism, or collusion with external forces, political freedoms in Hong Kong were degraded to a significant extent (BBC, 2020a). Under this new law, some cases from Hong Kong may be transferred to Mainland China, which marks lesser independence in the judiciary system of Hong Kong (BBC, 2020a). For example, China is already imposing regulations on journalists as it has expelled foreign correspondents from China and banned others from entering Hong Kong (*Wall Street Journal*, 2020a). Moreover, the possibility of the weakened status of Hong Kong as a global financial hub, as discussed previously, imposes another significant cost on Hong Kong.

On the flip side, the implementation of the national security law marks a critical opportunity for Hong Kong to tackle critical issues such as the overheated housing market. Projects like the "Lantau Vision Tomorrow," in which the government proposed to build an artificial island for housing, demonstrate the severity of housing shortages in Hong Kong. However, the Lantau project has been sharply criticized due to environmental and sustainability concerns as well as its high costs (HK\$624bn; 15–20 years of construction) to which critics stated that it would be literally "pouring money into the ocean" (*The Guardian*, 2019). On a more positive note, cities in the vicinity of Hong Kong would appear to have room to spare. The RBC Economics Housing Affordability Report points out that "per capita housing in Hong Kong is only 16 square meters, far below the 34 square meters per person in the neighboring province of Guangzhou" (*CGTN*, 2020a). Perhaps, this suggests one possible strategy for Hong Kong to tackle the housing problem which is to establish greater interconnection between Hong Kong and neighboring Chinese cities. The GBA will play a crucial role in this by enabling the physical integration of coastal cities with the Hong Kong–Zhuhai–Macau Bridge, the Express Rail Link (connecting Shenzhen–Guangdong), the Shenzhen–Zhongshan Corridor. These linkages will increase the mobility of Hong Kong citizens across the border between Hong Kong and the Mainland (*China Briefing News*, 2019).

Other than the housing problem, Hong Kong's economy has struggled with sharp income inequality for years. According to a recent taxation report by the Hong Kong government, the richest 10 percent of the population pays nearly 80 percent of taxes (*CGTN*, 2020a). In this sense, the growing interference of the central government in Hong Kong could be a positive sign for its economy as it might press for significantly more redistributive policies (e.g., a less stratified and more equitable education system, more affordable housing, and so on) that will target the poorest and most vulnerable (The Diplomat, 2020). Overall, the national security law marks a transition for Hong Kong, which offers opportunities to reorganize old policies and possibly improve the structural problems that may have been inducing severe income disparity in Hong Kong.

Impacts on other countries

Western countries: Supportive or against?

Interestingly, Western countries — the US and European countries — have employed contrasting viewpoints toward the Hong Kong issue. While the US confirmed its criticism of the Chinese government's policies by supporting the Hong Kong protesters, many European countries adopted a different approach toward China's decision. Center for American Progress has shown that there is a level of mistrust among EU countries toward the US citing the 2018 Pew Research Center survey result indicating that "the global community had less confidence in US President Trump than in Chinese President Xi ... to do the right thing" in global affairs (Hart and Johnson, 2019). Indeed, the EU and China had recently reached the investment deal, stating US allies [including themselves] can't be sure of America's long-term commitment to an international alliance, given four years of a unilateral approach (*Wall Street Journal*, 2020a).

By contrast, the US has strongly objected to China's tightened control over Hong Kong as the national security law degrades democratic values in Hong Kong. For the US, the rising presence of China on the global stage is a great threat to its democratic principles and also to its economic outlook: China's ambitious plan to build a "digital silk road" is a potential threat to the US dominance in the technology market and at the same time, it raises security concerns. Hence, "an increasing number of developed countries, including the US, Australia, Japan, and some European countries banned Chinese tech firms from their 5G infrastructure ... to limit Chinese tech giants' expansion and [as an attempt] to prevent China from setting standards for the internet, 5G networking, and other areas" (Kurlantzick and West, 2020).

Due to this structural barrier established by many developed countries, China's access to the technology market is largely limited, which has pushed it to launch the digital silk road project. This project involves technology investment, agreement on joint research, and the provision of education on Chinese technology in developing countries with the ultimate goal to establish a digital infrastructure around the world (Defense One, 2021). Yet, despite the present concerns of security risks, which many developed countries have been reluctantly emphasizing, China's digital silk road still offers an appealing option for many developing countries. Regarding this, Hillman (2021) shared his view pointing out "even wealthy democracies were reluctant to swallow the additional costs of safer alternatives. In the developing world, [where] resources are even more limited," it is more unrealistic to expect the abstract fear on cybersecurity to discourage the developing counties' participations to China's digital silk road. Moreover, this case displays a clear association between the US–China conflict and future business opportunities for each side, which implies that neither side will be likely to compromise.

Taiwan: Its status at risk

The situation in Hong Kong is of great concern for Taiwan. It has long been a clear goal for China to unify Taiwan with the Mainland. President Xi declared that it is now a time to "explore a Taiwan plan for one country, two systems," thus offering a similar approach to how Hong Kong is administered (Lawrence and Martin, 2020). From its recent experience in Hong Kong, this may imply China's direct insistence that Taiwan is "part of its territory" (*Maizland*, 2021). In fact, many forecasts that at some point in the future, China will undertake all measures to regain Taiwan (*AEI*, 2020). China views Taiwan as a threat to its legitimacy since it "emerged as a vibrant democracy" in the past 40 years (*Brookings*, 2021). In this respect, China's current stance to view Taiwan as "part of its country" signals the possibility of China's growing pressure on Taiwan. Once again, at any time under any circumstances, China will be ready to pay the price to get rid of any possible threat challenging its central authority and political stability.

Implications

For Hong Kong

Regardless of the disruption to daily life brought on by the 2019 Hong Kong protests, in the long run, Hong Kong is likely to still play a crucial role in the broader Chinese economy. The dominance of Mainland companies in Hong Kong's IPO market is one example representing its importance. It should be noted that it was not the intention of China to disrupt the Hong Kong economy, which has been its prominent cash cow for the last few decades. Rather, the reason for China to tighten its control over Hong Kong is simple and clear: ensuring the political legitimacy of the central government even if it may come at the cost of the functionality of the Hong Kong economy.

For China

The linkage between the two regions, Hong Kong and the Mainland, is significant to the extent that any negative economic impact in Hong Kong is also likely to affect the Chinese economy. However, the sanctions imposed by the US on Hong Kong will not critically damage the Chinese economy since there is a limitation to the extent of regulations the US can impose on Hong Kong, given the interdependency between the US and Hong Kong, which makes it more of a challenge if it is seeking to punish China's actions through Hong Kong (*Fortune*, 2020). Thus, the economic consequence of the national security law on the Mainland should not be exaggerated. The current dispute over the Hong Kong issue is likely to impose negative impacts on both Chinese and the US economy. However, the consequence is unlikely to be as large as to devastate the second largest economy of the world.

Where should China compromise?

China's interest is clear. It values the Hong Kong economy, however, the priority is on securing political stability, no matter how great the economic cost will be. In this regard, Hong Kong should understand that the "one country two systems" principle does not grant — and has never granted — Hong Kong's independent sovereignty. Even though Hong Kong was able to retain some democratic features in its administration, it is still part of China. Once China feels that the principle of 'one country' is undermined, the consequence will be the collapse of the latter principle, 'two systems,' which has been witnessed recently in Hong Kong.

The compromising point between Mainland China and Hong Kong should be where Hong Kong does not demand political independence and accepts the loss of some of its cultural and political distinctions, while China guarantees economic independence to Hong Kong (for example, by establishing relevant measures). This will be the best, and perhaps the only, middle-ground for both parties to settle the dispute. If Hong Kong agrees to this, Hong Kong will secure its economic independence and receive security from the central government in return. Despite the unique components of Hong Kong's culture and system, it is still part of China. The core of the strategy is to attain a goal by minimizing the cost of conflict (Moon, 2018). To do so, both China and Hong Kong have to understand that they have to separate economy from politics.

Conclusion

The US–China trade war, the BRI, and Hong Kong's national security law are three major issues which China is confronted with. These three issues all hold one common factor, which is that they are an economic challenge China has to address. On the surface level, the rising tension between the US and China and the recent clash between the Hong Kong protesters and the central government of China is often understood as a political problem since both conflicts are primarily derived from the great power competition. However, the economic rationales and implications associated with the two issues should never be downplayed. Similar to this, many argue that the rationale for China with the BRI is simply to extend its political influence over its neighboring countries. While this may be a valid argument, it is important to note that the solution, as well as the primary motive behind the BRI, is an economic one. Simply put, the recent conflicts between China and the other countries in the region are closely associated with economic perspectives.

Throughout the trade war, the US and China have been building walls between them which have been restricting the physical trade of products and the exchange of intellectual property between the two countries. However, this only inhibits the potential economic growth of both countries, thus the current barriers between them should be alleviated through collaborative measures — e.g., elimination of unnecessary sanctions and the conduct of collaborative research. Secondly, China's ambitious project, the BRI, highlights the significance of the economic rationale behind the initiative as it demonstrates that the outcome of the project will not be successful with a lack of economic opportunities. Therefore, the BRI offers an opportunity for China to establish an infrastructure cluster industry for the BRI-participating countries on top of the infrastructure investments. Lastly, the Hong Kong issue highlights the importance of separating economy and politics as the demand for political freedom in Hong Kong triggered the conflict between China and Hong Kong. Indeed, the conflict between the two parties will be mitigated when both parties successfully distinguish the politics and economy.

The trade war between the US and China exemplifies the tendency of the country to align the business and the national interest on the same line. However, business should not be the tool for the country to achieve its national objectives. The government should not expect the corporations to fulfill the government's aims or to be faithful to the country's regime. The corporation, of course, must meet and respect the legal, administrative, and cultural obligations and expectations of the country, where the corporations are willing to operate. However, business should be working for the business interest, not for the national interest. Similarly, the operation of multinational companies in one country does not grant the country any authority to interfere in the decision of the companies. To establish a sustainable and attractive business environment, the promise of the separation of those two factors is crucial.

The confusion between the interests of business and the country largely inhibits the cooperation of the firms and the countries around the world. The failure to distinguish between politics and economy is likely to lead to unexpected and unsuccessful outcomes when pursuing policies or initiatives. When policymakers understand this simple logic, many international conflicts, as well as the tension between the US and China, will be largely alleviated and the countries will be able to effectively attain their objectives that can be either political or economic.

References

AEI. 2020. Why the Hong Kong national security law matters for Taiwan. https://www.aei.org/articles/why-the-hong-kong-national-security-law-matters-for-taiwan/.

Ansar, A., Flyvbjerg, B., Budzier, A., and Lunn, D. 2016. China's infrastructure investments threaten its economic growth. *Saïd Business School.*

https://www.ox.ac.uk/news/2016-09-12-chinas-infrastructure-investments-threaten-its-economic-growth.

AP News. 2021. Biden declares 'America is back' in welcome words to allies. https://apnews.com/article/biden-foreign-policy-g7-summit-munich-cc10859-afd0f542fd268c0a7ddcd9bb6.

BBC. 2017. Will Kenya get value for money from its new railway? https://www.bbc.com/news/world-africa-40171095.

BBC. 2019a. Greater Bay Area: China's ambitious but vague economic plan. *BBC News*. https://www.bbc.com/news/business-47287387.

BBC. 2019b. Hong Kong: Timeline of extradition protests. *BBC News*. https://www.bbc.com/news/world-asia-china-49340717.

BBC. 2020a. Hong Kong security law: What is it and is it worrying? *BBC News*. https://www.bbc.com/news/world-asia-china-52765838.

BBC. 2020b. Michael Kovrig and Michael Spavor: China charges Canadians with spying. https://www.bbc.com/news/world-asia-china-53104303.

BBC. 2021. The Hong Kong migrants fleeing to start new lives in the UK. *BBC News*. https://www.bbc.com/news/world-asia-china-55357495.

Beijing Review. 2018. An Ungrounded Accusation. http://www.bjreview.com/Opinion/201808/t20180820_800138627.html.

Biden, J. 2020. Why America Must Lead Again. *Foreign Affairs*. https://www.foreignaffairs.com/articles/united-states/2020-01-23/why-america-must-lead-again

Brookings. 2020. Why now? Understanding Beijing's new assertiveness in Hong Kong.https://www.brookings.edu/blog/order-from-chaos/2020/07/17/why-now-understanding-beijings-new-assertiveness-in-hong-kong/.

Brookings. 2021. Understanding Beijing's motives regarding Taiwan, and America'srole.https://www.brookings.edu/on-the-record/understanding-beijings-motives-regarding-taiwan-and-americas-role/.

Bureau of Economic Analysis. 2019. 2018 Trade Gap is $621.0 Billion. https://www.bea.gov/news/blog/2019-03-06/2018-trade-gap-6210-billion. Accessed March 6, 2019.

Business Insider. 2020. Moody's downgrades Hong Kong's rating, citing the government's 'slow' response to protests. https://markets.businessinsider.com/news/stocks/moodys-cuts-hong-kong-ratings-on-protests-upgrades-outlook-to-stable-2020-1-1028829532.

CGTN. 2020a. HK security to help solve economy's structural problems. https://news.cgtn.com/news/2020-07-07/HK-security-to-help-solve-economy-s-structural-problems-RVw3U6iOf6/index.html.

CGTN. 2020b. How Trump was able to leverage CFIUS to block Chinese deals. https://news.cgtn.com/news/2020-08-27/How-Trump-was-able-to-leverage-CFIUS-to-block-Chinese-deals-ThgMQe1ndC/index.html.

Chance, A. 2017. American perspectives on the belt and road initiative. *Institute for China-America Studies*. https://chinaus-icas.org/wp-content/uploads/2017/02/American-Perspectives-on-the-Belt-and-Road-Initiative.pdf.

Chatzky, A. 2019. Will there be winners in the U.S.-China trade war? *Council on Foreign Relations*. https://www.cfr.org/in-brief/will-there-be-winners-us-china-trade-war.

Chatzky, A. and J. McBride. 2020. China's Massive Belt and Road Initiative. *Council on Foreign Relations*. https://www.cfr.org/backgrounder/chinas-massive-belt-and-road-initiative.

China Briefing News. 2019. The Greater Bay Area Plan — Integrating Hong Kong, Macau, Guangdong. https://www.china-briefing.com/news/the-greater-bay-area-plan-china/.

China Briefing News. 2020. What is Hong Kong's Special Status and What Could Change? https://www.china-briefing.com/news/us-position-hong-kong-special-status-possible-implications/.

China Daily HK. 2019. "HK seeks to play 'larger role' in BRI." https://www.chinadailyhk.com/articles/222/236/6/1556244136921.html.

Chong, T. and X. Li. 2019. Understanding the China–US trade war: causes, economic impact, and the worst-case scenario. Economic and Political Studies. 7 (2): 185–202.

Chosunbiz. 2020. Hong Kong Risk Peehaja, Singapore hyang ha nun Gobal Eunhangdul [Let's Flee the Hong kong Risk, Global banks are heading to Singapore] [in Korean]. https://biz.chosun.com/site/data/html_dir/2020/12/22/2020122201220.html?utm_source=naver&utm_medium=original&utm_campaign=biz.

CNBC. 2019. Hong Kong's IPO market has been hit by the protests, but it could see a turnaround. https://www.cnbc.com/2019/10/22/investing-hong-kongs-ipo-market-has-been-hit-by-protests.html.

CNBC. 2020. World leaders react to China's controversial national security bill in Hong Kong. https://www.cnbc.com/2020/05/29/world-leaders-react-to-chinas-controversial-national-security-bill-in-hong-kong.html. CNBC. 2021. Biden has promised not to raise taxes on people earning less than $400,000. Here's what he might push for instead. https://www.cnbc.com/2021/03/18/biden-tax-plan-what-people-making-under-and-over-400000-can-expect.html.

CNN. 2016. Donald Trump's speech: 'America first,' but an America absent from the world. https://edition.cnn.com/2016/07/22/opinions/donald-trump-speech-amanpour/index.html.

CNN. 2020a. Beijing may have built bases in the South China Sea, but that doesn't mean it can defend them, report claims. https://edition.cnn.com/2020/12/07/china/south-china-sea-bases-military-intl-hnk/index.html.

CNN. 2020b. Samsung slump makes Huawei the world's biggest smartphone brand for the first time, report says. https://edition.cnn.com/2020/07/30/tech/huawei-samsung-q2-hnk-intl/index.html.

CNN. 2020c. What you need to know about Hong Kong's controversial new national security law. https://edition.cnn.com/2020/06/25/asia/hong-kong-national-security-law-explainer-intl-hnk-scli/index.html.

CNN. 2021. Biden targets Trump's legacy with first-day executive Actions. https://edition.cnn.com/2021/01/20/politics/executive-actions-biden/index. html.

CRI. 2014. Xi Jinping's "One Belt, One Road" concept has far-reaching strategic significance. http://news.cri.cn/gb/42071/2014/10/10/882s4720906.htm.

Defense One. 2021. How China's Digital Silk Road Is Leading Countries Away from the United States. https://www.defenseone.com/technology/2021/02/ how-chinas-digital-silk-road-leading-countries-away-united-states/172219/.

Djankov, S. and S. Miner. 2016. China's Belt and Road Initiative Motives, Scope, and Challenges. PIIE Briefing 16, no.2: 7.

Djankov, S., S. Miner, C. S. Hendrix, R. Z. Lawrence, and F. Toohey. 2016. China's Belt and Road Initiative Motives, Scope, and Challenges. Peterson Institute for International Economics. https://www.piie.com/system/files/ documents/piieb16-2_1.pdf.

DWa. The implications of China's new security law. https://www.dw.com/en/the-implications-of-chinas-new-security-law/a-18557771. Accessed February 1, 2021.

DWb. Tariffs prompt US firms to rethink China business: survey. https://www. dw.com/en/tariffs-prompt-us-firms-to-rethink-china-business-survey/a-48824637. Accessed February 1, 2021.

DW. 2017. New Silk Road' and China's hegemonic ambitions. https://www. dw.com/en/new-silk-road-and-chinas-hegemonic-ambitions/a-38843212.

East Asia Forum. 2020. China's military modernisation. https://www.eastasia forum.org/2020/12/16/chinas-military-modernisation/#:~:text=Key%20 changes%20include%20the%20introduction,corruption%20and%20 improve%20Xi's%20control.

Financial Times. 2020. How 2020 turmoil will reshape the future of Hong Kong financial hub. https://www.ft.com/content/43ed7ebd-343e-46bf-b374-b3af8d5e7efe.

Fitch Ratings. 2020. Fitch Downgrades Hong Kong to 'AA-' from 'AA'; Outlook Stable. https://www.fitchratings.com/research/sovereigns/fitch-downgrades-hong-kong-to-aa-from-aa-outlook-stable-20-04-2020.

Foreign Policy. 2021. A New Pivot to Asia. https://foreignpolicy.com/2021/01/15/ biden-china-asia-allies-strategy-pivot/.

Fortune. 2020. Nuclear option:' How the U.S. could leverage Hong Kong to hurt Beijing. https://fortune.com/2020/05/29/trump-china-announcement-hong-kong/.

Frost & Sullivan. 2017. The One Belt One Road Initiative and its Implications for China and the Rest of the World. https://ww2.frost.com/frost-perspectives/ the-one-belt-one-road-initiative-and-its-implications-for-china-and-the-rest-of-the-world.

García-Herrero, A., Li, H., and Ng, G. 2021. Hong Kong's Intermediary Role on Funding the BRI: How Does it Fare Against Singapore? HKUST IEMS. https://papers.ssrn.com/sol3/papers.cfm?abstract_id=3721905.

General Office of Leading Group of Advancing the Building of the Belt and Road Initiative. 2016. Belt and Road in Big Data 2016. Beijing: The Commercial Press.

Global Times. 2019a. Calmness is the best response to US' fluctuation in trade talks. https://www.globaltimes.cn/page/201905/1148815.shtml.

Global Times. 2019b. View risks of a trade war objectively. https://www.globaltimes.cn/page/201905/1149090.shtml.

Goldman Sachs. 2016. The Stock Connect. https://www.goldmansachs.com/insights/pages/stock-connect/.

Guo, M., L. Lu, L. Sheng and M. Yu. 2018. The Day After Tomorrow: Evaluating the Burden of Trump's Trade War. Asian Economic Papers. 17(1): 101–120.

Hart, M., and B. Johnson. 2019. Mapping China's Global Governance Ambitions. Center for American Progress. https://www.americanprogress.org/issues/security/reports/2019/02/28/466768/mapping-chinas-global-governance-ambitions/.

Hillman, J. E. 2018. China's Belt and Road Initiative: Five Years Later. Center for Strategic & International Studies. https://www.csis.org/analysis/chinas-belt-and-road-initiative-five-years-later-0.

Hillman, J. E. 2021. Competing with China's Digital Silk Road. Center for Strategic and International Studies. https://www.csis.org/analysis/competing-chinas-digital-silk-road.

HRIC. 2021. Hong Kong Timeline 2019-2021: Anti-Extradition Protests & National Security Law. https://www.hrichina.org/en/hong-kong-timeline-2019-2021-anti-extradition-protests-national-security-law.

IMF. 2020. World Economic Outlook Database, October 2020. https://www.imf.org/en/Publications/WEO/weo-database/2020/October/weo-report?

Investopedia. 2020. One Belt One Road (OBOR). https://www.investopedia.com/terms/o/one-belt-one-road-obor.asp.

Investopedia. 2021. How Does a Currency Swap Work? https://www.investopedia.com/terms/c/currencyswap.asp.

Jalinous, F., K. Mildorf, K. Schomig, C. Brayton-Lewis and S. Jorgensen. 2018. CFIUS Reform Becomes Law: What FIRRMA Means for Industry. White & Case. https://www.whitecase.com/publications/alert/cfius-reform-becomes-law-what-firrma-means-industry.

Koenig, P. 2019. China – The Belt and Road Initiative – The Bridge that Spans the World. New Eastern Outlook. https://journal-neo.org/2019/11/23/china-the-belt-and-road-initiative-the-bridge-that-spans-the-world/.

Kokas, A. 2021. The Soft War That America Is Losing. Stanford University Freeman Spogli Institute for International Studies. https://fsi.stanford.edu/news/soft-war-america-losing.

Kurlantzick, J., and West, J. China's Digital Aid: The Risks and Rewards. Council on Foreign Relations. https://www.cfr.org/china-digital-silk-road/. Accessed February 1, 2020.

Kwong, Y. 2016. The Growth of "Localism" in Hong Kong. China perspectives. https://journals.openedition.org/chinaperspectives/7057?file=1.

Lawrence, S. V. and M. F. Martin. 2020. China's National Security Law for Hong Kong: Issues for Congress. Congressional Research Service (CRS). https://fas.org/sgp/crs/row/R46473.pdf.

Macro Polo. 2019. For Company and For Country: Boeing and US-China Relations. https://macropolo.org/analysis/boeing-us-china-relations-history/.

Maizland. 2021. Why China-Taiwan Relations Are So Tense. https://www.cfr.org/backgrounder/china-taiwan-relations-tension-us-policy. Accessed May 19, 2021.

Mint. 2017. One Belt, One Road has no basis in China's history. https://www.livemint.com/Opinion/lrHNZQcdLcDN2eTtmbC9cK/One-Belt-One-Road-has-no-basis-in-Chinas-history.html.

Moon, H. C. 2018. The Art of Strategy: Sun Tzu, Michael Porter, and Beyond, Cambridge University Press, Cambridge.

Morgan Stanley. 2018. Inside China's Plan to Create a Modern Silk Road. https://www.morganstanley.com/ideas/china-belt-and-road.

Network World. 2003. Cisco sues Huawei over intellectual property. https://www.networkworld.com/article/2339527/cisco-sues-huawei-over-intellectual-property.html.

New York Times. 2010. China Passes Japan as Second-Largest Economy. https://www.nytimes.com/2010/08/16/business/global/16yuan.html.

New York Times. 2013. Xi Jinping's Chinese Dream. https://www.nytimes.com/2013/06/05/opinion/global/xi-jinpings-chinese-dream.html.

New York Times. 2017a. Behind China's $1 Trillion Plan to Shake Up the Economic Order. https://www.nytimes.com/2017/05/13/business/china-railway-one-belt-one-road-1-trillion-plan.html#:~:text=VANG%20VIENG%2C%20Laos%20%E2%80%94%20Along%20the,eventually%20connect%20eight%20Asian%20countries.

New York Times. 2017b. Trump Proposes the Most Sweeping Tax Overhaul in Decades. https://www.nytimes.com/2017/09/27/us/politics/trump-tax-cut-plan-middle-class-deficit.html.

New York Times. 2018. How China Got Sri Lanka to Cough Up a Port. https://www.nytimes.com/2018/06/25/world/asia/china-sri-lanka-port.html.

New York Times. 2019. In Blow to Trump, America's Trade Deficit in Goods Hits Record $891 Billion. https://www.nytimes.com/2019/03/06/us/politics/us-trade-deficit.html.

New York Times. 2020a. F.C.C. Designates Huawei and ZTE as National Security Threats. https://www.nytimes.com/2020/06/30/technology/fcc-huawei-zte-national-security.html.

New York Times. 2020b. Why China's Move to Rein In Hong Kong Is Just the Start. https://www.nytimes.com/2020/05/24/world/asia/china-hong-kong-taiwan.html.

Nikkei Asia. 2020. Hong Kong seeks boost from China to jump-start economy. https://asia.nikkei.com/Politics/Hong-Kong-seeks-boost-from-China-to-jump-start-economy.

Nikkei Asia. 2021. Hong Kong's Joshua Wong and Agnes Chow jailed for protest roles. https://asia.nikkei.com/Spotlight/Hong-Kong-protests/Hong-Kong-s-Joshua-Wong-and-Agnes-Chow-jailed-for-protest-roles.

Pang, I. 2020. Hong Kong: Impact of losing special status from US. ING. https://think.ing.com/articles/hong-kong-impact-of-losing-special-status-from-us.

People's Daily Online. 2020. 2020 Two Sessions: The year that China eliminates poverty. http://en.people.cn/n3/2020/0529/c90000-9695947.html.

Policy Forum. 2019. The Free and Open Indo-Pacific strategy: A way forward. https://www.policyforum.net/the-free-and-open-indo-pacific-strategy-a-way-forward.

Reinsch, W. A., Martinez-Don, C., and Saumell, P. 2020. Hong Kong's Special Status: What's Happening and What's Next. Center for International Strategic and International Studies. https://www.csis.org/analysis/hong-kongs-special-status-whats-happening-and-whats-next.

RepTrak. 2021. Cisco Systems. https://www.reptrak.com/rankings/company/cisco. Accessed May 18, 2021.

Reuters. 2017. Exclusive: In China, the Party's push for influence inside foreign firms stirs fears. https://www.reuters.com/article/us-china-congress-companies/exclusive-in-china-the-partys-push-for-influence-inside-foreign-firms-stirs-fears-idUSKCN1B40JU.

Reuters. 2018a. Beijing eases back on 'Made in China 2025' amid trade talks with U.S. https://www.reuters.com/article/us-china-economy-priorities-idUSKBN1OB1T0.

Reuters. 2018b. U.S. restricts exports to Chinese semiconductor firm Fujian Jinhua. https://www.reuters.com/article/us-usa-trade-china-semiconductors-idUSKCN1N328E.

Reuters. 2020a. Breakingviews — War for Hong Kong talent is Taiwan's to lose. https://www.reuters.com/article/us-hongkong-protests-taiwan-breakingview-idUSKBN23A0EZ.

Reuters. 2020b. Leaving Hong Kong: A family's wrenching decision to emigrate. https://www.reuters.com/investigates/special-report/hongkong-security-emigration/#:~:text=The%20passports%20are%20a%20legacy,to%20a%20Home%20Office%20study.

Reuters. 2021. Biden set to rejoin Paris climate accord, impose curbs on U.S. oil industry. https://www.reuters.com/article/uk-usa-biden-climate/biden-set-to-rejoin-paris-climate-accord-impose-curbs-on-u-s-oil-industry-idUKKBN29P136.

South China Morning Post. 2019. Explainer: What is the Sino-British Joint Declaration and what does it have to do with Hong Kong's extradition crisis? https://www.scmp.com/news/hong-kong/politics/article/3017318/explainer-what-sino-british-joint-declaration-and-what-does.

SupChina. 2019. What do the Hong Kong protesters want? https://signal.sup-china.com/what-do-the-hong-kong-protesters-want/.

The Atlantic. 2018. The Elusive 'Better Deal' With China. https://www.theatlantic.com/international/archive/2018/08/china-trump-trade-united-states/567526/

The Conversation. 2020. Red capital: how Chinese companies wield political influence in Hong Kong. https://theconversation.com/red-capital-how-chinese-companies-wield-political-influence-in-hong-kong-140281.

The Conversation. 2021. Hong Kong: China crackdown is likely to boost migration to UK. https://theconversation.com/hong-kong-china-crackdown-is-likely-to-boost-migration-to-uk-152766.

The Diplomat. 2018. What Does China's Belt and Road Initiative Mean for US Grand Strategy? https://thediplomat.com/2018/06/what-does-chinas-belt-and-road-initiative-mean-for-us-grand-strategy.

The Diplomat. 2020. Beijing's Plan for a Post-National Security Law Hong Kong. https://thediplomat.com/2020/07/beijings-plan-for-a-post-national-security-law-hong-kong/.

The Guardian. 2018a. Huawei beats Apple to become second-largest smartphone maker. https://www.theguardian.com/technology/2018/aug/01/huawei-beats-apple-smartphone-manufacturer-samsung-iphone.

The Guardian. 2018b. What is China's Belt and Road Initiative? https://www.theguardian.com/cities/ng-interactive/2018/jul/30/what-china-belt-road-initiative-silk-road-explainer

The Guardian. 2019. Are artificial islands the answer to Hong Kong's housing crisis? https://www.theguardian.com/cities/2019/jul/12/are-artificial-islands-the-answer-to-hong-kongs-housing-crisis.

The Harvard Gazette. 2020. Hong Kong's future unsettled as China tightens the leash. https://news.harvard.edu/gazette/story/2020/07/hong-kongs-future-unsettled-as-china-tightens-the-leash/.

The Hill. 2016. Trump suggests leaving WTO over import tax proposal. https://thehill.com/policy/finance/289005-trump-suggests-leaving-wto-over-import-tax-proposal.

The Interpreter. 2020. The economics of national security in Hong Kong. https://www.lowyinstitute.org/the-interpreter/economics-national-security-hong-kong.

The Times. 2019. Chinese tech giant Huawei 'helps to persecute Uighurs.' https://www.thetimes.co.uk/article/chinese-tech-giant-huawei-helps-to-persecute-uighurs-7dfcb56nw.

The White House. 2021. Inaugural Address by President Joseph R. Biden, Jr. https://www.whitehouse.gov/briefing-room/speeches-remarks/2021/01/20/inaugural-address-by-president-joseph-r-biden-jr/.

Thorup, M. The Impact Of The US-China Trade War On Hong Kong. International Strategies for Globally Minded. https://www.escapeartist.com/blog/the-impact-the-us-china-trade-war-on-hong-kong/.

Tomotaka, S. 2021. "Belt and Road" vs. "Free and Open Indo-Pacific": Competition over Regional Order and ASEAN's Responses. Security & Strategy 1: 1.

TRT World. 2021. The United States' nuclear defense is lagging behind Russia andChina.https://www.trtworld.com/magazine/the-united-states-nuclear-defense-is-lagging-behind-russia-and-china-46127.

U.S. Citizenship and Immigration Services. 2021. Buy American and Hire American: Putting American Workers First. https://www.uscis.gov/archive/buy-american-and-hire-american-putting-american-workers-first

United States Census. 2021a. Trade in Goods with China. https://www.census.gov/foreign-trade/balance/c5700.html. Accessed February 1, 2021.

United States Census. 2021b. U.S. Exports to China by 5-digit End-Use Code 2011 - 2020. https://www.census.gov/foreign-trade/statistics/product/enduse/exports/c5700.html. Accessed February 1, 2021.

United States Census. 2021c. U.S. Imports from China by 5-digit End-Use Code 2011 - 2020. https://www.census.gov/foreign-trade/statistics/product/enduse/imports/c5700.html. Accessed February 1, 2021.

Vox. 2020. This is the future Joe Biden wants. https://www.vox.com/policy-and-politics/21340746/joe-biden-covid-19-coronavirus-recession-harris.

Wall Street Journal. 2012. China Tech Giant Under Fire. https://www.wsj.com/articles/SB10000872396390443615804578041931689859530.

Wall Street Journal. 2019. State Support Helped Fuel Huawei's Global Rise. https://www.wsj.com/articles/state-support-helped-fuel-huaweis-global-rise-11577280736.

Wall Street Journal. 2020a. *China's Expulsion of American Journalists Raises RedFlagsOverHongKong.*https://www.wsj.com/articles/chinas-expulsion-of-american-journalists-raises-red-flags-over-hong-kong-11584536325.

Wall Street Journal. 2020b. U.S. tightens restrictions on Huawei's access to chips. https://www.wsj.com/articles/commerce-department-tightens-restrictions-on-huaweis-access-to-chips-11597671747.

Wall Street Journal. 2021. China is the only major economy to report economic growthfor2020.https://www.wsj.com/articles/china-is-the-only-major-economy-to-report-economic-growth-for-2020-11610936187.

Washington Post. 2018. Trump got Mexico to pay for the wall by simply changing the meaning of 'pay' and 'Mexico.' https://www.washingtonpost.com/politics/2018/12/13/trump-got-mexico-pay-wall-by-simply-changing-meaning-pay-mexico/.

Washington Post. 2020. Huawei tested AI software that could recognize Uighur minorities and alert police, report says. https://www.washingtonpost.com/technology/2020/12/08/huawei-tested-ai-software-that-could-recognize-uighur-minorities-alert-police-report-says/.

Xinhua News Agency. 2020. HK exchange unveils plans to expand mutual market access. China.org.cn. http://www.china.org.cn/business/2020-11/28/content_76957583.htm.

Chapter 7

Building Resilient Global Value Chains in the Pandemic Era: A Conceptual Framework and Case Studies of Singapore and Vietnam

Wenyan Yin, Jeongmin Seo, and Aejung Kwon

Abstract

Despite the growing protectionist policies from major developed and developing countries, multinational corporations (MNCs) tend to adjust their current efficiency-oriented global value chains (GVCs) to more resilient ones, instead of reshoring overseas businesses back home. In this respect, this chapter seeks to introduce a comprehensive framework across four directions: agile response, alternative routes, diversification, and sustainability orientation, for establishing resilient GVCs in the pandemic era. In reviewing and reorganizing the suggestions of existing studies, this chapter argues firms need to be more globalized while maintaining the key principles of GVCs. As such, countries will also need to improve their national business environment and make it more attractive for firms to locate parts of the entire GVCs in their countries. This chapter takes two countries: Vietnam and Singapore — as examples which have been widely recognized as successful countries that have opened up their economies and utilized international resources for economic development. This chapter shows that despite the potential challenges from the global pandemic, both countries tend to push forward the globalization of their economy and introduce various measures, such as strengthening the global relations with other economies and investments for digital transformations, to upgrade their positions in the GVCs.

Keywords: Coronavirus pandemic, globalization, global value chains, resilience, Singapore, Vietnam

Introduction

As of April 2021, the confirmed number of COVID-19 cases worldwide has surpassed 130 million (WHO, 2021). Almost every country in the world has been affected by this pandemic. Many regions are encountering worse situations now than during the early stage of the pandemic in early 2020 as cases across continents are surging once again due to the emergence of COVID-19 variants (*Economist*, 2021). In order to contain the spread of the virus, some countries recently imposed lockdown restrictions while others are considering tightening regulations as well (NPR, 2021). The repeated lockdowns in many countries (e.g., Israel) has caused a massive economic shock. Except for a very small number of countries (e.g., China), the majority of countries worldwide posted negative economic growth in 2020. Global economic growth is projected to be at −4.4 percent — the worst recession since the Second World War (China Briefing, 2021). Furthermore, the pandemic has also delivered the biggest and broadest shock over the value chains (Mckinsey, 2020).

To overcome the global pandemic, a growing number of countries have been adopting protectionism and nationalism in order to address the supply chain reconfiguration (Evenett, 2020; Seric *et al.*, 2020). Many argue that globalization had been in decline before the pandemic, and it is time for governments to take measures to encourage firms to repatriate their overseas production to home countries or to stimulate domestic production for substituting foreign imports (*Economist*, 2020, 2021). However, despite government incentives and policy measures, in reality, there are only limited cases of firms reshoring their businesses back to their home countries; many of them continue to conduct their business abroad (Bloomberg, 2021; De Backer *et al.*, 2016; *Economist*, 2020).

On the other hand, the blockage of the Suez Canal by the cargo ship *Ever Given* for nearly two weeks severely disrupted the global supply chains in early 2021. The blockage resulted in billions of dollars of trade loss, and the negative impacts from the crisis could take months to return to normal[1] (SCMP, 2021). Despite the growing concern and criticism of globalization, *The Economist* (2021) stressed that "global supply chains are still a source of strength, not weakness.... Resilience comes not from autarky but from diverse sources of supply." Similarly, the BBC (2020) has also pointed out that globalization could be slowed down, but probably it will not be reversed, because it is too important for economic development. Therefore, the question is not *whether* to globalize or not, but *how* to efficiently globalize by learning the lessons from the pandemic and other crises (BBC, 2020).

Some studies (Miroudot, 2020; Sharma *et al.*, 2020) have argued that pre-pandemic global value chains (GVCs) have focused too much on efficiency but insufficiently prepared for risks. This thus requires firms to pay more attention to both efficiency and measures for sustainability issues. Gölgeci *et al.* (2020) pointed out that although there could be some trade-offs between efficiency and resilience in GVCs in the short run, they are not necessarily mutually exclusive with each other in the long run. In this respect, this chapter aims to introduce a comprehensive framework of building resilient GVCs via a thorough review of existing studies on a similar topic.

The following section begins by explaining the concept of GVCs and its historical development. The third presents the recent reshoring policies of major countries and firms' response and the analysis on the gap between government and businesses on international businesses. The fourth then introduces four aspects for building resilient GVCs by integrating and reorganizing the preceding studies. The fifth takes the two examples of Vietnam and Singapore, which continually promoted globalization and establishing GVCs even during the pandemic by building a better business environment, thereby attracting more MNCs.

---

[1]It is estimated that the blockage could cost global trade between US$6 billion to US$10 billion a week and reduce the annual trade growth by 0.2 to 0.4 percent. Moreover, the canal blockage does not only affect the global shipping industry but also other numerous businesses such as retailers, supermarkets, and manufacturers (BBC, 2021).

Global Value Chains: Conceptual Framework and Historical Development

Global value chains

GVC is extended from Porter's (1985) value chain framework, which aims to explain how discrete activities contribute to firms' competitive advantage — cost or differentiation. The value chain is composed of two broad categories of primary and support activities, which are further divided into nine activities. Five *primary* activities include inbound logistics, operations, outbound logistics, marketing and sales, and service. Four *support* activities comprise procurement, technology development, human resource development, and firm infrastructure. The analytical tool of the value chain is a widely accepted framework to identify the sources of competitive advantages and assess the firm performance (Moon, 2018).

Porter's value chain framework though only emphasizes the efficiency of conducting all value chain activities by one single firm in its home country. In reality, over the last few decades, firms have been increasingly locating various activities to foreign countries where each activity can be most efficiently performed by exploiting foreign locational advantages. Moreover, more firms are pursuing outsourcing or cooperative governance, rather than internalizing the entire value chain activities.

According, GVC conceptually extends Porter's value chain from two aspects. First, geographically, GVC extends the location from domestic to international scope. Second, the governance mechanism of the value chain is extended from one firm to many firms. There are three types of governance — trade, foreign direct investment (FDI), and non-equity mode (NEM) — for firms to choose to perform each value chain activity, driven by various factors at the firm, industry, and country level (Moon and Yin, 2017, 2020; Yin, 2017).

GVC examples: Apple and Samsung Electronics

Apple and Samsung Electronics are the two key players in the smartphone business, and both companies are good examples of adopting GVC to produce low-cost and high-quality products. On the back of Apple's signature iPhone, it is written as "Designed by Apple in California; Assembled in China." Apple is well known that it performs technology development internally in the US and outsources operations to other companies (e.g., Foxconn) of which factories are located in China. By offshoring the factories in China and outsourcing the majority of the parts and components to the global suppliers, Apple reduces production costs, and also improves product quality, thereby achieving higher competitiveness in the market. However, since 2017 the text on the back of its iPhones disappeared for iPhone 8 and X. This is because Apple's assembly factories are no longer located in China only, but their locations are now diversified to other countries such as India and Brazil. On the other hand, in addition to the US, Apple has established or announced its plans to establish R&D and/or design centers in regions such as Germany, China, Israel, Japan, and Taiwan.

Unlike Apple, Samsung internalizes most of the value chain activities, but it also outsources some key parts & components (e.g., battery, Google's Android operating system) and activities (e.g., marketing and services). Samsung's assembly factories of smartphones are located in Korea, India, Vietnam, and Indonesia. Yet, nearly 50 percent of its phones are manufactured in Vietnam. Recently, Samsung began to show a tendency to increase the production portion of low value-added parts and components in other firms to reduce production costs. On the other hand, Samsung's smartphone R&D and design centers are found in San Francisco, China, Delhi, London, Japan, Seoul, and Sao Paolo.

The evolution of GVC (1990s–2010s)

For the last two decades of 1990s and 2000s, the GVC has shown rapid growth driven by technology development which allows fine-slicing of value chain activities and better communication across partners from distant regions (UNCTAD, 2020). The growth of GVC is also supported by the liberalization of trade and investment policies of governments. In addition, emerging markets have played an increasingly important role in promoting globalization by attracting more MNCs into their markets (UNCTAD, 2020). The global FDI stock increased 10 times and global trade increased 5 times over the past two decades. In the same period, the GVC share of trade proxied by the share of foreign value-added in exports increased by more than 10 percentage points (*UNCTAD*, 2020).

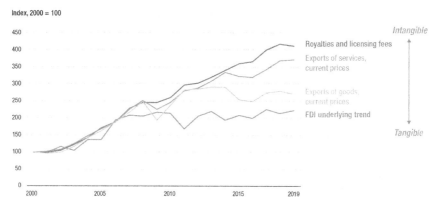

Figure 1.   Indicators of international production by tangibility, 2000–2019 (Indexed, 2000 = 100).

Source: UNCTAD (2020: 125).

After the global financial crisis in 2008 and 2010s in particular, the growth momentum of GVC has stalled. This was because of the global recession, protectionist measures, and the most recent COVID-19 pandemic. As shown in Figure 1, trade and FDI growth stagnated over the last decade. However, it has shown different patterns among various channels of globalization. For trade, the exports of goods slowed down but the exports of services witnessed strong growth. On the other hand, NEMs were firmly established by MNCs for globalization to bypass the governments' growing restrictive and regulatory measures on trade and investment.

Government Protectionist Policy and MNCs' Response Towards Globalization

Government protectionist policy

Among other factors, recent US–China tensions have particularly raised profound threats and uncertainty on the global economy and MNCs' global expansion. China's ambitious plan known as Made in China 2025 and expansive Belt and Road Initiative in the mid-2010s provoked the US. The relationship between China and the US has become more competitive than ever (*FT*, 2020). With the growing trade deficit against

China, the Trump administration kicked off a trade war in 2018, by imposing high tariffs against imports from China. The combative relationship has expanded into the investment and technology sectors.

Trump pushed the "Buy American, Hire American" policy before the trade war against China. Under an executive order, Trump encouraged American and foreign firms to invest in the US, hire American people, and sell the goods that were made in America. The first target of such reshoring policy was the American automobile industry. Trump threatened to impose high tariffs of 25 percent on automobile imports produced in foreign countries. Trump even tweeted by ordering American firms to move out of China and to immediately start looking for alternatives. In 2019, the Department of Commerce of the US also added 28 new companies and agencies to its "blacklist" of Chinese firms, which are banned from doing business in the US. These firms are the significant players in China's technology growth (CNBC, 2019a). This in fact has significantly reduced the FDI inflows from Chinese firms in the US.

The Biden administration has sought to overturn many Trump-era policies, such as immigration, climate, and tax policies. However, the "Buy American" order[2] signed on January 25, 2021 seems to echo Trump's policies. This executive order sought to re-shore and expand domestic supply chains, by increasing government purchases of American goods. On the same day, Biden also ordered a 100-day security review of US supply chains for critical items, including computer chips, medical gear, electric-vehicle batteries, and specialized minerals, to reduce its overdependence on foreign suppliers and avoid shortages of goods as experienced in the recent COVID-19 pandemic.

In addition to the US, many other policymakers in other countries have proposed that globalization has gone too far even before the outbreak of pandemic and argued for the necessity to back up the reconfiguration of supply chains. As shown in Table 1, major governments have taken measures for reshoring policies by encouraging the repatriation of production or stimulating domestic production to replace foreign imports.

---

[2]The Act requires that the goods purchased by federal entities for public use should be produced in the US and at least 50 percent of the cost of their components must be procured from the US.

Table 1.   Reshoring policies of major countries.

Country	Policies
US	• Deployed the Defense Production Act of 1950 to offer financial incentives to expand production within the US • Signed the Buy American order (2021/1/25) • Ordered a 100-day security review of America's supply chains (2021/1/25)
Japan	• Intended to relocate production bases to Japan, for products with high added value and for which it is highly dependent on a single country • Included 220 billion Yen (about US$2 billion) in financial grants for firms moving production facilities out of China
EU	• EU: talked about "strategic autonomy" and created a fund to buy stakes in regional firms • Germany and France: Advocated supply chain reform (Specific funds for repatriating supply chains)
China	• Launched "dual circulation", aimed at insulating China's economy from outside pressure (2020)
India	• Modi told the nation that a new era of economic self-reliance has begun • "Vocal for local"

Source: Information is abstracted from Evenett (2020), Economist (2020, 2021).

MNCs' response to government's anti-globalization policies

Apple's response to Trump administration

Apple has much at risk due to the US–China trade war, since the majority of iPhones, Apple Watches, and iPads are assembled in China. Trump once said to Apple's Tim Cook that he did not have to worry about tariffs if Apple builds factories in the US. Despite admonishments from the Trump administration, Apple has not built any new factories in the US so far. Instead, Apple invested in its American suppliers such as Corning, which produces the glass used in Apple displays, to enhance their quality and functional competitiveness (Intelligencer, 2017). Apple also built a new branch in Austin, Texas, seeking to support 15,000 employees in departments such as customer services, R&D, and operations.

Apple's reluctance to build factories in the US is not because of labor costs. In fact, the Chinese labor costs have started to rise already, and according to the analysis by *MIT Technology Review* on Apple's supply chain in 2015, the retail price would only increase about US$100 than it is now if it was produced in the US, instead of in China (Swearingen, 2017). The more critical reasons for Apple's choice of China for its production assembly are due to the combined advantages of scale, skills, infrastructure, and costs (*New York Times*, 2019). Apple has found no other country that can substitute China. In particular, Chinese factories operate at all hours, and workers are also possible to get up from sleep for production. Yet, this is never possible in the US. Due to these reasons, until just recently when Apple diversified its production to minimize the impact of a trade war by moving some iPhone assembly to India, and some iPad and MacBook assembly to Vietnam, China remained as a key location for the production of Apple products.

Automakers' response to Trump administration

Ford canceled its US$1.6 billion projects in Mexico and invested US$700 million in an existing plant in Michigan state of the US for electric and autonomous cars. Yet, for the new investment in the US, *The Economist* (2017) commented that Ford's maneuver seems "more wheel-spin than U-turn." This is because the original plan for the new Mexican plant aimed to build small passenger vehicles for which the US demand has fallen due to the decrease in oil price. Therefore, the decision to cancel the new plant is purely based on the shrinking market demand and the necessity of reducing its footprint in Mexico. On the other hand, Ford had already announced back in 2015 that it would invest in electric cars, which was before it faced pressured by the Trump administration.

Like Ford, other automakers also invested in the US as shown in Table 2, but these investments are all based on market analysis and their business necessity. In fact, these global automakers' investments in the US are driven by the locational advantages of the US such as access to advanced technology and large market, and the investments, which can further strengthen their market position and international competitiveness (Moon and Yin, 2017).

Table 2.   **The investment in the US announced by the MNCs.**

Firm	Investment	Motivations
Ford	US$700 million (2021–2023)	• To produce electric and autonomous cars
GM	US$6.5 billion (2020)	• To increase electronic vehicle production
Fiat Chrysler	US$1 billion (2017–2019)	• To upgrade its existing plants
	US$4.5 billion (2017–2019)	• To invest $4.5 billion in Michigan for new Jeep SUV models
Toyota	US$13 billion (2017–2020)	• To meet demand and upgrade plants to build more fuel-efficient models
Hyundai	US$3.1 billion (2017–2011)	• 30–40% of the investment for developing self-driving and eco-friendly cars
	₩2 trillion 2018	• To set up joint venture Motional with Aptiv, a US autonomous vehicle technology company
	₩770 billion 2021–2022	• To invest in US robot company Boston Dynamics to gain 60 percent ownership
Daimler	US$1.3 billion 2015	• To expand production facilities in Alabama (The increasing demand for SUV in the US)
Mercedes-Benz	US$53.6 million 2019–2022	• To boost EV production in Alabama

Other firms' response against the government policy

Without the significant benefits of doing business in the home country, firms will be less likely to move their overseas businesses back home. A survey of German manufacturers showed that only 2 percent brought production home during the period 2010–2012, whereas four times as many firms have shifted operations abroad during the same period (*Economist*, 2020). The study by OECD published in 2016 also found that despite the incentives provided by the governments for reshoring, the effects of reshoring policies were limited (*Economist*, 2020).

This trend remains during the pandemic. Most global businesses choose to remain global; the economic incentives to outsource still prevails among firms (*New York Times*, 2020). For example, only 80 South

Korean firms out of thousands with links in China have returned part of their operations back to their home countries since 2013 when the country introduced its U-Turn law. Even the Korean government extended its reshoring subsidies and incentives in early 2020, there have been only around 15 firms moved back home (Bloomberg, 2020a). The survey by the Korea Federation of SMEs showed that 70 percent of Korean firms in China have no interest in reshoring, and 90 percent of Korean firms in Vietnam also indicated they have no plans to move back to Korea. The top three reasons cited for "not to return home" include high production costs, reduced foreign market access, and reduced ties with foreign partners.

Similarly, previous studies (e.g., Bonadio *et al.*, 2020; OECD, 2020) have highlighted challenges or disadvantages accompanying with firms' reshoring practices, which include higher costs and higher volatility in output due to fewer channels for economic adjustment. Furthermore, the domestic economy could also face a natural disaster or other disruptions such as the 2011 Japanese earthquake. Before 2011, Japanese automobile firms used to locate the production of key parts and components at home, however, the earthquakes have significantly disrupted the supply chains of Japanese firms, automakers in particular. Hence, since the 2011 earthquake, Japanese firms moved to diversify their supply chains in other regions such as North America, Europe, and Asia to reduce the ripple effects from the shocks in any part of the world. In fact, when the 2016 earthquake hit Japan, Japanese firms saw much less downturn compared to when the 2011 earthquake hit (McKinsey, 2020).

Different perspectives on international business between government and business

The above comparative analysis showed that governments and business hold different perspectives on globalization (see Table 3) (Moon, 2016). Politicians mainly prioritize the domestic voters and their interests, whereas businessmen consider the interests of their global stakeholders including both domestic and foreign governments, partners, and consumers. Moreover, politicians tend to prioritize the fair distribution between rich and poor, job security, and welfare of voters, but business mainly aim to maximize profits for survival and sustainable growth of their industry. To achieve their goals, politicians will tend to pursue protectionist policies by emphasizing the "made in home country" slogan, while businessmen pursue efficiency via

Table 3.   Comparison of politicians and businessmen.

	Politicians	Businessmen
Scope of activities	Domestic	Domestic + Foreign
Interests	Voters	Stakeholders
Objective	Welfare: employment	Profit creation
Method	Protectionism	Efficiency
Production strategy	Made in home country	Made in the world
Global view	Competition	Competition + Cooperation
Result	Income distribution	Survival and growth

Source: Moon (2016b).

the "made in the world" strategy. Hence, multinational firms will possess both competitive and cooperative views, and consider global expansion as a key option for enhancing their competitiveness. In this regard, it is understandable that firms will not always follow the government policies as they find that the policies contradict their interests.

Four Directions for Building Resilient GVCs

Despite the growing criticism and concern about the risks and challenges of GVCs, many studies have acknowledged that the main GVC principles are less likely to change (Verbeke, 2020; Kano and Oh, 2020). In other words, the leading firms will continue to use both externalization and internalization modes to govern the fine-sliced value chain activities, which are dispersed across many countries in the world. Some argue that pre-pandemic GVCs are overly focused on efficiency and have not prepared well for risk management (Sharma *et al.*, 2020; Miroudot, 2020). Nevertheless, efficiency does not have to be sacrificed for building resilient GVCs (Miroudot, 2020). Gölgeci *et al.* (2020) argued that the two aspects of efficiency and resilience may be at odds in the short run, but there could be no trade-offs in the long run.

There have been an increasing number of studies that propose and suggest the ways of building resilient GVCs in the pandemic era. Table 4 summarizes and reorganizes them into four categories: agile response, alternative routes, diversification, and sustainability orientation. The following will explain each aspect in more detail.

Table 4. Four directions for building resilient GVCs.

Categories	Methods	Studies
Agile response	Dynamic response and digital transformation	Verbeke (2020), Miroudot (2020), Sharma *et al.* (2020)
Alternative routes	Alternative governance and methods	Contractor (2021), Strange (2020), Verbeke (2020)
Diversification	• Location (production/ market) • Supplier, research, and others • Product/industry	Verbeke (2020), Miroudot (2020), Strange (2020), UNCTAD (2020), Zhan (2021), Kano and Oh (2020), O'Neil (2020), Gereffi (2020)
Sustainability orientation	Social mechanism/ development (e.g., SDG, ESG)	Waldman and Javidan (2020), Gereffi (2020), Gölgeci *et al.* (2020)

Agile response

Conventional efficiency-oriented GVCs have emphasized lean manufacturing such as the Just in Time model. However, IB scholars have stressed that more emphasis needs to be put on "agility manufacturing," (Potdar *et al.*, 2017) which requires firms' dynamic capabilities in adapting to environmental changes to remain competitive in an uncertain environment (Miroudot, 2020). Furthermore, the agile response is particularly important for intra-GVC coordination and improvements of firms' information processing capability (Verbeke, 2020). Sharma *et al.* (2020) then stressed that firms need to evaluate sourcing strategies in real-time, so that they achieve operational flexibility and keep the supply chain agile (Sharma *et al.*, 2020).

Alternative routes

MNCs need to further "micro-modularize" their value chains which would allow for easier substitution of one module by another when they are facing uncertainties or disruptions (Verbeke, 2020). This can thus help firms to reduce the potential negative impacts upon the entire GVCs because of a specific problem in one of its activities. On the other hand, Strange (2020) suggested that firms should reevaluate the governance of their GVCs, i.e., internalization and externalization. Strange argued that as the future pandemic is as likely to impact domestic economies, greater externalization will facilitate responses to uncertainties more quickly and appropriately. He added that alternative methods such as establishing spare domestic capacity, stockpiling, and greater liquidity will help mitigate the adverse effects on GVCs. Similar to Strange (2020), Contractor (2021) articulated that despite the imposition of a greater degree of protectionist trade policies by major governments, these measures in fact have induced more tariff-jumping investments. Furthermore, alliances such as international joint ventures and contractual alliances have grown which are the alternative routes to exports or investment through FDI to reach global markets.

Diversification

Further diversification can be achieved from three perspectives: location, suppliers, and product/industry to diversify the risks from uncertainties. Strange (2020) stated due to the growing geopolitical tensions and protectionist sentiments, it has become more important to achieve resilience through diversification, which comes from more rather than less diversification of suppliers dispersed across many countries. On the other hand, Verbeke (2020) suggested that after decades of concentrating on their core business, firms could also diversify into other activities that share similar underlying competencies but are less likely to be negatively impacted by the crisis at the same time with the core business. Moreover, Miroudot (2020) added building redundancy in suppliers so that just in case of facing a crisis, other suppliers can provide the necessary inputs. Specifically, the same products/parts can be sourced from different suppliers. Furthermore, long-term relationships with suppliers are important as they ensure faster recovery and more commitment by suppliers for risk mitigation.

Sustainability orientation

Waldman and Javidan (2020) argued that it is false to view globalization and nationalism as a dichotomy, and therefore anyone should not be so hastened to lean toward one side or the other side. Instead, they can be integrated and pursued together. In the pre-pandemic period, firms often focused on global-oriented actions and benefitted from them but never took the integrative approach to address both global and national concerns when making decisions. Firms were only trying to pick the region in which their value chain activities can be most efferently performed, by only considering efficiency, not possible risk. Gereffi (2020) recommended the measure that it is necessary to bolster capacity in the home country with regards to the essential products to address the security concerns. The second issue is about firms' engagement with environmental, social, and governance (ESG) issues. Although there have been concerns about sustainability for several decades, not until recently have firms translated their words into action (Eccles and Klimenko, 2019). The purpose of firms should not just be profit maximization, but also a provision of solutions to the problems generated in the process of producing the profits (Eccles and Klimenko, 2019). Hence, it is no longer whether firms engage with sustainability issues but *how* to effectively commit to the sustainability issues. In this respect, Porter and Kramer's (2011) creating shared value (CSV) concept provides useful guidelines for firms who want to contribute to the social and environmental development as well as strengthening their financial performance.

Case Study: Vietnam and Singapore

The realignment of GVCs was accelerated due to US–China tensions and the global pandemic (*Wall Street Journal*, 2019; Shira and Associates, 2020). As firms seek to adopt a diversification strategy to reduce their dependence on China-centered GVCs, there are more opportunities for other countries to take a part in GVCs (Barhat, 2020; OECD, 2021). However, this will not happen automatically (Rovčanin, 2007). Countries need to build an attractive business environment for various business activities, as such an environment is important to firms' locational decisions. The following section takes the examples of Vietnam and Singapore to show how these two countries have adopted various measures to cope with the pandemic and strengthen their attractiveness for foreign firms to conduct business in Vietnam and Singapore in the pandemic era.

The case of Vietnam

The growing participation of Vietnam in GVCs before the pandemic

Vietnam has maintained a level of sustained growth over the last decade. The GDP of Vietnam was US$106 billion in 2009 and grew by more than

2.5 times to US$261 billion in 2019 (World Bank, 2021a). During the same period, Vietnamese exports of goods increased substantially from US$57 billion to US$264 billion, and imports of goods also jumped from US$70 billion to US$253 billion (*WTO*, 2021). Since 2012, Vietnam's exports have surpassed imports. Yet, the country needs to upgrade its structure of export components, as it still mainly exports low-tech goods (ADB, 2018: 247) and the trade in services accounts for a much smaller percentage (about 8.16 percent) of Vietnam's total trade in goods and services (see Figure 2).

In addition to its growing degree of globalization via trade, Vietnam has also emerged as an attractive FDI destination for MNCs. The Vietnamese government adopted its *Đổi Mới* policy in the late 1980s to attract more FDI by introducing elements of a market econ-omy, liberalizing trade, and easing foreign investment regulations (Le, 2019). As the inflows of FDI to Vietnam increased from US$8 billion in 2010 to US$16.1 billion in 2019 (see Figure 2), the Vietnamese rank in terms of FDI inflows among ASEAN countries increased from fifth to third position, by accounting for 10 percent of total FDI inflows to ASEAN in 2019.

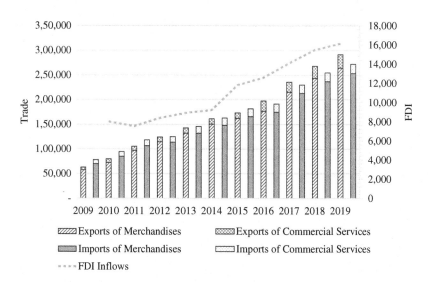

Figure 2.   The total trade and FDI inflows of Vietnam (Unit: million US$).

Source: WTO (2021) and ASEAN Statistics (2021).

Drivers behind the economic growth of Vietnam in the pandemic era

Although the majority of countries recorded negative economic growth during the pandemic, Vietnam maintained its positive GDP growth during this period. It recorded an economic growth of 2.9 percent in 2020, which was even higher than that of China, 2.3 percent (CNBC, 2021). Although several sectors showed negative growth, most of the industries in Vietnam remained resilient, showing positive growth. The following describes the contributing factors to Vietnam's resilient economy despite COVID-19.

First, Vietnam showed successful containment of the pandemic by adopting strong prevention policies at the national level. It has had many experiences in dealing with pandemics such as SARS in 2003 (*Financial Times*, 2021), and such preceding experiences have helped Vietnam to adopt a more efficient response to COVID-19. By April 14, 2021, there were only a total of 2,733 confirmed cases in Vietnam, recording the second smallest number of confirmed cases among ASEAN countries (Worldometer, 2021). Vietnam was thus identified as the second safest country in the COVID Performance Index[3] (Lowy Institute, 2021). Crisis management capability has actually become an increasingly crucial factor for firms' locational decisions. They have been more concerned about looking for a reliable destination that can respond better to the global health crisis, thereby improving the resilience of their GVCs (Lee, 2020a). The stability and dynamics of the Vietnamese economy have well demonstrated its capability to manage the crisis.

Second, effective government policies for attracting FDI helped the Vietnamese economy to remain resilient. The positive effects of FDI on the Vietnamese economy over the last two decades have been empirically proven (Nguyen, 2020a). Throughout 2020, FDI was one of the key factors for Vietnam's economic growth during the pandemic. By November

---

[3]The Covid Performance Index by Lowy Institute evaluated the six indicators of prevalence of COVID-19 with publicly available and comparable data: "Confirmed cases, confirmed deaths," "Confirmed cases per million people," "Confirmed deaths per million people," "Confirmed cases as a proportion of tests," and "Tests per thousand people." On 13 March 2021, 116 countries were evaluated and ranked based on their performance over 43 weeks. However, Vietnam was not included in the March ranking due to insufficient data. Instead, the January ranking was used in this part.

of that year, the estimated amount of FDI inflows reached US$17 billion, recording an increase of US$1 billion when compared to 2019 (*Vietnam Briefing News*, 2021). In addition to this, the regulative innovations implemented before the pandemic have contributed to the increase in FDI inflows. According to the US Department of State (2020a), the Vietnamese government introduced "Resolution 55" in 2019 with the aim to attract US$50 billion FDI by 2030. Furthermore, in January 2020, the government introduced reforms in the electronic payment procedures of foreign firms such as the removal of foreign ownership limits in the e-Wallet sector[4] (US Department of State, 2020a).

Moreover, the FDI in the manufacturing sector is expected to increase as many MNCs' manufacturing plants have recently been relocated to Vietnam. For example, Samsung Electronics registered 50 local supporting enterprises to assign them as first-tier suppliers; the number of its second-tier suppliers has increased from 157 to 192 during 2018–2020 (VietnamPlus, 2021a). Similar to this, Toyota developed 10 first-tier suppliers in Vietnam (VietnamPlus, 2021a). Apple also asked Foxconn to relocate production facilities for assembling some iPad and MacBooks from China to Vietnam to minimize the risk of dependence on China (Reuters, 2020).

Third, strengthening international relations with foreign economies was another factor that promoted positive economic growth in Vietnam. As part of efforts to improve its business environment, the government has provided opportunities to export more commodities and services by improving the degree of its economic openness. In this case, it has established ties with a wider variety of countries in recent years. A free trade agreement (UKVFTA) was signed with the UK in December 2020, which eliminated 99 percent of tariffs, promising the free flow of capital and investment and helped maintain a close tie between the two countries (Bloomberg, 2020b). In January 2019, the Comprehensive and Progressive Agreement for Trans-Pacific Partnership, a free trade agreement between 11 countries in the Asia-Pacific region, came into effect in Vietnam, which has positively influenced the trade relationship with other member countries (Government of Canada, 2020). On March 31, 2021, at the 48th anniversary of Vietnam-Australia diplomatic relations, Tran Phuoc Anh, director of the Ho Chi Minh City's Department of Foreign Affairs,

---

[4]"E-wallets" means a type of electronic card which is used for online transactions (*Economic Times*, 2021).

promised to enhance cooperation to overcome the pandemic and confirmed that development in their relationship can realize the goals established in Vietnam-Australia Strategic Partnership by 2023[5] (VietnamPlus, 2021b). In addition, there were also many other agreements and events to promote interdependence, which are all strategies by Vietnam to diversify its GVCs and secure flexibility in its economy.

Fourth, technological innovation and digital transformation have been key driving forces in the Vietnamese economy. Technology and production capabilities of Vietnamese companies, and sophisticated infrastructure are essential factors for MNCs to make an investment or contractual decisions. Tran Phuoc Anh noted that it is crucial to develop new technologies for participating in the GVCs, and thus promoting cooperation with foreign firms and encouraging technology transfer are necessary (VietnamPlus, 2021a). The Vietnamese government is also seeking to catch up with the leading countries in digitalization. The government announced the "National Digital Transformation Program to 2025, orientation to 2030" (Asem Connet Vietnam, 2021) to help Vietnam transition to a digital government, digital economy, and digital society, required for creating a competitive digital business environment.

The case of Singapore

Singapore is one of the most open countries and is known as possessing one of the most business-friendly environments in the world. It ranked as the highest country in the 2021 Index of Economic Freedom (Heritage Foundation, 2021), and second position in the World Bank's Doing Business 2020 (World Bank, 2020). Foreign investors can easily access the Singaporean market. Except for a few sectors, there are almost no discrimination between domestic and foreign investors in the Singaporean market. This open regulation system is one of the most attractive factors for foreign investors. Singapore has also many advantages including tax structure, customs facilitation, intellectual property protections, and

---

[5] Vietnam and Australia agreed that the Plan of Action for Vietnam-Australia Strategic Partnership for the period 2020–2023 in August 2019 and the plan focuses on three priorities: enhancing economic engagement; deepening strategic, defense and security cooperation; and building knowledge and innovation partnerships (Prime Minister of Australia, 2019).

well-developed infrastructure. In addition, transparency is one of the most attractive features among its investment climate (The U.S. Department of State, 2020b).

The platform role of Singapore in the GVCs before the pandemic

Singapore is considered the central hub of global logistics and the size of the trade going through Singapore is large. From 2010 to 2019, the annual total exports and imports of goods had remained above US$330 billion and US$280 billion respectively. The trade in commercial services has also increased steadily during the same period (see Figure 3) (WTO, 2021). According to *Financial Times* (2020), the volume of goods passed through Singaporean ports was the second-largest after Shanghai in 2018. Most merchandise imported by Singapore is re-exported to other destinations. As such, Singapore is regarded as a gateway to Asia. The amount of FDI inflows almost doubled from US$57 billion in 2010 to US$97 billion in 2019 (see Figure 3). Throughout this period, the percentage Singapore accounted for in ASEAN FDI inflows has increased from 53 percent to 58 percent (*ASEAN Statistics*, 2021).

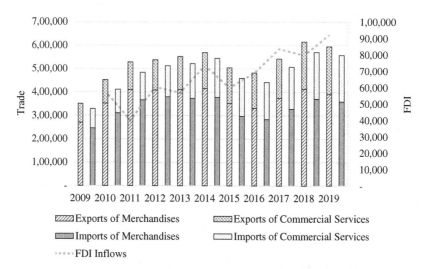

Figure 3.   The total trade and FDI inflows in Singapore (Unit: million US$).

Source: WTO (2021) and ASEAN Statistics (2021).

Challenges and opportunities of Singapore in the pandemic era

• *Challenges*

The total confirmed cases of COVID-19 in Singapore was 60,719 as of 14 April 2021, but the number of deaths was only 30 (Worldometer, 2021). The country has contained the spread of COVID-19 through various policies such as the telecommuting among workers, the provision of temporary residence for dormitory replacement, and "the TraceTogether Programme" (*INGSA*, 2020; TraceTogether, 2021). However, despite the successful containment, the Singaporean economy still experienced negative growth of GDP in 2020; its GDP shrank by 5.4 percent in 2020. Below we summarize some factors that contributed to the negative growth.

First, FDI accounts for a significant portion of Singapore's GDP. However, FDI inflows declined by the largest scale over the last 20 years. The recent growing protectionist policies adopted by some leading countries have largely affected the FDI inflows to Singapore. Alongside this, the prolonged US–China trade war has further contributed to the spread of protectionism among many other countries (Davies, 2020; Qiang *et al.*, 2020, Business Times, 2018).

Second, Singapore's heavy reliance on foreign workers has further deteriorated its economy. As of December 2019, 1,427,400 foreign workers were employed in Singapore (Ministry of Manpower Singapore, 2021), which was about one-fourth of the whole population of Singapore. Yet, according to the data presented by the Ministry of Health Singapore (2020), migrant laborers accounted for about 90 percent of the total confirmed COVID-19 cases in Singapore. As a result, the areas of low-wage or basic industries such as construction, cleaning, and food and beverage sectors, where the reliance on foreign labors was relatively high, were more severely affected.

Third, the decline in shipping and tourism is another factor that damaged the Singaporean economy. For example, air cargo decreased from 1,164,765.2 tons in 2018 to 824,578.7 tons in 2020 (Department of Statistics Singapore, 2021a), and sea freight transport decreased from 630,125.3 tons in 2018 to 590,738.3 tons in 2020 (Department of Statistics Singapore, 2021b). On the occasion of construction, there was also a setback in the import of materials due to the closing of Chinese factories (TODAY online, 2020). Singapore has been a major destination for tourism and for 2018 ranked fifth in Global Top 20 Destination Cities by International Overnight Visitors (Mastercard, 2019). But this sector suffered greatly as a result of the pandemic and related travel restrictions. As a result, there was a lot of damage in the tourism sector as well as the retail and hospitality sector.

• *Opportunity*
The de-coupling from China's supply chains has been increasing around the world due to China's rising labor costs and the US–China trade dispute. This trend has accelerated more with the pandemic. Singapore though has been one of the beneficiary countries from this shifting trend. Hong Kong, which is often considered as a rival of Singapore, has been somewhat losing its competitiveness and attractiveness for foreign firms. In this respect, many MNCs are considering Singapore as one of the alternatives for locating their value chain activities (Switow, 2021). As Southeast Asia, whose regional hub is Singapore, has a large population, abundant natural resources, and high potential market growth, many MNCs are choosing Singapore as the gateway when expanding into the ASEAN or even wider Asia-Pacific region (*Business Times*, 2019). Some financial companies, in particular, are considering or have completed their locational transition from Hong Kong to Singapore (CNBC, 2019b; World Bank, 2021b). The evidence can be found from the fact that the amount of FDI inflows in Singapore exceeded that in Hong Kong for the first time in 2019 over the last 15 years (see Figure 4).

Singapore has the competitiveness to seize the opportunity and has the potential to expand its growth. For example, Singapore has a world-class logistics system known as the Networked Trade Platform which is an efficient IT model for trade and logistics that connects businesses, community systems, platforms, and governments. These systems are essential to prepare for further globalization (Capri, 2020a).

Another strength of Singapore is its enhanced digital economy. There has been a growing demand for digitalization and industry 4.0 as the COVID-19 pandemic increases demand for contactless services, technologies, and digital infrastructure. In 2020, the Singaporean government invested US$2.5 billion in ICT, building modern ICT infrastructures such as cloud-based services, public data analytics, and AI utilization (GlobalData, 2020). New digital ecosystems such as fintech, medical services, and e-commerce are also growing due to social distancing (Capri, 2020b). This can contribute to the attraction of IT companies and the

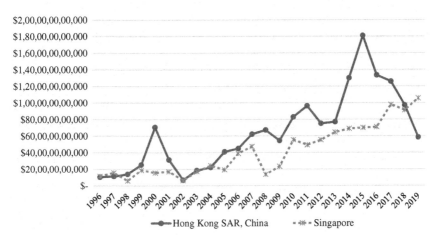

Figure 4.   The net FDI inflows to Singapore and Hong Kong (Unit: US$).

Source: World Bank (2021b).

support of online activities of companies by providing a ready digital experience.

Implications

Globalization has undoubtedly imposed positive effects on economic development. Vietnam and Singapore are the beneficiaries that have achieved substantial economic growth by pursuing open-door policies and integration with the global economy. Vietnam has now been the fastest growing economy among emerging countries, while Singapore has been the most open and attractive global business hub. Despite the challenges from the pandemic, Vietnam has maintained positive GDP growth. Although Singapore recorded negative growth in 2020, this decline is expected to be a temporary phenomenon, and the economy will shift to positive growth in the pandemic era. Both countries will make efforts to further integrate their economy into the global market, by linking their economy to MNCs' GVCs and raising their position within these networks. They will strengthen globalization policies by improving their relationship with other countries and strengthening the connectivity by establishing diverse FTAs. Moreover, through digital transformation and technological innovation, the governments have laid the foundation to attract higher value-added activities for MNCs. Accordingly, in contrast to countries pushing forward protectionism and nationalism, both countries have continuously sought to improve their business environment such as openness and global connectivity and advanced infrastructure. These efforts actually have helped them suffer less from the pandemic, and these countries are also expected to recover quicker when compared to other countries. If both countries have shifted toward self-reliance amid the pandemic, they could have suffered from more critical damage and would have experienced more difficulty in recovering from the disruptions.

On the other hand, it has been well acknowledged in the international business (IB) literature that MNCs' performance is significantly influenced by the locational environment where their business is performed (Porter, 1998; Rugman and Verbeke, 2001). Therefore, MNCs will seek the location which can not only help them better exploit their existing competitive advantages but also the places where they can explore new advantages, thereby the MNCs could further strengthen their competitive advantages. In the case studies of Vietnam and Singapore, this chapter has revealed that despite their difference in locational advantages, both countries are still attractive for MNCs. Over the past few decades, location advantage has shifted from inherited tangible assets to created intangible assets, and from disposal resources to sustainable location-bounded resources or clusters (Moon and Roehl, 2001; Moon, 2016a). In fact, both Vietnam and Singapore are attempting to further enhance their locational advantages by promoting digital transformation and developing technology capabilities, thereby they will be able to host more value-added activities in the future.

Bathelt *et al.* (2004) argued that the locational innovation advantage relies on both local resources and global linkages. Locations with a high degree of global connectivity such as global cities are preferred by MNCs for overseas expansion (Cano-Kollmann *et al.*, 2016; Turkina and Assche, 2018). The connectivity of locations in the GVC context has been particularly important to link with other value chain activities dispersed around the world, as a single location can affect the entire value chain. This then requires a high level of connectivity among the globally dispersed locations in order to effectively coordinate and deliver higher value to the consumers (Moon and Jung, 2010; Moon, 2016b).

The cross-border linkages are not just important for the sustainable competitiveness of host countries but for the firms' competitiveness as well. Competitive locations with knowledge and resources developed entirely in a local setting are no longer sufficient for firms to maintain competitiveness (Wolfe and Gertler, 2004), but rely more on their firms' linkages to their counterparts and other actors located abroad (Bathelt *et al.*, 2004; Cano-Kollmann *et al.*, 2016). More importantly, a successful firm does not just passively adjust to the environment but alter the setting by increasing the effectiveness of the value chain (Nightingale, 2008; Sarasvathy, 2001; Vahlne and Johanson, 2017). This is particularly true when MNCs invest in developing countries where the institutional and physical infrastructure are less developed. In these settings, they are not just satisfied with exploiting local resources but are committed to upgrading the local business environment. Therefore, MNCs seek to build more resilient GVCs in the pandemic era, as well as the host countries that look to attract more MNCs' value chain activities, should not only enhance their local resources but also strengthen their global linkages.

Conclusion

GVCs as one of the most visible "trademarks" of globalization has often been linked to economic development. However, due to the growing disruptions in the GVCs and the negative impact on involved economies as seen with the COVID-19 pandemic, many governments are concerned about the vulnerability of GVCs and risks of overreliance on foreign suppliers for key products and services. In this respect, growing government protectionism and nationalism seek to back up supply chain reconfiguration by encouraging the relocation of overseas production back home or stimulating domestic manufacturing. Yet despite the criticism raised by many politicians on global value chains, most global businesses chose to remain global.

Over the long run, firms will seek to adjust their GVCs from efficiency-oriented ones toward efficiency plus resilience oriented GVCs in order to sustain their global businesses. In this respect, this chapter contributed to the GVC literature by introducing a comprehensive framework of building resilient GVCs from four directions, including agile response, alternative routes, diversification, and sustainability orientation. This is in contrast to preceding studies on resilient GVCs that have only covered one or some parts of the four aspects. Accordingly, this chapter has argued that MNCs could be more globalized in the pandemic era by assisting firms to diversify the risks and maintain their global competitiveness.

On the other hand, in order to attract at least MNCs' partial activities among the entire GVCs, countries need to invest more or reduce unnecessary regulations to improve their business environment. Hence, countries should push forward globalization, and make their economies more integrated with the global one. This chapter takes two examples of Vietnam and Singapore, which have benefited much from globalization as they have achieved fast-growing and sustainable economic development over the past few decades. Despite the challenges from the pandemic, both countries performed well to contain the spread of the virus while they also maintained their open-door policies by strengthening the relationship with other countries and actively pushing digital transformation. Overall, this helped to adapt well to the changing environment and upgrade their positions in the GVCs.

References

Asian Development Bank (ADB). 2018. *Economic indicators for Southeastern Asia and the Pacific: Input-Output Tables.* Asian Development Bank. http://dx.doi.org/10.22617/TCS189780-2.

Asem Connet Vietnam. 2021. National digital transformation program to 2025, orientation to 2030. http://asemconnectvietnam.gov.vn/default.aspx?ZID1=14&ID8=99391&ID1=2. Accessed April 8, 2021.

ASEAN Statistics. 2021. Flows of inward foreign direct investment (FDI) to ASEAN countries (in million US$). https://data.aseanstats.org/indicator/FDI.AMS.TOT.INF. Accessed April 1, 2021.

Barhat, V. 2020. After China, where next? Morningstar. https://www.morningstar.ca/ca/news/201411/after-china-where-next.aspx. Accessed April 19, 2021.

Bathelt, H., A. Malmberg, and P. Maskell. 2004. Clusters and knowledge: Local buzz, global pipelines and the process of knowledge creation. *Progress in Human Geography* 28(1): 31–56.

BBC. 2020. Will coronavirus reverse globalisation? April 2.

BBC. 2021. The cost of the Suez Canal blockage. March 29. https://www.bbc.com/news/business-56559073. Accessed April 4, 2021.

Bloomberg. 2020a. South Korean firms reluctant to bring production back from China, October 6. https://www.bloombergquint.com/global-economics/south-korean-firms-reluctant-to-bring-production-back-from-china. Accessed March 11, 2021.

Bloomberg. 2020b. U.K., Vietnam reach free-trade deal as Brexit deadline looms. https://www.bloomberg.com/news/articles/2020-12-11/u-k-vietnam-reach-free-trade-deal-as-brexit-deadline-looms.

Business Times. 2018. US, China trade war to impact Singapore's economy in three ways: Chan Chun Sing in parliament. https://www.businesstimes.com.sg/government-economy/us-china-trade-war-to-impact-singapore%E2%80%99s-economy-in-three-ways-chan-chun-sing-in. Accessed April 20, 2021.

Business Times. 2019. Singapore's hook as a site for corporate treasuries. https://www.businesstimes.com.sg/opinion/singapores-hook-as-a-site-for-corporate-treasuries. Accessed April 29, 2021.

Cano-Kollmann, M., J. Cantwell, T. J. Hannigan, R. Mudambi, and J. Song. 2016. Knowledge connectivity: An agenda for innovation research in international business. *Journal of International Business Studies* 47: 255–262.

Capri, A. 2020a. Commentary: COVID-19 could redefine Singapore's place in the global economy. Channel News Asia. https://www.channelnewsasia.com/news/commentary/commentary-covid-19-could-redefine-singapore-s-place-in-the-12442140. Accessed April 1, 2021.

Capri, A. 2020b. Commentary: How Singapore will remain a top trading hub in a post-pandemic world. Channel News Asia. https://www.channelnewsasia.com/news/commentary/singapore-top-trading-hub-post-coronavirus-covid-19-pandemic-12715434. Accessed April 8, 2021.

China Briefing. 2021. What to expect as China's economy enters 2021. January 12. https://www.china-briefing.com/news/china-2021-economic-outlook-foreign-investor-expectations/.

CNBC. 2019a. Trump is now blacklisting several big Chinese companies — here's what they do and why they are important. October 8.

CNBC. 2019b. Firms may consider moving out of Hong Kong amid protests and political uncertainty, experts say. https://www.cnbc.com/2019/06/19/businesses-may-consider-moving-from-hong-kong-to-singapore.html. Accessed April 20, 2021.

CNBC. 2021. This is Asia's top-performing economy in the Covid pandemic — it's not China. https://www.cnbc.com/2021/01/28/vietnam-is-asias-top-performing-economy-in-2020-amid-covid-pandemic.html. Accessed April 8, 2021.

Contractor, F. J. 2021. The world economy will need even more globalization in the post-pandemic 2021 decade. *Journal of International Business Studies*, https://doi.org/10.1057/s41267-020-00394-y.

Davies, N. 2020. Foreign direct investment: Changes in Singapore. King & Wood Mallesons. https://www.kwm.com/en/au/knowledge/insights/fdi-singapore-20200724. Accessed April 20, 2021.

De Backer, K., C. Menon, I. Desnoyers-James, and L. Moussiegt. 2016. Reshoring: Myth or reality? *OECD Science, Technology and Industry Policy Paper* (27).

Department of Statistics Singapore. 2021a. Table builder: Air cargo discharged by region/country of Origing, Annual. https://www.tablebuilder.singstat.gov.sg/publicfacing/createDataTable.action?refId=15258. Accessed April 1, 2021.

Department of Statistics Singapore. 2021b. Table builder: Sea cargo and shipping statistics, annual. https://www.tablebuilder.singstat.gov.sg/publicfacing/createDataTable.action?refId=14599. Accessed April 1, 2021.

Department of Statistics Singapore. 2021c. Table builder: International visitor arrivals by inbound tourism markets, monthly. https://www.tablebuilder.singstat.gov.sg/publicfacing/createDataTable.action?refId=14599. Accessed April 1, 2021.

Economic Times. 2021. Definition of 'E-wallets'. https://economictimes.indiatimes.com/definition/e-wallets#:~:text=Definition%3A%20E%2Dwallet%20is%20a, bank%20account%20to%20make%20payments. Accessed May 17, 2021.

Economist. 2017. Ford Motors courts Donald Trump by scrapping a planned plant in Mexico. January 17.

Economist. 2020. Is a wave of supply-chain reshoring around the corner? December 16.

Economist. 2021. Almost one billion doses of covid-19 vaccines have been produced. April 3.

Evenett, S. J. 2020. Chinese whispers: COVID-19, global supply chains in essential goods, and public policy. *Journal of International Business Policy* 3: 408–429.

Financial Times. 2020. In charts: Singapore's trade. https://www.ft.com/content/193e1ddb-9e61-413f-ab7d-df7a52f30413. Accessed March 13, 2021

Financial Times. 2021. Asia's COVID recovery: Vietnam's breakout moment. https://www.ft.com/content/ffa50623-b86f-4456-a6f0-9abceeb1ef7a. Accessed April 8, 2021.

Gereffi, G. 2020. What does the COVID-19 pandemic teach us about global value chains? The case of medical supplies. *Journal of International Business Policy* 3: 287–301.

GlobalData. 2020. Government investment to aid post-COVID-19 recovery of ICT market in Singapore, says GlobalData. https://www.globaldata.com/government-investment-aid-post-covid-19-recovery-ict-market-singapore-says-globaldata/. Accessed April 8, 2021.

Government of Canada. 2020. CPTPP partner: Vietnam. https://www.international.gc.ca/trade-commerce/trade-agreements-accords-commerciaux/agr-acc/cptpp-ptpgp/countries-pays/vietnam.aspx?lang=eng. Accessed May 26, 2021.

Gölgeci, I., H. E. Yildiz, and U. Andersson. 2020. The rising tensions between efficiency and resilience in global value chains in the post-COVID-19 world. *Transnational Corporations* 27 (2): 127–141.

Heritage Foundation. 2021. 2021 Index of economic freedom: Singapore. https://www.heritage.org/index/country/singapore#regulatory-efficiency. Accessed March 26, 2021.

Intelligencer. 2017. Apple isn't building 3 factories in the U.S., no matter what Trump says. July 25.

INGSA. 2020. 14 April 2020 – Blue-collar workers moved from dormitories to alternative living arrangements. COVID-19 Policy Making Tracker. https://www.ingsa.org/covid/policymaking-tracker/asia/singapore/. Accessed March 30, 2021.

Kano, L. and C. H. Oh. 2020. Global value chains in the post-COVID world: Governance for reliability. *Journal of Management Studies* 57(8): 1773–1777.

Le, H. 2019. Economic reforms, external liberalization and macroeconomic performance in Vietnam. *International Research Journal of Finance and Economics*. November 2019(176): 129–155.

Lee, S. 2020a. Is Vietnam the next China? Preparing for the post-pandemic decoupling. Korea Institute for International Economic Policy.

Lowy Institute. 2021. Covid performance index — deconstructing pandemic responses. https://interactives.lowyinstitute.org/features/covid-performance/. Accessed April 7, 2021.

Mastercard. 2019. Global destination cities index report 2019.

Mckinsey. 2020. Risk, resilience, and rebalancing in global value chains. August 6. https://www.mckinsey.com/business-functions/operations/our-insights/risk-resilience-and-rebalancing-in-global-value-chains.

Ministry of Health Singapore. 2020. Measures to contain the Covid-19 outbreak in migrant worker dormitories. https://www.moh.gov.sg/news-highlights/details/measures-to-contain-the-covid-19-outbreak-in-migrant-worker-dormitories. Accessed April 2, 2021.

Ministry of Manpower Singapore. 2021. Foreign workforce numbers. https://www.mom.gov.sg/documents-and-publications/foreign-workforce-numbers. Accessed March 31, 2021.

Miroudot, S. 2020. Reshaping the policy debate on the implications of COVID-19 for global supply chains. *Journal of International Business Policy* 3: 430–442.

Moon, H. C. 2016a. *Foreign direct investment: A global perspective*. Singapore: World Scientific.

Moon, H. C. 2016b. *The strategy for Korea's economic success*. New York: Oxford University Press.

Moon, H. C. 2018. *The art of strategy: Sun Tzu, Michael Porter, and beyond*. Cambridge: Cambridge University Press.

Moon, H. C. and J. S. Jung. 2010. Northeast Asian cluster through business and cultural cooperation. *Journal of Korea Trade* 14(2): 29–53.

Moon, H. C. and T. W. Roehl. 2001. Unconventional foreign direct investment and the imbalance theory. *International Business Review* 10: 197–215.

Moon, H. C. and W. Yin. 2017. *Korea's Investment Promotion Strategy in Response to the New US Government* [in Korean]. Seoul: KOTRA.

New York Times. 2020. Companies may move supply chains out of China, but not necessarily to the U.S. July 22.

Nguyen, H. H. 2020a. Impact of foreign direct and international trade on economic growth: Empirical study in Vietnam. *The Journal of Asian Finance, Economics and Business* 7(3): 323–331.

Nightingale, P. 2008. Meta-paradigm change and the theory of the firm. *Industrial and Corporate Change* 17(3): 533–583.

NPR. 2021. New lockdowns in Europe as COVID-19 cases soar; Pakistan's PM tests positive. March 20.

OECD. 2020. *Shocks, risks and global value chains: Insights from the OECD METRO Model*. June 29. Paris: OECD.

OECD. 2021. *Global value chains: Efficiency and risks in the context of COVID-19. OECD Policy Responses to Coronavirus (COVID-19)*. Paris: OECD Publishing.

TODAY Online. 2020. Covid-19: Faced with labour crunch, supply disruptions, contractors in S'pore fear missing project deadlines. https://www.today online.com/singapore/covid-19-faced-labour-shortages-supply-disruptions-contractors-fear-missing-project. Accessed April 2, 2021.

O'Neil, S. K. 2020. How to pandemic-proof globalization: Redundancy, not re-shoring, is the key to supply-chain security. *Foreign Affairs*, April 1.

Porter, M. E. 1985. *Competitive Advantage: Creating and Sustaining Superior Performance*. New York: Free Press.

Porter, M. E. 1998. *On Competition*. Boston, MA: Harvard Business School Press.

Potdar, P. K., S. Routroy, and A. Behera. 2017. Agile manufacturing: A systematic review of literature and implications for future research. *Benchmarking: An International Journal* 24 (7): 2022–2048.

Prime Minister of Australia. 2019. Media release: Joint statement between Vietnam and Australia. https://www.pm.gov.au/media/joint-statement-between-viet-nam-and-australia. Accessed May 21, 2021.

Qiang, C. Z., V. Steenbergen, Y. Liu, Y. Li, and M. Paganini. 2020. Foreign direct investment and global value chains in the wake of COVID-19: Preparing for the new normal. World Bank Blogs. https://blogs.worldbank.org/psd/for-eign-direct-investment-and-global-value-chains-wake-covid-19-preparing-new-normal. Accessed April 20, 2021.

Reuters. 2020. Exclusive: Foxconn to shift some Apple production to Vietnam to minimise China risk. https://www.reuters.com/article/us-foxconn-vietnam-apple-exclusive-idUSKBN2860VN. Accessed April 8, 2021.

Rovčanin, A. 2007. Foreign direct investment and national competitiveness – financial aspects. *Economic Analysis* 40 (3–4). Institute of Economic Sciences: 28–40.

Rugman, A. M. and A. Verbeke. 2001. Subsidiary-specific advantages in multi-national enterprises. *Strategic Management Journal* 22 (3): 237–250

Sarasvathy, S. 2001. Causation and effectuation: Toward a theoretical shift from economic inevitability to entrepreneurial contingency. *Academy of Management Review* 26 (2): 243–263.

Seric, A., Görg, S. Mösle, and M. Windisch. 2020. How the pandemic disrupts global value chains. https://iap.unido.org/articles/how-pandemic-disrupts-global-value-chains. Accessed March 20, 2021.

Sharma, A., A. Adhikary, and S. B. Borah. 2020. Covid-19's impact on supply chain decisions: Strategic insights from NASDAQ 100 firms using Twitter data. *Journal of Business Research* 117: 443–449.

Shira, D. and Associates. 2020. A guide to Vietnam's supply chains – the China plus one strategy. *Vietnam Briefing* (41). Hong Kong: Asia Briefing: 4–6.

South China Morning Post (SCMP). 2021. Container backlog, global supply chain disruption from Suez Canal crisis could take months to clear. April 9.

Strange, R. 2020. The 2020 Covid-19 pandemic and global value chains. *Journal of Industrial and Business Economics* 47: 455–465.

The U.S. Department of State. 2020a. 2020 Investment climate statements: Vietnam. https://www.state.gov/reports/2020-investment-climate-statements/vietnam/. Accessed April 29, 2021.

The U.S. Department of State. 2020b. 2020 Investment climate statements: Singapore. https://www.state.gov/reports/2020-investment-climate-statements/singapore/. Accessed April 29, 2021.

TraceTogether. 2021. What is the TraceTogether programme?. https://support.tracetogether.gov.sg/hc/en-sg/articles/360053530773-What-is-the-TraceTogether-Programme-How-is-it-different-from-the-TraceTogether-App-. Accessed March 30, 2021.

UNCTAD. 2020. *World investment report 2020*. New York and Geneva: United Nations.

Vahlne, J. E. and J. Johanson. 2017. From internationalization to evolution: The Uppsala model at 40 years. *Journal of International Business Studies* 48: 1087–1102.

Verbeke, A. 2020. Will the COVID-19 pandemic really change the governance of global value chains? *British Journal of Management* 31 (3): 444–446.

VietnamPlus. 2021a. Better technologies help firms become entrenched in global value chains. https://en.vietnamplus.vn/better-technologies-help-firms-become-entrenched-in-global-value-chains/196628.vnp. Accessed April 8, 2021.

VietnamPlus. 2021b. Vietnam-Australia diplomatic ties marked in HCM city. https://en.vietnamplus.vn/vietnamaustralia-diplomatic-ties-marked-in-hcm-city/198401.vnp. Accessed April 8, 2021.

Vietnam Briefing News. 2021. FDI in Vietnam: A year in review and outlook for 2021. https://www.vietnam-briefing.com/news/fdi-in-vietnam-year-in-review-and-outlook-for-2021.html/. Accessed April 15, 2021.

Waldman, D. A. and M. Javidan. 2020. The false dichotomy between globalism and nationalism. *Harvard Business Review*, June 18. https://hbr.org/2020/06/the-false-dichotomy-between-globalism-and-nationalism. Accessed March 11, 2021.

Wall Street Journal. 2019. Manufacturers move supply chains out of China. https://www.wsj.com/articles/manufacturers-move-supply-chains-out-of-china-11563096601?reflink=desktopwebshare_permalink. Accessed April 19, 2021.

Wolfe, D. A. and M. S. Gertler. 2004. Clusters from the inside and out: Local dynamics and global linkages. *Urban Studies* 41 (5/6): 1071–1093.

World Bank. 2020. Economy profile of Singapore. Doing Business 2020. https://www.doingbusiness.org/en/data/exploreeconomies/singapore.

World Bank. 2021a. GDP (Current US$) – Vietnam. https://data.worldbank.org/indicator/NY.GDP.MKTP.CD?end=2019&locations=VN&start=2001.

World Bank. 2021b. Foreign direct investment, net inflows (BoP, current US$) - Singapore, Hong Kong SAR, China. https://data.worldbank.org/indicator/BX.KLT.DINV.CD.WD?contextual=default&end=2019&locations=SG-HK&most_recent_value_desc=true&start=1997. Accessed April 20, 2021.

Worldometer. 2021. COVID-19 CORONAVIRUS PANDEMIC - Reported Cases and Deaths by Country or Territory. https://www.worldometers.info/coronavirus/#countries. Accessed April 15, 2021.

World Health Organization. (WHO). https://covid19.who.int/. Accessed April 9, 2021.

World Trade Organization. (WTO). 2021. International trade statistics. https://data.wto.org/. Accessed March 30, 2021.

Yin, W. 2017. *Global value chain: Theoretical integration, extension, and empirical analysis.* Unpublished Ph.D. dissertation, Seoul National University.

Zhan, J. X. 2021. GVC transformation and a new investment landscape in the 2020s: Driving forces, directions, and a forward-looking research and policy agenda. *Journal of International Business Policy*, https://doi.org/10.1057/s42214-020-00088-0.

Part III

Country Cases: Introduction

The last part of the book, Part III Country Cases, discusses strategies to enhance national competitiveness across various fields by examining examples in real life and evaluating the application of theoretical ideas presented in the previous part. Part III is composed of eight invited chapters that address a wide range of topics to provide useful implications for academia and practitioners. The authors of these chapters identify digitalization, the role of government, business ecosystem and innovation, and cooperation with other institutions as necessary conditions to enhance national competitiveness.

The first two chapters, "Digitalization: The Norm of the 'New Normal' Impact of Digital Economy Ventures on the National Competitiveness of an Emerging Market" and "Digital Innovations and AI in Mental Health as Facilitators of Sustainable Competitive Economy in Post-COVID-19 recovery" highlight the current trend of digitalization. In the first chapter, the author emphasizes the crucial role of digital ventures in leading the successful transformation of the digital economy with striking examples of such ventures in Turkey. The second chapter assesses the severity of worsened psychological conditions amid the spread of COVID-19 and signals the need for governments to incorporate digital innovations in mental health treatment to provide more effective and affordable treatments in Croatia with implications for the rest of the world.

The two chapters, "National Competitiveness and Response to COVID-19: The Political Factor in Mexico and Brazil" and "National Competitiveness and the Role of the Government: The Case of Korea" underline the role of government in assessing or enhancing national competitiveness. The former points out the significance of political factors in benchmarking the practice of strategies for enhancing national competitiveness in Latin American countries, specifically Mexico and Brazil. The latter chapter highlights the three key conditions to practice policies to enhance national competitiveness which includes political continuity, social dialogue capabilities, and the ability to prohibit the politicization of the economy. By discussing this, the author analyzes the Korean government's operation of such policies and points out the governments' incapability to implement mid to long-term policies.

The next two chapters, "Trends in Competitiveness of India: Exploring the Role of Start-ups and Entrepreneurial Ecosystem" and "Open Innovation and China's Competitiveness Improvement" emphasize the business ecosystem and innovation as essential factors for sustaining national competitiveness. Although both chapters highlight the significance of innovative technologies in enhancing national competitiveness, the former one puts greater emphasis on the role of start-ups or ventures and emerging technologies by addressing the example of India. For its part, the latter chapter points out the adoption of open innovation as one of the largest contributing factors to the economic development in China.

The last two chapters, "Reinvigorating Policy and Modifying Practices: Lessons Learned from Indonesia's South–South Cooperation during COVID-19" and "From Fundamental Research to Industrial Application: The Global Competitiveness of Swiss Universities" argue that cooperation with other institutions will enhance national competitiveness. The former chapter stresses the significance of promoting cooperation by addressing the specific example of South–South Cooperation (SSC) in Indonesia. Similar to this, the latter one depicts the key role of higher education to enable the cooperation between scholars and entrepreneurs in creating market value with the example of Switzerland.

Chapter 8

Digitalization: The Norm of the "New Normal"

Impact of Digital Economy Ventures on the National Competitiveness of an Emerging Market

Pınar Büyükbalcı

Abstract

The challenges presented by the COVID-19 pandemic have made it an undeniable fact that digital technologies provide the strongest means to transform industries and markets. Technology ventures bear a notable role in supplying these tools to incumbents, governments, and indeed to small conventional companies, which all thrive to adjust themselves to the "new normal." Thereupon, this chapter seeks to examine the impact of digital economy ventures by demonstrating their role to advance digital transformation efforts in an emerging market context. In doing so, it depicts striking examples from Turkey regarding; (i) the collaboration between incumbents and digital economy ventures, (ii) the rise of new stars exploiting digital economy opportunities, and (iii) the ventures using digitalization to create social impact for extremely vulnerable actors.

Keywords: Digital transformation, digital economy ventures, technology ventures, emerging market, the COVID-19 Pandemic

Introduction

History has shown many times that advancing technology can change both industry and society in a revolutionary way, a process which coined the term "industrial revolution." Relatedly, Autio *et al.* (2021) argue that digitalization, a general-purpose technology (GPT), like the steam engine or electricity, transforms not only the business landscape but also reshapes the societal context. Thus, just like its revolutionary predecessors, digitalization has become a pivotal factor in firm-level and national-level competitiveness.

There has been a dramatic increase in using digital technologies in almost every industry, with the COVID-19 pandemic amplifying their relevance in new market conditions. Delivery services, remote working systems, remote education supporting infrastructure, and payment systems are just a few of those technologies that business organizations strive to adopt in the rush of the pandemic. As expressed by Kane *et al.* (2020) in a recent Deloitte Insights commentary, "slow and steady don't work, given the dynamics of a pandemic."

Saliola and Islam (2020) underline that we have previously witnessed the use of digital technologies disrupting production processes, challenging the boundaries of the firms, and restructuring of global value chains. The COVID-19 pandemic has amplified all of these trends. The pace of digitalization has sped up so swiftly that, in order to respond to relentlessly emerging disruptions — in the supply chain, workforce, consumer shopping behavior, and other areas — firms had to adopt new practices in just a few months, and sometimes even in weeks.

The power of digitalization to transform industries has become unquestioned with the so-called "new normal" brought on by the pandemic. Digital transformation now has a strong strategic inference for both countries and companies as it provides the tools to increase flexibility and thus to take action under constantly changing conditions. Technology ventures particularly bear a significant role in providing these tools to incumbents, governments, and even to small conventional companies, which all thrive to become a part of the new game.

The issues raised by the COVID-19 pandemic have particularly led to severe economic and social consequences in emerging markets, which are already subject to several resource constraints as well as institutional deficiencies. Also, there is a high chance that the impact of a possible global economic recession will be more devastating, and probably more long-lasting, for these economies. Thus, developing tools to stay competitive both domestically and internationally has become even more crucial for these economies, and particularly for the firms originating from these markets.

Building on these remarks, this chapter first discusses how digital transformation enables competitiveness, especially during crisis times. Consequently, it highlights the role of digital economy ventures by portraying their entrepreneurial moves to speed up such transformation in an emerging country context by presenting examples from Turkey.

Putting Digital Transformation into the Business Context

The term "digital economy" reflects the impact of digitalization on the changing nature of economic activities. By definition, "digital economy" refers to the economy being increasingly affected by digital technologies promoted by the use of artificial intelligence (AI), cloud computing, data analytics, blockchain, machine learning, and other such areas (Soto-Acosta, 2020). Similarly, Bukht and Heeks (2017) relate digital economy to, "that part of economic output derived solely or primarily from digital technologies with a business model based on digital goods or services."

To further discuss specific implications regarding the very nature of the digital economy, it is important to maintain conceptual clarity by distinguishing between the key terms: digitization, digitalization, and digital transformation.

Digitization refers to the conversion of analog information into a digital format, enabling computers to store, process, and transmit accumulated data (Verhoef *et al.*, 2021; Yoo *et al.*, 2010). Digitalization, by contrast, reflects the use of digital technologies to alter current processes (Autio *et al.*, 2021; Verhoef *et al.*, 2021). And for its part, digital transformation is the end-state of digitization and digitalization, which is very much "pervasive" in nature and reflects "company-wide change" (Iansiti and Lakhani, 2014; Kane *et al.*, 2015; Verhoef *et al.*, 2021). Briefly, it refers the use of digital tools to transform how companies create and capture value (Correani *et al.*, 2020).

According to Merriam-Webster, "transformation" stems from the transitive verb of "transform," meaning "to change in composition or structure." Thus, transformation requires a sustained change with implications for the functioning and organization of a system, in this case, the business organization and the economic context. It is important to mention that transformation is not temporary but rather a permanent process. In line with this conceptual reasoning, the related literature notes that the result of digital transformation is to reach a digital maturity that requires long-term orientation (Fletcher and Griffiths, 2020).

Recent research by IBM Institute of Business Value (IBV) puts forth that, during the turmoil caused by the pandemic, executives feel the need to "prioritize digital transformation." The executives further listed several obstacles delaying their full digital transformation — with low digital maturity, inadequate digital integration, and poor interoperability as the most prominent ones (Bieck and Marshall, 2020).

Finally, there are system-level concerns to address in order to prepare the ground for a smooth digital transition. For instance, George *et al.* (2020), incisively, relate the extremely varying impact of the pandemic on industries to system-level mismatches, such as problems arising when exponentially growing systems put high demands on fixed-capacity systems (for example the COVID-19 pandemic vs. healthcare system). Specifically, the authors note that, when systems with network-enabled exponential growth collide with fixed-capacity, this will obviously hamper both firm-level and national-level competitiveness. The authors discuss that, in such cases, well-designed organizational and industrial strategies should be used to avoid disastrous consequences. While crises cause system-level inconsistencies and gaps to be more visible, the COVID-19 pandemic, in a way, legitimized digital transformation as a calibrator.

Fostering Digitalization in an Emerging Economy

The case of Turkey: Contextual framework

Compared to their developed counterparts, emerging markets are subject to limitations such as relatively low levels of capital accumulation, immaturity of the institutional context, and political uncertainties challenging stability and future economic prospects. Affected by these, regarding its national competitiveness scores, Turkey ranks 40th among 62 countries, and thus, considered as a rather vulnerable emerging economy, currently classified as "ordinary" striving to be an "advancer" (IPS National Competitiveness Research, 2019–2020).

Regarding digital transformation, recent research confirms that the country still has a way to go. For example, according to the Digital

Transformation Index (2020) of Turkey Informatics Industry Association (TUBISAD), Turkey ranks average in its overall score. However, a closer look at the sub-index scores reveals important deficiencies emerging as obstacles for the digital transformation of the country. Especially, inadequate support of political and regulatory mechanisms, the inefficiency of government procurement of advanced technology products, low levels of university-industry cooperation in ICT, and hardships of venture capital availability emerge as the weak chains of the system. It has identified rather stronger pillars like the availability of latest technologies and affordable usage costs of internet technologies as the eases of doing business. Finally, the scores in the economic impact dimension hint at a relatively promising picture for Turkey. Despite the still low scores of international trade in ICT and digitally-deliverables services, the positive scores reflect the impact of digitalization on improving organizational models and business models.

This rather pessimistic picture informs us about the critical role of entrepreneurial technology ventures and their support to national competitiveness. Highlighting this, a recent Endeavor report evidenced the positive impact of big (having over 50 employees), entrepreneurial, super-productive, and technology-enabled firms (coined with the acronym "BEST") by underlining their strong association with local economic growth (Barto and Morris, 2020).

It is already well-known that firms in emerging economies are more vulnerable because of limited institutional means, which become even more problematic during times of crisis. Furthermore, the scant amount of financial aids provided to firms in those countries is another challenge when compared to advanced economies. Despite these drawbacks, several examples have showcased how digital transformation creates new opportunities to overcome these challenges and thus to improve competitiveness. A common feature of these examples lies in their entrepreneurial profile. Thus, the following section will elaborate on the impact of digital economy ventures in increasing the resilience of companies in different industrial domains during the COVID-19 pandemic.

Lead actors in managing the COVID-19 crisis: Digital economy ventures

The impact of digital economy ventures in leading digital transformation has been underlined by some recent papers, such as Sussan and Acs

(2017). These ventures portray new practices and agile business models and thus provide evidence for the opportunities, tools, and outcomes of digitalization in different industrial domains. They are also remarked among the most effective actors in any entrepreneurial ecosystem (EE) as they lead high value-added activities.

Digital economy ventures are entrepreneurial in their very nature as their growth path revolves around monitoring constantly changing technology and spotting any occasion to meet emerging needs and thus to fill market gaps. Doing this without losing momentum requires a practice of high-level entrepreneurship, featuring Covin and Slevin's (1989, 1991) pro-activeness, risk-taking, and innovativeness trilogy.

The active role digital economy ventures take within the entrepreneurial ecosystem is important as it is the main domain that inherits the physical factors and the human factors that a venture interacts with while running its operations (Mason and Brown, 2014; Spigel, 2017; Stam, 2015, 2018). In other words, the number of successful digital economy ventures an EE inherits and supports is important in reflecting its potential to enhance national competitiveness.

The expected outcome of any ecosystem is the positive spillover effects of interactions (Audretsch *et al.,* 2016; Kuratko *et al.,* 2017). Specifying the impact of entrepreneurial ecosystems, Audretsch *et al.* (2019: 315) refer to the roots of the concept — as described by the Greek philosopher Hesiod — and underline its salient features as being related to economic, technological, and societal dimensions. Thus, according to the authors, the impact of an ecosystem can be studied by "untangling" how entrepreneurial firms shape and influence these aspects.

Following Audretsch *et al.* (2019), the current chapter attempts to trace how technology ventures have affected the economic, technological, and societal dimensions of the national context during the COVID-19 pandemic. It is a significant endeavor to understand how these ventures create spillover effects improving national competitiveness. As framed by the Institute for Policy and Strategy (IPS), the National Competitiveness Index covers several criteria under the "physical factors" and "human factors" dimensions which closely stick to economic, technological, and societal aspects. Thus, the purpose here is to provide a picture of how technology ventures shape and influence economic, technological, and societal thinking via fostering digitalization. Under this attempt, the following subsections will clarify the role of technology ventures during the pandemic by exemplifying, (i) collaboration between incumbents and digital economy ventures, (ii) the rise of new stars exploiting digital economy opportunities, and, (iii) ventures using digitalization to create social impact for highly vulnerable actors.

Collaboration between incumbents and digital economy ventures

Kane *et al.* (2020) remind us of the infamous "knowing-doing gap," a term introduced by Jeffrey Pfeffer and Robert Sutton, to explain what we observe about the digitalization efforts of the incumbents in various industries. The "knowing-doing gap" emerges from, "the challenge of turning knowledge about how to enhance organizational performance into actions consistent with that knowledge" (Pfeffer and Sutton, 1999: 4). Kane *et al.* (2020) further underline the results of a recent Deloitte survey showing that 87 percent of survey respondents "knows" that the industry will be disrupted by digital technologies, while only 44 percent thinks that their company is appropriately responding to these disruptive voids, which is a view perfectly framing the "knowing-doing gap."

The COVID-19 pandemic made such gaps more visible and more painful, if not existential angst, for companies. We witnessed several incumbents collaborating with high-growth technology ventures to close these gaps. The need to adapt to the new context is obvious, which brings the need for recontextualizing all aspects including, the operating model, and sometimes even the complete business model. But how to do it remains an unsolved question, for both public and business companies.

Technology ventures frequently step into the scene as enabling big companies to take action for digital disruption, and thus to become "doers." Since the beginning of the COVID-19 pandemic, several such collaborations have started. The prominent examples showcase how these collaborations pay off by increasing the resilience of incumbents and leading to value creation, not only in terms of technological outcomes but also regarding the economic and societal domains.

A very noticeable example is the case of Medianova, a Turkish-originated technology startup, and now a global Content Delivery Network (CDN) company. Technically, CDN is a distributed cloud product and a digital backbone increasing the performance and the redundancy of internet traffic. The case of Medianova portrays how collaborations between technology ventures and government, as well as with private companies, lead to value creation.

During the initial days of the pandemic, Medianova got a call from the Turkish Education Ministry asking about the possibility of moving all classes to the Ministry's online education platform in a week. The idea was to use live and on-demand videos as a way to keep schools open during the lockdown. Still, it was very challenging as, with a potential 17 million active students, the platform was never tested and never scaled that much. Thanks to Medianova's scalable cloud CDN and the support of local operators, the schools went online in just six days.

Next was a call, again from the government, about the Turkish "e-government project" (E-Devlet), serving 85 million people. They wanted to speed up the delivery process of face masks to the country's citizens. Medianova CDN platform supported the process and helped it to flow smoothly and in order.

Apart from its collaboration with government projects, Medianova also provided support to privately-owned companies again in education and in other industries. For instance, the company supported the technology infrastructure transformation of a well-known private school chain with about 200,000 students. Their specific need was to replace the Zoom platform with the open-source Jitsi meeting platform and to integrate it into the school's online education system. Jitsi was hosted on Medianova edge-cloud platform at speed, which was a great use case of edge-computing enabling education to run in digital platforms.

Finally, a holding company benefited from the live streaming platform of Medianova to reach out to its 40,000 employees and made sure that the communication between the C-Suite and the employees is not disrupted. People could attend meetings, ask questions, and interact with senior management, which is extremely critical to lower anxiety during times of crisis. After a while, the company managers admitted that employee performance was even better than before, thanks to live-streamed communication enabling continuous contact between the managers and employees.

With the motto, "commence your next digital evolution," Commencis has emerged as another prominent case demonstrating the positive spillover effects of collaborations during the pandemic. Commencis is a technology venture enabling firms to grow and scale in the digital sector by providing them big data analytics and cloud products. The company serves a global array of businesses in several industries ranging from banking to airlines and retail.

With the pandemic placing urgent needs in nearly all industrial domains the company serves, it has become crucial for Commencis to provide its customers with a versatile enough digital partnership to lead their digital transformation. In doing so, Commencis helped companies to shift their operational processes and services to digital products and thus enabled them to improve customer engagement. The company created value for its clients by accelerating their digitalization to stay responsive despite pandemic-related challenges.

For instance, the company supported its clients from the banking industry to improve their services by building data-driven, customer-focused digital channels enabling them to respond to the needs of a large customer base via a digital medium. The company also provided its clients with the digital tools to foster credit card usage, which became especially critical during the pandemic, and to manage financial transactions of their customers securely.

During the pandemic, tracing, and predicting abruptly changing patterns in consumer behavior have become strategic necessities, especially for retail companies. With sales channels shifting from offline to online and frequently purchased products moving from outdoor-social ones to indoor-individual comfort ones, it has become a real challenge for companies to design a proper combination of operational and marketing strategies. To speed up the digital transformation among customers in the retail business, Commencis provided a wide array of digital products and services, including the design of e-commerce platforms supported by digital analytics and engagement tools that can help companies to understand how customers interact with the brand.

For the consumer goods and services industry, besides providing an e-commerce platform, the company also supported several clients by providing them with the digital tools to monitor, and thus to increase, their sales teams' performance, and to process the information on dealers to improve company sales performance.

Finally, Commencis has been an important supporter of its clients in the aviation industry in leading their digital transformation, which has become a matter of utmost concern for these companies to sustain already hampered operations. The company specifically assisted leading brands in the aviation industry in building a digital technology-supported travel experience for their consumers and to trace real-time customer interaction with digital analytics tools. These efforts enabled aviation companies to build flexible and agile digital business processes which is deemed strategic to achieve a rather quick recovery in the post-pandemic period.

Collaborating with Commencis allowed several incumbents to build a competitive edge despite the tough conditions in their industrial domains. Evidently, the company empowered its customers by offering them several digital tools with an integrated approach, thus making it possible for them to quickly take action and to meet abruptly changing market needs.

Inveon, a digital commerce software developing company, led value creation during the pandemic, for both business customers and their end-users. In an era when the use of e-commerce surged, Inveon, specifically provided B2B and B2C e-commerce infrastructure software, m-commerce applications, and several other digital performance growth services.

With the increasing e-commerce traffic, scalability and agility have become pre-requisites of competitiveness. Enhancing these skills, the company especially created a competitive edge for its customers via "InCommerce," a digital commerce software infrastructure tool, which enables firms to respond to e-commerce demands with utmost efficiency.

Another differentiating feature for those companies collaborating with Inveon has been the digital growth consultancy provided. Inveon's consultancy specifically revolves around operational support enabling the use of digital tools to foster the journey of digital transformation of their customers. This support service has been extremely important during the pandemic, as unexpected circumstances have prompted unforeseeable needs and sudden changes in consumer behavior. Staying responsive under these conditions has required the effective use of digital tools, which would have been very challenging for incumbents were it not for the support of Inveon, acting as their digital performance management consultant.

A related example here is Inveon's collaboration with the diamond line of a jewelry company to lead several special day campaigns. In particular, Inveon provided support to track campaign performance and thus to adjust marketing mix strategies accordingly. The aim here is to trigger consumer behavior that would lead to increased sales. The usage of advertisements through effective, target-oriented campaigns and the processing of data retrieved to spot changing consumer behavior during the pandemic resulted in an exceptional increase in the transaction, conversion rate, and revenue for the Gülaylar Diamond Line.

Similarly, Inveon improved the competitive strength of a kids-wear brand in Turkey, by helping them launch a new "Mother and Baby Care" category on its digital commerce website. Inveon GrowthLab specifically supported B&G Store by collaborating with them in designing a communication strategy for the category which boosted cross-sales. With data analytics, the Inveon GrowthLab team detected the most relevant categories for B&G customers during the pandemic period. They designed a much easier shopping experience, increased digital channel variety, and enhanced focus on social media channels.

Finally, as an internationally operating venture, Inveon also created value for its customers by sharing best-practice examples with them picturing how firms in their industries cope with the pandemic-related industrial challenges. In doing so, they specifically share brand new practices for the use of digital tools to improve operational performance.

Digital economy opportunities and the rise of new stars

As well as the need to enhance the already famous global brands like Zoom and Netflix, the emerging needs that came with the pandemic has created several opportunities for newly founded firms — such as Carbon Health, a health-technologies US-based startup founded by a Turkish entrepreneur, Eren Bali — to speed up his expansion plans. There are also noteworthy examples of Istanbul-based digital economy ventures exploiting opportunities during the pandemic crisis and, thus, ensuring a high-growth — encompassing international market expansion.

Getir, meaning "bring" in Turkish, is an online delivery startup, which has been demonstrated as one of the most remarkable growth stories in recent times. As an already successful and growing company, Getir used its digital technology-based optimization tools to design, improve, and manage the entire delivery process including the coordination of its motorbike fleet and fulfillment centers. In a recent interview, the co-founder of the company emphasized that, with the use of AI technology the company has ensured that their 1,500 stock-keeping units (SKUs) always have the right assortment for the region they operate in. The company, thus, differentiates itself with its fast delivery promise (delivery within 10 minutes), order live-track option, and a wide range of grocery products it offers to its customers.

With the COVID-19 lockdowns prompting radical changes in shopping behavior, the consumer perceives online grocery shopping as the new normal, which also resulted in sky-rocketing demand for Getir. Thanks to high levels of investment made in the pre-pandemic era to build a robust digital platform infrastructure, the company managed to cope with the increasing demand and ensured a sustained growth rate.

The results were noticeable with a tremendous increase in downloads of the Getir app, as well as the growth in the average shopping cart expenditures and overall transaction volume. With increasing sales numbers and the injection of new investment, the company gave a start to its previously set international expansion plans. At the beginning of 2021, the company launched operations in London, justified by the co-founders with "London being a very crowded, highly digitalized world city." Another investment round followed London operations and made the company the second unicorn of the Turkish entrepreneurial ecosystem. According to recent press releases, the near-term international expansion plan includes several other cities all around the world.

Using digitalization to support highly vulnerable industries

As underlined by the World Economic Forum (2020: 6), since the beginning of the pandemic, most small businesses have been at a disadvantageous position as they lack "the resources or capabilities to adjust to this new, more digitally demanding world". Nevertheless, just as for large companies, possessing a strong digital presence has become a pre-condition for these small businesses to thrive in the future.

In Turkey, one of the most damaged industries during the COVID-19 pandemic has been the food and beverages business, as was the case in several other countries. Despite strong vocal demands, government support fell short of providing satisfactory amounts of aid to businesses in the industry. Turkey has over one hundred thousand companies operating in the food and beverages industry, employing over 2 million people. Among several other factors like supply chain and workforce-related ones, the disruption in the sector is mainly due to two major issues: the government's decision to temporarily stop in-place service to prevent the spread of the virus and a change in consumer behavior, specifically people feeling anxious about dining in closed spaces with other people. Thus, home-delivery and take-home options became the only viable option for restaurants to continue their operations.

The difficult period for restaurants began on March 16, 2020, with the government's decision to restrict in-place services in restaurants, cafes, entertainment venues, along with all other non-essential service providers until a second announcement. This first lockdown period for restaurants lasted until June 1, 2020. And even after in-place operations resumed, it did not last long. With a surge in COVID-19 cases towards the end of the year, restaurants were again told to stop all in-place operations by November 20, 2020. During the lockdowns, restaurants were only allowed to serve via food delivery systems.

Yemek Sepeti or "food basket" in Turkish, is among the best-known marketplace business models in Turkey as it provides a digital platform for customers to place orders from restaurants. Its outstanding growth and strong digital platform caught the attention of the leading international players in this sector, and finally, the company was acquired by Delivery Hero in 2015.

Its digital platform enables over tens of thousands of restaurants all over Turkey to process online food orders, which has become a lifesaver especially for those mom-and-pop restaurants for which it would have been impossible to go digital otherwise. According to company press releases, the number of new restaurants joining the platform only in 2020 reached nearly 33,000.

Still, finding a digital medium to process online orders was not the only challenge for all those small restaurants operating at low capacity. Their cash flow balance was completely broken as they were trying to pay for the ingredients and other supplies, as well as the wages of their employees, at a time when sales were dropping because of lock down measures. Yemek Sepeti, made several bold decisions at this point to ensure the survival of these mom-and-pop shops, which would otherwise have gone bankrupt.

For instance, the company launched a campaign with the Union of Chambers and the Commodity Exchanges in Turkey and presented an option to customers to make advanced payments to restaurants in their neighborhoods. They would save these advanced payments in the customers' digital wallets which could then be spent at a later date, with some bonus options. The company increased the frequency of payments that restaurants get from the platform and removed several cost items for them like the additional fees they normally pay for when being listed. It further initiated another campaign presenting an option for customers to place their orders via Yemek Sepeti platform but collect the "take-away" package themselves from the restaurants, instead of waiting for home delivery. In that case, the company declared that they will charge zero commission to the restaurants. The company also made donations to struggling shop employees in the food and beverages sector. These endeavors provided considerable impact for a very disadvantaged sector and contributed to its competitiveness in times of crisis.

Conclusion

The resilience of an economy is largely dependent on how resilient its firms are. The COVID-19 pandemic has provided unique insights to show that winners of the "new normal" will be those companies who adopt an opportunity-driven focus, rather than a necessity-driven one. To put it more specifically, thriving companies will be the ones who anticipate the chaotic environment as an opportunity to transform themselves.

From the viewpoint of a business organization, if digitization addresses the technical core, then digitalization relates to the operational core, and finally, digital transformation encompasses the strategic core. The pandemic is credited with harnessing digital technologies to various business functions. Therefore, it is not too assertive to say that, to create a competitive edge, a company should embed digitization into its fabric, foster digitalization of its operations, and achieve digital transformation to prosper in the long term.

In recent research by Deloitte (2020), a senior executive commented on the digital transformation of businesses by saying that, "when the tide goes out, you see who has been swimming naked." This is a coherent statement signaling that the use of digital tools does not necessarily mean that companies intend to adopt them to serve their long-term strategic needs. Some companies just use these tools simply to "save the day," while others attempt to embed them into their business models. We should note that it is the latter what we coin with the term "digital transformation."

This chapter is an endeavor to illustrate the critical role of technology ventures — the pioneers of the digital economy — in creating value for several stakeholders in the market. The cases illustrated previously show that firms with a varied range of profiles stick to digital technologies to stay responsive in the face of disruptive events. Using digital tools enables firms to meet changing needs, exploit new opportunities, and support malfunctioning industries, especially in emerging markets with limited resources.

The pandemic provides several lessons for Turkey. For instance, the abrupt needs that emerged under crisis conditions fostered collaborations between technology ventures and government bodies. Future initiatives should provide more favorable conditions for such collaborations, enabling digital technology ventures to fix the inadequacies of public services, a matter frequently observed in emerging markets. Making available political and regulatory mechanisms to ease up such collaborations would be a critical action to take.

Digitalization enables firms to design state-of-the-art business models to reshape conventional industries and easily adapt to new market domains, which empowers the emergence of high-growth firms. It is also important to underline how digitalization leads to exploiting opportunities around the world. As illustrated by the cases above, building digitalized business models enables better market fit in the international domain and thus paves the way for attracting funds from international investors, which is vital for emerging country firms challenged by the hardship of venture capital (VC) availability.

Furthermore, the striking examples of technology ventures as solution partners in supporting the digitalization process of incumbents showcase a huge potential. Such collaborations enable these otherwise "obsolete" corporations to achieve a competitive edge in the changing and digitalizing business landscape. Finally, technology ventures make it possible for traditional mom-pop shops to become a player in the digital economy. This obviously, has contributed to national competitiveness, considering the high proportion of these small firms in emerging markets.

The cases illustrated here, along with several untold others, clarify that if it was not for the active presence of these digital economy ventures, national competitiveness would be even more severely damaged with several companies and institutions failing to continue their operations. One thing the COVID-19 pandemic has rather shown is that what matters is not just adapting to the "new normal," but rather, being prepared for the "next normal," as exactly promised by digital transformation.

Acknowledgments

I would like to extend my special thanks to *Serkan Sevim* (the founder and the CEO of Medianova), *Fatih İşbecer* (the co-founder and chairperson of Commencis), and *Yomi Kastro* (the founder and managing partner of Inveon) for sharing information on company practices which provided great insight for this chapter.

References

Audretsch, D. B., E. E. Lehmann, and M. Menter. 2016. Public cluster policy and new venture creation. *Economia e Politica Industriale* 43(4): 357–381.

Audretsch, D. B., J. A. Cunningham, D. F. Kuratko, E. E. Lehmann, and M. Menter. 2019. Entrepreneurial ecosystems: Economic, technological, and societal impacts. *The Journal of Technology Transfer* 44: 313–325.

Autio, E., R. Mudambi, and Y. Yoo. 2021. Digitalization and globalization in a turbulent world: Centrifugal and centripetal forces. *Global Strategy Journal* 11: 3–16.

Barto, L. D. and R. Morris. 2020. *How Cities Can Identify the Best Businesses for Local Economic Growth.* Endeavor Insight. https://endeavor.org/content/uploads/2015/06/BEST-Report-Endeavor-Insight.pdf.

Bieck, C. and A. Marshall. 2020. Redirecting resources to promote post-pandemic growth. *Strategy & Leadership* 48(6): 45–50.

Bukht, R. and R. Heeks. 2017. Defining, conceptualising and measuring the digital economy. *Development Informatics Working Paper* (68). http://dx.doi.org/10.2139/ssrn.3431732.

Correani, A., A. De Massi, F. Frattini, A. Petruzzelli, and A. Natalicchio. 2020. Implementing a digital strategy: Learning from the experience of three digital transformation projects. *California Management Review* 62(4): 37–56.

Covin, J. G. and D. P. Slevin. 1989. Strategic management of small firms in hostile and benign environments. *Strategic Management Journal* 10(1): 75–87.

Covin, J. G. and D. P. Slevin. 1991. A conceptual model of entrepreneurship as firm behavior. *Entrepreneurship: Theory and Practice* 16(1): 7–25.

Fletcher, G. and M. Griffiths. 2020. Digital transformation during a lockdown. *International Journal of Information Management* 55: 1–3.

George, G., K. R. Lakhani, and P. Puranam. 2020. What has changed? The impact of Covid pandemic on the technology and innovation management research agenda. *Journal of Management Studies* 57: 1754–1758.

Iansiti, M. and K. R. Lakhani. 2014. Digital ubiquity: How connections, sensors, and data are revolutionizing business. *Harvard Business Review* 92(11): 90–99.

Kane, G. C., D. Palmer, A. N. Philips, D. Kiron, and N. Buckley. 2015. Strategy, not technology, drives digital transformation. *MIT Sloan Management Review* 14: 1–25.

Kane, G. C., A. N. Philips, J. Copulsky, and R. Nanda. 2020. *A Case of Acute Disruption: Digital Transformation through the Lens of Covid-19.* Deloitte Insights. https://www2.deloitte.com/us/en/insights/topics/digital-transformation/digital-transformation-COVID-19.html. Accessed January, 2021.

Kuratko, D. F., G. Fisher, J. M. Bloodgood, and J. S. Hornsby. 2017. The paradox of new venture legitimation within an entrepreneurial ecosystem. *Small Business Economics* 49(1): 119–140.

OECD Leed Programme Workshop paper by Mason, C., and Brown, R. C. 2014. *Entrepreneurial Ecosystems and Growth-oriented Entrepreneurship.* https://www.oecd.org/cfe/leed/Entrepreneurial-ecosystems.pdf.

Pfeffer, J. and R. Sutton. 1999. *The Knowing-doing Gap: How Smart Companies Turn Knowledge into Action.* Boston, MA: Harvard Business School Press.

Saliola, F. and A. M. Islam. 2020. How to harness the digital transformation of the Covid era. *Harvard Business Review* (September): 2–4.

Soto-Acosta, P. 2020. Covid-19 Pandemic: Shifting digital transformation to a high-speed gear. *Information Systems Management* 37(4): 260–266.

Soto-Acosta, P., S. Popa, and D. Palacios-Marques. 2016. E-business, organizational innovation and firm performance in manufacturing SMEs: An empirical study in Spain. *Technological and Economic Development of Economy* 22(6): 885–904.

Spiegel, B. 2017. The relational organization of entrepreneurial ecosystems. *Entrepreneurship Theory and Practice* 41(1): 49–72.

Stam, E. 2015. Entrepreneurial ecosystems and regional policy: A sympathetic critique. *European Planning Studies* 23(9): 1759–1769.

Stam, E. 2018. Measuring entrepreneurial ecosystems. In A. O'Connor, E. Stam, F. Sussan, and D. B. Audretsch (Eds.), *Entrepreneurial Ecosystems: Place-based Transformations and Transitions.* New York: Springer Publications (173–196).

Sussan, F. and Z. J. Acs. 2017. The digital entrepreneurial ecosystem. *Small Business Economics* 49: 55–73.

The Institute for Policy & Strategy on National Competitiveness (IPSNC). 2020. *IPS National Competitiveness Research 2019–2020.* Seoul: The Institute for Policy & Strategy on National Competitiveness. http://ipsnc.org/research.html.

Turkey Informatics Industry Association (TUBISAD). 2020. Turkey's digital transformation index. http://www.tubisad.org.tr/en/images/pdf/tubisad_dde_endeks_report_eng.pdf.

Verhoef, P. C., T. Broekhuizen, Y. Bart, A. Bhattacharya, J. Qi Dong, N. Fabian, and M. Haenlein. 2021. Digital transformation: A multidisciplinary reflection and research agenda. *Journal of Business Research* 122: 889–901.

World Economic Forum. 2020. Digital transformation: Powering the great reset. https://www.weforum.org/reports/digital-transformation-powering-the-great-reset.

Yoo, Y., O. Henfridsson, and K. Lyytinen. 2010. The new organizing logic of digital innovation: An agenda for information systems research. *Information Systems Research* 21(4): 724–735.

Chapter 9

Digital Innovations and AI in Mental Health as Facilitators of Sustainable Competitive Economy in Post-COVID-19 Recovery

Damir Kušen

Abstract

The COVID-19 pandemic has presented a serious threat to mental health on a global scale. With unemployment worldwide reaching staggering highs and the loss of job security for millions of people, recent studies suggest that the pandemic can be linked to elevated anxiety levels, psychological distress, depression, PTSD, and suicidal behavior. While the case number of those infected by the COVID-19 virus (more than 170 million infected and more than 3.5 million deaths on May 30, 2021) certainly poses an unprecedented global health challenge, the detrimental effects on the population's mental health are far more difficult to measure, and thus address. Governments around the world are therefore tasked with providing more effective and affordable solutions to tackling both aspects of the pandemic's impact via increased investment in healthcare, medication, and vaccine distribution, as well as through an emphasis on innovative approaches to improve mental healthcare. Digital innovation and AI have already shown their potential for both prevention and treatment of mental health problems, as valid supplements for mental health practitioners.

Effective combatting of the pandemic's consequences on mental health is crucial for rebuilding sustainable and competitive economies in the post-COVID-19 recovery.

Keywords: COVID-19, mental health, AI and big data analysis, digital psychiatry, economic recovery, competitiveness, Croatia

Introduction

The World Health Organization (WHO) defines mental health as "a state of well-being in which the individual realizes his or her own abilities, can cope with the normal stresses of life, can work productively and fruitfully, and is able to make a contribution to his or her community" (WHO, 2004). While this definition is certainly holistic, it is difficult to imagine that a large number of people in society can fully agree with each aspect of it for their own lives. Such people who are not in a state of well-being have increased in number during the current pandemic when working "productively and fruitfully" has simply not been an option for many. Therefore, in this chapter, we use a somewhat more concise definition of mental health. Specifically, we adopt the definition from the Oxford Dictionary that it is "a person's condition with regard to their psychological and emotional well-being" (Lexica Oxford Dictionary, 2020).

Mental health disorders are generally multifaceted and result from complex interactions of psychological, physical, biological, genetic, social, economic, and environmental factors. Depression is a common mood disorder characterized by extended periods of feeling extremely low, which are significant enough to cause disruptions to the individual's daily life. Furthermore, depression is a leading cause of disability, which directly and seriously affects the national economy. Anxiety causes people to feel distressed, fearful, and uneasy for sometimes inexplicable or irrational reasons. Both mood disorders, if persistent for an extended period of time or with high intensity, may lead to suicidal or self-harming behavior.

The figures describing the levels of global mental health, even before the COVID-19 pandemic, suggest an alarming situation that demands urgent and fundamental changes to public mental health policies. According to WHO statistics published in January 2020, around 264 million people in the world at the time suffered from depression and 284 million from anxiety (WHO, 2020). Left untreated, depression can affect one's ability to work, contribute to social and familial problems, prompt frequent and long-term sick leave, and might ultimately lead to suicide. More than 800,000 people worldwide commit suicide each year and, in the age category between 15 and 29, suicide is the second leading cause of death (WHO, 2020).

During the World Economic Forum in Davos in 2019, experts estimated that one in four people would experience mental illness during their lifetimes, costing the global economy an estimated $16 trillion by 2030. Now, following the COVID-19 pandemic, these figures will undoubtedly be much higher, making mental health one of the main problems for society globally. Similar warning figures have also been produced by the WHO. This situation with mental health is even worse in low-income countries where more than 75 percent of people with mental disorders do not receive any medical treatment.

Thus, the mental health of society has significant effects on economic performance, competitiveness, and overall prosperity of a nation. It is not surprising that every severe economic crisis has had devastating impact upon people's overall mental health. This complex, but fundamental mutual interaction is a crucial indicator of national prosperity and overall economic affluence, but also of the general mental well-being of a nation (Beddington *et al.*, 2008).

History has shown that every severe crisis has had the potential to disrupt the complex and sensitive dynamic of a country's socio-economic life and has produced disastrous outcomes for human wealth. The Great Depression from 1929 to 1933 caused millions of people to become unemployed, putting them in desperate situations and generating severe mental health problems, such as depression and anxiety. It had a tremendous social, familial, and psychological impact. Similarly, the serious worldwide financial crisis of 2008 led to the deepest recession since the Great Depression, with a global economic loss of more than $2 trillion, which caused a proliferation of unemployment rates and severely endangered the mental health of millions of people.

Since the beginning of 2020, the COVID-19 pandemic has taken a drastic toll on human capital, with more than 170 million people infected while 3.5 million people have died (Johns Hopkins University, 2021, as on May 30, 2021). The associated psychological and mental trauma produced by this pandemic is practically immeasurable. COVID-19 has been a disease of isolation and its prevention of social contact has placed tremendous stress on people and their health. Throughout 2020, all countries have been affected by travel restrictions in some way. Quarantine and self-isolation measures have affected many people from all walks of life, generating significant stress, fear, depression, and anxiety on a global scale.

According to a WHO report from January 2020, before the spread of the COVID-19 pandemic, around 264 million people in the world suffered from depression (WHO, 2020). Indeed, in one of their first reports, during the early phase of the COVID-19 pandemic's spread, they stated that: "Good mental health is critical to the functioning of society at the best of times. It must be front and center of every country's response to and recovery from the COVID-19 pandemic" (WHO, 2020). Now, following the pandemic, the number of people suffering from depression and other mental illnesses is likely to have increased immensely. However, the number of mental health practitioners and psychological care providers was far less than the number society needs, even during normal times. And unfortunately, there is no significant indicator or trend suggesting that the number of mental health practitioners might be increased in the near future, despite their crucial role in the post-COVID-19 pandemic recovery.

The world is clearly faced with a very complex situation that requires rapid policy changes to orientate toward more efficient systems for providing mental healthcare for rapidly increasing and complex needs. The research for this chapter will seek to analyze and answer whether the development of advanced technology, artificial intelligence (AI), machine learning, and tele-psychiatry could be valid supplements to mental health practitioners. This chapter argues that AI-based devices and methods are useful additions to medical practitioners and should be developed on a much larger scale and utilized more in the prevention, diagnosis, and therapy of mental illness. Furthermore, governments and relevant international organizations should invest significantly in the research and utilization of new innovative technologies in the public health sector.

The vitality and sustainability of national economies, economic performance, and competitiveness strongly depend upon human capital and the mental health of the work force. However, people across the world have been strongly affected by the COVID-19 pandemic, with widespread trauma and stress, job insecurity, income decline, social isolation, depression, anxiety, and post-traumatic stress disorder (PTSD). It is only through considerable government relief programs and support mechanisms, as well as comprehensive approaches to mental health, that society will be able to overcome the serious consequences of COVID-19 and facilitate faster and ameliorated economic recovery.

Teams of experts in many countries have developed new and innovative technologies and applications that might be used online to aid the public's mental health. Among them, a multidisciplinary team in Croatia has also contributed to the development of advanced digital psychiatry and mental health based on AI and psychiatric practice for more efficient predictions and diagnosis of mental health disorders, founded on decades-long comprehensive research.

Key Aspects of Mental Health Exacerbated by the COVID-19 Pandemic

Although the world has previously been subjected to several pandemic-level threats, the global spread of the COVID-19 virus, and its highly contagious characteristics, have presented an unprecedented crisis. In addition to the physical illness that has affected more than 170 million people (as of May 30, 2021), it has also severely disrupted people's mental health on a global scale. According to a survey concerning the impact of the COVID-19 pandemic on mental, neurological, and substance abuse services, performed by the WHO in 2020 across 130 countries, it has supposedly disrupted or halted health services in 93 percent of those surveyed (WHO, 2020). As a global pandemic that has struck almost all countries around the world with disastrous consequences, COVID-19 is perceived by people as a serious threat. The pandemic has affected their daily lives by changing routines and restricting social contact. By disrupting business and trade, exports, and travels, it has generated a deep and global economic crisis that consequently presents high-level risks for job security and income loss. A natural response to a direct threat to personal economic security is a higher level of stress, anxiety, fear, and depression. With such a staggeringly high number of COVID-19 positive cases worldwide, this fear has become very real and could easily provoke mental disturbances or endanger the mental health of millions of people.

The consequences of COVID-19 pose a global danger to public health. In all of modern history, it is unlikely that the mental health of people on a global scale has been under such a threat. Certainly, the world has experienced two world wars that obviously generated enormous destruction and millions of deaths, creating an incalculable human toll.

Nevertheless, the world has never experienced such devastation in a period of peace and otherwise normal life. The global pandemic has brought the world to a complete lockdown with rigorous restrictions on travel and movement, and a ban on social contact, altogether posing a direct health risk for the world's population.

During its early stages, in late January 2020, the novel coronavirus SARS-CoV-2, which would later be known as COVID-19, was defined by the WHO as a public health emergency of international concern. However, it quickly evolved into a global pandemic by mid-March 2020. As a result, governments around the world were only given limited time to respond, and therefore many of them lacked efficient tools, measures, policies, and knowledge for containment. The consequences of this rapid and extensive pandemic spread included partial or total collapse of national health systems, huge shortages of medical practitioners, as well as a lack of necessary equipment and medications to treat the millions of patients, many of whom experienced serious and life-threatening symptoms. This unprecedented global crisis, which has been considered to be far worse than the 1918 Spanish flu pandemic, has caused a fundamental disruption to normal life throughout the entire world.

Increased levels of depression, anxiety, and suicide rates

A stark warning that both depression and anxiety have increased dramatically throughout the COVID-19 pandemic is provided in a survey result based on a representative sample of 60,000 Americans who completed a self-assessment report on these symptoms (Patient Health Questionnaire (PHQ-2 Scale, and Generalized Anxiety Disorder — GAD-2 Scale)). It shows that the number of Americans responding to mental health problems increased from 11.0 percent in the first half of 2019 to 42.4 percent in late 2020 (Terlizzi and Shiller, 2021; Vahratin *et al.*, 2021). According to the WHO, nearly 800,000 people across the world commit suicide every year. These suicide rates are staggering; 23.0 per 100,000 in the Republic of Korea, 14.9 in Japan, and 14.5 in the US. In 2017, the average suicide rate in the EU was 4.2, with significant differences among its member states, ranging from Lithuania (13.5), Finland (10.4), and Norway (10.2), to Greece (1.5), Portugal (2.1), Spain (2.2), and Italy (2.4) on the lower side of the scale (Eurostat, 2020). Suicide is especially the leading cause of death among young people in the age range of 15–29. For each person who commits suicide, there are more than 20 others who attempt to end their lives (WHO, 2020). As the COVID-19 pandemic brought about unprecedented changes in daily life and has enforced rigorous restrictions on travel, social gatherings, and personal contact, people have had to self-isolate and quarantine. It is likely that these circumstances might increase depression, anxiety, alcohol and substance abuse, and subsequently the suicide rate.

Historically, increased suicide rates have seen a correlation with global crises. For instance, during the Great Depression between 1928 and 1932, suicide rates rose to more than 30 percent. Additionally, the number of people who were hospitalized and required medical assistance increased three-fold (*Nature*, 2014). This same trend was seen throughout East Asia during the 2003 SARS pandemic. During the financial and banking crisis of 2008, there were an estimated 1,000 additional deaths from suicide in England between 2008 and 2010 (Barret *et al.*, 2012). Similar rises occurred in many other countries, especially in Europe and North America due to the high rise of unemployment. The greatest rise in the incidence of suicide appeared to be in young men. Furthermore, for each registered suicide, there were 30–40 people who ended up in hospitals following attempts to end their lives, usually with evident self-harm. This 2008 crisis was the deepest recession since World War II in many countries and was particularly detrimental to young people, many of whom fell into debt or lost their properties and livelihoods. The increased suicide rates can largely be attributed to being a consequence of that.

Some initial studies suggest that COVID-19 has also increased the suicide rate, with many arguing that a pandemic creates the ideal conditions for a decline in people's mental health. Another argument suggests that the pandemic's social-contact restrictions make it far more difficult to approach and obtain mental health services. A frequently cited study in Nepal, based on police reports, suggests a sharp increase in suicide incidents during the COVID-19 pandemic (Ueda *et al.*, 2020). Some studies (Tanaka and Okamoto, 2021) suggest that the rate of suicide incidents in Japan has significantly increased (16.5 percent) during the second wave of the pandemic.

The Republic of Korea ranks at the top of countries with the highest per capita suicide rate among OECD countries. Statistical data from the Korean Ministry of Health and Welfare shows an increase in the suicide rate among young women by 17.9 percent in April 2020, which was the peak month of the COVID-19 pandemic in Korea, in comparison to April 2019.

In the first half of 2020, almost 600,000 Korean people asked for medical help because of depression, which presented a 5.8 percent increase compared to the previous year. The number of those who deliberately harmed themselves in this period increased by nearly 36 percent.

Nevertheless, stay-at-home measures to curb the spread of COVID-19 have increased the time spent at home with family or close friends, which has predominantly had a contrasting effect as it has proven to be a positive factor in the prevention of suicidal thoughts. Many non-essential jobs switched to online work, which was a relief to those who usually have to commute and spend significant amounts of time travelling between their home and their workplace. This situation has thus opened up the possibility to increase quality time spent with family members or close friends and to potentially allot more time to hobbies or other recreational activities.

Studies in Norway (Qin and Mehlum, 2020), UK (Appleby *et al.*, 2021), Germany (Radeloff *et al.*, 2020), and Peru (Calderon-Alyosa and Kaufman, 2021) contrasts the study results mentioned previously, suggesting that suicide rates have actually fallen during the COVID-19 pandemic. Overall, any interpretation of the first available reports and studies analyzing the link between suicide and the COVID-19 pandemic should be regarded with caution, and more scientific studies are certainly needed. As is always the case in the social sciences, a causal link should not be misinterpreted with mere correlation or association indications, and evidence cannot be replaced by supposition.

Shortage of mental health practitioners and insufficient mental health budgets

Professional face-to-face medical treatment and therapy to help people with depression or other stress-related clinical symptoms is the most effective method for combatting mental illness. However, the huge shortage of mental health practitioners in all countries around the world presents a rapidly emerging global health problem, in which the serious consequences of the COVID-19 pandemic can create a severe global mental health crisis. Despite the obvious evidence that severe economic crises, pandemics, and natural disasters have devastating effects on public mental health and might be even considered as an issue of national security, the budgets available to researchers in this area are still very small. Researchers across the world are vocal in stating that projects on psychological treatments remain "scandalously under-supported" (Holmes *et al.*, 2014).

The number of psychiatrists per 100,000 people even in the most advanced economies is extremely low. According to the WHO's latest data available, there are 18.9 in the UK, 17.6 (average) in EU countries, 12.3 in the Russian Federation, 11.9 in Japan, 10.5 in the US, 5.7 in the Republic of Korea, 2.2 in China, and 0.75 in India. In the majority of the countries in the world, this number is below 1 per 100,000. The latest available data from Eurostat shows that the largest number of psychiatrists per 100,000 citizens in Europe is in Switzerland (51.7), Germany (27.4), the Nordic countries (above 20), France (17.4), and in Italy (16.1) (Eurostat, 2020).

The national budgets for mental health care across the world are also concerningly low. In 2001, the WHO collected data based on a questionnaire distributed to all its member states in order to get a better overview of the amounts allocated to mental healthcare. The results showed that almost one-third of the 191 countries did not have a specified budget allocated for mental health, while 36 percent spent less than 1 percent of their total health budgets on mental health (Saxena *et al.*, 2003).

All EU member countries have mental health policy plans and corresponding budgets. In the EU pre-2004, $200 per capita was allocated to mental health, which was significantly more than in many other countries or regions around the world. In 2016, the EU had 50 mental health workers per 100,000 people, including psychiatrists, nurses, social workers, and speech therapists. In 2018, of all hospital beds available in the EU, 13.5 percent were psychiatric care beds (Eurostat, 2020).

OECD countries spend an average of $4,000 per person for health services. In 2018, health spending made up 8.8 percent of the GDP, with projections that by 2030 this proportion could increase to 10.2 percent. In the US, actual healthcare spending is much larger with $10,000 per capita (OECD, 2019). The Republic of Korea is an exemplar country with significant achievements in providing mental healthcare for its citizens. A special Act on Mental Health, with an allocated budget of $253.4 million, was passed in 2019 and enabled the expansion of psychiatric facilities.

COVID-19 as a disease that prevents social contact and minimizes face-to-face interactions presents an additional obstacle in providing necessary psychological help and adequate counselling. This is another valid reason for putting more effort into designing effective online mental health services. A rising number of cognitive scientists question the validity, reliability, and sensitivity of traditional diagnostic methods in psychiatry, suggesting that they are outdated, subjective, and do not represent the complex reality. Rather than on objective markers of illness, traditional methods of diagnostics in psychiatry are predominantly based on human interpretations reduced to conventionally drafted descriptive categories and verbal constructs.

Digital Innovations and AI in Prevention, Diagnosis, and Treatment of Mental Health Disorders

When the world was first faced with the COVID-19 pandemic, 15.5 percent of the global population was already affected by some type of mental disorder (WHO, 2020). Between 2017 and 2018, in the US, 19 percent of adults who experienced mental illness and 60 percent of youths who experienced major symptoms of depression did not receive any mental health treatment (MHA, 2021). With a rise in the number of people seeking mental health support as a result of the pandemic, the serious shortage of mental health practitioners could be supplemented by digital and AI-based platforms, programs and applications, jointly developed by computer scientists and mental health experts.

The national budget allocated to mental healthcare in many countries is insufficient and lacking in contingency planning. The emerging advanced technology provides numerous possibilities for innovative solutions and for the utilization of AI and machine learning, digital psychiatry, online platforms, and apps especially designed for screening, prevention, consulting, diagnostics, and therapy of mental disorders. The number of these applications is increasing daily and these are generally becoming available to all internet users. At the same time, government agencies responsible for health and mental care are tasked with defining precise regulations, standards, and rules that must be followed in all digital solutions and applications that have the potential for clinical impact. As a sign of recognition of the new trend of digital psychiatry, the European Psychiatric Association decided to organize the 29th European Congress of Psychiatry on April 10–13, 2021 under the motto "Personalising and Integrating Mental Health Care in the Digital Era."

Screening and prevention of mental health disorders

In 2014, Mental Health America created an Internet-based comprehensive mental health-related diagnostic screening set of ten screens, based on existing clinically validated diagnostic tests for depression *Patient Health Questionnaire-9 Item* (PHQ-9), and for anxiety *Generalized Anxiety Disorder-7 Item* (GAD-7), as well as the *US Household Pulse Survey*. Since 2014, through this Online Screening Program (www.mhascreening. org), over 6 million people have actively participated in providing data about their own mental health. Access to the screening set is free and the data collected throughout the test will be anonymous and confidential. From January to September 2020, during the pandemic, over 1.5 million people voluntarily participated in the screening. By using these large datasets, experts from Mental Health America have prepared one of the first COVID-19-related extensive descriptive reports of mental health screening, coming to the dramatic conclusion that the "… the number of people looking for help with anxiety and depression has skyrocketed." (MHA, 2021). Alongside the variety of screening methods adapted for online use, the Internet and smartphone-based applications could be used for comprehensive public data-collection and awareness campaigns aimed at empowering the prevention capacity of society to resist COVID-19 and any negative consequences of the pandemic.

Diagnostics of mental health disorders

According to new approaches to diagnostic systems in psychiatry, which highlights the utilization of machine learning, big data analysis, and AI, generating measurable data-based psychiatry tailored to individual patients has the potential to be a game changer for the further development of mental health diagnostics. Digital psychiatry, by using machine learning in the form of multiclass prediction and multitask learning, could allow the use of predictive models to obtain answers and data from individual patients.

Yet, the development of new AI-based devices and methods in digital psychiatry remain seriously challenged by many issues. First on the list of obstacles is the size of the dataset on patients that is available today. In their study, Singh and Reynolds (2016) pointed out that the phenotypic details and datasets in psychiatry are much larger than in many other medical specialties, but that the lack of shared information still imposes restrictions to further improvements in digital psychiatry and big data analysis (Longo and Drazen, 2016). Sharing information in this area is always sensitive due to personal data protection regulations. In their paper published in *Nature*'s neuroscience section, Poldrack and Gorgolewski (2014), introduced the benefits and obstacles in data-sharing systems in neuroimaging, suggesting that big data sharing models might help in the development of more reliable AI-based predictive models, but that the ethical issues of patient confidentiality when combined with possible facial recognition software still possesses a reasonable threat (Poldrack and Gorgolewski, 2014).

In non-medical domains, the predictive power of machine learning and sophisticated learning algorithms are based on more than a million subjects. In psychiatry, the data set is usually significantly smaller, reducing the predictive power and consequently deteriorating the actual potential of AI-based diagnostic solutions. Norwegian neuroscientists Brita Elvevag and Peter Foltz, from the Institute of Cognitive Science at the University of Tromso, have tried to develop machine learning devices that will be more accurate in the detection of changes or irregular patterns in the speech of patient that might indicate mental health problems. Scientists from the Department of Psychiatry at NYU Langone Health have developed AI solutions aimed at increasing the level of objectivity in PTSD diagnosis. They introduced a new method for analyzing voice oscillations as a possible valid and more objective set of indicators for the presence of PTSD symptoms. In April 2019, they published their study in the *Depression and Anxiety Journal*, presenting initial evidence that speech analysis might be a useful tool in PTSD diagnostics (Marmar *et al.*, 2019).

Self-reported assessments always face challenges due to the high levels of subjectivity and distorted self-perception of the participants. For instance, veterans returning from combat situations have been exposed to extraordinary experiences with very strong emotional burdens, and their stories are not just descriptions of events, but rather their own views, mixed with their emotional interpretations and political perspectives that reduce the objectivity of their reports.

Treatment and therapy of mental health disorders

The utilization of new advanced technology in psychological help and care-providing systems has been profiled as a possible useful contribution to widely available, cost-effective, and easier treatment for millions of mental health patients who do not have access to health practitioners or cannot financially afford it. Computerized and Internet-based cognitive behavior therapy (CBT) is based on big data analysis, machine learning, AI, and previous extensive clinical experience. Internet-based cognitive behavioral therapy (ICBT) is a relatively new method of psychotherapy that provides psychological assistance to patients with depression, anxiety, panic disorder, PTSD, or obsessive-compulsive disorder. The first impressions and results obtained have mainly supported the further development of this method, with patients showing positive attitudes toward ICBT. Because face-to-face therapy is more expensive and less convenient for patients who live far from the clinics, and for those with a lower socioeconomic status, there is a significant factor of cost-effectiveness that supports the further development of using AI in providing psychological and psychiatric services online.

Since the 1960s, computer scientists and engineers have been trying to design software solutions capable of communication. Robots capable of simple, short conversations were first designed at the MIT Artificial Intelligence Laboratory with the famous Eliza program. The current big data processing power, AI, and new knowledge in neuroscience and machine learning have facilitated the development of a new concept of chatbots or virtual therapists, examples include Stanford psychologists who developed *Woebot* and *Elli,* which has been developed by the University of Southern California. A large number of chatbots have, however, been developed as commercial products and usually lack clinical approval, which might make them more suitable for entertainment purposes rather than for serious clinical diagnosis or therapy, which could in itself be dangerous if those using them do not recognize the difference.

Self-guided ICBT requires patients to use apps or internet programs such as "MoodHacker" while some apps, like *e-Ouch,* are designed to provide assistance in the management and treatment of chronic pain. There are also websites such as "Living Life to The Full," which delivers cognitive behavioral therapy (CBT) for maladaptive thoughts, sleeping disorders, anxiety control, relaxation techniques, exercise, and diet. However, a large majority of newly developed software applications, programs, and virtual therapists lack clinical approval from national health authorities and are still more often seen as relaxation and amusement, rather than serious clinical tools.

Case Study: Croatian Initiative for AI and Digital Mental Health: International Centre of Excellence for Resilience and Mental Health

Three decades of research in PTSD, stress resilience, and the further development of digital psychiatry

Croatia, like many other countries, has been trying to develop an efficient multidimensional model and comprehensive approach for the utilization of AI and machine learning in conjunction with expertise in mental health, psychiatry, and psychology. All massive stressful events, large-scale human and natural disasters, or global pandemics pose significant threats to public mental health and the mental well-being of people. Croatian mental-health experts together with computer scientists from the Faculty of Electrical Engineering and Computing at the University of Zagreb significantly contributed to this field of stress-related mental health during and after Croatia's War of Independence (1991–1995). Since then, large teams of experts have initiated comprehensive studies in the areas of PTSD and trauma-related disorders. The experience of war and war-related events is disastrous for the mental health of people directly affected by them. An overwhelming majority of Croatian defenders did not have any previous special military training to cope with high levels of stress and life-threatening situations that are frequent and common in war and battle situations. As a result of these stressful events, many veterans, and also civilians, later developed symptoms of PTSD, depression, and anxiety. In multiple research papers, the authors have sought to develop efficient diagnostic systems, combining medical, psychological, and physiological data (Ivezić *et al.*, 2000; Kozarić-Kovačić *et al.*, 2001).

From the early 1990s, an interdisciplinary group of Croatian experts, scientists, and practitioners in the fields of medicine, mental health, psychology, psychiatry, cognitive science, neuropsychology, computer science, AI, and machine learning have initiated a wide range of research projects to find optimal solutions for providing necessary psychological care. The number of mental health practitioners was disproportionately smaller than the public's need and the country had limited resources for mental health services. As a result, the active search for tele-medical and digital solutions in psychiatry and Croatia's mental healthcare system has been extensively developed in the past twenty years. Three decades of

Croatia's intensive multidisciplinary research on PTSD and stress-related behavior has amassed extensive knowledge and research-based data in the area of public mental health.

In that context, Croatia initiated a proposal to host NATO's Centre of Excellence for Resilience and Mental Health. In 2013, NATO's Allied Transformation Command in Norfolk, Virginia included this Croatian initiative on its list of potential future NATO centers of excellence. This initiative, which remains under consideration, was based on a presentation by Croatian experts at the annual NATO Military Mental Health Expert Panel session that was previously held in Brussels. Additionally, in 2005, the Croatian Government organized an international NATO conference on "Novel Approaches to the Diagnosis and Treatment of PTSD." Since 2008, in cooperation with the Virtual Reality Medical Centre in San Diego and the Interactive Media Institute in Brussels, Croatia organized a series of international conferences and seminars on the topic of the utilization of digital technology in the prevention and mitigation of mental disorders provoked by stress for soldiers and war veterans. This project was sponsored by the NATO Science for Peace and Security Program (Wiederhold, 2013).

Over the past fifteen years, the Laboratory for Interactive Simulation Systems, from the Faculty of Electronic Engineering and Computing, at the University of Zagreb has cooperated closely with numerous mental health institutions in joint research efforts to develop new models, methods, and devices to incorporate advanced ICT technology, AI, VR, and machine learning in the treatment of mental health disorders, PTSD, emotional dysfunctions, and stress-related problems. (Popovic *et al.*, 2009; Ćosić *et al.*, 2010, 2013; Kukolja *et al.*, 2014; Horvat and Jagušt, 2020). Three year-long joint international projects on the development of metrics for soldier resilience prediction and training were additionally completed in 2019 by cooperation between Zagreb University and Hadassah Hebrew University Hospital in Jerusalem, Israel, and Emory University School of Medicine, Atlanta, Georgia.

Emphasis on digital psychiatry after the simultaneous impact of COVID-19 and earthquakes on Croatia in 2020

Decades of research in the areas of mental health and applications of AI and tele-psychiatry systems in mitigating stress, depression, and anxiety, have shown their practical value during the COVID-19 pandemic. Croatia, like all other countries, has been affected by the pandemic, but due to the low level of demographic density and the imposition of strict measures in the early phases of the ongoing crisis, Croatia managed to withstand it relatively well. The country did not experience any total lockdowns, but restrictions of movement and social distancing measures were implemented throughout the pandemic, with their severity depending on the crisis level. Croatia also did not extensively employ the quarantine model, but rather encouraged people to be responsible and avoid situations that might increase the risks of infection.

On top of this public health challenge, an additional source of unpredictable high-level stress upon the population of Zagreb, Croatia's capital, was inflicted by the disastrous 5.3Mw magnitude earthquake that hit the city on March 22, 2020. In the six months following the main earthquake, hundreds of smaller, but still detectable, aftershocks hit Zagreb and other areas in Croatia, provoking long-term stress, fear, and anxiety in its citizens. According to an estimate by the World Bank, the scale of destruction, involving substantial damage to the historic city center, was around 11.3 billion EUR (WB, 2020). Additionally, a second strong earthquake (6.4 Mw magnitude) hit the city of Petrinja, 80 km south of Zagreb, on December 29, 2020, inflicting disastrous damage to the buildings and infrastructure of the city and its surrounding.

These two simultaneous disasters, COVID-19 and the strong earthquakes, as well as their respective consequences, persisted for many months further provoked higher levels of stress for the citizens of Croatia. These encouraged the government and other relevant institutions to further invest in research and projects aimed at providing optimal models and tools for more accurate predictions, diagnostics, and treatments of mental disorders (Jakovljevic *et al.*, 2020).

The Croatian multidisciplinary team of experts led by Professor Krešimir Ćosić, from the Laboratory for Interactive Simulation Systems, at the Faculty of Electrical Engineering and Computing of the University of Zagreb, has also proposed cooperation with Seoul National University as well as with other institutions. It is only through the sharing of knowledge, data, and methodology that the world will be able to effectively respond to and combat the negative consequences of the COVID-19 pandemic, as well as to increase the level of preparedness and resilience for any future cases of the next global pandemic or serious natural disasters.

Social and Economic Consequences of the COVID-19 Pandemic and Addressing Its Aftermath

Social and economic consequences of the COVID-19 pandemic

The World Economic Outlook projected that the global economic growth for 2020 would decline by 4.9 percent (IMF, 2021). In the majority of countries, as a result of the pandemic and its consequences, 2020 ended with estimated budget deficits of around 10 percent of GDP, further burdening the already high public debt. The IMF estimates that in many countries, the economic output of 2020 was reduced at a rate of between −3 and −10 percent. Nevertheless, a positive return is projected in 2021, between 3 and 6 percent (IMF, 2021).

COVID-19 has strongly affected labor markets around the world, resulting in millions of jobs being lost. The unemployment rate in the US for February 2020 was 3.5 percent, but by April 2020 it had peaked to about 14.8 percent. In the following months, the US labor market experienced a gradual recovery, and by December 2020 the unemployment rate was 6.5 percent. Comparatively, in the Eurozone, unemployment in December 2020 was 8.5 percent. The leading economies in Asia managed to perform well whilst navigating through the 2020 COVID-19 crisis. However, lockdowns, travel and movement restrictions, social distancing measures, and overall stress brought on by the COVID-19 pandemic have affected the mental well-being for many people.

The Great Depression between 1929 and 1933 resulted in hundreds of millions of people losing their jobs. The unemployment rate in 1929 was just 3.2 percent. However, this crisis increased that number almost eightfold by 1932. Millions of people lost their jobs and livelihoods, ending up in desperate situations; this facilitated the development of depression, anxiety, and severe mental health problems, causing tremendous negative social, familial, and psychological impacts. During the years of the Great Depression, suicide rates in the US increased from 13.9 per 100,000 to 17.4 per 100,000 (Bernstein, 1987). Additionally, the global GDP declined by 26.7 percent, and employment rates in the peak period of the crisis reached only 25 percent (*Nature*, 2014). Industrial production faced a downturn of 46 percent in the US, 41 percent in Germany, and 23 percent in the UK. Foreign trade fell 70 percent in the US and around 60 percent in European countries. For over a decade following the Great Depression, the most developed western countries did not return to pre-crisis period levels.

The New Deal relief program, initiated by President Franklin D. Roosevelt, did not only offer economic recovery but also facilitated support for the mental health of the nation, suggesting that the collapse was not their personal economic failure, but rather a societal one, thereby alleviating the psychological pressure on individuals. This experience should pose a valid precedent for government policymaking and planning measures after each serious economic crisis.

The scope of the consequences of COVID-19 to the global economy is incalculable. Almost all nations in the world (192 countries) were directly affected, with more than 141 million confirmed cases, and more than 3 million deaths by the middle of April 2021 (John Hopkins, 2021). Daily life for much of the global population was disrupted by travel restrictions, lockdowns, and limited social contact, causing a high level of anxiety in individuals' lives. According to the World Bank, the COVID-19 pandemic initiated the worst global recession since World War II (World Bank Group, 2020). With billions of jobs under direct threat, the economic and social security of practically all nations has come under unprecedented challenges. As a result of this, hundreds of millions of people across the world fell under the threat of financial decline and poverty. The poor, who are even more vulnerable, lost most of their long-term prospects for getting their families out of poverty. Many research papers suggest a noticeable link between these financial difficulties and higher suicide rates.

This rapid economic decline at a global scale has generated significantly more social destruction, family violence, alcoholism, drug consumption, aggressive behavior and higher crime rates, psychological disorders, anxiety, depression, and suicidal tendencies. There is an estimation that every 1 percent increase in the level of unemployment is associated with a 0.79 percent rise in suicides among people below 65 years old (Stuckler *et al.*, 2009). A rise in unemployment may also be associated with higher homicide rates, as reported in Greece between 2007 and 2009, where homicides were doubled when the unemployment rate was surging (Giotakos *et al.*, 2011).

The rapid socioeconomic decline caused by the COVID-19 pandemic and the stagnation of economic activities can seriously influence people's mental health through direct loss of jobs, low chance of reemployment, and significant income decline. Long-term unemployment, impoverishment, and the resulting familial disruptions can be responsible for a deterioration of mental health, most prominently depression, anxiety, suicide, and substance abuse.

Ultimately, the COVID-19 pandemic will have long-term impact in all spheres of people's lives. More than 1.5 billion children in many parts of the world will miss out on a proper education, which will in turn have a strong negative effect on their future employability and efficiency in the workplace. Companies will be faced with lower skill levels among the work force, which could additionally weaken their competitiveness.

Economic recovery after COVID-19

The pace of economic recovery after COVID-19 will probably depend on the amount of financial relief and stimulus packages, the level of investment in R&D, new innovative technologies and solutions, as well as on human capital and the mental health of the labor force. The financial measures implemented to lead economic recovery will probably be stronger in developed countries. In developing countries, the financial and economic crisis provoked by the COVID-19 pandemic might take a longer time to recover. A significant proportion of international development assistant aid programs might be reduced because the provider countries will redirect their spending to their own national recovery.

The relief stage is based on the introduction of emergency measures and policies, primarily in the area of public health and direct assistance packages seeking to help people directly affected by the pandemic. There is a wide spectrum of relief mechanisms and measures provided for small company owners, like microcredit schemes based on low interest, and additional education, training, or therapy for entrepreneurs with a history of mental illness or substance addiction. It is crucial to extend advisory services, such as the citizen's advice bureau, specialized job centers, debt advisory agencies, housing agencies, and other relevant service providers.

Once the pandemic is under control, the restructuring phase requests serious reforms and institutional changes in health and social security systems. Perhaps, the restructuring of entire economic systems may be necessary due to the company's accumulated debt during the pandemic and business disruption, as well as in the overall adjustments to the new socio-economic reality. Particular attention should be paid to the restoration of human resources and labor. In the long run, each government should develop efficient national resilience strategies to protect their countries from future pandemics. This period of recovery should be the time to strengthen relevant policies and plans, institutions and tools, activities, and measures that can improve the resilience of the nation and readiness for possible future disruptions.

The US has responded to the COVID-19 pandemic with sizeable relief packages. The US$8.3 billion Coronavirus Preparedness and Response Supplemental Appropriations Act was passed on March 6, 2020, which was allocated for coronavirus vaccine research and development. The Families First Coronavirus Response Act, passed on March 18, 2020, provides US$104 billion relief. On March 27, 2020, the US Congress passed the Coronavirus Aid, Relief, and Economic Security Act (CARES Act) in response to the huge economic fallouts due to the COVID-19 pandemic, which is composed of a US$2.2 trillion economic stimulus bill. This bill provides emergency assistance and healthcare for businesses, families, and individuals who were directly affected by COVID-19. This is the largest economic stimulus package in the US history, equaling to about 10 percent of the total GDP. An additional amount of US$900 million in relief was provided by the Consolidated Appropriation Act 2021, passed by Congress on December 21, 2020. Finally, on March 5, 2021, the US Senate passed the US$1.9 trillion coronavirus relief bill, which provides US$350 billion for state aid, supporting jobless people, child allowance, stimulus checks, and vaccine distribution.

Altogether, according to the World Bank Group (WBG), industrialized countries have spent up to 15–20 percent of their GDPs on stimulus packages, whilst for emerging markets, the size of the stimulus package was only close to 6 percent of their GDPs. The poorest countries invested less than 2 percent in providing financial stimuli to help their companies (WBG, 2020). On June 30, 2020, the WBG announced the Emergency Response Program to support micro, small, and medium-sized companies in India, with an amount of US$650 million. The SME sector in India, which employs approximately 150–180 million people, contributes to 30 percent of India's GDP and 40 percent of total exports (WBG, 2020). Furthermore, since the outbreak of the COVID-19 pandemic, the International Monetary Fund (IMF) has provided assistance to more than 100 countries that asked for emergency financial assistance, such as the Rapid Credit Facility (RCF) and Rapid Financing Instrument (RFI) facilities. Additionally, the IMF's Catastrophe Containment and Relief Trust (CCRT) helps to relieve the debt of the poorest countries (IMF, 2020).

In 2020, the Republic of Korea provided pandemic rescue packages totaling US$28.2 billion, with a supplementary relief aid budget of

US$60.2 billion. In early March 2021, the Korean government provided an extra US$13.3 billion, as another round of relief programs to help small merchants, the self-employed, and the underprivileged segments of society, all of whom might be classified as those hardest hit by the pandemic. In addition, Korea has delivered a total of US$12.8 billion stimuli checks to all households. In comparison to the relief amounts given during the Global Financial Crisis, when the total stimulus package was US$53.7 billion (Hur and Kim, 2012), the financial assistance related to COVID-19 has indeed been significant.

Financial stimuli could be crucial aid for the recovery of the national economy. Without direct financial assistance, it is very difficult for companies to survive and stay profitable. The innovative capacity of these companies could be significantly reduced, with less capacity for improvements and novel solutions. In such a desperate situation, the competitiveness of companies and the overall national economy will come under direct threat. Hence, governments could design stimulus packages that would support innovation-related business activities. For example, in June 2020, Germany announced a second stimulus package with US$55.8 billion directed to future focus technologies. In France, a stimulus package from September 2020 has targeted US$8.4 billion for digital investment and US$13 billion for investment in R&D.

Recovery of human capital after the COVID-19 pandemic

Alongside the impact of the financial crisis on the competitiveness and profitability of companies, the post-crisis period causes a huge decline in human capital. The rapid increases in unemployment, job insecurity, income decline, depression, anxiety, stress, mental disorders especially PTSD, and serious emotional or cognitive dysfunctions present serious obstacles to the efficiency of human capital. The pandemic's impact on mental health is likely to persist long after the threat of infection is tamed. Previous research suggests that the psychological toll can persist for up to three years after the outbreak of the pandemic. Recovery of human capital is therefore a crucial element in the post-pandemic period. Economic progress in a society that is heavily affected by a huge economic crisis, disastrous pandemic, and global health crisis or by natural catastrophes directly depends on human capital and its capacity for change.

The World Bank Group (WBG) has a key role in international efforts for helping developing countries to establish more resilient and effective health systems to these countries by providing both financial assistance and expertise. The WBG supports developing countries in purchasing COVID-19 vaccines, in accessing tests and treatments, and in improving the governments' prevention, diagnostics, and immunization policies, and practices. With US$160 billion of direct financial support allocated to more than 100 developing countries, the WBG will strengthen economic recovery programs, support business and trade, and help those in need: the poor, vulnerable, and those with mental disorders (WBG, 2020). The WBG responded to the COVID-19 pandemic in its very early phase and with substantial emergency assistance. First the preparedness and response projects with a value of $1.9 billion were launched on April 2, 2020, with the aim to help 25 of the most vulnerable countries. Only a month later, on May 19, the WBG announced that its emergency assistant operations to strengthen the preparedness and response in fighting COVID-19 includes 100 developing countries that make up 70 percent of the global population (WBG, 2020). Some of these projects were especially designed to help people dealing with the negative psychological effects associated with the pandemic. The total value of the financial support for these Global Health Emergency Response Programs is US$6 billion.

Alongside the WBG, the national governments in a number of countries have formulated programs to help their citizens in handling the negative consequences of the COVID-19 pandemic and its influence on mental health. It is crucial to include mental health services as a part of the National Health Insurance scheme or in basic healthcare benefits packages as it promotes higher productivity of workforce The WHO estimates that every US$1 invested in mental health could yield a US$4 return on investment (WHO, 2016), through better health and the ability to work more efficiently.

The entertainment industry could facilitate the recovery of a mental health of a nation that has been weakened by the pandemic and severe economic crisis. Intensive use of digital devices, gadgets, internet-based activities, and social networks have a therapeutic effect by diverting attention and distracting people from their difficulties. In the period following the Great Depression, the newly emerging entertainment industry (radio entertainers like Bing Crosby, Gracie Allen, George Burns, and others), and the boom period of the Hollywood film industry helped people in the same way. However, using this method requires close attention as it also may pose a new global threat of digital-addictive behavior.

Nowadays, an increasing number of companies are offering wellness programs for their employees. For example, some companies integrate health promotion programs at the workplace, such as cognitive-behavioral therapy. In addition to increasing productivity, these programs could be effective in tackling the stigma associated with mental disorders. Innovation-driven SME companies could establish small innovation and creativity hubs inside their companies, encouraging employees to share their experiences and ideas, as well as discuss possible solutions for new innovative or competitive products, goods, and services. With more informal social interactions, employees with certain mental difficulties could feel more accepted and appreciated by others, and the stigma associated with mental illnesses will be reduced.

Digital platforms, frequently community-led, designed as a smartphone or computer-based applications, allow the easy sharing of relevant information at the global level, which could be very useful in the period of the post-COVID-19 pandemic recovery. One of the most comprehensive digital platforms that lists more than 900 different innovations organized in nine categories and from worldwide contributions, is the COVID-19 Innovation Hub. Its target is to help the most vulnerable segments of the global economy — SMEs in developing countries, farmers, small company owners, people in need, and other areas. Some of these excellent innovative and society-oriented projects are recognized and appreciated by a number of sponsors and have managed to raise significant amounts (data updated in March 2021) for their operations, the most prominent of which are now listed: the One Acre Fund raised US$44.4 million (March 2021) to provide financial support and services for small farmers, which was implemented mainly in African countries; Living Goods raised US$16.7 million through community health programs focusing on help with new-born babies and child health; Healthy entrepreneurs raised US$5.3 million for delivering health products and services to hard-to-reach areas; AskNivi raised US$4.1 million for AI-based digital health advisors, providing relevant health-related information; Lista raised US$1.9 million for the assistance and improvement of financial capabilities and knowledge of low-income people living in rural areas; Ideas42 raised US$1.4 million, for the development of mobile financial management training for micro-entrepreneurs; and We Care Solar raised US$300,000, for aid in saving lives in childbirth with innovative solar suitcases, to areas without electricity.

Some of the aforementioned initiatives are community-based approaches or oriented to provide psychological support through friendly chats (*TuConsejerija*), while others are more sophisticated and expert-based in providing digital psychiatry or psychology assistance, like IMPACT — offering psychiatric services through tele-psychiatry based at primary care centers to bridge the mental health treatment gap in India. Other platforms are oriented to providing mental health services in under-resourced settings (Happy Life), providing basic mental health support (Wysa), or offering support for effective online teaching.

Finally, COVID-19 vaccinations might be the first real signal that the end of the pandemic is in the near future. According to COVAX, the first round of vaccine delivery gave out 237 million doses of the AZ/Oxford vaccine — manufactured by AstraZeneca (AZ) and licensed and manufactured by the Serum Institute of India (SII/AZ), and they have been delivered to 142 participating facilities. According to WHO data, 1.87 billion people have already been vaccinated by end of May 2021 (Johns Hopkins, 2021).

Conclusion

The trends in global mental health over the past three decades have experienced rapid deterioration, which has been immeasurably worsened by the advent of the COVID-19 pandemic. This has further presented a serious risk for the weakening of human capital and has threatened the psychological well-being of citizens worldwide. These detrimental consequences on mental health are also inextricably and co-dependently linked with global economic competitiveness and sustainability. Namely, degeneration in the mental health of the working population certainly leads to weaker performance in the workplace, with ultimate adverse effects on the economy as a whole. Simultaneously, an economic decline leads to higher levels of unemployment and job insecurity, causing high levels of stress for the population, which leads to further deterioration of mental health. Thus, it is critical for governments and other institutions around the world to find and adopt effective solutions to combat the multifaceted nature of this crisis.

The research presented in this chapter argues that, due to the critical shortage of mental health practitioners even in the most developed countries, perhaps the most promising pathways for improving people's overall mental health is through innovations based on AI, machine learning, big data processing, and VR, designed in close cooperation with mental health experts. These internet or smartphone-based solutions, if they are designed and programmed professionally and in line with strict health standards and criteria, could be a vital aid that could supplement mental health practitioners in diagnostics and psychological therapy. One of the valid examples of the implementation and development of these approaches can be seen in Croatia. Over the past three decades, multidisciplinary teams of Croatian scientists have developed a wide range of effective systems for providing optimal psychological care, particularly aimed at veterans from Croatia's War of Independence who are at a disproportionately higher risk of suffering from PTSD, depression, and other stress-related disorders. Through the Laboratory for Interactive Simulation Systems at the University of Zagreb, experts have spent the past 15 years closely cooperating with mental health institutions to develop new models, methods, and devices for treating and addressing mental health issues based on technologies at the forefront of innovation such as AI, virtual reality, and machine learning.

The economic, social, and psychological damage has continuously heightened amidst the COVID-19 pandemic and the global economy will face a worse recession than during the Great Depression. Millions of people will lose their job and a large number of companies will be at risk of bankruptcy or unbearable debt. This chapter argues that mental health is not only a public healthcare issue, but also a global economic, social, and developmental priority. It demands global initiatives and comprehensive, multi-sectoral, and integral approaches. The World Bank, and many developed countries, have already initiated huge relief and recovery programs to help national economies overcome the COVID-19 crisis. The World Health Organization is appealing to all countries to invest more in mental health prevention and protection of people with the central message that mental health should be fully included as a part of basic healthcare systems.

A sustainable and competitive economy requires a healthy and innovative society. The lessons learned from this destructive pandemic period suggest that the global economy can only function well if the physical and mental health of the global population is under sufficient care. It is the responsibility of the whole international community to collaborate and implement policies to provide optimal healthcare. Imposing more responsible investment in the mental wellbeing of the people is the best countermeasure to increase the resilience of countries against future pandemics and natural disasters and to contribute to the world's overall prosperity.

References

Appleby, L., N. Richards, S. Ibrahim, P. Turnbull, C. Rodway, and N. Kapur. 2021. Suicide in England in the COVID-19 pandemics: Early observational data from real time surveillance. *The Lancet Regional Health — Europe 4* (2021) 100110. *Research Paper*, Vol 4, 100110, May 01, 2021.

Barr, B., D. Taylor-Robinson, A. Scott-Samuel, M. McKee, and D. Stuckler. 2012. Suicides associated with the 2008–2010 economic recession in England: Time trend analysis. *BMJ* 2012;345:e5142.

Beddington, J., C. L. Cooper, J. Field., U. Goswami., F. A. Huppert., R. Jenkins., H. S. Jones., T. B. L. Kirkwood., B. J. Sahakians, and S. M. Thomas. 2008. The mental wealth of nations. *Nature* 455: 1057–1060.

Bernstein, M.A. 1987. *The Great Depression: Delayed Recovery and Economic Change in America, 1929–1939*. New York: Cambridge University Press.

Calderon-Anyosa, R. and J. Kaufman. 2021. Impact of COVID-19 lockdown policy on homicide, suicide, and motor vehicle deaths in Peru. *Preventive Medicine* 143: 106–331. https://www.cdc.gov/nchs/covid19/pulse/mental-health.htm.

Ćosić, K., S. Popović, D. Kukolja, M. Horvat, and B. Dropuljić. 2010. Physiology-driven adaptive virtual reality stimulation for prevention and treatment of stress related disorders. *Cyberpsychology, Behavior, and Social Networking* 13: 73–78.

Ćosić K., S. Popović, M. Horvat, D. Kukolja, B. Dropuljić, B. Kovač, and M. Jakovljević. 2013. Computer-aided psychotherapy based on multimodal elicitation, estimation, and regulation of emotion. *Psychiatria Danubina* 25 (3): 340–346.

Eurostat. 2020. *Mental Health and Related Issues Statistics*. Health in the European Union — facts and figures. https://ec.europa.eu/eurostat/statisticsexplained/index.php?title=Mental_health_and_related_issues_statistics.

Eyre, H. A., A. B. Singh, and C. Reynolds 3rd. 2016. Tech giants enter mental health. *World Psychiatry* 15(1): 21–22.

Giotakos O, D. Karabelas, and A. Kafkas. 2011. Financial crisis and mental health in Greece. *Modern Greek* 22: 109–119.

Holmes E. A., M. G. Craske, and A. M. Graybiel. 2014. Psychological treatments: A call for mental health science. *Nature* 511: 287–289.

Horvat, M. and T. Jagust. 2020. Emerging opportunities for education in the time of COVID-19: Adaptive e-learning intelligent agent based on assessment of emotion and attention. *Conference on Central European Conference on Intelligent and Information Systems (CECIIS 2020)*. October 7–9, 2020, Zagreb (online).

Hur, S and S. Kim. 2012. Fiscal policies of Korea through the global financial crisis. *Korea and the World Economy* 13(3): 395–418.

International Monetary Fund (IMF). 2020. IMF executive board approves proposals to enhance. 20: 189.

International Monetary Fund (IMF). 2021. *World Economic Outlook Update.* https://www.imf.org.

Ivezić, S., A. Bagarić., L. S. Oruc., N. Mimica, and T. L. Golub. 2000. Psychotic symptoms and comorbid psychiatric disorders in Croatian combat-related posttraumatic stress disorder patients. *Croatian Medical Journal* 41(2): 179–183.

Jakovljević, M., S. Bjedov., N. Jakšić, and I. Jakovljević. 2020. COVID-19 Pandemia and public and global mental health from the perspective of global health security. *Psychiatry Danubiana* 32(1): 6–14.

Johns Hopkins Coronavirus Resource Center. 2021. Johns Hopkins Coronavirus Resource Center. https://coronavirus.jhu.edu/. Accessed on May 30, 2021.

Kozarić-Kovačić, D., D. K. Hercigonja, and M. Grubišić-Ilić. 2001. Posttraumatic stress disorder and depression in soldiers with combat experiences. *Croatian Medical Journal* 42 (2):165–170.

Kukolja, D., S. Popović., M. Horvat., B. Kovač, and K. Ćosić. 2014. Comparative analysis of emotion estimation methods based on physiological measurements for real-time applications. *International Journal of Human-Computer Studies* 72 (10–11): 717–727.

Longo, D. and J. Drazen. 2016. Data sharing. *New England Journal of Medicine* 374 (3): 276–277.

Nature. 2014. Mental health: The great depression. *Nature* 515 (7526): 179.

Marmar C. R., A. D. Brown., M. Qian., E. Laska., C. Siegel., M. Li., D. Abu-Amara., A. Tsiartas., C. Richey., J. Smith., B. Knoth, and B. Virgyri. 2019. Speech-based markers for posttraumatic stress disorder in US veterans. *Depress Anxiety* 36:607–616.

Mental Health America. 2020. Mental Health Information; COVID-19 and Mental Crisis; The State of Mental Health in America; Prevalence of Mental Illness. https://mhanational.org. Accessed on 15 April 2021.

OECD. 2019. *Health at a glance 2019: OECD indicators.* Paris: OECD Publishing.

Poldrack, R. A. and K. J. Gorgolewski. 2014. Making big data open: Data sharing in neuroimaging. *Nature Neuroscence* 17(11):1510–1517.

Popović, S., M. Horvat, D. Kukolja, B. Dropuljić, and K. Ćosić. 2009. Stress inoculation training supported by physiology-driven adaptive virtual reality stimulation. *Annual Review of CyberTherapy and Telemedicine 7:* 50–54.

Qin, P. and L. Mehlum. 2021. National observation of death by suicide in the first 3 months under COVID-19 pandemic. *Acta Psychiatrica Scandinavica* 143: 92.

Radeloff, D., R. Papsdorf, K. Uhlig, A. Vasilache, K. Putnam, and K. von Klitzing. 2020. Trends in suicide rates during the COVID-19 pandemic restrictions in a major German city.

Saxena S., P. Sharan, and B. Saraceno. 2003. Budget and financing of mental health services: baseline information on 89 countries from WHO's project atlas. *Epidemiology and Psychiatric Sciences* 30(16): 1–5.

Stuckler D., S. Basu, M. Suhrcke, A. Coutts, and M. McKee. 2009. The public health effect of economic crises and alternative policy responses in Europe: An empirical analysis. *Lancet* 374(9686): 315–323.

Tanaka, T. and S. Okamoto. 2021. Increase in suicide following an initial decline during the COVID-19 pandemic in Japan. *Nature Human Behavior* 5: 229–238.

Terlizzi, E. P. and J. S. Schiller. 2021. Estimates of mental health symptomatology, by month of interview: United States, 2019. *National Center for Health Statistics.*

Ueda M., R. Nordström, and T. Matsubayashi. 2020. Suicide and mental health during the COVID-19 pandemic in Japan. *Journal of Public Health. medRxiv preprint doi:* https://www.medrxiv.org/content/10.1101/2020.10.06 .20207530v5. Accessed on 29 May 2021.

Vahratian, A., S. J. Blumberg, E. P. Terlizzi, and J. S. Schiller. 2021. Symptoms of Anxiety or Depressive Disorder and Use of Mental Health Care Among Adults During the COVID-19 Pandemic — United States, August 2020–February 2021. *MMWR Morb Mortal Wkly Rep* 2021;70:490–494.

Wiederhold, B. 2013. *New Tools to Enhance Posttraumatic Stress Disorder Diagnosis and Treatment.* Amsterdam: IOS Press.

World Bank Group. 2020a. *Saving Lives, Scaling-up Impact and Getting Back on Track: World Bank Group COVID-19 Crisis Response Approach Paper.* The World Bank.

World Bank Group. 2020b. *World Bank Group's Operational Response to COVID-19 (coronavirus) — Projects List.* Caribbean: World Bank Group.

World Bank Group. 2021a. *World Bank Approves $750 million Emergency Response Program for Micro, Small, and Medium Enterprises in India.* Caribbean: World Bank Group.

World Bank Group. 2021b. *World Bank Supports Croatia to Weather Difficult Times Caused by COVID-19 Pandemic and Recent Earthquake.* Caribbean: World Bank Group.

World Health Organization. 2004. *Promoting Mental Health: Summary Report.* Geneva: WHO.

World Health Organization. 2016. *Investing in Treatment for Depression and Anxiety Leads to Fourfold Return.* Geneva: WHO.

World Health Organization. 2020. *Fact Sheet on Depression.* Geneva: WHO.

Chapter 10

National Competitiveness and Response to COVID-19: The Political Factor in Mexico and Brazil

Francisco J. Valderrey, Evodio Kaltenecker, and
Miguel A. Montoya

Abstract

Emerging markets face a challenging recovery from the COVID-19 pandemic. Although most nations strive to improve their competitiveness to escape from the economic downturn caused by the pandemic, the results may be different from the expectations of these governments. In this chapter, we analyze competitiveness in Mexico and Brazil. We attempt to go beyond the interpretation of results collected in well-known reports, such as the Global Economic Index, to demonstrate the need for further analysis in those countries where political factors may carry a non-comparable weight. We use the DD-Based 9-Factor Model, which considers the impact of politics in public policymaking. We compare Mexico and Brazil, as both nations are undergoing substantial political change, with personal leadership and geopolitical impact unmatched in the region. International managers should be aware of the impact of strong leadership upon public policy and national competitiveness. Those findings are no novelty in Latin America, a region where the political dimension may turn the table on investors without warning. Indeed, political factors should not be adequately addressed by competitiveness benchmarks in those nations where the rule of man may replace the rule of law.

Keywords: Brazil, competitiveness, COVID-19, Mexico, political risk, public policy

Introduction

The events of 2020 challenged every theoretical framework intended to explain changes in competitiveness, either nationally or globally. Indeed, the appearance of a health and economic crisis of unseen scale caused by the COVID-19 pandemic has demonstrated the limitations of predictive tools for unexpected events of such magnitude. Despite some constraints, the DD-Based 9-Factor Model provides plausible answers, primarily related to human factors and political decisions.

In this chapter, we establish a comparison between two emerging economies, Mexico and Brazil, based on the decisions made by policy-makers and the effects on their economies throughout 2020. These are the two leading countries in Latin America across several dimensions, such as GDP, total population, and international trade. Furthermore, both nations are undergoing substantial political changes, with personal leadership and geopolitical impact unmatched in the region.

The two largest economies in Latin America are pursuing strikingly different strategies. On the one hand, Mexico, led by the leftist president Andrés M. López-Obrador, refused to mitigate the pandemic's economic impact by boosting public spending, which will probably leave the country lagging in terms of economic recovery. On the other hand, Brazil's far-right president, Jair Bolsonaro, an early skeptic of COVID-19, strongly supported cash transfers and emergency bailouts from the federal budget. While the emergency assistance prevented the Brazilian economy from collapsing, it created economic uncertainty due to an unstable debt trajectory, which will probably weaken the currency and increase inflation and interest rates, which are formulas for poor economic performance in the long run.

Indeed, the governments of both nations have drawn international attention due to their unconventional responses to the pandemic. Although decisions from each country's leaders may look peculiar, the responsibility for those decisions is by no means limited to the highest representatives of each nation as the consequences compose a more extended political apparatus. Furthermore, similar policies are often implemented in economies of different political contexts, thus demonstrating the need to include ideological and personal factors into national competitiveness analysis.

In following the DD-Based 9-Factor Model's methodological approach, we first analyze the competitive structure of each country's market, aiming to identify and compare those elements that may result in each nation's strengths and weaknesses. We then look into different sub-factors to evaluate the impacts of decisions made by politicians and bureaucrats, such as general profiling, their legislative activities, and the results of decisions. Additionally, we enhanced the survey results with qualitative information from international institutions and relevant media sources.

We draw our comparative conclusions from the public policies of both administrations related to the pandemic's macroeconomic consequences, mainly looking at the political system, regulation, and arbitrary intervention. Finally, we share our findings and provide a set of recommendations for policymakers and multinational companies (MNCs) dealing with emerging markets.

Mexico and Brazil, Leading Latin America

A comparison of the two largest economies in the region

Undoubtedly, Mexico and Brazil are the leading nations in Latin America. The size of their population and economies dwarf any other in the region. Additionally, over the past few decades, both nations have been providing a reference to other countries in the region's most pressing geopolitical issue, the relationship with the US. Whereas Mexico has maintained a closer relationship with its northern neighbor, Brazil has established closer ties with other South American countries, looking to improve trade and economic relationships with other blocks or countries, such as the EU or China. Recently, though, these longstanding positions are changing due to the ideologies of the leading political parties in Mexico and Brazil. Those geopolitical shifts may profoundly impact Latin America, thus demonstrating the importance of the political factors in those countries where institutions may not be as effective as to limit the impact of strong political influence. Generally speaking, emerging countries face "higher contextual uncertainty in the form of higher corruption and political risk" (Cuervo-Cazurra *et al.*, 2016).

As Table 1 shows, both nations occupy vast territories, although Brazil is more than four times larger than Mexico. In terms of population, Mexico has roughly 127 million people, which is a lot less than the 211 million people living in Brazil. However, in Latin America, no other country has such large population size, which has led to the two nations taking a leading regional role across multiple issues. The population is one of the fundamental factors for market size, although the importance of technological innovation, international trade, and attraction of foreign direct investment may transcend this. The comparison is also favorable to Brazil in terms of GDP with US$1.84 trillion compared to US$1.27 trillion from Mexico. In the end, the difference in population creates a similar GDP per capita, with US$8,717 in Brazil and US$9,946 in Mexico. Such a similar income level is associated with human development, as both nations have an almost identical score in the Human Development Index.

Differences become more apparent in foreign dependency since the Brazilian economy is self-sufficient in many sectors, while the Mexican economy is hugely dependent on the US: the percentage of foreign trade in the Mexican economy (78 percent) is disproportionately higher than that in the Brazilian economy (29 percent). Foreign direct investment does not show a clear difference, but once again, the imbalance becomes very evident in the trade balance, where Brazil outperforms its competitor by

Table 1.   Mexico and Brazil, the leading economies in Latin America.

Criteria	Mexico	Brazil
Territory (thousand km²)	1,964	8,516
Population (million people)	127	211
Urban population (percent)	80.4	86.8
GDP (trillion USD)	1.27	1.84
Per capita GDP (USD)	9,946	8,717
Foreign trade (percent of GDP)	78.2	29
Trade balance (including services) (million USD)	−548	40,782
Foreign direct investment (billion USD)	78	69
Competitiveness	48/141	71/141
Human Development Index (World Rank)	74/188	75/188

Source: Data from Santander Trade, World Bank, Global Competitiveness Report, 2019.

approximately 40 billion dollars. Additionally, Brazil is characterized by diverse trade partners, spreading the risk of imports and exports over China, the US, the EU, and their neighboring countries, thus avoiding Mexico's overdependence on its northern neighbor. This is one of the significant comparative strengths for Brazil, with more of an even distribution in its foreign commerce as well as its membership in Mercosur, the most crucial regional integration initiative in South America. As appealing as Mercosur might be, the reality shows quite a different result, meager trade figures and less innovation and investment among its member states. Mexico, instead, is a member of the recently signed US–Mexico–Canada (USMCA) Treaty (formerly North America Free Trade Area) where, perhaps, the Latin American nation is the weakest link in the chain.

Nevertheless, the trade figures, business opportunities, technological spill-over effects, and innovations coming from this agreement compensate for Mexico's weaker position within the treaty. As a result, even if Mercosur is a more comprehensive integration agreement than the USMCA is, the access to the largest market in the world — that USMCA enables — makes a noticeable difference. This explains the reason why in the Global Competitiveness Index (2019) Mexico ranks higher (48) than Brazil (71) out of the 141 countries measured.

Competitiveness in Mexico and Brazil

Regardless of the differences between the two countries' economies mentioned above, the improvement of competitiveness is crucial for both countries and the entire region. Table 2 shows a more detailed evaluation of the 12 pillars of competitiveness, according to the Global Competitiveness Report, 2019. The pillars can be divided into four categories: enabling environment, human capital, markets, and innovation ecosystems. Each of those categories contains different component factors as follows:

- Enabling environment: *Institutions* (1), *Infrastructure* (2), *ICT adoption* (3), and *Macroeconomic stability* (4).
- Human capital: *Health* (5) and *Skills* (6)
- Markets: *Product market* (7), *Labor market* (8), *Financial system* (9), and *Market size* (10).
- Innovation ecosystems: *Business dynamism* (11) and *Innovation capability* (12).

Table 2.   Mexico and Brazil, comparison of the 12 competitiveness pillars.

Pillar	Mexico		Brazil	
	Score	Rank/141	Score	Rank/141
Institutions	48	98	48	99
Infrastructure	72	54	65	78
ICT adoption	55	74	58	67
Macroeconomic stability	98	41	69	115
Health	82	60	79	75
Skills	58	89	56	96
Product market	58	53	46	124
Labor market	56	96	53	105
Financial system	62	64	65	55
Market size	81	11	81	10
Business dynamism	66	41	60	67
Innovation capability	44	52	49	40

Source: Data from *The Global Competitiveness Report*, 2019.

The differences between Mexico and Brazil are not so evident in the category of "enabling environment," except for in the component, "macroeconomic stability": Mexico offers a much more stable macroeconomic environment. In the second group, "human capital," the differences are few, although they play in favor of Mexico in general. The third group, "markets," demonstrates fundamental differences in the "product market" and "financial system," in which Brazil scores higher. Both countries show the highest performance in the indicator, "market size," in which Brazil ranks within the top 10 performers, leaving Mexico in 11th place. Unfortunately, little credit may be attributed to their governments for such a success since the market size is primarily composed of almost uncontrollable variables such as population. Finally, the fourth group, "Innovation ecosystems," shows somewhat contradicting results, with Mexico evidencing a more dynamic business environment, while Brazil possesses more innovation capability.

Methodology

Many rankings and tools offer a comparison of countries based on their competitiveness; amongst these arguably the Global Competitiveness

Index is not that well known. However, this index is handy when grouping many nations for general comparison (e.g., grouping countries by their development stages). Using the index, it is easy to look at nations, regions, or economic blocks and identify which of the three development stages the country may fall in. Those stages include factor-driven, efficiency-driven, and innovation-driven, as well as the intermediate categories between the stages, called transitions (Ogrean, 2010).

There is also other measures for comparing a country's competitiveness such as the DD-Based 9-Factor Model (Cho and Moon, 2013). Such a model has been evolving, adjusting to the reality among those nations being analyzed. One core quality of this model is that it points out the structural areas the governments should focus on improving. For example, a comparative study between South Korea and Dubai identified strategic areas each country should focus on and showed industries where both economies could induce complementary effects by collaborating (Cho *et al.*, 2016). A similar analysis conducted within a regional area provides valuable hints for identifying trade opportunities that may result in regional agreements supported by the mutually beneficial business exchange. Mexico is a member country of numerous trade blocks, perhaps the member of too many of them. Thus, by using the DD-Based 9-Factor Model, Mexico can make more strategic decisions when the country is looking to expand trade partnerships. In Brazil's case, the methodology is especially useful to evaluate the cost and opportunity for new members to Mercosur.

Table 3 juxtaposes the different factors and sub-factors of the model. For comparison, it is imperative to clarify a division between two sets of factors: physical and human. Factor conditions, demand conditions, related industries, and business context compose the physical factor group, while workers, politicians, bureaucrats, entrepreneurs, and professionals, compose the human factor group. Thus, the model assigns great importance to the human component. The physical factor group presents a broad view of a country, market conditions, natural endowment, industrial framework, infrastructure, communication, finance, technology, innovation, and some other elements to facilitate the understanding of the market's reality. The human factor group highlights the human capital and the country's potential to make proper use of these human resources.

Along with the physical factors, the human factors play an equally important role in the model. Thus, it may fit better when the human factor has a crucial impact on national competitiveness. Such is the case of

Table 3.   Factors and sub-factors of the DD-Based 9-Factor Model.

Factor	Sub-factors
Factor conditions	Energy resources (6), Other resources (13)
Demand conditions	Basic demand (12), Demand quality (8)
Related industries	Transportation (9), Communication (11), Finance (20), Education (10), Science and Technology (9), Cluster development (3), Overall living environment (14)
Business context	Strategy and structure (5), Globalization of local firms (5), Business culture (7) Foreign investment (13)
Workers	Quantity of labor force (10), Quality of labor force (6)
Politicians and bureaucrats	Politicians (7), Bureaucrats (8)
Entrepreneurs	Personal competence (6), Social context (5)
Professionals	Personal competence (7), Social context (6)

Source: Data from Cho and Moon (2008) and Cho *et al.* (2016).

Mexico and Brazil, as also happens in Latin America. The region is often subject to political leadership excessively controlled by individuals or specific population sectors rather than stable institutions. Unfortunately, those two countries and the region are the only few cases experiencing the rule of man vs. the rule of law; many other emerging economies suffer from political instability. Consequently, the DD-Based 9-Factor Model may enhance the analysis from the Global Competitiveness Index.

Some argue that the Global Competitiveness Index incorporates the impact of government and politics into its measure of national competitiveness. "Pillar 1, Institutions," includes Checks and Balances, Transparency, and Future Orientations of Government. These indicators do not include strong leadership in less politically stable markets. In Latin America, personal leadership in the government is critical, both in leading the administration and bureaucrats. Once again, the two Latin American countries under study are by no means the exception to this rule of law. Neither the action of an individual taking the political system to the brink of collapse is limited to the geographical realm of Latin America as the past experience of the US elections has shown.

Table 4 shows the result of the comparison between Mexico and Brazil, based on the methodology of the DD-Based 9-Factor Model, using data for the period 2017–2018 and 2019–2020. Although the data set used for comparison may not be very extensive, it is sufficient to point out yearly changes in some factors. For instance, factor conditions shifted dramatically in both nations, which sends a warning signal about the volatility of those factors. Such warning is not too modest as those factors are mostly related to energy, which is a susceptible sector to foreign investors and local governments. The changes in other factors during these periods were not very evident, although Brazil was generally more prone to variations.

Brazil scores favorably, when compared to Mexico, only on factor conditions. The comparison obtained with the DD-Based 9-Factor Model and those obtained using the Global Competitive Index appears to be consistent. Remarkably, politicians' and bureaucrats' roles may require further analysis, as conditions appear to worsen over time in the two countries. Indeed, the use of the Index of Economic Freedom and the Corruption Perception Index may complement the comparison results obtained using other frameworks (Miller *et al.*, 2019), such as the DD-Based 9-Factor Model.

Consequently, the combined use of the different models may present a clearer picture of impact of political factors on national competitiveness. Those enterprises who saw sizable investments at risk in Mexico or Brazil

Table 4. Mexico and Brazil, a comparison from the DD-Based 9-Factor Model.

Pillar	Mexico		Brazil	
	2017–2018	2019–2020	2017–2018	2019–2020
Factor conditions	21	37	6	19
Demand conditions	37	34	58	42
Related industries	42	43	40	53
Business context	32	45	42	46
Workers	17	13	46	48
Politicians and bureaucrats	53	57	50	60
Entrepreneurs	32	33	41	53
Professionals	31	28	59	53

Source: Data from IPSNC (2020).

(not to mention Venezuela or other Latin American countries), will surely appreciate such information. Finally, it is fundamental to clarify that national competitiveness is not a matter of study limited to economists, rating agencies, international institutions, or researchers. Managers who make business decisions may discover valuable information from competitiveness indicators.

The Cases of Mexico and Brazil

The political dimension is important in Mexico and Brazil. Ideological factors may impact society, often creating a divide among extreme political positions, resulting in political parties being somewhat inconsistent with their proposals to society. Political systems in both nations are rather complicated, mainly due to unresolved historical issues that impact upon contemporary society.

The political system

Throughout its history, Mexico has witnessed longstanding dictatorships, civil unrest, military coups, and civil war. Even today, ideology carries much weight in many relevant decisions. Presently, the country is a democracy organized as a federal republic with 32 states. Although the executive branch probably has a disproportionate weight in the national matters, there is a division of power. Indeed, the power of the President is not comparable to many democratic countries. The President is elected for 6 years, with no reelection, and he acts as the head of the government, the state, and the armed forces. The legislative power is also strong but is divided between the Chamber of Deputies and the Senate, which places a barrier to legislative action. Under the current administration, the leading party, MORENA, holds a majority vote in both chambers, which allows the party's legislative proposals to gain a "rubber stamp" approval. The leftist ideology of their supporters has become appealing to many millions of people.

Before the 2018 election, where Andrés Manuel López Obrador (AMLO) obtained an overwhelming victory, three political parties dominated Mexico's political system. Partido de Acción Nacional (PAN) represented moderate right-wing politics, Catholic followers, and the pro-business interest. Partido de la Revolución Institucional (PRI) is a center-left party that dominated the political scene for most of the last century, although the number of supporters has fallen dramatically (Santander Trade, 2021). Finally, the Partido de la Revolución Democrática (PRD) represented most of the leftist sympathizers until the advent of MORENA. The political scene in Mexico is shaped by profound ideological antagonism, although many critical voices point at the dominance of hidden interests over the accurate representation of the majority of citizens' interests. Corruption has been rampant for many years, and it is unclear whether or not the situation has improved with the new administration. The vicinity and strong dependence upon the US move political standings of people and some political parties, thus adding more dissension elements.

The political dimension is also of utmost importance in Brazil. The country had various experiences ever since its independence from Portugal, going through different forms of government and even experiencing military rule during extended periods. In 1985, democracy was restored, although the results have been disappointing for many years. Many scandals and rampant corruption have led to frequent moments of political change in Brazil until President Cardozo's administration (1994–2002) gave the country much-needed stability. After Cardozo, his leftist opponent Lula da Silva won the election and held power until 2010. His successor Dilma Rousseff gave continuity to his political project until 2016 when she faced impeachment. Following her removal from power, Bolsonaro won the subsequent presidential election in 2018. His policies represent the interests of business and many voices of those on the far right.

Brazil is a presidential federal republic composed of 26 states and a federal district. Despite a degree of autonomy among the states, the federal government holds power in those matters of national concern. The legislative branch is bicameral, with a House of Representatives with 513 members and a Senate with 81 members. Senators are elected for 8 years to provide stability to the National Congress, who are elected by decisions of both institutions (The Brazilian Report, 2017). The judiciary branch has a more loose organization, as state and federal levels both play essential roles. There are several jurisdictions, according to the legal matters of concern.

The response to the pandemic

As happened in many countries, the pandemic went unnoticed in Mexico during the first weeks of January 2020. News from Wuhan caused little concern.

Dramatic pictures came later from Europe, such as trucks delivering bodies to morgues in Italy during the night, drew attention to the severity of the issue. However, most people still felt safe as long as they are away from the centers of the spread of the disease. The official decision from President AMLO was made to minimize the potential consequences of COVID-19. It is unclear if such a strategy was an attempt to ease concerns among the people, as it was later explained, or was due to a complete lack of understanding about the potential damage that the pandemic would cause. Despite being a popular tourist destination, Mexico finally imposed limitations on flights placed from many nations.

As the coronavirus spread to almost every corner of Mexico, the government decided to appoint a pandemic czar, Dr. López-Gatell. While he possessed academic credentials as an epidemiologist, his prominent role was arguably in public relations. He demonstrated incomparable skills in communicating to the nation, explaining how the government controlled the pandemic with simple words and easy-to-read charts. Acting with self-confidence, he presented different scenarios with predictions for the total number of fatalities. His worst-case scenario pointed at 60,000 lives, while the actual numbers far exceeded his most pessimistic scenario. President AMLO supported the pandemic czar regardless of the widespread criticism directed at him. The government was establishing a strategy to combat the COVID-19 pandemic based on the availability of hospital beds. Unfortunately, many experts interpreted such attempts as failures, as COVID-19 patients could not receive sufficient medical care at public hospitals. A vast number of unexplained deaths suggest that many people were sent back home where they died.

The lack of response at the early stage of the spread of the virus eventually developed into an economic lockdown, where companies were forced to close business, and most people had to stay at home. The confinement lasted for over a year, although some activities were permitted depending on the severity of pandemic. Eventually, Dr. López-Gatell established a color code system lifting some restrictions according to each state's health situation. At first, the system worked smoothly, although many exemptions were added to allow some economic activities. Despite the government's complacency and the victorious messages from the government, reality proved a different situation. Mexico reached top positions in the world rankings in terms of the total number of victims, infected people, and other negative ratios. Many high-ranking officials eventually got infected, including President AMLO himself and Dr. López-Gatell.

Regardless of the authorities' official account, Mexico's new normality will show a country suffering from a human disaster and the worst economic crisis in almost a century.

As happened in Mexico, Brazil paid little attention to the warning signs coming first from China, then from Europe, and eventually from the US. Furthermore, the government minimized the potential impact of COVID-19, with President Bolsonaro fighting his crusade against those who believed in the severity of the disease. He portrayed an image of defiance against the pandemic, although he eventually got infected himself. His message runs across a large section of the population and certainly to those enterprises willing to keep business running as usual. Contrary to the Mexican case, he did not rely on one expert, expressing disagreements with medical professionals and state-level authorities. Eventually, the message came across to the population, communicating a sense of self-reliance that made matters worse. In a short time, Brazil emerged as one of the worst affected nations by the pandemic.

As result of the government's response, the spread of COVID-19 in Brazil is expected to reduce support for Bolsonaro significantly. At first, he went through a denial phase, lashing out at local officials who implemented severe lockdowns, accusing them of destroying the country (Friedman, 2020). Later, he adopted a more moderate tone seeking a balance between saving lives and keeping jobs (Aragao, 2020). Whereas AMLO distanced himself from the fight against the disease, Bolsonaro put himself in a leadership position amid the pandemic. From a political standpoint, the Mexican president transferred responsibility for management to someone else. Contrary to this, the Brazilian president probably placed too much political risk on his shoulders.

The importance of vaccines to fight the pandemic and ... political opposition!

Many people blamed China for the pandemic. As a result, decision-makers worldwide were able to escape from severe criticisms. However, the issue of vaccine distribution posed another threat to politicians, as many people believe that the governments are responsible for managing vaccination programs. Once pharmaceutical companies started to announce success on the different trials, millions of people began to put pressure on their governments to get the shot at the earliest possible moment that could be lifesaving. Countries raced to secure the highest possible number of doses, raising prices, and limiting vaccines' availability. Thus they started to compete vigorously against each other, making the import of vaccines a national priority.

In Mexico, the vaccination campaign was a slow process, with confusing information shared to the public and ineffective logistics. During the early stages, the central government maintained absolute control over the entire process, supported by health authorities and the military. Results were disappointing, but AMLO managed to avoid significant criticism. The government put health workers and the elderly as the first group to receive the vaccine. At the time of writing, it is unclear how the situation may evolve in the fight against the pandemic.

In Brazil, many people raised concerns about vaccines. While other Latin American countries such as Argentina, Chile, and Mexico began vaccinating the population, Brazil has not announced its plan to immunize its 210 million population (Leite and Beck, 2021). Bolsonaro reacted only after growing pressure to speed up Brazil's vaccine rollout shows (Reuters, 2021). However, Brazil's president survived the political storm, even if he was seen as one of the few prominent leaders denying the pandemic's severity (Watson, 2020). His public appearances where he shakes hands and refused to wear a facemask sends a clear message that, in Bolsonaro's view, the pandemic is not something to worry about. This paradoxical result can be attributed to the emergency voucher program set up by the Brazilian federal government to counter the economic impact of social distancing and self-isolation on families whose incomes are dependent on service-based informal work. Bolsonaro's emergency program favored millions of Brazilian families, which had their incomes diminished by the pandemic. Therefore, Bolsonaro's popularity among Brazilians comes from two fronts. On the one hand, the financial support boosted his image because many of the recipients of the relief checks saw him as their last resort to save them from hunger. On the other hand, half of the population did blame him for raising the pandemic's death toll due to his insufficient response (Ionova, 2020).

Brazil as Latin America's largest economy decreased the negative impact of coronavirus with a massive stimulus package worth more than 8 percent of GDP, resulting in a contraction of less than 5 percent of its GDP, smaller than other countries in the region (Harris, 2021). As a consequence, Bolsonaro's popularity has increased, but with a hefty price. The so-called "coronavirus voucher" has ballooned Brazil's already unsustainable public spending, fostering worries about the country's economy that is already under immense strain. FitchRatings showed that Brazil's fiscal position deteriorated sharply in 2020 and it has forecasted the general government deficit to rise to 16.7 percent of GDP from around 6.0 percent in 2019. In Fitch's view, the spending cap's flexibilization to accommodate new spending initiatives could undermine the fiscal anchor and damage market confidence. As a consequence, Brazil is far from recovering fiscal credibility (FitchRatings, 2020).

Conclusion

This chapter has looked into the human factors that shape a nation's competitiveness, focusing on political decisions. The impact of policy on the government and political parties and individuals' leadership may be a less exciting topic. Much less the impact of bureaucrats in the decision-making process. Still, we believe that those people and their immediate reality are strong contributing factors to overall competitiveness. This is exceptionally true in emerging countries where man's rule is well rooted in the government.

In Mexico and Brazil, civil servants have limited power. The government officials are by no means equivalent, but bureaucrats have a moderate degree of power in those two countries. In Mexico, the debate is still open to creating a professional career for civil servants, limiting the real power of government officials (Botello, 2020). In Brazil, government officials have become an obstacle to executive power, but it would be challenging to imagine such a group of people acting in the opposite direction to the president (Lima, 2018).

The examples we chose, Mexico and Brazil, are good representatives of emerging nations with stable institutions. Nevertheless, in both countries, political decisions carry much weight, and those decisions often go beyond institutions' power. Governance in many Latin American nations follows different rules from other latitudes. The decisions made by the presidents of Mexico and Brazil had a clear impact on their nations' fate during the pandemic. They followed different paths, although the commonality is that they made their own decisions. In the case of AMLO, he gave the lead role to one of his officials, although he did not cease to keep control over the situation. It is no secret to Mexican citizens that essential decisions need approval from the President. Bolsonaro, by contrast, attempted to include the epidemiologist's input into his decisions, although he openly criticized their views. Their decisions had a positive impact on the health and financial income of many.

Emerging markets usually face a delicate balancing regarding their public finances. Surprisingly, in Mexico, a leftist government made any possible attempt to keep foreign debt under control. To some extent, it succeeded, although at the cost of ignoring the calls for economic assistance from all corners of society. AMLO's obsession with running a tight ship, except for a handful of strategic projects, was a barrier to financial assistance to enterprises and people in need. In the end, unemployment figures skyrocketed, as well as the number of bankruptcies. The final figures for the year 2020 reveal an 8.5 percent decrease in GDP, 2.6 million people losing their jobs, and countless companies going out of business (El País, 2021).

In Brazil, the long-term damage to the public budget created by Bolsonaro's emergency voucher scheme spilled over into the country's currency and inflation-fighting credibility. As the focus of the global economy will shift from recovery from the pandemic to economic fundamentals, Brazil will yet again have to reconcile with its fiscal health, which has taken a hit during the pandemic as the government stepped in to offer support to those impacted by the downturn (Barua and Samaddar, 2020). In any case, the economic situation may improve due to exogenous circumstances. For instance, in 2021, Brazil's economy may benefit from a global economic recovery, primarily due to higher growth in China, Brazil's leading trade partner (Kaltenecker, 2018; Montoya *et al.*, 2019), and a very competitive exchange rate.

There are many lessons to draw from the comparative analyses of how Mexico and Brazil handled the COVID-19 pandemic. One of the lessons is the significance of including human factors in analyzing competitiveness. A second lesson is crucial to international institutions; there is a need to combine different methodologies to obtain a less blurry picture of a country. International institutions provide a framework for the advance of nations and their people; consequently, it is imperative to understand how to evaluate the political leaders and the impact of national competitiveness. As demonstrated through the use of the DD-Based 9-Factor Model, it is paramount to provide a deeper analysis of those political issues that may tilt the balance in favor of a political leader or a party. The model provides general information on significant factors but also elicits relevant details through the sub-factor analysis. Often, those factors are correctly perceived by political analysts, but most of the available methodologies leave little room for including those appreciations into a rigorous analysis. Specifically, in the cases of Mexico and Brazil, a broader approach to political factors may help MNEs and international investors to better assess financial risk and the desired return rate on their projects. The practical consequences include many, as viewed by the handling of the pandemic by both governments, such as unique hurdles to business people in Mexico or the changes in Brazil derived from economic recession. No matter how much information decision-makers may obtain from official statistics or reports from international organizations, it will not be sufficient to evaluate hidden issues invisible to outsiders. In the end, international managers are always in need of more detailed data that will help them to understand their markets better.

References

Aragao, T. 2020. Bolsonaro's erratic behavior on the COVID-19 threat increases his political isolation. https://www.csis.org. Accessed February 10, 2021.

Barua, A. and M. Samaddar. 2020. Brazil: It's still too early to cheer despite a rebound in the third quarter. https://www2.deloitte.com. Accessed February 11, 2021.

Botello, N. A. 2020. The populist transition and the civil sphere in Mexico. In *Populism in the Civil Sphere*. New Jersey: Wiley.

Cho, D. S. and C. Moon. 2013. *International Review of National Competitiveness: A Detailed Analysis of Sources and Rankings*. Massachusetts: Edward Elgar.

Cho, D. S., H. C. Moon, and M. Y. Kim. 2008. Characterizing international competitiveness in international business research: A MASI approach to national competitiveness. *Research in International Business and Finance* 22(2): 175–192.

Cho, D. S., H. C. Moon, and W. Yin. 2016. Enhancing national competitiveness through national cooperation. *Competitiveness Review* 26(5): 482–499.

Cuervo-Cazurra, A., L. Ciravegna, M. Melgarejo, and L. Lopez. 2018. Home country uncertainty and the internationalization-performance relationship: Building an uncertainty management capability. *Journal of World Business* 53(2): 209–221.

El País. 2021. La economía mexicana se desploma un 8,5% en 2020. https://elpais.com/mexico/2021-02-25/la-economia-mexicana-se-desploma-un-85-en-2020.html. Accessed March 13, 2021.

FitchRatings. 2020. Fitch affirms Brazil at 'BB-'; outlook negative. https://www.fitchratings.com/research/sovereigns/fitch-affirms-brazil-at-bb-outlook-negative-18-11-2020. Accessed February 9, 2021.

Friedman, U. 2020. The coronavirus-denial movement now has a leader. www. theatlantic.com. Accessed February 10, 2021.

Harris, B. 2021, January 28. Brazil's economic dilemma: Public debt restraint or sluggish recovery. www.ft.com. Accessed February 9, 2021.

Ionova, A. 2020. Political cost of coronavirus? For Brazil's Bolsonaro, not much. www.csmonitor.com. Accessed February 9, 2021.

IPSNC. 2020. Center for National Competitiveness Research: User guide. www. ipsnc.org. Accessed February 16, 2021.

Kaltenecker, E. 2018. The Chinese century: Is China-Brazil relationship a proxy or new global governance? www.evodiokaltenecker.com. Accessed February 9, 2021.

Leite, J. and M. V. Beck. 2021. Bloomberg.com. www.bloomberg.com. Accessed February 10, 2021.

Lima, Iana Alves de. 2018. The impact of the Brazilian institutional arrangement on political control over bureaucracy. *Cadernos EBAPE.BR* 16(4): 656–666.

Miller, T., A. B. Kim, and J. M. Roberts. 2019. *Index of Economic Freedom*. Washington, DC: The Heritage Foundation. www.heritage.org. Accessed February 10, 2021.

Montoya, M. A., D. Lemus, and E. Kaltenecker. 2019. The geopolitical factor of belt and road initiative in Latin America. *Latin American Journal of Trade Policy* 2(5): 6–21.

Ogrean, C. 2010. National competitiveness between concept and reality. Some insights for Romania. *Revista Economica* 49(1–2): 59–72.

Reuters. 2021. Bolsonaro thanks China for fast-tracking COVID-19 vaccine supplies. www.reuters.com. Accessed February 10, 2021.

Santander Trade. 2021. Economic and political outlay, Brazil. www.santander-trade.com. Accessed March 12, 2021.

Schwab, K. 2019. The global competitiveness report. *World Economic Forum*, 9–14.

The Brazilian Report 2017. So, just how does the Brazilian political system work? http://brazilian.report. Accessed March 10, 2021.

Watson, K. 2020. Coronavirus: Brazil's Bolsonaro in denial and out on a limb. http://www.bbc.com. Accessed February 9, 2021.

World Bank. 2020. *Global Investment Competitiveness Report 2019/2020: Rebuilding Investor Confidence in Times of Uncertainty*. www.worldbank.org. Accessed March 13, 2021.

Chapter 11

National Competitiveness and the Role of the Government: The Case of Korea

Tae-Shin Kwon

Abstract

This study discusses the role governments play in strengthening national competitiveness based on Korea's own experience. Building on national competitiveness policies and past cases involving the Korean Presidential Council on National Competitiveness (PCNC), this study sets forth three crucial elements to explore: policy continuity, social dialogue capabilities, and prohibition from the politicization of the economy. National competitiveness policies are mid-to-long-term policies and entail comprehensive tasks in a socioeconomic context. In addition, highly controversial issues such as labor market flexibility underscore the importance of the government's ability to facilitate social dialogue to build a social consensus advantageous to strengthening national competitiveness, while refraining from politicizing the economy. National competitiveness policies that can be classified as industrial policies often lead to politicizing the economy, which is why public–private cooperation and checks and balances are crucial to deter potential side effects.

Keywords: National competitiveness, policy continuity, social dialogue, politicization of economy

Introduction

Since the rise of globalization in the 1990s, countries around the world have been vying to strengthen their competitiveness as the international environment has become increasingly fierce. The US Competitiveness Policy Council (CPC) — comprising representatives from industry, labor, government, academia, and non-governmental organizations — was launched in 1991 as an independent council of the federal government. The CPC released various policy reports aimed at strengthening the US national development and competitiveness during its six years of operations before its activities came to an end in 1997. Since then, the Council on Competitiveness, a private organization established in 1986 before the CPC, took on the baton. In Ireland, the government established the National Competitiveness Council under the Prime Minister's Office in 1997 and has since been examining the country's competitiveness and drafting an annual competitiveness report entitled "Ireland's Competitiveness Challenge." Aside from these government-established councils, organizations such as Japan's Innovation Network (established in 2013) and Malaysia's MIGHT (founded in 1993) from both public and private sectors evaluate their own countries' competitiveness and conduct research on relevant policies. Furthermore, an international network dedicated to national competitiveness has been formed by the Global Federation of Competitiveness Councils (established in 2010) led by the US CPC.

The reason why these countries established these organizations is that national competitiveness is a pivotal yardstick in measuring a country's present status, which provides insight into what will be of future concern. Reflecting this interest, several international bodies periodically release national competitiveness rankings. After experiencing a slowdown in growth and struggling to find new engines for growth, Korea launched the Presidential Council on National Competitiveness (PCNC) in March 2008 which was co-chaired by President Lee Myung-Bak. The PCNC is a joint public–private council that plays a role to identify agendas for strengthening national competitiveness and making policy recommendations. The PCNC was the first governmental body in Korea to specialize in agenda selection and policy execution to enhance Korea's competitiveness. The strength of power and effectiveness of decision-making of the PCNC was verified by the fact that the President himself was directly involved. However, it was abolished in February 2013 when the new administration took office.

Every country seeks to bolster economic growth and industrial com-petitiveness through various policies. Nonetheless, policy discussions over national competitiveness are required to design and implement policy agendas and policies in a more systematic manner at a pan-governmental level. Since the PCNC was established and operated as an official government body for this very purpose, it is necessary to discuss and evaluate its progress. The author of this chapter served as the vice chairman of the PCNC, which is why the purpose of this study goes beyond simply evaluating its role, to build on the experience of PCNC, and outline the role of government in strengthening national competitiveness.

Although there is no unified definition for national competitiveness, it is generally understood as a country's "holistic" capability to create added value (or economic growth). Here, the word "holistic" is inextrica-bly associated with the role of government explored throughout this study. Individual companies can contribute to the competitiveness of industries through technological innovation and enhanced human resources as well as other factors; still, the government's role is vital in strengthening the holistic competitiveness of a country. This explains why governments launch institutions that can help fortify national competitiveness, and Korea's PCNC is a prime example.

This chapter also compares industrial policies with national competi-tiveness policies to examine the role of governments. Industrial policy is a traditional and typical governmental policy that has been used to enhance production capabilities. National competitiveness policy and industrial policy inevitably coincide, as both policies are geared toward delivering added value. However, national competitiveness policies have a broader definition than industrial policies. Therefore, the government may play a different role when implementing national competitiveness policies and industrial policies. This study clarifies the role of government in strengthening national competitiveness by analyzing the different responsibilities of government in implementing these two types of policies.

The following is an outline of this study. The following section pro-vides an overview and experiences of Korea's PCNC. The third section presents an analysis of the government's role in strengthening national competitiveness. The fourth section details the lessons learned from Korea's own experiences, and the final section consists of a summary and conclusion.

The Presidential Council on National Competitiveness

Background

Lee Myung-Bak was inaugurated in February of 2008 amidst heightened expectations that the new administration would be able to revive the economy. Before he took office, both economic and capital investment growth were markedly in decline (see Figure 1). Given that a decline in investment growth rate tends to paint a grim picture for the economic outlook, getting the economy back on track was a critical concern for the new government. On top of this, declining birth rates and an aging population urged the need for the Korean government to be equipped with economic capabilities that would enable the country to cope these demographic challenges. There was a consensus that the existing input-driven growth model would fall short in overcoming these challenges, which highlighted the urgent need for stronger innovative capabilities. Accordingly, the Lee administration established the PCNC as a presidential advisory body upon its inauguration. Although the PCNC took on an advisory role, the fact that it was established directly under the President represents the administration's steadfast determination to enhance national competitiveness as a core policy agenda.

Organizational structure

The PCNC was organized in such a way that three subcommittees were formed under the Chairman and Vice Chairman. Members of the Council were largely divided into members from the private sector and the government. To enhance the level of expertise and diversity, 35 members from the private sector, consisting of the heads of major economic organizations, heads of major state-run research institutes, and representatives from the labor sector, consumers, press/media, and foreign companies in Korea, were recruited. The Minister of Economy and Finance and the Senior Secretary for Economy for the President served as *ex-officio* members representing government, and the ministers of other departments participated in council meetings when agendas relevant to their ministry were on the table. The three subcommittees were each responsible for regulatory reform, investment promotion, and law and institutional development; every member belonged to a subcommittee aligned with their expertise and representation. Each subcommittee was based on a

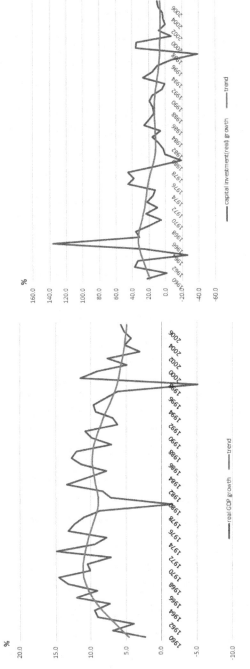

Figure 1. GDP and capital investment growth rate 1960–2007.

Note: The trend curves have been extracted by the author using the Hodrick–Prescott filter method.

Source: Bank of Korea.

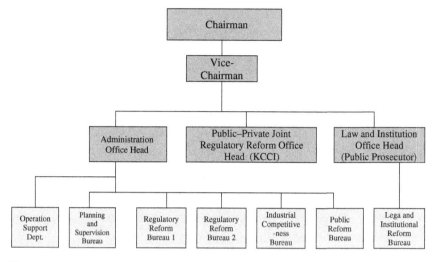

Figure 2.   Organizational chart of the PCNC working group.

Source: Building advanced Korea through reinforcing national competitiveness, PCNC, 2012.

public–private partnership to map out agendas regarding major issues and reform/innovation tasks from each sector, and designed policy improvement plans.

Alongside this, a working group was also organized to support the activities of the PCNC. Since the actual regulatory reform and various policies geared toward strengthening national competitiveness were carried out by the working group, it was in effect the PCNC's core organization. The working group possessed three leaders (Figure 2) — heads of the Administration Office, Public–Private Joint Regulatory Reform Office, and Law and Institution Office — and six bureaus and one department (the Planning and Supervision Bureau, Regulatory Reform Bureau 1, Regulatory Reform Bureau 2, Industrial Competitiveness Bureau, Public Reform Bureau, Legal and Institutional Reform Bureau, and Operational Support Department), where 50 public officials and relevant experts from 19 ministries and institutions were assigned.

The Public–Private Joint Regulatory Reform Office merits additional explanation because it exemplifies the nature of the PCNC. This office was established jointly by the PCNC and Korea Chamber of Commerce and Industry (KCCI) in April 2008 and consisted of a dual leadership system (a high-ranking public official and Vice Chairman of KCCI).

Promptly identifying onsite challenges that impede corporate activities and incorporating remedies into regulatory reform[1] were the main tasks of this office. KCCI represented the private sector because it possessed the most extensive corporate network nationwide, which helped incorporate a wide range of opinions from companies in an effective manner. The office helped establish a bottom-up approach to selecting agendas and identifying regulations at the PCNC, and top-down and bottom-up methods to operations were well coordinated throughout the PCNC.

Operation

The PCNC operated on four major principles. The first principle was systematic and step-by-step sequencing. The PCNC prioritized urgent tasks that could deliver quick results. Complex tasks, namely ones that needed a social consensus and required long-term efforts, were to be carried out once the PCNC reached a certain level of maturity. The second principle was policy implementation in accordance with global standards. Looking into the experiences and institutions of advanced countries with higher national competitiveness helped the PCNC benchmark policies and adapt them to Korea while reducing the need for trial and error. The third principle was a two-track approach. This included pursuing system reform and searching for onsite solutions at the same time so that the PCNC could make recommendations for socioeconomic institutional reform while also paying attention to the difficulties experienced by businesses as well as providing solutions to strengthen the validity of policies. The fourth principle focused on consumer and quality-oriented reform. As described above, the Public–Private Joint Regulatory Reform Office helped to swiftly incorporate onsite solutions into policies, which focused on improving customer satisfaction on the qualitative aspects of policies.

Performance

The PCNC set forth 88 agendas over 30 meetings held from 2008 to 2012 and carried out activities to deliver on these agendas (Table 1). Reforms aimed at increasing national competitiveness were largely

---

[1] For more details about regulatory reform during the Lee Myung-Bak administration, see Ryu (2015).

Table 1.   Meetings held and number of agendas

Year	Total	2008	2009	2010	2011	2012
Meetings held	30	9	10	4	3	4
Agendas	88	24	28	11	10	15

Source: Building advanced Korea through reinforcing national competitiveness, 2012.

divided into three parts: business environment improvement, discovering new growth engines, and social capital accumulation.

Business environment improvement

Regulatory reform was the number one priority for improving Korea's business environment. Although every new administration put forth regulatory reform as a major national agenda, they have failed to deliver substantive changes that would make a real difference for businesses. The PCNC recognized regulatory reform as the foremost task to enhance corporate competitiveness. In addition, regulatory reform was necessary not just for businesses, but also for the public as excessive regulations were a hindrance to people's everyday lives. As such, the PCNC promoted a negative regulatory system, expansion of the regulatory sunset clause, streamlining business startup procedures, and improving restrictive entry barriers. Strengthening the competitiveness of small and medium enterprises (SMEs) that account for the majority of businesses and employment was also an urgent task. Therefore, a shift was made from protection-oriented policies to policies that promote innovation among SMEs.

The PCNC also reformed regulations on land use, which helped provide more space for factories. Furthermore, overall improvements were made to the national land management system, such as easing regulations in the Seoul metropolitan area, simplifying licensing procedures for industrial complexes, and revamping zoning systems. In pursuing the above policies, the PCNC placed great emphasis on public–private partnerships. In this effort, the Public–Private Joint Regulatory Reform Office went on local site visits, held meetings with industrial representatives, and gathered recommendations from economic organizations.

New growth engines

Persistent low growth underscored the importance of identifying new growth engines in sectors outside of Korea's key manufacturing industry. The country was in desperate need of new growth industries to recover from the Global Financial Crisis and secure market share in the post-crisis world. Therefore, fostering new growth engines was a key task for the PCNC. It endeavored to strengthen competitiveness in new frontiers, such as engineering, beauty, franchise, and meeting, incentives, convention, and exhibition (MICE) industries. Additional focus was on strengthening the competitiveness of legacy industries, such as construction, tourism, and banking, which had significant room for improvement. In this case, supplying companies with talented human resources was an essential task in promoting growth. The PCNC therefore made efforts to attract talented foreign workers, foster skilled manpower in Korea, and establish an education system that provides a balance between study and work.

Social capital accumulation

There is ample empirical evidence that social capital is an essential contributor to a country's overall productivity.[2] Therefore, the PCNC came up with strategies to strengthen law and order, promote a law-abiding culture for assemblies and demonstrations, and rationalized administrative penalties and sanctions. Various institutional improvements were also made to enhance the quality of administrative practices. The online civil petition service was introduced to make it more convenient for petitioners and the Council to voice their needs, successfully reducing the administrative workload of the personal authentication by 60 percent. The PCNC believed that making civil petitions more convenient was an important part of accumulating social capital. As such, the PCNC made institutional improvements to advance the transportation system, most notably by introducing the Intelligent Transportation System (ITS), improving the transportation operation system, and making road projects more efficient (Table 2).

---

[2]The relevant studies include Knack and Keefer (1997), Giacinto and Nuzzo (2006), Dettori *et al.* (2012), Ng *et al.* (2015), Jalles and Tavares (2015), and Bengoa *et al.* (2017).

Table 2.   Major projects of PCNC (2008–2012)

Theme	Detailed tasks
Improving the business environment through regulatory reform	• Improving industrial complex regulations • Streamlining business startup procedures • SME regulatory reform • Expanding the regulatory sunset clause • Improving competition-restrictive entry barriers • Improving technical regulations • Introducing the negative regulatory system • Improving the behavior and awareness of public officials • Improving regulations and systems for job creation • Reorganizing subordinate laws to achieve 5 percent economic growth
Discovering new growth engines for sustainable growth	• Attracting talented human resources from across the world • Revitalizing free economic zones • Strengthening the competitiveness of the following industries: finance, tourism industry, agriculture, construction, franchise, beauty, MICE, engineering • Improving the nationality system • Innovating SME productivity • Establishing a market-friendly vocational competency development system • Establishing an education system that promotes balance between study and work
Accumulating social capital and promoting public benefits	• Promote a sophisticated culture for assemblies and demonstrations to establish law and order • Rationalization of administrative penalties and sanctions • Rationalization of fines and penalties • Reforming public institutions operations • Efficient use of land • Advancement of online civil petition administration • Advancement of transportation operation systems • Advancement of basic administrative infrastructure • Establishment of the ITS • Advancement of the national standard certification system • Improvement of transportation convenience and safety

Evaluation

Although it is difficult to quantify the performance of the PCNC, we can still deduce a rough evaluation of its performance during the period 2008–2012 based on the rankings released by organizations that evaluate competitiveness (Figure 3).[3] According to IMD World Competitiveness Rankings (IMD World Competitiveness Yearbook, 2007–2020), Korea climbed up to 22nd in 2012 from 31st in 2007, the year before the PCNC was launched. According to the World Economic Forum (WEF) Global Competitiveness Report, 2007–2019, Korea fell from 11th in 2007 to 19th in 2012. The fluctuating rankings of Korea's national competitiveness provided by these two organizations is due to the employment of different evaluation methods and standards. Therefore, looking at the overall trends will provide a more accurate picture than solely relying on the evaluation provided by each institution.

If we extend the evaluation period from 2007 up to the latest year, IMD's rating for Korea improved from 31st in 2007 to 23rd in 2019 while for the WEF, its rankings fell from 11th in 2007 to 13th in 2019. On the other hand, if we draw a linear curve for the changes year on year, the trendlines of the results for both institutions curves upward showing an increasing trend in ranking numbers. In other words, the national competitiveness ranking shows a downward trend. The pattern over the past decade indicates that Korea's national competitiveness has not improved in the least. In conclusion, the effect of the PCNC on national competitiveness ranking during its operation is unclear, but considering the long-term ranking trend, it would be difficult to conclude that the Korean government's efforts to strengthen national competitiveness were successful.

Although the PCNC's policy agendas were all meaningful, efforts made to generate social capital should be held in high regard. Social capital was never before set as an official national policy agenda. The PCNC recognized social capital as an important national competitiveness factor, drawing up and pushing forward concrete policy agendas and tasks. Due to the nature of social capital, it takes a long time to improve such a factor. Therefore, it is unfortunate that the PCNC was dismantled and its efforts to generate social capital were cut short. However, PCNC's attempt to set social capital as an important axis of national competitiveness for the first time in the history of the Korean economy and make pan-governmental efforts merits applause.

---

[3]There is criticism that the ratings of major competitiveness evaluation institutions, International Institute for Management Development (IMD) and World Economic Forum (WEF), are subjective as these are based on the data obtained from questionnaires. Therefore, data provided by these institutions are merely a part of the wider range of information taken into consideration.

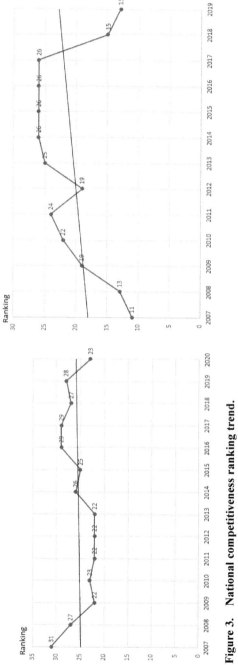

Figure 3.   National competitiveness ranking trend.

Note: The solid line indicates a linear trend.

Source: Annual competitiveness reports released by IMD and WEF.

National Competitiveness and the Role of the Government

Industrial policy characteristics of national competitiveness policy

Return of industrial policy

The most fundamental goal of strengthening national competitiveness is to enhance a country's ability to create added economic value from various industries. Traditionally, industrial policies were implemented to this end and encompass a government's various explicit and implicit support for policies aimed at promoting the growth of competitiveness in specific industries. Most industrial and corporate support policies, such as subsidies, financial support, and human resources development, can be classified as industrial policies. In terms of fostering industries and strengthening industrial competitiveness, industrial policy and national competitiveness policy share almost identical values.

Industrial policy was once relegated as a peripheral economic policy amid the growth of interest in neoliberalism. Criticism about the effectiveness of industrial policy has been raised by academia and political circles in major countries as support for international organizations and strong government intervention in most developing countries such as in South America and Africa failed to make transition into the stages of economic development. In addition, since the so-called "Washington Consensus" gained broader appeal in economics and policymaking from the 1990s, industrial policy has been degraded into an outdated policy tool. The waning validity of industrial policies as they were increasingly seen as potential violations to the growing number of trade agreements between countries contributed to this negative outlook. In such an environment, the successful economic development in some East Asian countries such as Korea and Taiwan were regarded as anomalies that resulted from development under an autocratic regime.

Meanwhile, innovation-driven growth came to the fore due to protracted low growth, particularly in developed countries, and declining productivity owing to demographic changes such as an aging society. The spread of the international division of labor due to globalization placed low-value-added product manufacturing in developing countries and in effect made it difficult for developed countries to achieve growth through input-driven growth models. As a result, the governments of major countries attempted to support high-value-added creation through innovation. In addition, increased focus on global climate action and environmental regulations highlighted the need for carbon emissions reduction, low-carbon technology, clean energy, environmental R&D, and other "green" industrial policies, where the government plays an important role.

China's commitment to cutting-edge technology sectors also triggered other countries to competitively promote industrial policies. As China is rapidly catching up with developed countries in legacy industries, the Chinese government's heavy investment in the high-tech industries (new materials, renewable energy, cutting-edge medicine, and other advanced sectors) has led to fierce competition among countries to gain market dominance. Furthermore, the state interventions based on industrial policies were a natural course of action following the decline in liberal economic policies and increasing stimulus packages introduced by governments after the Global Financial Crisis.

New industrial policy and national competitiveness policy

After industrial policy started to gain attention again, interest in national competitiveness began to rise in earnest. While industrial policies were once criticized for choosing winners, they have now been rebranded. The nature of industrial policies have changed from supporting a select few companies (winners), which caused controversy over preferential treatment and back-scratching alliances between government and businesses in the past, to policies aimed at enhancing industrial innovation and productivity. Scholars such as Rodrik (2004, 2008) who advocated for new industrial policies emphasized that new approaches can help reduce or share risk borne by the enterprises in the innovation process. He further asserts that "competition" is an important element of policy and that industrial policies should not restrict competition. New industrial policy is in line with the strengthening of national competitiveness as it emphasizes innovation and competition, which is different from the old industrial policy paradigm of protecting infant industries. When we scale up the range of industrial policy from specific industries to the entire country, it becomes a national competitiveness policy. Due to prolonged low growth and the rise of China, the discovery of new growth engines through industrial policy rose as a national task in developed countries, which resulted in fierce competition between countries over new industries. In this process, various countries have naturally recognized the importance of national competitiveness, and policy efforts to strengthen such efforts have spread.

Role of the government: National competitiveness policy vs. industrial policy

Although the national competitiveness policy holds similarity with the industrial policy, it tends to encompasses a broader scope. Due to this contrast between the two approaches, the government's role is different for each one. National competitiveness includes not only the competitiveness of individual economic units such as industries and companies but also socioeconomic competitiveness. As such, the PCNC made efforts to accumulate social capital. As the term, social capital may sound quite broad, the government's role in accumulating social capital is inevitably extensive. Promoting fair law enforcement, efficiency and stability of laws and institutions, transparency of policy-making and implementation, and other diverse socioeconomic factors related to economic performance are all targets for national competitiveness policies. Since socioeconomic elements are not generally covered by industrial policy, in terms of the role of the government, national competitiveness policy is broader than industrial policy. At the same time, national competitiveness policies aimed at enhancing socioeconomic competitiveness are intrinsically much more obscure than industrial policies. For example, national competitiveness policies for enhancing the efficiency and stability of laws and institutions are more difficult to flesh out and standardize than industrial policies, which are geared toward improving the productivity of specific industries. Therefore, national competitiveness policy can be highly influenced by the political, cultural, and social context of a country and the ideological characteristics of the government at a specific time.

From the perspective of national competitiveness, specific industrial policies may not be consistent with enhancing national competitiveness. For example, considering technological developments and economic structural changes, specific industrial policies may hinder structural change in industries where it is necessary. The government needs to make a call in favor of national competitiveness if an industrial policy does not help to improve national competitiveness from a long-term perspective. However, due to the limitations set by a democratic system, the government is more likely to choose industrial policies that bring about political benefits — a more populist option — over the policies enhancing national competitiveness in the long run. Therefore, the performance of a national competitiveness policy depends on how effectively a country's government operates for the benefit of the country in the long term. In other words, the success of national competitiveness policies is determined by the government's own competitiveness. This means that the competitiveness of the government should be maintained regardless of political ideologies or dominance of a single political party. Even if the government changes through elections, aspects such as efficiency and dedication to innovation should remain unchanged for a government to stay competitive.

Lessons from Korea's Experience

Each country employs a wide range of national competitiveness policies, although they may not explicitly set national competitiveness as a policy agenda. However, increasing national competitiveness in a short period is a challenge. This chapter intends to outline the lessons learned from the author's field experience at the PCNC and policies related to national competitiveness. The lessons presented here encompass areas of improvement for the government in carrying out the national competitiveness policy, and successful elements that can be applied universally in national competitiveness policies.

Policy continuity

Upgrading national competitiveness in an increasingly competitive world is not easy and requires a lot of time. The search for new growth engines and social capital accumulation that the PCNC focused on was mid-to-long-term tasks. For mid-to-long-term tasks to produce results, policy continuity is necessary. Several factors, such as competitive companies and human resources that make up the industry and a system that can support corporate growth, are required for an industry to become a growth engine. This does not happen overnight. New growth engines can be obtained only when the vision, detailed plans that fit the vision, and execution are sustained for a considerable time. The same is true for social capital accumulation. Since social capital is path-dependent, it is difficult to deliver tangible results in a short time. Therefore, a mid- and long-term outlook is essential to accumulate social capital.

One of the challenges though is the fact that presidents serve a five-year term in Korea, resulting in policy discontinuity. Even if the ruling political party wins the presidential election (thus no change in regime), in many cases, there is still disconnection in the practice of many policies. For example, although the ruling party won the presidential election in 2013, the PCNC was still abolished. Since its closure, policies explicitly aimed at strengthening national competitiveness have been non-existent. Of course, this does not mean that national competitiveness policies cannot be carried out without an organization like the PCNC. However, individual and decentralized policies that are not grounded in a systematic and comprehensive framework are unlikely to deliver tangible outcomes. In particular, since national competitiveness policies generally require pan-governmental cooperation, the government should promote integration and coordination in policy implementation.

The PCNC was launched as a result of President Lee's strong interest in national competitiveness. To move forward with different interests and integrate and coordinate on a variety of different policies, government officials must recognize that strengthening national competitiveness is a national agenda strongly promoted by the head of state. The Hartz Reform, promoted by the former German Chancellor Gerhard Schroeder and the treatment of the "British disease" by the UK Prime Minister Margaret Thatcher, shows that the role of the leader is critical for the success of national reform. Even if power changes hands, if the head of national policy recognizes national competitiveness as an important policy agenda and has the will to implement relevant policies, a pan-governmental organization such as the PCNC can be maintained and policy continuity can be achieved.

Meanwhile, for mid-to-long-term policies, performance should be evaluated over a certain period of time in the implementation process, based on which the content and direction of the policy should be modified and managed. However, the lack of policy continuity makes evaluation and management of policy performance difficult. The Korean government has a strong tendency to overlook the significance of policy continuity. There have been many cases where each new government seeks to repromote national agendas from the point of ground zero, which hinders mid-to-long-term policies from delivering results. Given this context, it is very important to ensure continuity of policies for mid-to-long-term national tasks such as national competitiveness policies.

Social dialogue capabilities

Labor has been pointed out by foreign investors as the weak link in the Korean economy. Due to the country's labor regulations such as excessive protection of regular workers and uncooperative labor-management relations, the rigidity in the Korean labor market has significantly degraded its national competitiveness. This in turn means that the Korean government has failed to alleviate the severe rigidity of the labor market. Such a condition reinforces the duality in the labor market, which is a major cause of employment instability and the declining number of jobs. The high youth unemployment rate in Korea and the large income gap between non-regular and regular workers are also closely related to the exacerbated dual structure of the labor market.

According to the WEF's 2019 Global Competitiveness Report (GCR), which provides a relatively detailed classification of the elements that constitute national competitiveness, Korea's labor market flexibility is ranked 97th; Korea ranks around 100th in most of the subcategories (Table 3). In particular, cooperation in labor–employer relations is among the lowest in the world, ranking 130th among 141 countries. Moreover, the problem is that Korea's labor market flexibility is showing no signs of improvement. Comparing 2008, 2012, and 2019, respectively, the rankings in the detailed areas of labor market flexibility are becoming worse. Since the PCNC was launched in 2008, the rankings for labor–management relations have remained the lowest among the other countries measured. Flexibility in employment and layoff processes has deteriorated significantly compared to 2008. The ranking in this category in 2008 was 45th (134 countries in total), but the rankings plunged by more than double to 109th in 2012 (144 countries in total) and 102nd in 2019 (141 countries in total).

Table 3. Korea's WEF labor market flexibility ranking

	2008	2012	2019
Labor market flexibility	Ranking/134th	Ranking/144th	Ranking/141st
Redundancy costs	108	117	116
Hiring and firing practices	45	109	102
Cooperation in labor–employer relations	95	129	130
The flexibility of wage determination	43	63	84

Source: Annual global competitiveness reports, 2019.

The issue of labor market inflexibility was not addressed by the PCNC as a major agenda. It was one of the most important factors in strengthening national competitiveness, but it was not adopted as a priority task due to the complexity and difficulty of solving the problem. However, since a rigid labor market is an endemic problem plaguing the Korean economy, some previous governments have attempted to carry out reform. In particular, the previous Park Geun-hye administration attempted to reform the labor market, but the results were unsuccessful. Labor market reforms, especially those aimed at increasing labor flexibility, require the consent of large groups of stakeholders, such as workers and labor unions. In particular, when sizeable and formidable militant labor unions and left-leaning political forces work in solidarity, it is almost impossible to force the labor markets to be flexible. After all, since workers and labor unions cannot easily agree on labor market reform, consensus must be reached through constant negotiation and communication.

Meanwhile, in the process of reforming the labor market, the government should be able to exert social pressure on the labor unions while exerting an ability of persuasion at the same time. Applying social pressure is possible only when there is a sufficient social consensus that labor market reform is ultimately necessary for the Korean economy and also for the benefit of the workers. Here, labor market flexibility is feasible only through dialogue and persuasion with the labor community based on a social consensus about labor market reform. Therefore, the government must actively carry out social dialogue to create a consensus.

Based on the current status of the Korean labor market flexibility, it is obvious that efforts to promote social dialogue were not successful. Here, social dialogue is not simply communication to understand the other party's position, but social communication that helps enhance national competitiveness. In other words, the ability to facilitate social dialogue to strengthen national competitiveness refers to the "government's capability to form public opinion in a direction conducive to strengthening national competitiveness." A government that is better at leading social dialogue holds a better capability to solve problems involving complex interests and strengthen national competitiveness. In addition, the higher the social dialogue ability of the government is, the higher the level of social capital accumulation there will be, and vice versa. This means that these two aspects are complementary and can form a positive cycle.

Korea lacks social dialogue capabilities, as is attested by its 54th ranking in social cohesion based on IMD evaluations (as of 2019) and 78th ranking in social capital according to WEF (as of 2019). This ranking is considerably lower than the overall national competitiveness ranking. The PCNC also made a number of institutional improvements to enhance social capital, but it did not succeed in equipping the government with social dialogue skills to build a consensus on issues with inherent conflict. The ability of the government to actively communicate with stakeholders and reduce disagreements to reach consensus in a direction favoring the future of the country does not necessarily highlight the ability of a specific individual. It is the ability of the social system. Of course, an outstanding political leader can do the job better, but no matter which political leader (or government) takes office, the capacity for social dialogue is determined by its ability to systematically resolve conflicts. This social dialogue ability is an ability that is embedded in the system of a society, and therefore it takes time to improve this ability. This, in turn, is linked to the aforementioned problem of policy continuity.

Politicization of economy

The government needs to avoid the politicization of the economy. In other words, the economy should be managed through economic logic (or market logic), not political logic. However, despite the numerous side effects from the politicization of the economy, this trend is quite a common phenomenon among governments. Reinforcing national competitiveness means pursuing efficiency and innovation, but the politicization of the economy indicates a complete opposite approach. In principle, the governments of democratic countries do not accept economic politicization. The primary intention of the government, of course, is to increase national competitiveness by operating the economy based on economic logic to produce better results. Nonetheless, sometimes the government tends to politicize the economy, especially during election periods or in times of political difficulties.

Since strengthening national competitiveness is a mid-to-long-term task, the government will face the temptation to politicize the economy as they pursue these policies and will sometimes act on this temptation. While governments advocate productivity improvement and innovation as a national agenda, sometimes, the details of individual policies do not align with what they advocate. This occurs frequently while promoting industrial policies. For example, despite advocating for advancing the retail and distribution industry, the government will regulate operations of large-scale retail and distribution businesses to protect small business owners, and despite advocating for financial innovation, the government will restrict the autonomy of financial institutions. These cases are frequently observed in the Korean economy.

For national competitiveness policies to produce the desired outcomes, the politicization of the economy should be kept to a minimum level. In fact, such an intervention should be considered as one of the major reasons for the failure in strengthening national competitiveness. When it becomes widespread, economic agents' confidence in government policies will fade. At the same time, the lack of trust in the government damages social capital. In the end, the politicization of the economy itself is a drawback on national competitiveness, but the loss of social capital and trust in the government inflicts deeper damage to national competitiveness. Public–private organizations such as the PCNC can help ease this problem. Public–private partnerships can keep government policies that promote politicization of the economy in check while creating synergies between government policies.

Conclusion

Modern global competition is not just between companies. It is about the ability of the state to support competition between companies, that is, competition between countries based on national competitiveness. In order to reinforce the various elements of national competitiveness in a systematic and efficient way, governments and private sectors in various countries have established and operated institutions. In Korea, the PCNC under the President's Office was assigned this responsibility from 2008 to 2013. Even though strengthening national competitiveness is a mid-to-long-term task, the PCNC was soon scrapped by the successor government. Thereafter, a number of national tasks for economic growth were promoted, but there was never a comprehensive and systematic policy initiative under the single theme of national competitiveness. Although the results announced by international competitiveness rating institutions do not represent an absolute value, the long-term trend of Korea's national competitiveness rankings over the past decade — despite the recent rise in rankings — shows that various efforts to strengthen national competitiveness have not been very successful. The reasons behind this failure are largely three-fold: lack of policy continuity, lack of social dialogue capabilities, and politicization of the economy. These are the lessons learned from Korea's experience, are universally applicable to other countries as well.

Policy continuity is critical for mid-to-long-term tasks such as strengthening national competitiveness. The PCNC's abolishment is a prime example of the lack of policy continuity in pursuit of national competitiveness policies. Due to the intrinsic nature of mid-to-long-term tasks, policy continuity is essential for national competitiveness. This continuity is even more vital when the national competitiveness policy is a comprehensive pan-governmental national agenda. The lack of continuity is a problem not just for national competitiveness policies but also for many other policies. Resolving this has been one of the long-standing challenges of the Korean government.

The ability to communicate socially to elicit a consensus is an important element of a competitive government in solving endemic problems that erode national competitiveness. While labor market rigidity hinders Korea's national competitiveness, it is still showing little signs of improvement. Unlike problems such as regulatory reform that the government can solve through sheer will, labor market policies require social consensus because there are significant stakeholders, such as workers and their unions, who are opposed to increasing flexibility in the labor market. Therefore, the government must be capable of communicating with these stakeholders to produce a social consensus. Such a capability requires considerable time to be established. In our context of a discussion, the social dialogue capability refers to the government's ability to draw a social consensus in the direction of strengthening national competitiveness. In other words, the government should be able to persuade opponents by forming a social opinion in a direction to pursue stronger national competitiveness. In this respect, the Korean government has thus far failed to demonstrate an ability to draw a social consensus from the labor market in the direction of strengthening national competitiveness. The more rigid the labor market becomes, the more important this ability will be in assessing the competence of the government.

The politicization of the economy is not limited to the policy of national competitiveness. It is one of the drawbacks of a modern democracy and it is difficult for political leaders to resist the temptation of politicizing the economy because of the potential political gains. Although the intensity and frequency of the politicization of the economy varies across countries, the general trend is that more conscientious and competent governments are, the less the tendency to politicize the economy. In connection with national competitiveness, the more national competitiveness policies fall under the category of industrial policies, the more likely the economy will be politicized. Industrial policy is an area where government support is inevitable, however, such support can be designed for political gains, contrary to the fundamental purpose of industrial policy. In the past, industrial policies in underdeveloped countries failed because of this very reason which ultimately led to skepticism about industrial policy. Therefore, an organization dedicated to national competitiveness policies that can promote public–private partnerships and keep governments in check is needed. If a public–private organization that receives policy support from the government but allows the private sector to check the possible political motive of the government, can promote national competitiveness policies with a mid-to-long-term perspective, and thus the politicization of the economy can be significantly deterred.

These three are factors that must be improved in the Korean government's pursuit of national competitiveness policies. The core areas of focus for national competitiveness are labor reform and the fourth industrial revolution. First of all, labor reform is a necessary task to strengthen Korea's national competitiveness. The labor environment and labor-management issues have consistently been pointed out as the biggest problem in numerous surveys conducted by foreign companies about Korea's economic environment. Making these matters worse, there have been no signs of improvement, while the politicization of the economy has exacerbated the dual structure in the labor market. Labor market dualism not only intensifies rigidity in the labor market but also contributes to unemployment. Ultimately, labor reform is urgently needed to solve the problem of job creation as well. In this respect, Korea needs to benchmark Germany's success in increasing employment through labor reform, known as the Hartz Reform (2003–2005).

If labor reform is vital for strengthening institutional competitiveness, the fourth industrial revolution is crucial for enhancing industrial competitiveness. In particular, various types of regulatory reform catering toward the fourth industrial revolution are needed, but human resource development is also an important task. For example, artificial intelligence is at the core of the fourth industrial revolution, but in Korea, artificial intelligence experts are in short supply. Since artificial intelligence is now applied across almost all industries, the success of the fourth industrial revolution relies heavily on relevant experts. It is worth recalling that while promoting heavy and chemical industrial policies in the 1970s, significant investments were made to foster technical and skilled manpower in these industries. As we face transformative changes in science and technology with the fourth industrial revolution, we need to reform educational systems and human resource development programs to supply the manpower needed.

References

Bengoa, M., V. M.-S. Román, and P. Pérez. 2017. Do R&D activities matter for productivity? A regional spatial approach assessing the role of human and social capital. *Economic Modelling* 60: 448–461.

Dettori, B., E. Marrocu, and R. Paci. 2012. Total factor productivity, intangible assets and spatial dependence in the European regions. *Regional Studies* 46: 1401–1416.

Giacinto, V. D. and G. Nuzzo. 2006. Explaining labour productivity differentials across Italian regions: The role of socio-economic structure and factor endowments. *Papers in Regional Science* 85: 299–320.

International Institute of Management Development. *IMD World Competitiveness Yearbook, 2007–2020.* Lausanne: International Institute of Management Development.

Jalles, J. T. and J. Tavares. 2015. Trade, scale or social capital? Technological progress in poor and rich countries. *Journal of International Trade & Economic Development* 24: 767–808.

Knack, S. and P. Keefer. 1997. Does social capital have an economic payoff? A cross-country investigation. *Quarterly Journal of Economics* 112: 1251–1288.

Ng, A., M. H. Ibrahim, and A. Mirakhor. 2015. Ethical behavior and trustworthiness in the stock market-growth nexus. *Research in International Business & Finance* 33: 44–58.

Presidential Council on National Competitiveness. 2012. *Building Advanced Korea through Reinforcing National Competitiveness* (in Korean). Seoul: Presidential Council on National Competitiveness.

Rodrik, D. 2004. *Industrial Policy for the Twenty-First Century. Faculty Research Working Paper Series RWP04-047.* Cambridge: Harvard University.

Rodrik, D. 2008. Industrial policy: Don't ask why, ask how. *Middle East Development Journal* Demo Issue: 1–29.

Ryu, C.R. 2015. *Pharmacon of Regulations* (in Korean). Goyang: Daeyoung Munhwasa Book Publishing.

World Economic Forum. *The Global Competitiveness Report, 2007–2019.* Geneva: World Economic Forum.

Chapter 12

Trends in Competitiveness of India: Exploring the Role of Start-Ups and Entrepreneurial Ecosystem

Kirankumar S. Momaya

Abstract

India has climbed several steps on the ladder of competitiveness throughout its developmental journey in its post-independence era. The journey
toward the next stage can be very different and demand thinking beyond
a factor-driven attitude to address complex problems. Start-ups can
play a very important role to address the relevant parts of such issues.
Focusing on south and west India, we provide examples of start-ups or
ventures that are building capabilities to scale-up. The key objective
of this chapter is to provide perspectives and identify some examples
of ventures that may be able to leverage emerging technologies such
as artificial intelligence (AI) for competitiveness. We adapt qualitative
analysis and use a variety of data sources to identify trends and patterns
to complement longitudinal insights about competitiveness. With several
innovative ideas, India is seeking to help many countries. Focal firms or
institutes can play a major role if they can adapt fast, and learn to leverage discontinuities such as corona crisis to enhance strategic flexibility
and build differentiating capabilities. We conclude with implications for
leaders in politics and business, as well as topics for further studies.

Keywords: Country competitiveness ranking, start-up ecosystem, entrepreneurial ventures, technology-based innovation, stages of competitiveness, sustainability of emerging industries, responsible AI

Introduction

India has climbed several steps on the ladder of competitiveness through-out its developmental journey in its post-independence era. With a long rich heritage, India is emerging rapidly as an entrepreneurial greener country with a tremendous untapped potential for development and also expanding its contribution to the world business, investment, innovation, trade, and development. A perspective on the world economy (Maddison, 2003) shows that India had been contributing 32.9 percent of the world's GDP at the beginning of the common era. Since gaining its independence in 1947, India has advanced significantly on several fronts — from agri-culture, dairy, and infrastructure to services, software, and space explora-tion. In this context, competitiveness — a multidimensional concept having relevance across levels (country, industry, and firm) — is becoming important for a large country with a population of more than 1.36 billion. A growing range of modern industries, a multitude of services, and start-ups that drive job creation can become major strengths to advance the economy if the aspects of competitiveness are better understood. Country competitiveness, which is often measured on more than 100 criteria, can provide a comprehensive picture of the resources and capabilities of a country and help with important policy decisions.

Among multiple reports on a country's competitiveness, the National Competitiveness Report (IPS–NCR, henceforth referred to as NCR) has been providing a more comprehensive framework for enhancing national competitiveness compared to the World Competitiveness Yearbook (WCY). A glimpse of the trends in the competitiveness rankings of India and those of selected large countries (Table 1) indicates a significant jump for India, despite a very large population base and many other constraints. India has been slowly, but steadily climbing to the top 20 ranking of the NCR. This is in contrast to its performance in other reports, where its rankings fluctuate widely. A strong theoretical basis, as well as possibili-ties of applying various analytical tools, enhances the utility of NCR.

The journey toward the next stages of competitiveness can be quite different and demand thinking that goes beyond a factor-driven mindset

Table 1. Trends in competitiveness ranking of India and some selected countries in 2000s.

Country	Population density (per km2) 2010	Per capita GNI/GDP (US$) 2018	Per capita GNI/GDP (US$) 2009	Ranks as per WCY 2020	Ranks as per WCY 2018	Ranking as per National Competitiveness Research, year of survey 2012	2009	2008	2005	2003
USA	33	62,850	46,381	10	7	4	2	1	1	1
Canada	4	44,860	39,669	8	1	2	3	4	2	8
Australia	3	53,190	45,587	18	9	7	7	10	15	14
Japan	336	41,340	39,731	34	18	23	20	16	19	30
Korea	485	30,600	17,074	23	25	18	23	22	22	27
China	141	9,470	3,678	20	13	15	17	20	24	31
India	369	2,020	1,031	43	22	21	28	33	47	42
Out of no. of countries				63	72	65	67	67	66	56

Notes: 1. WCY = World Competitiveness Yearbook. 2. Per capita 2009 numbers are nominal GDP.

Sources: Developed based on data from National Competitiveness Research (various years), WCY (2020), and data from World Bank (various years).

to one that is focused on innovation-based capabilities. Based on the driving factors of development, a typology of country development was proposed which includes — factor condition-based, investment-based, and innovation-based conditions (Momaya, 2011). Most emerging countries remain trapped in the factor condition-based stage. Major infrastructure investment that countries such as India are doing can be viewed as seeking to break out from factor-driven stage of competitiveness in the investment-based phase. But this demands massive domestic savings or international borrowings with associated risks. The innovation-based stage is aspired by some countries, but this stage requires new thinking, innovation capabilities, and emerging multinational eneterprises (EMNEs; Bhat, 2020); stronger facets of the competitiveness Assets-Processes-Performance (Competitiveness APP; Momaya, 2001) framework; and dynamic interactions among relevant factors of competitiveness like the '9 factors model' (Cho and Moon, 2013). The vital role of entrepreneurship in strengthening related and supporting industries that can then help to transform semi-developed countries has been recognized by scholars of competitiveness (IPS, 2020; Momaya, 2016).

Korea's economic success has inspired numerous studies (Moon, 2016) and provided useful frameworks to measure competitiveness (NCR, 2020). Based on the popular Diamond Model (Porter, 1990) and its extensions, NCR takes on a different approach by incorporating both human and physical factors, which enhance the analytical capabilities; this is more useful to evaluate the competitiveness of developing and advanced countries of varying sizes. Building on extensive analysis and experiences, Moon (2016) detailed four factors — agility (speed + precision), benchmarking (learning + best practices), convergence (mixing + synergy), and dedication (diligence + goal-orientation) — of the ABCD model that has strong utility.

Taking a context of mega cluster spanning from Western to Southern India — an entrepreneurial hub of industry and economy — this chapter provides examples of start-ups or ventures that are striving to facilitate the responsible digital transformation needed for the shift toward an entrepreneurial rebound from discontinuities such as COVID-19, and to enhance competitiveness. Tech start-ups have enormous potential to invent, innovate, commercialize new products or services, providing opportunities to youth and contributing to the economic development of regions (Subrahmanya, 2021). The findings presented here may help draw implications for leaders in politics and business, as well as topics for further studies.

Objectives

The key objective for this chapter is to provide perspectives and identify some examples of the leading technological firms — in emerging industries such as digital and artificial intelligence (AI) — that can help other firms (including start-ups) to recover from the pandemic quickly and start to climb the ladder of international competitiveness (IC; Momaya, 2017). In this chapter, we adapt qualitative analysis and use a variety of data sources to show the trends and patterns in India's competitiveness. With several innovative ideas, India is seeking to help other countries with emergency and healthcare needs (from drugs to vaccines) over a long period of time, despite massive internal needs and constraints (e.g. politics, agitations). Focal firms[1] or institutes can play a major role if they try to leverage such discontinuities to enhance strategic flexibility and build differentiating capabilities (e.g., cooperative strategies among key stakeholders in Asia) (Momaya, 2011).

Start-ups can play a key role due to their flexibility, agility, and speed. The COVID-19 pandemic has provided an opportunity for some focal firms (e.g., TCS, Wipro, Serum Institute of India[2]) and start-ups (e.g., one accelerating innovation through transaction platforms such as Ola) to contribute positively. Focal institutes such as Indian Institutes of Technology (IITs) and focal firms can play a major role if they try to leverage such discontinuities to enhance strategic flexibility (Momaya, Bhat, and Lalwani, 2017) and build differentiating capabilities (e.g., cooperative strategies among key stakeholders and in Asia, particularly with technology-based democracies such as Japan, Korea, and others in Southeast Asia {SEA}).

---

[1]Focal firms are capable firms positioned on critical parts of an industry value system (series of value chains of individual firms) or value network that play a crucial role for competitiveness and growth of that industry. For instance, Samsung is a classic example of a focal firm for technology hardware and equipment industry due to its massive contributions to R&D, design, engineering, and manufacturing of electronics, computer peripherals, including mobile phones, semiconductors, and other critical devices or components.

[2]SII is the world's largest vaccine manufacturer by number of doses produced and sold globally (more than 1.5 billion doses) which includes vaccines for Polio as well as Diphtheria, Tetanus, Pertussis, Hib, BCG, r-Hepatitis B, Measles, Mumps, and Rubella. It is estimated that about 65% of the children in the world receive at least one vaccine manufactured by Serum Institute. It exports corona vaccine to more than 50 countries.

For this chapter, we have adapted qualitative methods, particularly a longitudinal design (Bryman and Bell, 2011) to make sense of the trends in country competitiveness over the past two decades for select large countries. Such "çontextualist" study helps to examine the competitiveness processes (Momaya, 2001) and mechanisms by showing on which competitiveness factors, enhancements are being achieved. For instance, the shift from the factor-driven stage toward cooperation or innovation-driven stage of competitiveness (Momaya, 2011) is observed from such longitudinal study. For insights on competitiveness, we have explored the development process that has occurred over the past three decades since liberalization of 1991 in India based on a variety of data sources — from archival data to reports, books, papers, databases — for fact finding.

Emerging Findings from Examples

Start-ups can play a very important role in solving the complex problems, such as ones related to discontinuity of the pandemic highlighted previously, if cooperative strategies with focal firms are executed effectively. With the growing importance of start-ups in enhancing the competitiveness of clusters, states, and even countries (Momaya, 2017; Wenyan *et al.*, 2019), there is an increasing interest in strengthening the competitiveness of start-ups. The research results (e.g., Momaya, 2016, 2019) point out the leading role of focal firms in western India for the break-out of India from the "middle-income trap." For instance, firms from western India accounted for the lion's share of corporate taxes, revenues, and profits in a sample from the survey *Global 2000* (Momaya, 2016). Cities in western India are also hubs for start-up activities due to the strong entrepreneurial values in those cities.

Installing entrepreneurial values, skills, and culture among students, recent graduates, and knowledge workers to form a cluster can help to close the gaps — *vis-à-vis* the famous clusters such as Silicon Valley in the US. India has shown a successful path (GCR, 2020), thanks to its technology hubs in the valley spanning from Mumbai to Bangalore with further clusters around cities such as Pune and Hubli-Dharwad. Technology institutes such as IITs (e.g., Momaya *et al.*, 2017) can play a key role in upgrading the capabilities of entrepreneurs with high potential in the region and strengthening the ecosystem for technology innovation that provides support for innovation — from education, skill sets, and incubation to acceleration.

AI may provide a useful example of an emerging industry (EI) that can help start-ups and firms of Indian origin (FIOs) to become scale-ups. India is emerging as an AI accelerator, thanks to academic research and proprietary capabilities being built by technology service providers and niche AI-based technology firms. Several software FIOs have been investing steadily to build their capabilities related to AI. Table 2 provides a small glimpse of the product offering of the FIOs that are related to AI. Technology companies of Indian origin exhibit strong AI capabilities and over the years have developed a full stack of AI platforms that are used by over 700 clients across more than 15 sectors. For instance, AI platform HOLMES by Wipro can offer real-time insights by analyzing log data

Table 2.   Examples of AI-related digital platforms offered by selected ICT FIOs.

Company	AI-related entity	AI platforms	Focus segments	Verticals	No. of clients
TCS	Digitate (subsidiary)	Ignio	Process automation AI segment	BFSI, retail, telco, utilities, airlines	50+
Infosys	Edgeverve (subsidiary)	Nia	Process automation AI segment	BFSI, retail, telco, manufacturing, utilities, airlines	50+
Wipro	Wipro Holmes (division)	HOLMES	Process automation AI segment	BFSI, retail, telco, manufacturing, utilities	350+
HCL	DRYiCE (subsidiary)	iAssure	Service assurance platform	NA	100+
		MTaaS	Hosted platform for enterprise tools	NA	70+

Note: Data such as no. of clients is a conservative approximate as of June 2020. Some may have multiples of that no. in 2022, as some platforms are in customer scale-up stage.
Source: Developed based on company annual reports, media reports, Shivakumar and Momaya (2019) and Momaya *et al.* (2020).

directly from multiple cloud applications to enhance productivity. Through better management of skilled human resources, the FIOs are likely to produce a responsible AI that has better balances about the role of humans and machines.

Among the many challenges that a start-up faces on the journey to unicorn status, gaps in the entrepreneurial ecosystem are perhaps the most important. Despite efforts by key stakeholders of the industries and governments, as well as the major improvements in the ecosystem over the last two decades, the number of scale-ups from India climbing up the ladder of international competitiveness remains low. This is reflected by the data revealing that a few number of FIOs are on lists such as Global 2000. Despite many factor advantages, the contribution of India in Global 2000 has remained less than 80 companies (e.g., in the range of 50–70 over the last few years). Even if it crosses 80 (4 percent of the sample), it is still quite low for the country with a large entrepreneurial base. This suggests that there might be bigger underlying problems. For instance, start-ups in important segments such as deep-tech often have longer lead times, multiple valleys of death to cross, and have to rely mostly on borrowed capital from abroad, which imposes several limitations. In this sense, some industrial houses in India are coming forward to support start-ups or scale-ups. For instance, chemical-to-e-com industrial house Reliance Industries Ltd. (RIL) has mentioned that it is committed to supporting the build-up of a thriving start-up ecosystem in India and has been investing in several start-ups (e.g., Reverie Tech., the AI start-up Haptik, and the online pharmacy Netmeds). Such options can provide win-win opportunities to start-ups, as well as focal firms, by reducing over-dependence on international venture capitalists (VCs) or private equity (PEs).

Hence, focal institutes can play a key role in shaping the innovation ecosystem. The significant role of institutions such as Stanford University or UCLA in shaping Silicon Valley has been discussed adequately, but there is only a limited understanding of similar phenomena in the context of Asian countries. Carefully selected examples of start-ups or ventures in Western India that are related to the innovation valley in India that spans Tamil Nadu, Kerala, Karnataka, and Maharashtra up to Gujarat are represented in Table 3. While start-ups related to IIT Bombay are still at an early stage, corporate-supported ones such as Jio and Byju's seem to be growing quite well at the early level such as customer acquisition. Zoho has a quite different approach and has sustained and scaled-up quite well

Table 3. Examples of start-ups working on projects related to pandemics.

Start-up	Broad area (e.g. AI, DA)	Extent of scale-up	Highest stage of funding received	Example of initiatives to rebound from C-19	Remarks, for example, cooperative strategy, achievements
Atomberg	Energy efficiency	Medium, for example, 1 million fans/year		IoT-enabled products	Have also started cooperating with RIL, Tata, Infosys
IdeaForge	Unmanned aerial vehicle (UAV)	Medium, for example, 150,000+ customer flights; 20+ patents	Acquired contracts to tune of $20 million	Not relevant	An international leader in (UAV) tech.
Zoho	Suite of productivity software products	High, for example, more than 60 million users worldwide	Less dependent on VC funding	Digital productivity tools helping millions	25 years of life's work
Byju's	Education	High, for example, 900,000+ paid users	$785 million	Providing online tuitions to millions affected by the pandemic	
Jio	Telecom: mobile, broadband	Very high, for example, 10,000+ employees, 350+ subscribers	Raised US$21 billion	Mobility solutions by the firm helped millions work or study from home in corona times	Firm promises to provide affordable 4G and biz solutions to facilitate digital transformation for millions

Notes: 1. SINE is technology business incubator of IIT Bombay. 2. Pandemic-related services are not core services of the start-ups, but these are seeking to adapt their services to help customers cope with the crisis created by the COVID-19 pandemic.

in a difficult arena for FIOs such as software products, and that too without going for external venture capital.

Opportunities for Further Studies

Strategic discontinuities provide opportunities to think differently about the traditional business models and make suggestions for advanced studies to identify the cause of devastation. Scholars — from Adam Smith to Michael Porter — have developed frameworks to better explain the competitiveness of countries and firms, but none of these models could adequately explain the success of Asian economies (Moon, 2016: 5). Hence, the need to develop the traditional frameworks to the ones that provide better explanation — such as the ABCD model, Competitiveness APP framework — arises.

Here are examples of topics of high relevance for the competitiveness and sustainability of the countries, firms, start-ups, and other organizations.

The inability of the current innovation to address the many complex problems provides opportunities for start-ups and ventures. There has been a lack of sustained creation of breakthrough technologies; where there has been innovation, it has not been adequately successful at delivering solutions (GCR, 2020) to the current problems such as increasing consumption, emissions, and reducing carbon footprints. Stakeholders have not invested properly in the right type of innovation that could make campuses, clusters, and societies more sustainable, flexible, and resilient. As such, how can we shift the focus toward innovations that can address these problems? And what sources of funding provide the flexibility to do so?

The examples of start-ups and scale-ups presented in Table 3 provide a glimpse of the diverse opportunities and challenges faced by new ventures from emerging countries. For instance, firms from emerging countries have very limited capabilities to compete only in simple arenas such as transaction platforms (e.g., e-commerce). While India has a greater number of unicorns now (as of 2020, 42 for India; as compared to 12 each for Brazil and Korea), most of them were acquired prematurely. Marquee investors, which help the unicorns enter the $1 billion valuation, were in full control of the strings throughout the journey and phase out the founders (many of the founders are IITians). For instance, several start-ups such as Flipkart were acquired, and many others may be acquired by international giants due to gaps in the entrepreneurial ecosystem in India, such as a small amount of venture capital (incl. private equity), less sophisticated lead customers, and internationally less competitive domestic focal firms. Then, how can emerging countries develop capabilities to achieve better balances for sustainable innovation ecosystems that link to industrial clusters?

Models such as the Diamond Model were tested in the context of competitiveness of several industries, however, they could only partly explain the situation. On the other hand, the competitiveness Assets-Processes-Performance (APP) framework was able to explain the competitiveness of several industries in India, including emerging industries such as nanotechnology (Momaya, 2011). How can such frameworks be adapted to diagnose recovery and "Return from COVID-19" for large states of India, providing interesting opportunities for studies?

The many problems discussed previously induce significant risk derived from over-spending due to the GOI's stimulus package that was adopted in response to the COVID-19 pandemic. While fiscal balances may still be manageable, high risks associated with the greater overall debt (e.g., general government gross debt as a percentage of GDP in 2020 was 89.3 for India, as compared to 61.7 for China, 38.5 for Indonesia, and 18.9 for Russia) (Kwatra and Bhattacharya, 2021) should be addressed shortly. The Asian Financial Crisis in 1997 has taught some valuable lessons for many Asian countries and such discontinuities are bound to be repeated. In this situation, what are sustainable options to achieve better balances among jobs, productivity, savings, and spending?

By addressing the gaps in extant literature to explain Korea's economic success, Moon (2016) proposed the innovative ABCD Model based on four factors (Agility, Benchmarking, Convergence, and Dedication). An example to explain the dynamics of competitiveness of a business group was also shared by the authors (Moon *et al.*, 2015). With the growing importance of start-ups in contributing to a country's competitiveness, governments among several active economies like Korea have been promoting a number of new initiatives (Yin *et al.*, 2019). When looking at the comparative case of three Korean start-ups there is an indication of the high utility for some factors of the ABCD Model.

Higher labor productivity, agility, benchmarking, and flexibility are needed in India for multiple reasons. Some sub-factors such as diligence, precision, and synergy creation are quite difficult for most executives in emerging countries such as India and have become even more challenging to implement due to the disruptions derived from the COVID-19 pandemic.

In this case, what approaches toward training should be employed in such context?

With many innovative ideas, India is seeking to help a number of countries despite massive internal needs and constraints such political disputes. For instance, firms of Indian origin (FIOs), such as SII, have supplied more than 60 million doses of vaccines to 80 countries, including 17.7 million doses through the Covax facility to low-income countries as of March 2021 (ET, 2021). This in spite of the needs among many people domestically. With SII planning to raise production to 100 million a month (from 60) and Bharat Biotech to 20 million a month (from 4), the contribution of these FIOs is projected to be larger. Focal firms/IITs can play a major role if they try to leverage such discontinuities to enhance strategic flexibility (Momaya *et al.*, 2017) and build differentiating capabilities (e.g. cooperative strategies in Asia, particularly technology-based democracies such as Japan, Korea, or those in Southeast Asia). Unfortunately, cooperative strategies of FIOs in contexts in East Asia have not been very effective. This raises the question, how can the cooperative strategies between focal firms and IITs be strengthened to boost innovative programs involving short immersions with East Asian countries?

India and China — two major economies with large population bases that have been beneficial to the world (Sheth, 2008) — have been facing significant challenges, particularly in terms of sustainability. Adopting the Western levels of economic development in key aspects such as per capita consumption can be ineffective. Hence, focal firms in India need to innovate greatly for sustainable manufacturing, services, and supply chains which will help to conserve resources for the future. Functioning economic, business, and management models push India to move forward amid many difficulties of less development (Kanagasabapathi, 2013). Given this context, how can such capabilities be adapted to address challenges on fronts such as manufacturing of electronics, EV batteries, and other key components including APIs like Penicillin-G, which India imported more than 95 percent of.

Implications for Leaders

Many leaders in all walks — for example, business, entrepreneurship, industry, society, science and technology, political — have been contributing to the development of India, but there seem to be enormous opportunities for improvement, especially for the leaders of engineering and management of technology and innovation (MoT). For instance, each of the successful focal firms from Korea such as POSCO, Samsung, Hyundai (Moon, 2016: 113), have many exceptional leaders in engineering. In a review of a sample of 25 "Builders of Modern India" (RobinAge, 2019), about 12 (e.g., APJ Abdul Kalam, CV Raman, E Sreedharan, Homi Bhabha, Jayant Narlikar, JRD Tata, M Visvesvaraya, MS Swaminathan, NR Narayana Murthy, Sam Manekshaw, Verghese Kurien, V Sarabhai) appear to have capabilities to lead MoT. However, despite such capacity, the gaps in knowledge, innovation, and technology between India and the relevant benchmark countries remain vast, perhaps due to gaps in the quality of business leaders. Although the country has woefully fewer international competitive focal firms and indus-tries to help achieve balances, it still has an enormous reservoir of young workers seeking opportunities. In this case, India needs to increase the num-ber of focal firms and industries with international competitiveness such as software services to support the country's growth. Indeed, nurturing quality business leaders (such as Vikram Sarabhai, JRD Tata, and E Sreedharan) demands different approaches in the education system.

Here are some implications for leaders that were built on our findings and interactions with selected leaders of competitiveness in India, East Asia, and North America over the past three decades:

The IPS-NCR international review (Cho and Moon, 2013) suggests an interesting clustering of countries. India falls in the group of large countries with intermediary competitiveness along with some other highly competitive countries such as Brazil, Japan, Vietnam, which are the coun-tries with the vast potential to improve competitiveness very rapidly according to select factors. Leaders in India need to think differently and execute sound choices to boost balances, such as on savings, external trade, finance, and data, in order to move up to the "strong competitive-ness" group where more capable countries such as China, Germany, and France are positioned.

Yet despite considerable efforts to reform and internationalize the country (e.g., by the National Democratic Alliance (NDA) governments in the 2010s), it is not easy to achieve balances among several critical dimensions — from trade, fiscal, investments, technology to economy, environment, and equity. The central government may focus on early ones to sustain success with trade balances while at the regional level the focus may be more on manageable problems related to fiscal area and investments; corporate leaders may prioritize mitigating the challenges of management of human resources and technology and innovation (MoT). The main focus of the other stakeholders — including academia — may include creating and sharing the knowledge related to the sustainability of start-ups, ventures, and enterprises so that India can contribute a bigger share to the resolution of various sustainability problems such as those from rising pollution, climate change, and other environmental issues that can affect health.

While India seems to have a good quantity of human capital (e.g., particularly professionals, entrepreneurs) (Cho and Moon, 2013), the levels of quality, endurance, and sustainability are questionable. Discontinuities such as COVID-19 can help identify real leaders and "álso-ran." At this point, undertaking an independent diagnostic (e.g., in cooperation with leading competitiveness researchers) to acquire more accurate information to make determined decisions about the training of high-potential leaders is necessary.

Many professionals should learn and build on continuous innovation such as *Kaizen*.[3] While firms and organizations in India may be good at carrying out constraint-based innovations, such as *jugaad* or frugal (Agarwal *et al.*, 2016), the need for leading systematic innovation (Krishnan, 2010) is an urgent issue in India if capable product-based or technology-based start-ups are to be at least domestic leaders. The presence of firms such as Zoho is still too few to mitigate the many vexing problems arising in India and most firms of Indian origin (FIOs) have expanded abroad too slowly.

The scalability and internationalization of capable start-ups are necessary to create opportunities for skilled youth, a key enabler of competitiveness for countries including India. Nowadays, not just those from Silicon Valley but also those from the start-ups in Asian countries are also scaling up through internationalization (e.g., Yin *et al.*, 2019). Pre-mature stagnation in scale-up or failure of ventures can have devastating impacts for thousands of direct and indirect employees in the value chain. While highly successful decacorns such as Byju's have begun internationalization, it is

---

[3] *Kaizen* (改善), the Japanese word for "improvement," is a concept referring to business activities that continuously strive to improve functions and involve all employees from the CEO to the assembly line workers. By improving standardized programs and processes, kaizen aims to eliminate waste and redundancies (e.g., lean manufacturing) (adapted from books on Lean).

too early to comment on the effectiveness of their international strategy at this point.

Most emerging technologies are widely adopted by FIOs in the hope of improvements in productivity and international competitiveness, but real improvements are often marginal or even negative (e.g., cases of ICT, ERP) (Chaurasiya, 2015). The surveys have concluded several anomalies in India's markets (e.g., Share Market; Harshita *et al.*, 2018). Among the root causes of low maturity, perhaps, a key issue may be a low sophistication of customers and stagnation in their maturity. Hence, there is a need to develop a shared understanding about responsible AI such as machine intelligence (MI, e.g., being cooperatively developed at institutes such as IIT Bombay) and adapt MoT practices to help the focal firms and start-ups break out in international competitiveness.

Conclusion

Populous countries like India hold a responsibility to provide opportunities for millions of young workers by improving their competitiveness while mitigating global problems such as gaps in health and education, balances, and sustainability of cities. In this context, focal firms, institutes and start-ups, particularly in emerging industries (Momaya, 2011) with relevant stakeholders, can play a key role in competitiveness. As part of this effort, IITs, the leading universities from India, are striving hard to incubate many start-ups that are scalable and will contribute to the competitiveness of clusters, cities, and states.

Leaders in firms need to reexamine the strategies for gaining competitiveness. By thinking beyond factor-driven progress, the leaders should inculcate capabilities such as diligence, flexibility, and endurance to scale up the quality of people, processes, and breakout performance. Since in-house training processes hold inadequacies in many firms of Indian origin, the leaders may try to promote the cooperation of institutes to design and pilot "Leadership Development Programmes" related to Competitiveness.

Acknowledgments

I thank anonymous reviewers of IPS-NCR and Prof. H. C. Moon and Dr. Wenyan Yin and copy editors for their comments. I acknowledge cooperation from researchers (Ph.D./M. Mgt./MBA/Alumni/) at SJMSOM,

IITB. Particularly associates of Group on Competitiveness (GoC) Shivakumar, Dr. Ajitabh, Padmanav, Divyang, and Pranusha have started contributing. Cooperation from other members of Group on Competitiveness (GoC) at IIT Bombay, and participating companies for interactions for research and data collection is acknowledged. Infrastructure support from SJMSOM, IIT Bombay, and IRCC is acknowledged for the longitudinal study.

References

Agarwal, N., M. Grottke, S. Mishra, and A. Brem. 2016. A systematic literature review of constraint-based innovations: State of the art and future perspectives. *IEEE Transactions on Engineering Management* 64(1): 3–15.

Bell, E., A. Bryman, and E. Bell. 2011. *Business Research Methods*. New Delhi: Oxford University Press.

Chaurasiya N. नीरज कुमार चौरसयि 2015. पुस्तकालय और सूचना सेवाओं में सूचना एवं संचार प्रौद्योगिकी (ICT) का (in English: Information and communication technology {ICT} use in Library and information services), जज्ञिासा, हिंदी वज्ञिान पत्रिका (Jigyasha), an artefact of IIT Delhi, Vol. 29, 113–117.

Cho, D. S. and H. C. Moon. 2013. *International Review of National Competitiveness: A Detailed Analysis of Sources and Rankings*. Edward Elgar.

The Economic Times. 2021. Boosting vaccine supply — India's job: Tap unutilised capacity, lift export curbs. March 26: 14.

Harshita, Singh S. and S. S. Yadav. 2018. शेयर बाजार वसिंगतयिां: भारत में सर्वेक्षण (Share market anomaly: a survey in India), जज्ञिासा, हिंदी वज्ञिान पत्रिका (Jigyasha), an artefact of IIT Delhi, Vol. 32, 73–84.

IPS. 2020. *National Competitiveness Research*. Seoul: The Institute for Policy & Strategy on National Competitiveness.

Kanagasabapathi, P. 2013. *Indian Models of Economy, Business and Management*. PHI Learning Pvt. Ltd.

Krishnan, R. T. (2010). *From Jugaad to Systematic Innovation: The Challenge for India*. Rishikesha T Krishnan.

Kwatra N. and P. Bhattacharya. 2021. Getting the recovery budget right. Plain Facts, Mint, Mumbai. https://epst.livemint.com/Home/ShareArticle?OrgId= 121e8d857ed. Accessed January 16, 2021.

Momaya, K. S. 2011. Cooperation for competitiveness of emerging countries: Learning from a case of nanotechnology. *Competitiveness Review: An International Business Journal* 21(2): 152–170. https://doi.org/10.1108/10595421111117443.

Momaya, K. S. 2017. Scale-up and quality of ventures: Exploring the role of international capabilities. *International Journal of Global Business and Competitiveness*, 12(1): 3–5.

Momaya, K. S. 2019. The past and the future of competitiveness research: A review in an emerging context of innovation and EMNEs. *International Journal of Global Business and Competitiveness* 14(1): 1–10. https://doi.org/10.1007/s42943-019-00002-3.

Momaya, K. S., S. Bhat, and L. Lalwani. 2017. Institutional growth and industrial competitiveness: Exploring the role of strategic flexibility taking the case of select institutes in India. *Global Journal of Flexible Systems Management* 18(2): 111–122. https://doi.org/10.1007/s40171-016-0144-2.

Momaya K. S., S. Malagihal, A. Bodduri, A. Vartak and J. Dharamsey. 2020. Measuring competitiveness of select firms in AI segments: Exploring softer dimensions of technology management. *Proc. International Association for Management of Technology IAMOT*, 284–295.

Moon, H. C. 2016. *The Strategy for Korea's Economic Success*. Oxford University Press.

Moon, H. C., Y. W. Lee, and W. Yin. 2015. A new approach to analysing the growth strategy of business groups in developing countries: The case study of India's Tata Group. *International Journal of Global Business and Competitiveness* 10(1): 1–15.

NASSCOM. 2020. AI platforms: Next frontier for Indian IT services.

RobinAge. 2019. *Builders of Modern India*. New Delhi: Scholastic.

Sheth, J. N. 2008. *Chindia Rising: How China and India will Benefit Your Business*. Tata McGraw-Hill Education.

Shivakumar, S. M. and Momaya, K. S. 2019. Digital platforms and competitiveness of firms in the disruptive era: A study on ICT firms of Indian origin, 19th Global Conference Glogift, IIT Roorkee.

Subrahmanya, M. B. 2021. *Entrepreneurial Ecosystems for Tech Start-ups in India*. De Gruyter.

Yin, W., H. C. Moon, and Y. W. Lee. 2019. The success factors of Korean global start-ups in the digital sectors through internationalization. *International Journal of Global Business and Competitiveness* 14(1): 42–53.

Chapter 13

Open Innovation and Improvement of China's Competitiveness

Feihu Zheng

Abstract

The past fifty years have witnessed the rise of China to become one of the world's largest economies. China's achievements rest in its unique path of socialist development, which emphasizes the dual role of the visible hand of government (fairness) and the invisible hand of the market (efficiency). It has also demonstrated the flexible adoption of open innovation not only in crossing the firm's boundary but also spanning over national borders. Through the historical depiction of China's economic development and strategic analysis of China's macro policy and micro operational features, we find that a triangle governance mode can be used to represent China's remarkable performance, behind which it conforms to the same logic of the ABCD model.

Keywords: Competitiveness, open innovation, triangle governance mode, ABCD model, development strategy

Introduction

The past few decades have witnessed China's emergence as the largest developing economy in the world (China has now gained many first positions in the world: imports and exports, foreign reserves, and output in more than 70 branches of industries). This has not only reshaped global governance but also provided a new example for many developing countries. When the People's Republic of China was established in 1949, the country's economy was in a poor state and was closed off from the outside world. After more than half a century, great changes have taken place following the reforms launched by Deng Xiaoping. In 2018, when China's GDP approached 60 percent of the US, Trump administration announced a number of protectionist measures seeking to discourage China's economic growth; but in 2020, despite the sanctions against hi-tech firms by the US and the threat of COVID-19 global pandemic, China's GDP continued to improve and reached 75 percent of US GDP. During the same time, China announced its progress in overall poverty reduction. With the formulation of the new 14th Five-Year Plan by the Communist Party of China (CPC), the country is now striding toward the fulfillment of the two Centennial Goals (celebrating the 100th anniversary of CPC in 2021 and the 100th anniversary of the People's Republic of China in 2049). These indicate as well that under the leadership of the CPC, China will soon realize its goal of bringing the Chinese people's living standard to a level similar to that of middle-income developed countries by the mid-point of the twenty-first century. Considering the future promise of the common prosperity goal for China's 1.4 billion population, it is a unique achievement as no other country has ever experienced such a tremendous change (or a rapid development) with such a large population over a short period of time. Hereinafter we will review and explain how the above achievements were attained and what good hints other countries can take away from China's success.

Open Innovation and China's Arduous Exploration of Socialist Construction

Open innovation (OI) has become widely adopted as a new business strategy by firms across many industries (Gassmann *et al.*, 2010). OI is introduced as the opposite to closed innovation and requires firms to integrate internal and external sources by undertaking extensive cooperation with external organizations to improve both their innovative and financial performance (Chesbrough, 2003, 2006). Since Chesbrough developed this term, the analysis of OI has extended from the individual firm to the networks between organizations, from bilateral to multi-layer relationships, and even to the national innovation system, which constitutes the context and background for the firms' innovation nowadays. If we refine Chesbrough's idea of OI and apply it to the national level, it means a country should combine internal and external resources into architectures and systems with a national openness mode. This is precisely what China has done over the past half century, and China's successful exploration of socialist development really amplifies the scope of OI theories and practices. The following are the characteristics of the historical development of China's socialist development based on the OI principle, demonstrating the flexibility in the absorption and leveraging of external resources and opportunities, which is also referred to as the inbound/coupled openness and innovation.

Period 1 (1950s–1960s): Planned economy with certain autonomy

When the People's Republic of China was established in 1949, the Cold War emerged between the Eastern camp and the Western one. As part of the Eastern camp, China used the Soviet Union as a benchmark and adopted its planned economy, which led to some recovery under the First Five-Year Plan. Despite setbacks, the CPC remained committed to the planned economy. Similar to the later shrewd and decisive measures adopted by Deng Xiaoping, a hybrid model was then created for the Chinese economy which would stick to state planning as the core, but also permit limited freedom to the outside as the peripheral.[1] In so doing, China could then activate limited mobility of resources in the planned economy system. This "core-peripheral" economic development idea later proved to be timely and effective.

For example, during the difficult period in the 1960s, China imported some yellow beans from abroad to cure the outbreak of edema disease. Similarly, after the Cultural Revolution, faced with an extreme lack of grain, oil, and cotton. China tried to import these items to effectively deal

---

[1]At that time, even the planned economy was dominant, there still existed different understanding about the planned economy for the central government officials, which brought some flexibility in application. The peripheral implicates limited flexibility.

with their shortages. The initial limited "inbound openness" in a planned economy system has in fact brought the market mechanism to simply allocate the resources in China; such primitive reform shows the gene of openness embedded in China's development.

Period 2 (1970s–1990s): China's openness with the steady evolution of a dual economic system

Today, when we summarize China's success in economic development, one of the unique features is its incremental reform with a dual economic system since the end of the 1970s, which averted the type of radical transformation witnessed among former communist regimes who suffered economic difficulties as a result. The secret of China's step-by-step transformation lies in a balanced arrangement between the restrictions of the planned economy and the openness of a new market economy (Lin, 2014). As these two actions go on simultaneously (while planned economic activity is weakening and releases the resources, the market economic activity benefits and strengthens itself), economic transformation was able to occur smoothly.

Let us consider some examples. On one hand, in order to expand the market economy, the Chinese government has reduced and later aborted the national purchase of agricultural and sideline products at a lower fixed price; meanwhile, a more efficient "inbound openness" measure was adopted where China continued to import main foods after the 3rd Session of the 11th CPC Meeting in 1978. Such action not only solved the food supply issue for city residents but also provided room for peasants to bring their grains to the free market for a transaction. This allowed the flexibility to market price adjustment and greater autonomy for household production, which immediately activated China's rural land reform and ensured the successive agricultural harvest. In addition, with the development of township enterprises, individual economy, and private firms, as well as the joint ventures, the part of the market economy was thus developed from nothing, to small, and to a large one.

On the other hand, for the planned economy, the ratio of direct planning has been diminished and the ratio of indirect planning has been enlarged. At that time, as the productive materials were entirely controlled by state-owned firms, it was critical to relax the control of some of the productive materials. This process involved the reform of the planned economic system and the reform of state-owned firms' mechanism. During this period, the Chinese government's efforts to push the steady transformation from planned economy to market economy proved to be valuable and successful.

The inbound knowledge of comparative advantages for the agriculture and manufacturing industries was another driver for economic development. Before 1978, China pursued policies to maintain the independence of its domestic economy and ensured a closed internal cycle, which proved to be inefficient. For example, China emphasized the essentials of self-reliance in producing grains. Hence, the traditional method to produce grain was to plant corn, wheat, or any grains regardless of the local endowments. When the local environmental conditions were not suitable for farming, the government simply constructed water conservancy facilities to improve and adapted the production of crops. In so doing, China found itself trapped in an unproductive recycle system: the greater the investment spent on the production, the fewer the output, which impacted negatively upon the people.

Like more grains were planted, the same outmoded thought also prevailed in the manufacturing field. The Chinese government used to encourage building the whole value chains at home when they were developing new industries. But after a visit to Europe, Chinese government officials realized that most developed countries were open to the outside world and operated through international trade or Foreign Direct Investment (FDI), thus they maximized their output by making full use of their comparative advantages. This approach proved to be very illuminating for China. As a result, Chinese firms began to establish the value chains from the downstream as it could quickly get the feedback from customers. Then with the accumulated profits or assets, the firms could enlarge their upstream investment. This learning, obtained from the outside by participating in the global market through trade or FDI, greatly amplified China's prospects and benefited its socialist development.

Period 3 (since 2001): China's coupled innovation with a cluster of FDI and rapid outward FDI

The year 2001 was a special time as China joined the World Trade Organization (WTO). With this membership, more opportunities were available for the multilateral exchange of products and factors between China and other countries and deeper involvement in the global economy (Li, 2014). As a result of greater economic integration, in less than twenty years, the average GDP per capita for China has improved from US$1,053 (2001) to US$10,000 (2019), which is an increase of nearly ten times. China is now striding toward its goal of US$12,000 GDP per capita — the minimal threshold for a high-income developed country.

Another trend that appeared since China joined the WTO was that many Multinational Corporations (MNCs) have upgraded their resource allocation in the Chinese market. An increasing number of MNCs' regional or even global R&D centers have moved to China. Alongside this, two-thirds of the Fortune 500 companies have established branches in China. As MNCs first entered China in the 1990s, their value chains that were developed from sale agencies to manufacturing factories, have now extended to R&D centers. The integration of value chains in China does not only indicate the optimization of MNCs' resource allocation, it is a new kind of competition mode of industry cluster or the innovation cluster, which is featured with the typical phenomenon of "onshore reverse R&D outsourcing" in China (Zheng and Chang, 2016), where foreign MNCs act as the vendor firms and local firms are contract clients. It is found that during these R&D outsourcing activities, MNCs entered the Chinese market with multiple capabilities (Zheng *et al.*, 2019); they not only exploited their mature technology to serve the local clients (exploitation) but also added more inputs to explore their unused technology (Zheng *et al.*, 2018) to meet the local clients' sophisticated demands (Exploration). While in so doing, it demonstrated another new solution for technology scattering in host countries (host countries' firms can benefit from both exploitation and exploration behavior by MNCs), which is the new feature and effect of "onshore reverse outsourcing" under the context of open innovation in China over the past few decades. It has demonstrated that China has become the largest market by attracting an increasingly large number of global MNCs.

Based on the above circumstances, we can summarize two new features about China's rapid development: one is that with more inbound innovation, China's absorptive capabilities have improved and rising cluster innovation in China has thus supported the global competitiveness among Chinese firms (from 1995 to 2020, Chinese firms listed in Fortune 500 have increased from 2 to 133, China is now ranked in first place in terms of the number of listed firms). Another one is that many Chinese firms have gone abroad to compete in the global market by coupling inbound innovation and its own unique endowments, which increases Chinese firms' adaptation to the dynamic changes and velocity in an external environment.

A Macro Perspective for the Drivers behind Improvement of China's Competitiveness

When China's opening and reform policies are mentioned in discussion, people are often impressed by the Chinese government's decisive leadership. But such views are also challenged by the suitability of government interference. By using a different perspective, we hereby depict some typical cases from the macro dimension to address the essentials behind China's improvement in competitiveness.

China's success in land reform: A metaphor of triangle governance

At the end of the 1970s, reforms in the countryside, especially with the practice of household production, helped to reduce the perennial problem of grain shortages. This achievement was generally unexpected among most people. When we review this process, we find that it is featured by three distinctive characteristics, each of which is interconnected.

The first two features are the central regulation guidance but with an incremental and flexible degree of autonomy. Although China issued its "sixty regulations"[2] to guide rural economic development and prohibited the break-up of land and working it alone (typical of collectivized farming), some exemptions were made for some special occasions, such as single families in a remote areas. In fact, the practice of household production was not completely prohibited, it was just slightly frowned upon. This subtle change that did not outright ban household production left certain freedom and precious room for poorer areas to become more innovative. The third feature is the timely communication and reflective behavior between central and local governments. At that time, the central government was concerned about the possible emergence of unbalanced development amongst its rural areas: from the strong collectivized economy to a more independent middle-level area, to

---

[2]"Sixty regulations" is also called "work regulations of People's commune", it's revised and passed in the 3rd Session of the 11th CPC Meeting in 1978.

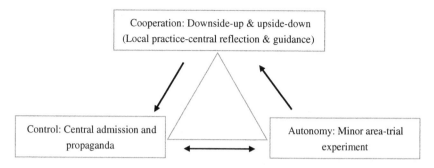

Figure 1.   Triangle governance of land reform.

some of the poorest areas with resource shortages. For the poorest areas, the most effective way of promoting economic development was to allow house-hold production for the local people. Therefore, the central government finally allowed local government to make their own choices; which surely permitted local people to pursue household production. Meanwhile, the central government paid close attention to the development of local practices and made a timely summary and guidance.

The above methods proved to be flexible and effective; they didn't impede the speed of this change (land reform). As a matter of fact, it gave the local organization (leader and officials) flexibility of time, thus led this change on the voluntary base and greatly reduced unnecessary negative effects. This is why the land reform trend evolved from the poorest areas to the middle-level areas, then to the wealthy areas, during which the new practice of household production was in the transition from imperfection to gradual improvement.

Using a model of triangle governance (Keidel, 2010), the above expe-rience can be demonstrated as follows. We use a triangle to depict the different meanings of vertex: control, cooperation, and autonomy (Figure 1); usually, the natural relationship of any complicated phenomenon can be demonstrated from these three dimensions.

China's coast city strategy and FTZ practices: A model of triangle governance

China's development of its coastal areas was one of the key strategies for the government during the 1980s. Previously under the country's planned economy, the coastal areas had strong processing capacity but a lack of resources, which made it reliant on the central government's transfer of resources from the western areas. But this kind of mode was unsustainable because there was a growing scarcity of resources, which resulted in sharp conflicts between different regions. Hence, the coastal areas had to transform their economic development strategy to an export-oriented one, which produced both economic and political values. On the economic side, such transformation conforms to international opportunities. As industrial value chains shifted from advanced countries to countries in East Asia, China happened to gain a pioneer advantage because of its timely opening policy practiced in the coastal areas. Plus its natural advantages of convenient transport and good infrastructure, the coastal cities are growing fast with an abundance of labor and adjacent convenience. Therefore, it is expected that as the coastal areas develop further, they will also play the role of a growth engine for the development of the interior areas. On the political side, since China has long maintained a planned economy, all economic opportunities were distributed equally around the country so that there was no chance for the coastal areas to utilize their comparative advantages. This thought produced a significant economic gap between Mainland China and Hong Kong, Taiwan, and other regions, raising the question about the socialist economy's international advantage. Therefore, a quick transformation to the export-oriented economy would encourage people to sustain a better life standard and increase their confidence obviously in the economy that was now featured by "socialism with Chinese characteristics."

The process of this transformation followed a reasonable logic: first, the province of Guangdong as a bridgehead with Hong Kong was suitable for processing and manufacturing industries. This experience then spread to other coastal areas. During this period, there was nationwide debate about the effect of pursuing such a transformation. Despite this debate, this strategy was formally adopted at the meeting of the Political Bureau of the CPC, which laid the foundation for the coastal area's development.[3] Using a metaphor of triangle governance, we describe the above experience as follows (Figure 2).

Over the past ten years, in order to open up further to the outside world, China not only put forward the Belt and Road Initiative but also accelerated Pilot Free Trade Zone (Pilot FTZ) construction. When we review China's

---

[3]Despite the different worries about the coastal area's development, the central government finally issued a series of policies promoting the development of the special economic zone and coastal opening cities by formulating the opening order from the east to the hinterland, from coastal to the riverside, etc.

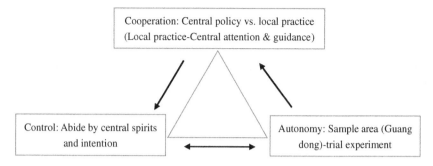

Figure 2.   Triangle governance of coastal city reform.

Pilot FTZ development, we find it follows the similar triangle logic: first, establishing a high-level FTZ domestically was one of the visions of the Chinese central government, and Shanghai was chosen to trial this process. Then based upon its experiences, the Ministry of Commerce encouraged other areas to apply for FTZ, which accelerated its growth from the coastal areas to the interior. Throughout this process, the central and local governments paid close attention and provided the necessary support.

Why did so many of China's innovations and development modes share these common triangle features? Are there any robust theories to support its logic? Hereinafter we will use the ABCD model by Hwychang Moon (2016) to make a comparison between the development strategy adopted by coastal and interior areas.

China's success in the macro reform: The comparison between ABCD model and triangle governance

The ABCD model, which was put forward by Korean economist Hwychang Moon (2016), serves as a strategic framework not only with successful growth for emerging economies but also for advanced countries that are losing their competitiveness. This model emphasizes four dimensions as key to developing a successful economy: agility-efficient management of time and accuracy; benchmarking incremental innovation through learning best practices; convergence-dominant diversification for maximizing synergies; and dedication-strengthened commitment toward an optimal goal. Table 1 summarizes the ABCD model and its relation to the dimensions and subfactors; we further list some of China's macro-management cases on the right to make a comparison.

Table 1. Distinction and comprehensiveness of the ABCD model vs. triangle governance.

ABCD model and features	Application for land reform	Application for coastal development strategy
Agility (speed)	Initial quick trial of household production in the poorest area (**Autonomy**)	Initial quick trial of processing trade in Guangdong (sample city) (**Autonomy**)
Agility (precision)	Discrimination to the different areas' practices by files (**Control**)	Using abundant labors to establish processing manufacturing for the international capital (**Control**)
Benchmarking (learning)	Factor endowments of the area; activate the potentials (**Cooperation: exploitation and exploration**)	Transportation facility and labor resource, absorptive capacity (**Cooperation: exploitation and exploration**)
Benchmarking (best practice)	Trial experiment's practices summarized for propaganda (**Control**)	"Three-plus-one" trading mixes was the initial focuses (**Control**)
Convergence (mixing)	The upside-down guidance (central files) mixed with downside-up experience (local practices) (**Cooperation**)	The coastal market chances mixed with the hinterland's labor transfer (**Cooperation**)
Convergence (synergy creation)	The sequent propaganda of experiences from the poorest area to the middle level and wealthy area with new improvement (**Cooperation**)	The sequent propaganda of experiences from the coastal area to the riverside area and hinterland with new improvement (**Cooperation**)
Dedication (diligence)	Inherited perspiration (**Autonomy**)	Inspiration of undertaking the opportunity of international industry transfer, inherited perspiration (**Autonomy**)
Dedication (goal orientation)	Improvement of agricultural production efficiency and better Chinese people's living standard (**Control**)	Highlight the unique advantage of coastal area, and set up the bright star of socialism construction (**Control**)

A Micro-Perspective on the Drivers behind the Improvement of China's Competitiveness

Since the 1990s, China has been accelerating its opening to the outside world by adopting its "going out" strategy. At that time, most Chinese firms were labeled as the "enterprise of nothing in three items," which meant they lacked brand, channel, and technology in the international market. How then could Chinese firms succeed in the international market? The following summarizes the case of a Chinese state-owned firm called Zhenhua Port Machine in the 1990s. We use the LLL model[4] (Mathews, 2006) and ABCD model to depict its comprehensive competitiveness capability (Table 2).

Based on our findings, Zhenhua's internationalization is more suited for the ABCD model than the LLL model. The LLL model usually emphasizes that MNCs from the Newly Industrializing Countries (NICs) should try to link themselves to the international market, especially by embedding themselves to Global Value Chains. The next step after making this linkage is to move and combine the resources internally and externally in order to strengthen its own position through the leveraged vehicle. Here, maintaining trust and balance are key points while trying to cooperate with other partners. In the end, based on the continuous linkage and leverage, MNCs can accumulate their advantages to a critical point and get its endogenous advantages. But Zhenhua case has revealed complicated circumstances. Once Zhenhua established its linkages with the international market. At the end of 1992, despite competition with many international port brands for Vancouver Port's tender offer, Zhenhua won the contract with 30 percent discount of its bidding price and assuming millions of US dollars for the freight, which meant through the low-cost strategy, Zhenhua successfully linked itself to the international port market. We can also find Zhenhua's Agility speed here, as low-cost strategy can usually bring the first-mover advantages for firms.)

At that time, the American buyer's strict demand (no component but the whole port machine to be transferred) and the Dutch shipping company's firm shipping contract constituted great challenges for Zhenhua. We also found no leverage resources for Zhenhua to exploit although Zhenhua immediately bought an old and super big transport vehicle, and

---

[4]LLL model indicates that international expansion is driven by resource linkage, leverage, and learning.

Table 2. Distinction and comprehensiveness of the ABCD model and LLL model: Zhenhua case.

	Zhenhua case	LLL model
Agility (speed)	Low-cost strategy for the first bidding in Vancouver (30 percent discount, burdened with millions of US$ of freight)	**Linkage** (low cost strategy made Zhenhua squeeze into international port machine market)
Agility (precision)	Improve the quality of peasants employee (build the welding training school, implement the strict regulations)	Zhenhua's hints behind Linkage: Educating the employee, transferring the peasants into the industrial workers.
Benchmarking (learning)	Internally, Zhenhua's workers are fond of learning with high rewards; externally, their workers mimic and overrun the competitors	**Leverage** (decompose other ship and mimic Holland's transport vehicles and form its own special carrier)
Benchmarking (best practice)	The independent R&D and innovation build Zhenhua's practice as the world standard	Zhenhua's uniqueness: innovate with world first rate technology, involving the carrier and port machine
Convergence (MIXING)	Zhenhua combine its superior location advantages with its own special carrier	**Learning** (improving and accumulating the advantages to reach the qualitative change, thus forming the endogenous advantages)
Convergence (synergy creation)	Zhenhua get both the low cost and differentiation advantages (its own special carrier + port machine products + convenient port transportation)	N.
Dedication (diligence)	Strict regulation to ensure and encourage inherited perspiration	N.
Dedication (goal orientation)	Innovation oriented culture and policy (high reward for the contribution, no retirement based on age)	N.

repacked it according to the Dutch special carrier (Benchmarking learning). Despite the difficulties, Zhenhua finally succeeded by making massive investment in the R&D sector. In fact, as part of Zhenhua's growth, it paid much attention to the R&D input (its yearly R&D input approached 2% of its output value and formed a 2,000-researcher team). Their vision was to get "at least one world no. 1 invention each year." (Benchmarking best practice) That is how Zhenhua finally got to the global summit of port machine technology. Here the ABCD model accurately depicts Zhenhua's growth and its competitiveness improvement as shown in Table 2.

Another successful case in the 2000s is with the emergence of China's high-speed rail network (Lu, 2013). Not only was there a six times increase in rail speed (from 120 kilometers in 1997 to over 200 kilometers in 2007), but also it witnessed a great extension of rail operating mileages (from 1035 kilometers in 2008 to 30,000 kilometers till 2018) and a big reduction of travel time (on average, 2/3 travel time was economized). That is why within 20 years, the high-speed rail network has become a part of people's daily life who enjoy a fast and convenient service. Furthermore, the high-speed rail industry's intellectual property rights have been distributed and recognized internationally. How was China able to achieve such a rapid transformation of its rail network? If we use the triangle governance model (Figure 3), we can discover a clear and comprehensive logic behind this remarkable achievement.

For the autonomy vertex, since the 1950s, China began to develop its own diesel locomotives; since 1978, China paid more attention to high-speed rail technology, but was limited by its economic level and engineering capability. China was at last able to begin construction of its first high-speed rail line in 1999. Up until 2005, the *Star of China* train ran for 536,000 kilometers and had achieved a satisfactory operating level, which established a strong foundation for China's independent R&D in the rail industry. When the Beijing–Tianjin high-speed railroad (2008), Zhengzhou–Xi'an railroad (2010), Wuhan–Guangzhou railroad (2009), and Beijing–Shanghai railroad (2011) were all completed, the government was satisfied with the development of this autonomous innovation by the rail industry to the extent that it would expand it further.

For the cooperation vertex, encouraged by the rail industry's excellent performance, the Ministry of Railways then implemented a strategy by opening the industry to the international joint ventures who could bid for future railroad construction contracts. Through such a mechanism,

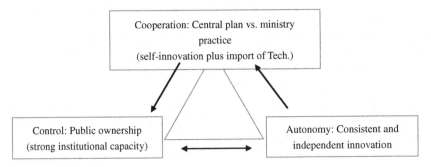

Figure 3.   Triangle governance of high-speed rail industry.

Chinese firms attending the ventures could learn much from their international partners. This implementation of open innovation proved to be effective.

Of course, during this rapid development process, there were many uncertainties lingering in China's rail industry — such as the Yongwen rail accident in July 2011, and the arrest of the Minister of Railways in the same year, which challenged the ministry and China's high-speed industry. At this critical moment, the central government played an important role: the State Council first disbanded the Ministry of Railways, and organized a new state-owned enterprise called China Railway to take up responsibility for the entire high-speed rail network and its expansion. In this respect, China Railway did not only submit a convincing report for the accident but also addressed the problems identified which helped it to regain the trust of the public and the government. In addition, this is the vivid description of the strong institutional capacity in China's socialist economic system where the vertex of control is the demonstration of the effects of public ownership.

Conclusion

In summary, we can use the famous Confucius approach to describe the drivers behind China's competitiveness. Confucius put forward the three classical questions in "Learning" which is part of the *Analects* (Nan, 2018). First, the idea of "learning and then practicing at every moment" highlights learning applied efficiently in daily life, a concept of self-control, and continuous improvements. Second, the notion that "the friend appreciating you may come from somewhere far away," urges you to be open-minded and patiently sticking to what you trust until it finally deserves you even if it may cost you a long time of waiting. Here, devotion and confirmation are the virtue. Third, the principle "do not get angry even when others don't understand you," urges you to just do the right thing, and do what you think is right, caring little for the remarks or disturbances around you. If we review the process of China's socialist development, its competitiveness conforms to the above wisdom from Confucius. We briefly summarize them as follows:

Period 1 (1950s–1970s): The transformation from a closed economy to an open one

In 1949, when the People's Republic of China was founded, it was part of the Soviet camp. Despite such an environment, we can still identify China's unique development features: while the whole economic system was a planned economy, a degree of autonomy was permitted in certain fields; while China was modeling itself on the Soviet Union's planned economic system (Learning), it further sought to approach the international market to mitigate scarcity of certain products (Practicing). Here, the mixing governance of dominant control and limited autonomy was a key feature. China also used the Soviet Union's advanced experience as a benchmark and sought to mimic its best practice, which brought some recovery into the first Five-Year Plan. In fact, the most precious legacy of this decade's development was the establishment of China's independent and comprehensive manufacturing system, which laid the foundation for China's future global manufacturing center.

Period 2 (1970s–2000s): The transformation from the planned economy to a market economy

The 3rd Session of the 11th CPC Meeting in 1978 was a historical turning point in China's modernization development. Since then, opening and reform have become the theme of China's economic strategy as its involvement in the global economy (cooperation with Western countries) has been the priority and key objective. Here, we can witness the simultaneous changes in the triangle governance mode: while China has relaxed strict macro-control of central government policy and micro-control of state-owned firms, more autonomy has been delegated or transferred to local governments and township enterprises or private firms. If we make an evaluation using the ABCD model, Agility can be found widely in micro organizations, rural households, or city firms, given the incremental autonomy. These organizations quickly set the targets to benchmark at home and abroad and mimic best practice as soon as possible. At the same time, they have dived into the market to leverage the resources and try to lead toward synergy creation. The famous "three-plus-one" trading mix was the creation of that time. This period also witnessed the summit of China's demographic dividend. The inherited perspiration from China's culture, combined with more opportunities for openness and the positive high reward for the contribution all promoted the rapid development of China's economy. To some degree, China's dedication to its market economy transformation in this period was appreciated and welcomed by the WTO.

Period 3 (2001–): The integration into the world economy and China's unique revival road
At the end of 2001, the WTO welcomed China as the largest developing country in the world. In joining the WTO, it not only opened the door for Chinese firms/products to the global market but also brought the world product/service to the Chinese market. This marked the real beginning of open innovation in China. China's development since its reentry into the WTO produced three big effects on the world: first, China, as the biggest developing country, has successfully strode into the threshold of a middle-income developed country, which brings important hints for developing countries to consider. China's mixed experience may even contribute to other countries' development, which is the popular driver behind China's Belt and Road Initiative. Second, with China's rise, it has exerted more positive actions in dealing with its population growth, economic development, climate, and environmental protection. Moreover, the international governance system is being reshaped to be a more comprehensive and fairer one, in which developing countries will have their own independent voices and receive fair treatment. Third, China's economic development path was neither the former Soviet Union's mode nor a Western one. Its vision is beyond the narrow competition to surpass other developed countries; the original aspiration of China's socialist development is to strengthen its economic growth for a more sustainable future and make China better year by year. The political scientist Samuel Huntington stated in his book *Conflicts of Civilization* that China is a civilization disguised as a country, which really grasp the nature and driver of the legacy of China's long-term development (Huntington, 1996).

References

Chesbrough, H. 2003. *Open Innovation: The New Imperative for Creating and Profiting from Technology.* Boston: Harvard Business School Press.

Chesbrough, H. 2006. *Open Business Models: How to Thrive in the New Innovation Landscape.* Boston: Harvard Business School Press.

Gassmann, O., E. Enkel., and H. Chesbrough. 2010. The future of open innovation. *R&D Management* 40(3): 213–221.

Huntington, S. P. 1996. *The Clash of Civilizations and the Remaking of the World Order.* New York: Simon & Schuster.

Keidel, R. W. 2010. *The Geometry of Strategy: Concepts for Strategic Management.* New York: Routledge.

Li, C. 2014. Will market openness bring foreign technology? Path analysis on the advancement in science and technology. *Comparative Economic & Social Systems* 5:12–19.

Lin, Y. 2014. *New Structural Economics — A Framework for Rethinking Development and Policy.* Beijing: Peking University Press.

Lu, F. 2013. High-speed rail miracle beyond policy expectations. *Outlook Weekly* 12: 30–47.

Mathews, J. A. 2006. Dragon multinationals: New players in 21st century globalization. *Asia Pacific Journal of Management* 23(1): 5–27.

Moon, H. C. 2016. *The Strategy for Korea's Economic Success.* UK: Oxford University Press.

Nan, H. 2018. *A Selection of the Analects of Confucius.* Beijing: The East Publishing Press.

Zheng, F. and L. Chang. 2016. MNCs' innovation outsourcing research: empirical analysis and new discovery in China, *Nankai Economic Studies* 4: 99–114.

Zheng, F., H. Cai., and X. Zhong. 2019. Open innovation and new mechanism of 'technology marketization' by MNCs. *Nankai Economic Studies* 5: 180–197.

Zheng, F., H. Jiao., and H. Cai. 2018. Reappraisal of outbound open innovation under the policy of China's market for technology. *Technology Analysis & Strategic Management* 30(1): 1–14.

Chapter 14

Reinvigorating Policy and Modifying Practices: Lessons Learned from Indonesia's South–South Cooperation during COVID-19

Vimala Asty F. T. Jaya and Miranda Tahalele

Abstract

The COVID-19 global pandemic has severely impacted and challenged the globalized world. In the pre-pandemic era, human mobility and connectivity became the beacon toward developing cooperation, but now, countries are facing the consequences of lockdowns and other restrictions. However, this chapter argues that the global crisis still highlights the need for countries to continually expand cooperation as in the case of Indonesia. This chapter addresses critical questions: how the Indonesian government regulates and implements its South–South Cooperation (SSC) policy during the pandemic and what are the implications for future cooperation. Adjustment and alteration to Indonesia's SSC policy cannot be avoided in response to President Joko Widodo's policy directions. Therefore, the implementations of the development cooperation program have been modified with a new approach like the online technical cooperation training program. The challenges and opportunities for developing a coherent policy and implementing it during the COVID-19 pandemic should be acknowledged as it gives value to Indonesia's roles in SSC. With the lessons learned from the implementation of the program, the roles of the state in extending national policy became more significant during this crisis.

Keywords: South–South Cooperation, COVID-19, Indonesia's government policy, development cooperation, knowledge sharing

Introduction

With the rise of many countries in the Global South as emerging powers and middle-income countries, the capacity to cooperate and to make connections among them in economic, political, and social–cultural contexts has also increased and expanded. However, these conditions changed dramatically with the spread of the COVID-19 global pandemic. During this crisis, countries were forced to adapt to specific health protocols and readjust their policies to include re-programming and budget reallocation. Several activities had to be modified toward specific public health measures and protocols applied: many countries imposed travel restrictions, closed borders, and imposed regional or local lockdown measures. Almost all countries have utilized their resources to address the pandemic while other programs have been left in limbo amidst the general uncertainty regarding the pandemic.

During this difficult time, the Government of Indonesia was expected to respond with approaches beyond their day-to-day activities. The pandemic has created a sense of uncertainty with the increasing number of infection and death rates in many countries, including Indonesia. Therefore, it cannot be denied that an adequate policy response is very critical to be practical and pragmatic during this challenging time.

It is noticeable that this crisis has not only impacted the public health of the people but also the government's other development programs. However, it should not be neglected that despite this public health crisis that has subsequently resulted in an economic crisis, the government still needs to conduct and implement its broader national program in order to achieve its targeted activities, improve living conditions, and remain committed to the ties with other stakeholders. During this turbulent time, the Government of Indonesia (GOI) has conducted several re-programming of its development policies in order to respond to the crisis. Therefore, this chapter intends to explore and analyze the approaches implemented by the GOI in conducting the South–South Cooperation (SSC) program during this pandemic crisis. It discusses the questions on how the government is regulating and implementing its SSC policy (as a non-public health issue) during the crisis, and what are the implications for future development cooperation. Furthermore, this chapter is divided into three sections which explore the implications of the pandemic to a global setting and national policy of international development cooperation; it discusses the implementation of Indonesia's SSC programs during the pandemic; analyze the implications of the pandemic upon the future of SSC as well as offer the policy recommendations.

Global and National Policy of Development Cooperation

In the past decade, the countries of the Global South have displayed their role in international development cooperation. They managed to develop a cooperation structure that is often considered as a challenge to the traditional development cooperation structure of North–South Cooperation. SSC has elevated the narratives and debates on the contribution and the role of the Global South in international development cooperation, especially with their rise as (re)emerging donor countries. Such cooperation has expanded the model not only from cooperation through the exchange of knowledge, expert dispatch, and technical cooperation but also to the cooperation through the expansion in economic cooperation and trade (UNOSSC, 2021). With its strong narratives of solidarity, win-win solution, and mutual benefit, SSC was built and developed into a horizontal partnership that differs from the top-down approach or vertical relationship that is often associated with North–South Cooperation (Kilby, 2017, 2018; Madwsley, 2012). This cooperation structure showcases that some countries have gained hegemony over others and drives further debate on the shape of global development cooperation. The rise of the Global South has challenged the traditional structure, intending to minimize the structural gap in development cooperation.

During the COVID-19 pandemic, global conditions have changed drastically, as all countries in the world face a great threat to public health. It is very evident that the role of governments in navigating and managing their domestic situation is becoming more relevant and important as a result. Some of the government's approaches include developing sound policy and establishing crisis management systems that are relevant and safe in guiding the country to pass through the pandemic. Several public health restrictions and protocols, as was mentioned earlier, have been applied to reduce the spread of the virus in the community. The obvious impact of these policies was that it has promoted more isolation amongst many countries. The effect of the pandemic and the adjustment made in the national policy have also, directly and indirectly, influenced the degree of commitment that the country makes to other countries. It cannot be neglected that this global pandemic has amplified the effect of the global development cooperation to the extent that it can change its future trajectory. Therefore, the current situation raises further questions on how the COVID-19 crisis impacted the global setting and national policy of development cooperation, especially with SSC, and how the country should modify its development cooperation policy to remain relevant and resilient during this global health crisis.

Global pandemic and the setting of international development cooperation

The global structure of international development cooperation, previously dominated by the vertical structure and geopolitical hegemony of northern countries to those in the Global South, is becoming obscured during the COVID-19 pandemic (Campbell and Doshi, 2020; Lemus-Delgado, 2020; Sidiropoulos, 2020). This condition showcases that there is a gap in the regulation and mechanism of global development cooperation, which is becoming more difficult to be managed by international cooperation. For example, COVID-19 vaccine distribution gap between developing and developed countries that remains challenging to the efforts for a global solution through development cooperation as many developed countries hesitant to join the COVAX Facility[1] (Oh, 2021). Countries are becoming more vulnerable and isolated than before as they now focus more on their domestic issues (Sidiropoulos, 2020). The current trend highlights that geopolitical domination is no longer relevant. Only a few countries can

---

[1]COVAX Facility is one of the pillars of Access to COVID-19 Tools (ACT) related to procurement and distribution for global vaccine to all countries in the world, led by Coalition for Epidemic Preparedness Coalition (CEPI), GAVI, and WHO as well as UNICEF as delivery partner (https://www.gavi.org/covax-facility, accessed on May 30, 2021).

still maintain their balance and relevance in global politics, with their capacity to support other countries as well as manage their national health challenges (Lemus-Delgado, 2020). The relevance of north–south relations is also being questioned as several emerging countries, such as China and South Korea, are playing more active roles in handling the global pandemic by supporting international organizations such as WHO and other countries in need (Igoe and Chadwick, 2020; Lemus-Delgado, 2020). Therefore, many northern countries have struggled to assert their dominance, as several countries from the Global South have contributed significantly to global development cooperation during the pandemic (Campbell and Doshi, 2020; Lemus-Delgado, 2020). This situation stimulates further discussion on whether this global structure will remain significant in the post-pandemic era.

It is very clear that this global health crisis has severely impacted upon the economic conditions of many countries that could possibly induce a recession. The International Monetary Fund (IMF) has projected that this crisis has caused global economic growth of around −4% in 2020, worse than the 2008–2009 financial crisis. (IMF, 2020; Lemus-Delgado, 2020). To support countries in need, the IMF and several regional financial organizations have promised to offer support by providing and allocating stimulus programs to handle the crisis (Stubbs *et al.*, 2021). Global financial schemes are also being reallocated, refocusing on public health and economic recovery — rather than on aid for development purposes (Lemus-Delgado, 2020). As many countries have to deal with severe financial problems derived from the pandemic, the national budget allocation for international aid has further been rearranged to prioritize the national needs among countries. The Development Assistance Committee (DAC) of Organisation for Economic Cooperation and Development (OECD) 2019 and 2020 reports on the financial projection of development aid have identified that budget rationalization cannot be avoided despite several estimations that have projected an increase of aid allocation from member countries (Lemus-Delgado, 2020; Wood, 2021). Furthermore, the amount of aid and loans provided by non-DAC OECD members, especially those from the Global South, which has been significant during this crisis and needs to be acknowledged (Campbell and Doshi, 2020).

Looking at the conditions of the global financial system, it can be identified that in the next few years, development cooperation might refocus its themes, issues, approaches, and modalities. For example, the issues of mitigating future health crises, developing a resilient health program and system, global vaccination program, and economic recovery program are going to be significant and relevant issues for global development cooperation. Furthermore, knowledge sharing in handling the pandemic crisis and post-pandemic crisis will also be essential as countries face challenges and problems that can be solved through the sharing of knowledge on containment measures and other countries' experiences (Igoe and Chadwick, 2020). Therefore, international development cooperation — including SSC — remains relevant in contributing and supporting countries during and after the crisis. The significance of SSC in the future depends on how the Global South can continue to recognize the value of learning and sharing knowledge with other countries, which have become a foundation of SSC over many years.

The implications of COVID-19 on the national policy of development cooperation

As Christensen and Lægreid (2020) argue that crisis management in public policy has become an important arena for leaders and bureaucrats to address, specifically to minimize the impact of this COVID-19 pandemic. Government approaches to the crisis can be discussed in terms of their legitimacy and capacity to modify and implement their policies and programs (Christensen and Lægreid, 2020). At the same time, government responses can be explored through the application of their crisis management policy at the strategic and operational levels (Boin and t'Hart, 2010; Weible et al., 2020). Policy application can directly or indirectly impact upon public policy in general, not just public health policy. Therefore, strong coordination is necessary during the crisis to assess the conditions and incorporate all layers of government bodies as well as the private sector, NGOs, and communities (Boin and Bynander, 2015; Weible et al., 2020). Given the COVID-19 crisis that occurred in Indonesia, President Joko Widodo has appointed the head of Indonesian National Board for Disaster Management (*Badan Nasional Penanggulangan Bencana*) Doni Monardo to lead the crisis management team for handling the COVID-19 pandemic (Gorbiano, 2020). Later, a specific task force for handling the situation was established. This task force's main responsibilities include minimizing the impact of the pandemic upon public health, economic, and socio-cultural sectors, and limiting its damage upon other parts of society.

During the pandemic, political leaders and government officials tended to conduct a pragmatic approach especially by adjusting regulations based upon their knowledge and understanding (Christensen and Lægreid, 2020). For example, several policies had to be reshaped to deal with health and economic problems. One of the necessary adjustments conducted by the GOI was budget reallocation specifically to cover the public health and economic stimulus programs (Official 3 [interview], 2021). This modification was implemented as part of the government's strategy to minimize the extension of the health crisis to economic and financial issues (Christensen and Lægreid, 2020). The direct impact of budget reallocation was that ministries and government institutions had to revise and readjust several activities and programs including those for SSC (Official 2 [interview], 2021). However, some programs might not be able to be implemented, despite the budget reallocation, because of the limitation of mobility and health protocols that need to be followed. As a result, exploring different approaches to the activities and programs becomes necessary.

The challenge to implement a sound policy and program becomes necessary — and needs to be explored further — especially on how non-health-related policies were impacted during the pandemic, and how governments have adjusted their programs. According to Boin and t'Hart (2010), there are at least five steps that need to be conducted during crises, which are as follows: diagnosing and deciding, mobilizing and organizing, containing and mitigating, informing and empowering, and coordinating and collaborating. These approaches can also be applied to other issues as this pandemic has impacted non-public health issues. In this context, policy, budget, and activities modification cannot be avoided and cooperation commitment with other countries in relation to SSC needs to be re-negotiated and re-communicated. Plans for the programs and activities need to be rearranged as well. Therefore, it is important to explore the application of non-public health policy and implementation, including the opportunities and challenges, during the crisis through the analysis of the GOI's reformulation of its SSC policy and the implication of this crisis to the non-public health issue.

Indonesia's South–South Cooperation during COVID-19

Indonesia's SSC is rooted in the history and principles that resulted from the 1955 Bandung Conference, an event which provided significant milestones for the narratives and direction of Indonesia's development cooperation. Soekarno, Indonesia's first President, and other Global South leaders who attended the Bandung Conference, envisioned Asian-African cooperation or Global South cooperation as a way to build a horizontal and equal developmental relationship with the spirits of anti-colonialism, solidarity, mutual benefits, and a win-win solution (Carmody, 2013; Mawdsley, 2012). After the 1955 Bandung Conference, Indonesia actively participated in the Non-Alignment Movement (NAM) and later established the NAM Centre of South-South Technical Cooperation (NAMC-SSTC) in 1995 (Engel, 2017). With the emergence of the NAM and G77 in the 1970s, the United Nations (UN) responded in 1978 by enacting the Buenos Aires Action Plan (BAPA) on Technical Cooperation as a mechanism to expand SSC and other cooperation among developing countries (Engel, 2017). The GOI adopted the resolution and expanded its SSC policy and management with the development of Indonesia's Technical Cooperation Program (ITCP) under the Cabinet Secretariat in 1981 (Engel, 2017; Hosono, 2018; Muhibat, 2016). ITCP was managing the SSC program and activities to other developing and under-developing countries, including facilitating the Triangular Cooperation supported by donor countries (Hosono, 2018).

With the end of the Soeharto regime in 1998 and later the Asia financial crisis in 1999, Indonesia's SSC program was swept under the radar as the GOI focused on recovering its economy. Indonesia's SSC was reinitiated after the enactment of the Jakarta Commitment in 2009, followed by the raising of Indonesia's status to Middle-Income Country (MIC) and a member of the G20 (Hosono, 2018). The idea to scale up SSC was additionally manifested by the GOI with the establishment of the National Coordination Team (NCT)[2] on South–South and Triangular Cooperation in 2010 (Hosono, 2018; NCT-SSTC, 2015). The notion to expand SSC was not only identified as a way to bring up the diplomatic value of development cooperation but also as a way to expand Indonesia's position within other developing countries and in global development fora. Since then, the GOI applied specific approaches to SSC including identifying SSC in a national development planning document, allocating a special budget for SSC programs and activities, improving management and governance of SSC, and extending its participation in global forums and regional cooperation (Hosono, 2018). These initiatives highlighted the

---

[2]The NCT SSC consists of the Ministry of Foreign Affairs, the Ministry of National Development Planning, the Ministry of State Secretariat, and the Ministry of Finance.

importance of SSC for Indonesia's development cooperation policies and signified SSC as one of the government's prioritized programs.

In recent years, Indonesia's SSC manifested its strong commitment and contribution to global development with the principle of "Better Partnership for Prosperity (NCT-SSTC, 2015)." Such cooperation continues to emphasize the narratives of solidarity, mutual respect, and equal partnership in working together to achieve common development goals. From 2014 to 2019, Indonesia has engaged in SSC programs comprised of 326 programs that have benefited 5870 participants from 134 countries with a budget of more than 100 million USD (NCT-SSTC, 2015, 2016, 2017, 2018, 2019a). The main modality of Indonesia's SSC is a capacity-building training program, where the GOI has invited officials and practitioners from other developing countries to share and exchange knowledge on specific thematic issues. In 2019, Indonesia conducted 74 SSC training programs and established around 30 training centers and centers of excellences (Indonesia began with 14 centers in 2014) with specific on-site technology and ready-made training modules or tailor-made programs (NCT-SSTC, 2019b).

The GOI has recognized the need to strengthen the implementation of SSC in the National Medium Term Development Plan (*Rencana Pembangunan Jangka Menengah Nasional* — RPJMN) 2020–2024, under priority seven[3] "Strengthening stability of political, legal and security affairs and transformation of public services" (Government of Indonesia, 2020). This expresses the strong commitment by the government to expand and scale up SSC and its contribution to global development cooperation fora. In RPJMN 2020–2024, the GOI further identifies the goals of SSC for implementing 553 SSC programs with a budget allocation of IDR 777 billion. For 2020, the GOI additionally planned to implement 86 SSC programs in three focus areas: development (poverty alleviation, animal husbandry and agriculture, disaster risk management, infrastructure planning and budgeting, and education), economics (macroeconomic management, public finance, microfinance, and

---

[3]The Government of Indonesia's Working Plan under RPJMN 2020–2024 covers seven national development priorities, which are as follows: (1) strengthening economic resilience, (2) developing regions, (3) improving human resources, (4) spreading the mental revolution spirit, (5) improving disaster resilience, (6) supporting climate change agenda, and (7) strengthening stability of political, legal, and security affairs and transformation of public services (Government of Indonesia, 2020).

micro–small–medium enterprises), and good governance and peacebuilding (democracy, peace, conflict resolution, law enforcement, and central and regional government relations) (NCT-SSTC, 2019b). However, the situation changed drastically with the outbreak of the COVID-19 pandemic which affected the planning and implementation of the program.

Like many other countries, the global pandemic has thrown the country into a state of confusion and uncertainty. This situation has forced the GOI to shift its policy. Several adjustments have been made by the GOI, and most notably two regulations were enacted by re-establishing a national policy and budget allocation to handle the pandemic. The first regulation was Government Regulation Number 1, which was issued on March 13, 2020 (*Peraturan Pemerintah Pengganti Undang-Undang — Perppu*, 1/2020) on the State Financial Policy and Stability of Financial Systems for the Management of COVID-19 Virus Disease 2019 and/or Encounter the Threats to National Economy and/or Stability of Financial Systems. This regulation stipulates the policy and actions taken by the GOI, including to allocate state fund of around IDR 405.1 trillion to handle the impact of COVID-19. The second regulation is Presidential Regulation Number 54 that was introduced on April 3, 2020 (*Peraturan Presiden — Perpres*, 54/2020) on the Revision of Allocation and Details in the Income and Expenses of the State Budget 2020. This regulation outlines the detailed budget spending for various policy designs to mitigate the economic effects of the COVID-19 pandemic.

The GOI policies to manage the COVID-19 pandemic have affected the implementation of national programs, including international development cooperation and the SSC program. For example, the budget allocation of several ministries has also been reduced by IDR 97.42 trillion due to the spending on the COVID-19 response program. With the reallocation of the national budget to respond to the pandemic, ministries and government agencies had to reprioritize their budget allocation for programs to the ones that are aligned with the government's policy in handling the COVID-19 pandemic. Therefore, the allocation of the budget toward SSC programs has been significantly reduced, resulting in the revision of their target implementation for 2020, from 86 programs to 68 programs (Official 1 [interview], 2021). However, Indonesia is still maintaining its commitment to contribute to the global development cooperation, especially to support other developing countries in handling the pandemic. Indonesia has distributed aid grants and conducted online training programs for several countries including Fiji, PNG, Timor Leste,

Solomon Island, and Palestine during this time (Official 2 [interview], 2021).

With the modality of SSC that depends on an in-person learning process, the limitations of mobility due to the pandemic caused several setbacks in the implementation of activities. At the beginning of the outbreak, not a single SSC program could be implemented as people could not travel abroad during the pandemic. This has led to several planned programs being either cancelled or postponed while the GOI seeks possible ways to implement new ones. After the New Normal policy was launched, the GOI began to encourage ministries and agencies to continue with their regular activities as long as they comply with standard health protocols. For instance, the central government also urged ministries and institutions to continue working by changing the way people work including shifting from offline to online platforms. In the second half of 2020, Indonesia's ministries and agencies finally managed to implement several SSC programs with new approaches — developed under the New Normal policy. These programs were conducted virtually with adjustment to the learning schemes and curriculum. Some of the contents include Training on Strategic Partnership with Muslim Religious Leaders in Family Planning and Knowledge Sharing Program for BARMM (Bangsamoro Autonomous Region for Muslim Mindanao) of the Philippines Youth Muslim Leaders implemented by the National Population and Family Planning Board (*Badan Kependudukan dan Keluarga Berencana Nasional* — BKKBN); Knowledge Sharing Program on Enhancing the Development of Small and Medium Industry implemented by Ministry of Industry; Training on Impact-Based Forecast implemented by Agency for Meteorology, Climatology, and Geophysics; and Webinar on Aquaculture Development for Shrimp, Sea Cucumber, Seaweeds implemented by Ministry of Agriculture. These SSC programs would normally be conducted as in-person training programs but had to be changed and adjusted into online training programs during the pandemic.

Compared to the in-person training methods, online ones have both strengths and weaknesses. Based on the results of the evaluation conducted by the Ministry of State Secretariat as a member of NCT SSC, there are several challenges in conducting online training. The most common issue is unstable internet connections, as online training requires all organizer, instructors, and participants to have reliable internet speeds. However, most of Indonesia's SSC beneficiary countries are from developing countries that have challenges with communication and information technology infrastructures (Official 2 [interview], 2021). Therefore, before the program is conducted, both training organizers and participants need to ensure the availability of required infrastructure including a stable internet connection and the availability of supporting tools such as computers.

Furthermore, it was discovered that not all in-person training programs can be fully converted into online ones, specifically the training programs that involve practice-based learning. As a result, online training programs are limited to sharing knowledge and experience to off line program participants only. For example, before the pandemic, most SSC programs offered a field trip training for participants in order to enhance their practical understanding, knowledge, and skills of the issues. These methods have been the strength of Indonesia's SSC program; however, such practice-based activity was not possible through the online training program. Another challenge when implementing the SSC program online is that obtaining the full commitment from participants to attend the entire training program is often challenging. Several training participants often did not fully participate in the whole program or were doing other tasks at the same time while participating in the training program. This induced extra efforts among the training organizers to communicate with participants who missed the training program through email or other communication tools. One of the alternative solutions to ensure full participation was to require participants to have a full attendance record in order to receive a training certificate. However, despite this requirement, there were still a few participants who did not demonstrate complete attendance of the program.

Despite all of these challenges, there are several opportunities to expand and conduct the online SSC training programs. Indonesia was able to invite more participants as online training programs do not require traveling to Indonesia. For example, the training on Strategic Partnership with Muslim Religious Leaders in Family Planning was attended by 30 participants in 2020 (Bureau for Foreign Technical Cooperation, 2020b) compared to 23 participants in 2019 that was conducted through the in-person session (Bureau for Foreign Technical Cooperation, 2019b). Another program, the Knowledge Sharing Program on Enhancing the Development of Small and Medium Industries, was joined by 40 participants in 2020 (Bureau for Foreign Technical Cooperation, 2020a) compared to only 19 participants in 2019 (Bureau for Foreign Technical Cooperation, 2019a). With more participants, Indonesia was able to widen its scope of collaboration in sharing knowledge and experiences. Another positive aspect is that the online training program was less costly than doing so in person. These benefits both training organizers and participants as the organizers do not need to prepare logistics and accommodation for participants, and the participants do not need to spend extra on travel expenses and commit additional travel time. With these explorations of challenges and opportunities on the implementation of Indonesia's SSC during the pandemic, the debate continues on what lessons can be learned and how SSC and development cooperation can be expanded in the post-pandemic environment.

Development Cooperation beyond COVID-19

Despite the plan that was proposed in 2019, adjustment and changes in Indonesia's SSC program was unavoidable when the COVID-19 pandemic hit the country. It has exposed the limitations and strengths of a country, including the unsustainability of some activities during and after the crisis. As SSC, especially its technical cooperation program involves interaction with other countries, the modification of the modalities of the program cannot be avoided. Upon the first glance, the implementation of Indonesia's SSC program during the pandemic can be considered to be functioning (or somewhat successful). However, there are possible risks that can be challenging for the future implementation of SSC. Three issues can be identified from the experiences which contribute to the debate on how to expand and sustain the SSC program and cooperation in the future.

The first issue is that modification of the program is most likely to take place at the level of activities, not at the level of overall policy. The general policy of SSC has not changed because it is still considered as a national priority program. However, funding allocation has been slashed and reallocated in 2020 due to the spending on the COVID-19 response program, and the activities also need to be modified and changed. In 2021, all SSC programs would be conducted within the new normal setting and its 2021 budget will be fully allocated as planned (Official 3 [interview], 2021). Nonetheless, it is important to note that the impact of the crisis on the implementation of the program and activities proved the unsustainability of SSC. Therefore, there is a need to develop contingency or an alternative national program, that is tangible to be achieved during and after the crisis. The government response to the crisis shall not be a "panic" response but a pragmatic and tangible one. The future policy should be able to identify several alternative models of cooperation and activities that can be implemented during the crisis. For example, expanding the alternative model of technical cooperation including by combining face-to-face or in-person training program with online programs. As most general policies remain the same, this alternative method signals possible alternations that can be undertaken for future programs.

The second issue is that consolidation and communication between stakeholders to conduct activities in a safe environment remains relevant. Working with conditions that allow the limitation of mobility and tight health protocols is likely to be still applicable in several years to come. Therefore, the online model for training programs that has been utilized, will still be relevant for future cooperation, because it effectively gains more participants and also can minimize cost. However, the program and its activities need to be better planned in order to achieve their target; this attempt includes developing a better curriculum and delivering an interesting training program. Therefore, the agency and training organizer have to develop a way to communicate more effectively with partners and participants as well as within their own institutions to gain the full benefit from a hybrid online program.

The third issue is that the technical and infrastructure issues of the online training program need to be mitigated. From the current experience, it can be identified that there are wide gaps in countries' capacity in accessing and utilizing digital devices including limited access to Wi-Fi that affects the connection quality as well as the limited digital literacy and infrastructures such as the capacity to access an online device. Therefore, online technology, digital literacy, and digital infrastructure devices become important factors for the implementation of SSC activities in the future, especially in developing a model of a program that is more sustainable. This experience also captured the importance of assessing and reviewing the technical and infrastructure capacity of the training participants before conducting an online program.

Looking in the context of global cooperation, regional and multilateral dialogues become important for countries to stay connected during the pandemic specially to understand how other countries deal with similar challenges. Since the GOI still identifies SSC as a national priority, its practice of SSC during the pandemic remains relevant to be explored and it additionally highlights Indonesia's commitment to the development cooperation agenda. Therefore, the model of knowledge sharing applied by SSC can still be relevant to provide a platform for regional and multilateral cooperation and dialogue. SSC can be utilized and extended as a forum for countries to expand connections and gain knowledge from other countries' experiences, such as developing alternative policies based on the lessons learned from other countries. Therefore, the experiences during the crisis and the government responses need to be documented because the experiences of modifying and readjusting policy implementation will not only benefit the country but also others.

Conclusion

The COVID-19 global pandemic has witnessed countries face uncertainty amidst difficult conditions. This crisis has forced governments to adjust their approaches, policies, programs, and national budget allocation. The condition acknowledges that the sovereignty of a country becomes more important, especially in managing the crisis that impacted society massively. It cannot be denied that this crisis has changed and challenged development cooperation mechanisms especially when mobility and restriction became problems. Facing many limitations, governments have taken necessary actions to be admissible during the crisis including modifying policies and utilizing digital technology. The case of Indonesia's SSC shows not only the challenges but also opportunities for the implementation of the program during the pandemic, including why it is important to modify the program and continue the activities. It points out that creativity, collaboration, and willingness to take risks to become the main factors for the SSC program, therefore, it can still be relevant during and after the crisis. SSC can be utilized as a platform for countries to learn from each other through a training program as it facilitates each country to explore an alternative policy based on countries' experiences while leading and learning by the examples.

References

Boin, A. and F. Bynander. 2015. Explaining success and failure in crisis coordination. *Geografiska Annaler: Series A, Physical Geography* 97(1): 123–135.

Boin, A. and P. t'Hart. 2010. Organising for effective emergency management: Lessons from research 1. *Australian Journal of Public Administration* 69(4): 357–371.

Bureau for Foreign Technical Cooperation. 2019a. *Report on Capacity Building Program on Enhancing the Development of Small and Medium Industry*. Jakarta: Ministry of State Secretariat.

Bureau for Foreign Technical Cooperation. 2019b. *Report on Training on Strategic Partnership with Muslim Religious Leaders in Family Planning*. Jakarta: Ministry of State Secretariat.

Bureau for Foreign Technical Cooperation. 2020a. *Report on Knowledge Sharing Program on Enhancing the Development of Small and Medium Industry.* Jakarta: Ministry of State Secretariat.

Bureau for Foreign Technical Cooperation. 2020b. *Report on Training on Strategic Partnership with Muslim Religious Leaders in Family Planning.* Jakarta: Ministry of State Secretariat.

Campbell, K. M. and R. Doshi. 2020. The coronavirus could reshape global order: China is manoeuvring for international leadership as United States falters. *Foreign Affairs.* https://www.foreignaffairs.com/articles/china/2020-03-18/coronavirus-could-reshape-global-order. (Accessed on 20 March 2021).

Carmody, D. P. 2013. *The Rise of the BRICS in Africa: The Geopolitics of South–South Relations.* London: Zed Books.

Christensen, T. and P. Lægreid. 2020. Balancing governance capacity and legitimacy: How the Norwegian government handled the COVID-19 crisis as a high performer. *Public Administration Review* 80(5): 774–779.

Engel, S. 2017. South-South Cooperation Strategies in Indonesia: Domestic and International Drivers. Graf, A. & Hashim, A (Eds). *African-Asian Encounters: New Cooperations and New Dependencies.* pp. 155–182. Amsterdam: Amsterdam University Press, IIAS.

Gorbiano, M. I. 2020. Covid 19: Jokowi forms fast-response team to contain virus. *The Jakarta Post.* https://www.thejakartapost.com/news/2020/03/13/covid-19-jokowi-forms-fast-response-team-to-contain-virus.html. (Accessed on the 21 March 2021).

Government of Indonesia 2020. *National Medium-Term Development Plan (Rencanan pembangunan jangka menengah nasional – RPJMN) 2020–2024.* Jakarta: Ministry of National Development Planning.

Hosono, A. 2018. Potential and challenges for emerging development partners: The case of Indonesia. *IDS Bulletin* 49(2): 13–29.

Igoe, M. and Chadwick, V. 2020. After the pandemic: How will COVID-19 transform global health and development? Devex. https://www.devex.com/news/after-the-pandemic-how-will-covid-19-transform-global-health-and-development-96936. (Accessed on 19 March 2021).

International Monetary Fund. 2020. World Economic Outlook, October 2020: A Long and Difficult Ascent. World Economic Outlook Reports. https://www.imf.org/en/Publications/WEO/Issues/2020/09/30/world-economic-outlook-october-2020. (Accessed on 30 March 2021).

Kilby, P. 2017. *China and the United States as Aid Donors: Past and Future Trajectories.* Washington, DC: East-West Center.

Kilby, P. 2018. DAC is dead? Implications for teaching development studies. *Asia Pacific Viewpoint* 59(2): 226–234.

Lemus-Delgado, D. 2020. South–South cooperation: A solution for the post-pandemic. *NIICE Special Report* 1005 (June 2020). Kathmandu: Nepal Institute for International Cooperation and Engagement.

Mawdsley, E. D. 2012. *From Recipients to Donors: Emerging Powers and the Changing Development Landscape*. London: Zed Books.

Muhibat, S. 2016. Charting the path to development effectiveness: Indonesia's SSC challenges. In A. Mulakala (Ed.), *Contemporary Asian Perspectives on South–South Cooperation*. Korea: KDI — TAF. pp. 118–136.

Oh, W. 2021. Rethinking global vaccine inequality: Lessons from game theory. *Georgetown Journal of International Affairs*. https://gjia.georgetown.edu/2021/04/10/rethinking-global-vaccine-inequality-lessons-from-game-theory/. (Accessed on 22 March 2021).

Sidiropoulos, E. 2020. Africa after COVID-19 and the retreat of globalism. *Policy Insights* 83 (April 2020). Johannesburg: South African Institute of International Affairs.

SSTC, NCT. 2015. *Annual Report of Indonesia's South–South and Triangular Cooperation (SSTC) 2014*. Jakarta: NCT SSTC.

SSTC, NCT. 2016. *Annual Report of Indonesia's South–South and Triangular Cooperation (SSTC) 2015*. Jakarta: NCT SSTC.

SSTC, NCT. 2017. *Annual Report of Indonesia's South–South and Triangular Cooperation (SSTC) 2016*. Jakarta: NCT SSTC.

SSC, NCT. 2018. *Annual Report of Indonesia's South–South Cooperation 2017: Moving towards Better SSC Management*. Jakarta: NCT SSC.

SSC, NCT. 2019a. *Annual Report of Indonesia's South–South Cooperation 2018*. Jakarta: NCT SSC.

SSC, NCT. 2019b. *Indonesia's Progress in South–South Cooperation: Advancing Together to a Better World*. Jakarta: NCT SSC.

SSC, NCT. 2020. *Annual Report of Indonesia's South–South Cooperation 2019*. Jakarta: NCT SSC.

Stubbs, T., W. Kring, C. Laskaridis, A. Kentikelenis, and K. Gallagher. 2021. Whatever it takes? The global financial safety net, Covid-19, and developing countries. *World Development* 137: 105171.

UN Office of South-South Cooperation. 2021. About UN Office of South-South and Triangular Cooperation. https://www.unsouthsouth.org/about/about-sstc/ (Accessed on 20 March 2021).

Weible, C. M., D. Nohrstedt, P. Cairney, D. P. Carter, D. A. Crow, A. P. Durnová, T. Heikkila, K. Ingold, A. McConnell, and D. Stone. 2020. COVID-19 and the policy sciences: Initial reactions and perspectives. *Policy Sciences* 53(2): 225–241.

Wood, T. 2021. Global aid increase in 2020. *Development Policy Blog*. https://devpolicy.org/global-aid-2020-20210414-4/. (Accessed on 15 April 2021).

Chapter 15

From Fundamental Research to Industrial Application: The Global Competitiveness of Swiss Universities

Christoph A. von Arb

Abstract

The pivotal role that academic institutions play today as essential drivers of innovation, which creates market value and warrants a high standard of living in a fiercely competitive global economy, is unparalleled. For Switzerland, where the cost of living is among the highest in the world, it is a must to perform at the very top now as the impact of deficits will only be felt years later. Therefore, one needs to ask if the academic institutions are performing at the required level? In a benchmark study, Swiss universities were compared with some of the world's leading research institutions through the analysis of 40 performance indicators with a focus on the efforts "Science to Market." Looking at higher education in Switzerland, it is notable that the student population has been growing disproportionally since 2010 due to the higher enrolment of foreign students. Furthermore, Swiss universities are known for their excellence in fundamental research including public/private partnership projects. This was confirmed with the two Swiss Federal Institutes of Technology leading in front. However, when focusing on "Science to Market" efforts, the rankings were pretty low. Whether looking at invention disclosures, patent applications, technology licensing, university spin-offs, or venture capital deals, a significant weakness in the competitive position of Swiss universities *vis-à-vis* its global competitors became apparent.

Keywords: Swiss universities, international benchmark, global competition, war for talent, quality of academic research, Science to Market, public–private partnerships

Introduction

Today, academia is often at the epicenter of innovation. At every "Innovation Hotspot" of the world, there is at least one top-performing research university. Alongside this, past innovations under "Made in Switzerland," such as "Velcro" or the "World Wide Web," were the results of a synergistic interplay between university and industry. The surrounding businesses and industries are the primary beneficiaries of these efforts whether through the employment of emerging talents, research cooperation, or university spin-off companies. For decades, there was a disconnection between academic research and market application. While Swiss universities were expected to perform their fundamental research at a very high level, they were rather discouraged to look at opportunities for commercial application. So-called applied research was left entirely to the private sector. While this system seemed to work well in the past, academic research in many fields of science has become crucial for the market to lead in innovations. At the same time, the globalization of science and market has added a new element of competition among academic institutions worldwide and it is affecting the recruitment of talent, the overall economic development, and the standard of living at large.

Since Swiss universities are primarily financed by the public sector, the funding agencies are obligated to provide evidence that the taxpayers' investments are paying off by assessing the following questions: (a) Is academic research in Switzerland performing at a top level from a global point of view? (b) Are the world's brightest talents studying in Switzerland? and (c) Do the universities actively seek the exploitation of the resulting innovation potential by industry? If so, the traditional funding mechanism of Swiss universities, in which the funding from the public sector accounts for about 70 percent or more of the universities' overall expenditures, is reasonable because the university locations will generate dynamic visibility beyond national borders, trigger the interest of the champions in the global innovation economy, and motivate them to seek collaborations at Swiss locations.

In a recent international benchmark study[1] on behalf of the private foundation Fondation CH2048, the consulting firm TRIPLEYE Inc. analyzed the transfer of scientific discoveries among Swiss universities to the market based on 40 performance indicators. The eight largest Swiss universities were compared with 22 of the world's leading universities in the US, Europe, and Asia (Figure 1).

Swiss Universities are Small but Growing

Swiss universities are among the smallest in the CH2048 Innovations monitoring 2020 benchmark study. However, the assumption that the

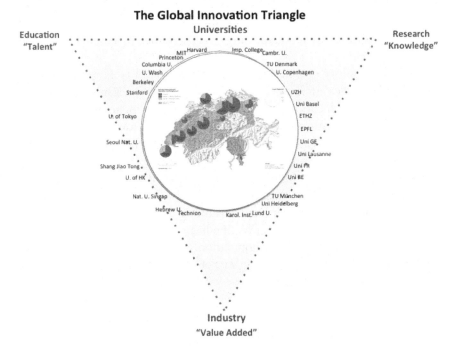

Figure 1. The global innovation triangle including all universities analyzed in the benchmark study.

Note: The insert is a map of Switzerland with the locations of its universities.

Source: von Arb (2020).

---

[1] This chapter is based entirely on the findings and original illustrations of the report CH2048 Innovationsmonitoring 2020 by the author Christoph A. von Arb.

student per professor/faculty ratio would be equally small is wrong. While small universities in the US such as Princeton and Stanford have a student per professor/faculty ratio of less than 10, the ratio at the University of Geneva is more than 20 and at the Federal Institute of Technology in Zurich (ETHZ), there are 40 students per professor/faculty. Interestingly, a smaller student per professor ratio does not seem to impact the "employer reputation" of an academic institution in the private sector. It appears that it is primarily the "brand," the global reputation and recognition of an academic institution that shapes the "employer reputation." This may well be the reason why particularly the elite universities in the US, Cambridge University and Imperial College in the UK, and Technical University in Munich are all highly ranked in this survey. They actively promote their global visibility and are thus able to position themselves ahead of the best Asian institutions in Japan, Singapore, and China. Regarding Switzerland, only ETHZ (rank 28) is among the top 50 in the world.

The availability of a highly educated talent pool is extremely important for an innovation-driven economy. In Switzerland, the highly regarded "Dual Education System" used in the past meant that the enrollment levels and graduation rates in the tertiary sector remained low by international standards. It took federal reform of Swiss law on Vocational Training and Education at the Universities of Applied Sciences to initiate radical change. Since 2006, student enrollment at universities in Switzerland has been increasing dramatically (Figure 2) and today the number of awarded Bachelor Degrees among the 25 to 34-year-olds is the highest of all OECD countries (Wikipedia).

The growth in the student population is most pronounced at the two Federal Institutes of Technology in Zurich (ETHZ) and Lausanne (EPFL). At EPFL, for instance, the number of students has almost doubled since 2006. It is important to note that this growth is to a large extent due to an increase in the enrollment of students from abroad (BFS, 2020).

Academic education and research cost a lot of money. If the expenditures of the universities are calculated on a "Per Faculty" basis, the values differ to a great extent: the Federal Institute of Technology in Zurich (ETHZ) and the Massachusetts Institute of Technology (MIT) are on top with USD 3.5 million each, while the Swiss universities in Fribourg and Geneva, as well as Imperial College in London and the University of Tokyo, have value, which is slightly below USD 1 million per faculty.

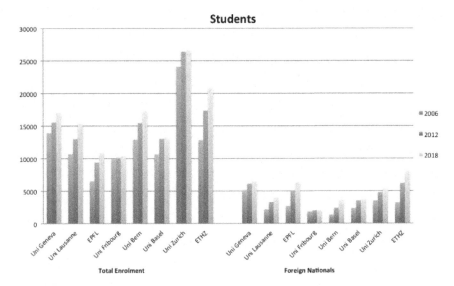

Figure 2. Total number of students enrolled at Swiss universities in 2006, 2012, and 2018 and the number of students originating from countries outside of Switzerland.
Source: von Arb (2020).

One might suspect that there would be a correlation between the number of students and financial expenditures, but that is not the case. This is particularly surprising from a Swiss perspective, where a significant part of the public sector's subsidies is actually calculated according to the enrollment of students. Nevertheless, the high level of government support may very well contribute to the fact that the income generated from private donations and gifts by academic institutions in Switzerland is among the lowest of all universities in this study; this could be interpreted as a disincentive for universities to actively seek to expand this kind of revenue stream.

Top Performance in Fundamental Research

In general, publications in highly selective peer review journals with a large number of citations are a must in order to gain recognition in academic research (Figure 3).

These lists of publications greatly influence the decision-making process in research grant applications. Looking at the so-called citation index,

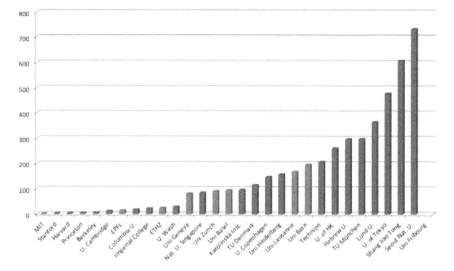

Figure 3.   Ranking of universities according to the percentage of most cited scientific publications among the top 1 percent.

Source: von Arb (2020).

the quality of fundamental research at Swiss universities must be pretty high, which also confirms the relatively high rankings of Swiss academia in Academic Ranking of World Universities (ARWU, 2007 & 2017).

Nevertheless, here, too, the differences among the institutions are substantial and show the two Swiss Federal Institutes of Technology often on top in the most relevant fields of science. Among the most important research areas from an industrial application point of view are the Medical and Pharmaceutical Sciences, Biology, Earth Sciences, Physics as well as the Computer Sciences and Engineering. In three of them — namely in Computer Sciences and Engineering, in Physics, and the Earth Sciences — ETHZ ranks among the top 50 in the world, while EPFL ranks among the top 50 in two areas. The Universities of Basel (Pharmaceutical Sciences), Bern (Earth Sciences), Geneva (Physics), and Zurich (Biology) rank among the top 50 in the world in one research area (Leiden Index, 2019).

In one of the most prominent and very quickly evolving research areas of today — Mathematics and Computer Sciences — the two Swiss Federal Institutes of Technology have been able to improve their ranking in recent years, while the University of Zurich lost terrain. With a global ranking of 250 in 2019, the largest Swiss University was at the end of all benchmark universities.

Interestingly, a similar trend can be observed when looking at the patent literature. In the period of 1980–2015, the high quality of fundamental research at Swiss universities resulted in a strong resonance in the patent literature with the University of Geneva at the forefront. However, when looking at the year 2019, only the two Federal Institutes of Technology are still showing a good performance. The University of Zurich dropped from 6th position in the study to number 14, while all other Swiss universities were not even included in the top 100 institutions (Reuters Index, 2018).

Public–Private Partnerships in Research: University of Basel in Front

Another important indicator showing the universities' active pursuit to take their science research results to the market is the number of joint projects between universities and private sector entities. In a survey of more than 1,000 universities, the University of Basel is the front-runner in Switzerland: 9 percent of its scientific publications are co-publications with an author from the private sector, the same as Stanford University and MIT. Seoul National University has 7.5 percent, which is by far the highest value of all Asian benchmark universities and it ranks 7th in the world when comparing the PPP numbers in Physical Sciences and Engineering. The excellent position of the University of Basel is primarily due to Biomedical and Health-related research collaborations. Furthermore, the University of Zurich ranks among the top 50 in the world for this area. The two Swiss Federal Institutes of Technology have a strong focus on Mathematics and Computer Sciences with the global rankings 9 (ETHZ) and 48 (EPFL), while the other Swiss universities are all at the end of the benchmark comparison in this prominent field.

The income generated by the universities with PPP projects is considerable: in 2018, the relatively small EPFL took in USD 70 million. This is significantly more than ETHZ received (USD 55 million). But the income of the University of Zurich (USD 120 million) was by far the highest in Switzerland, which is remarkable from a global perspective. For instance, MIT took in USD 140 million, Tokyo University USD 80 million, Seoul National University USD 62 million. At the University of Basel, the funding amounted to a mere USD 42 million.

Only a Few Proven Innovations

Nowadays, at many universities, it is mandatory for scientists to report significant discoveries in research work. The employing academic institutions are, in most cases, the owners of the intellectual property (or the research work) unless it is privately mandated. Making the number of the invention declarations public and showcasing their performance in this sector on the global market has become a valuable asset for many universities, however, there are also other universities, including Seoul National University, that do not even publish related numbers in their annual reports. Of the ones that do, it is not surprising that technical universities such as the Swiss Federal Institutes of Technology have the highest numbers of invention declarations among the chosen benchmark universities, while at the University of Lausanne for instance it is only a small percentage of that.

If an invention is considered to have a significant potential for a commercial application, universities move a step further and submit a formal application to patent the invention. The results for the patent applications (Figure 4) are comparable to the invention declarations. When the patent applications are based on the number of faculty, both Swiss Federal Institutes of Technology are ranked right behind MIT. However, the fact that only 12 percent of their patent applications are in the field of Engineering and Computer Sciences, while a good 25 percent are in the field of Medical and Pharmaceutical Sciences is rather surprising. Of all the other Swiss universities, none is included in the world's top 100 for patent applications per faculty except for the formidable value of the University of Zurich. It is ranked as number 10 in the benchmark study. Even more impressive is the value of Seoul National University (ranking 6) ahead of Stanford University and the University of Tokyo.

A further important step to incorporate scientific research into the market is the active promotion of a start-up culture at academic institutions. The results of the Swiss universities are not impressive considering the institutions have not been actively engaged in promoting such innovative culture. The current status of universities' venture capital activities is rather sobering: The numbers of VC deals (Figure 5) at the four Swiss locations Zurich, Basel, Geneva, and Lausanne are 50–100 times lower than at the locations in the US, London, or Shanghai. The differences are even more dramatic when it comes to a comparison of actual VC investments, where the values differ by a factor of 1,000. The only positive note is that the VC investments at the locations in Zurich, Basel, and Lausanne

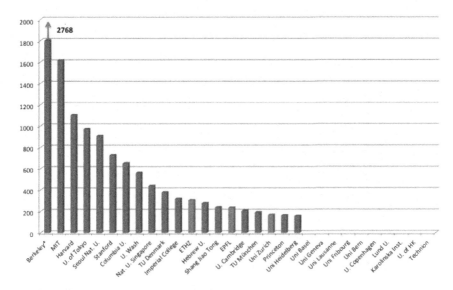

Figure 4.   Number of patent applications by universities between 2012 and 2017. The value for the University of Berkeley represents the amount of patent applications of the entire University of California system.

Source: von Arb (2020).

have seen an above-average increase (between 400 and 700 percent) in the years 2007–2017, although the increase is still lagging behind all Asian locations including Seoul (+1,500 percent) (Center for American Entrepreneurship, 2018).

When it comes to the comparison of the numbers of start-up companies, it is important to remember that most of them are not spin-offs from universities (Figure 6). True spin-offs originating from an academic institution must be verified as such. Unfortunately, many universities do not publish relevant information about their spin-offs. Among the ones that do, the two Swiss Federal Institutes of Technology have been showing a positive trend since 2006, recording 25 spin-offs in 2018 at which they are not much behind MIT and Stanford University. This is quite contrary to the other Swiss universities, where the number of spin-offs varied between 0 and 5 (Startup.ch).

Yet even launching a spin-off company does not guarantee that innovation will be successful in the market. Still, many founders of start-up companies dream of becoming a Unicorn. This refers to a start-up company

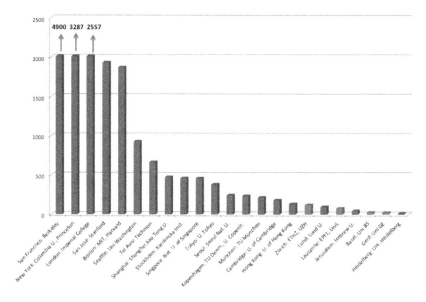

Figure 5. **Number of venture capital deals at locations of benchmark universities between 2015 and 2017.**

Source: von Arb (2020).

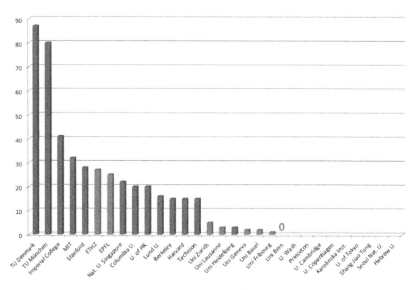

Figure 6. Number of university spin-off companies founded in 2018.

Source: von Arb (2020).

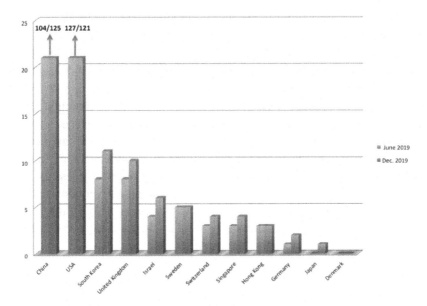

Figure 7. Number of start-up companies in benchmark countries reaching the valuation of a unicorn status according to a global survey from June 2019 and in December 2019.

Source: von Arb (2020).

with a market valuation of US$1 billion or more, a status the company will lose if the company goes public or is sold. A specific category for start-up companies with an estimated market potential valuation of that magnitude did not even exist 20 years ago, which indicates how much the dynamics in the start-up sector have changed. In 2019, more than 350 start-ups across the world attained the Unicorns status (Figure 7). Two-thirds were located in the US and China, 10 each in South Korea and the UK, and 2 in Germany. In Switzerland, there were 4 and at least one was a direct university spin-off (EPFL). This is clear progress considering that only 3 years earlier, in 2016, no start-ups had earned the Unicorn title in Switzerland. The very dynamic evolution of Unicorns was also exemplified by the two readings, which were done only half a year apart (Wikipedia).

Conclusion

The international benchmark study "CH2048 Innovationsmonitoring 2020," which uses 40 different performance indicators, yields a highly detailed "Science to Market" profile of some of the world's top research universities. Regarding the Swiss universities, the findings confirm, on the one hand, the traditional strengths mainly in fundamental research. On the other hand, they point to some distinct weaknesses in the "Science to Market" sector. Since developed countries are increasingly "science based" and are dependent on its contributions in order to maintain a high standard of living, it is very important to watch and monitor the evolution on a continuous basis from a global point of view. The universities, which are among the main providers of new scientific knowledge need to completely abandon any "Ivory Tower" mentality and take all necessary measures to facilitate the symbiotic process between universities and the corporate sector to eliminate existing deficiencies and also for the sake of securing their own global competitiveness as their counterparts, particularly in Asian countries, are catching up.

Swiss universities seem to be increasingly aware of these challenges and have begun to take action in recent years. This becomes apparent when looking at their long-term strategies. Recently, concrete measures and projects are already being formulated and implemented. In order to maintain a competitive position, it is a must to encourage the efforts to screen academic research results that provide economic merits, to run fundraising campaigns, and to promote public–private partnerships from which society at large, the principal funder of the universities in Switzerland, can benefit.

To that end, policymakers need to constantly look for new and creative approaches and funding opportunities to encourage universities to shape their academic portfolio in a way that will facilitate a comprehensive and holistic academic advancement to secure a sustainable future for the world from a longer perspective. In this way, Swiss universities will continue to maintain their impartial position and contribute to lead essential reflections and understanding in a perpetually changing world.

References

ARWU. Academic ranking of world universities. www.shanghairanking.com.
BFS. 2020. Bundesamt für Statistik. Swiss Federal Office for Statistics. www.bfs.admin.ch.
Center for American Entrepreneurship. 2018. Rise of the global startup city. http://startupsusa.org/global-startup-cities/.

Fondation CH2048. Allianz für eine global wettbewerbsfähige und verantwortliche Schweiz. [Alliance for a globally competitive and responsible Switzerland]. www.CH2048.ch.

Leiden Index. 2019. CWTS Leiden ranking. www.leidenranking.com.

Reuters Index. 2018. The world's most innovative universities. https://www.reuters.com/innovative-universities-2018/.

Startup.ch. The Swiss startup platform. https://www.startup.ch/.

von Arb, C. A. 2020. CH2048 Innovationsmonitoring. (Complete version — Modul A — in German language). https://www.ch2048.ch/download/.

Wikipedia. Free online encyclopedia. www.wikipedia.org.

Appendix

Appendix 1: Factor-Level Rankings

In this section, world rankings for the eight factors (Factor Conditions, Demand Conditions, Related Industries, Business Context, Workers, Policymakers and Administrators, Entrepreneurs, and Professionals) and 16 sub-factors (two for each factor) are presented. Statistical tables for the criteria level are provided in the website (ipsncr.org).

World Rankings: Factor Conditions

Factor conditions			Natural resources			Produced resources		
Rank	Region	Index	Rank	Region	Index	Rank	Region	Index
1	Australia	42.48	1	Australia	48.84	1	Australia	36.13
2	Canada	36.42	2	Canada	42.02	2	New Zealand	32.11
3	Kuwait	32.41	3	Kuwait	33.92	3	Kuwait	30.90
4	New Zealand	29.57	4	Russia	29.42	4	Canada	30.83
5	U.A.E.	27.75	5	U.A.E.	28.75	5	U.A.E.	26.76
6	Russia	25.33	6	New Zealand	27.02	6	Oman	25.60
7	Saudi Arabia	17.96	7	Saudi Arabia	18.72	7	Finland	21.84
8	Oman	17.81	8	Peru	16.58	8	Russia	21.23
9	Finland	15.13	9	Chile	15.33	9	Sweden	18.69

(Continued)

(Continued)

Factor conditions			Natural resources			Produced resources		
Rank	Region	Index	Rank	Region	Index	Rank	Region	Index
10	Sweden	12.84	10	Colombia	13.20	10	Saudi Arabia	17.20
11	United States	10.37	11	Oman	10.01	11	United States	13.14
12	Chile	10.04	12	Panama	9.85	12	Austria	12.92
13	Peru	9.12	13	Brazil	9.74	13	Czech Republic	8.97
14	Colombia	8.09	14	Finland	8.42	14	Netherlands	7.78
15	Austria	7.57	15	United States	7.61	15	Malaysia	7.45
16	Malaysia	7.13	16	Sweden	6.99	16	Germany	6.74
17	Brazil	5.55	17	Malaysia	6.80	17	Slovenia	6.06
18	Czech Republic	5.38	18	Argentina	5.99	18	Poland	5.93
19	Panama	5.11	19	Ukraine	4.52	19	Denmark	5.28
20	Argentina	5.01	20	Slovenia	3.48	20	South Africa	5.08
21	Netherlands	4.78	21	Poland	3.34	21	Croatia	4.90
22	Slovenia	4.77	22	Croatia	3.29	22	Chile	4.74
23	Poland	4.63	23	Indonesia	3.18	23	Belgium	4.15
24	Germany	4.39	24	Greece	3.01	24	Argentina	4.04
25	Croatia	4.10	25	Cambodia	2.66	25	China	3.60
26	South Africa	3.83	26	South Africa	2.57	26	Israel	3.34
27	Ukraine	3.78	27	Austria	2.22	27	Greece	3.31
28	Greece	3.16	28	Guatemala	2.11	28	United Kingdom	3.16
29	Indonesia	3.10	29	Germany	2.05	29	Ukraine	3.04
30	Denmark	3.09	30	Mexico	1.97	30	Indonesia	3.02
31	China	2.51	31	Turkey	1.81	31	Colombia	2.98
32	Belgium	2.29	32	Czech Republic	1.79	32	Slovak Republic	2.95

(Continued)

(*Continued*)

Factor conditions			Natural resources			Produced resources		
Rank	Region	Index	Rank	Region	Index	Rank	Region	Index
33	Turkey	2.20	33	Netherlands	1.78	33	France	2.93
34	Slovak Republic	2.13	34	Hungary	1.77	34	Turkey	2.60
35	France	2.11	35	Nigeria	1.65	35	Switzerland	2.39
36	Israel	2.07	36	Vietnam	1.57	36	Hungary	2.25
37	United Kingdom	2.03	37	Switzerland	1.52	37	Thailand	2.05
38	Hungary	2.01	38	Thailand	1.43	38	Egypt	1.83
39	Switzerland	1.95	39	China	1.42	39	Peru	1.66
40	Thailand	1.74	40	Philippines	1.40	40	Mexico	1.48
41	Mexico	1.73	41	Spain	1.36	41	Vietnam	1.36
42	Egypt	1.57	42	Slovak Republic	1.31	42	Brazil	1.35
43	Vietnam	1.46	43	Egypt	1.30	43	Spain	1.13
44	Cambodia	1.40	44	France	1.28	44	Italy	1.12
45	Nigeria	1.32	45	Italy	1.09	45	Nigeria	0.98
46	Spain	1.25	46	Japan	1.03	46	Japan	0.88
47	Guatemala	1.16	47	Morocco	1.01	47	India	0.73
48	Italy	1.10	48	United Kingdom	0.91	48	Korea	0.73
49	Japan	0.96	49	Denmark	0.89	49	Bangladesh	0.49
50	Philippines	0.83	50	Dominican Republic	0.86	50	Pakistan	0.40
51	India	0.72	51	Kenya	0.83	51	Panama	0.36
52	Morocco	0.64	52	Sri Lanka	0.81	52	Singapore	0.29
53	Korea	0.60	53	Israel	0.80	53	Morocco	0.28
54	Kenya	0.50	54	India	0.71	54	Philippines	0.26
55	Dominican Republic	0.48	55	Jordan	0.61	55	Guatemala	0.22
56	Sri Lanka	0.43	56	Korea	0.46	56	Kenya	0.17
57	Pakistan	0.42	57	Belgium	0.43	57	Cambodia	0.14
58	Bangladesh	0.37	58	Pakistan	0.43	58	Dominican Republic	0.09

(*Continued*)

(Continued)

Factor conditions			Natural resources			Produced resources		
Rank	Region	Index	Rank	Region	Index	Rank	Region	Index
59	Jordan	0.32	59	Taiwan, China	0.31	59	Taiwan, China	0.05
60	Taiwan, China	0.18	60	Bangladesh	0.26	60	Hong Kong SAR	0.05
61	Singapore	0.16	61	Singapore	0.03	61	Sri Lanka	0.04
62	Hong Kong SAR	0.02	62	Hong Kong SAR	0.00	62	Jordan	0.03

Note: The top five countries for *Factor Conditions* are Australia, Canada, Kuwait, New Zealand, and United Arab Emirates (U.A.E.). These countries showed high competitiveness in both sub-factors of *Energy Resources* and *Produced Resources*. The sub-factor, *Energy Resources*, is measured by the amount of reserves in natural resources per capita such as oil, natural gas, and coal. Land area and freshwater resources are also included. The other sub-factor, *Produced Resources*, is measured by the amount of energy resources produced per capita such as oil, natural gas, and coal. The productions of wood and meat are also included.

World Rankings: Demand Conditions

Demand conditions			Demand size			Demand quality		
Rank	Region	Index	Rank	Region	Index	Rank	Region	Index
1	United States	81.40	1	United States	92.93	1	Finland	85.58
2	China	64.35	2	China	63.65	2	Denmark	84.69
3	Switzerland	58.43	3	Germany	48.71	3	Sweden	84.54
4	Germany	55.89	4	Japan	33.55	4	Switzerland	83.73
5	Denmark	53.08	5	Switzerland	33.13	5	Austria	80.06
6	Sweden	52.70	6	United Kingdom	31.43	6	Korea	77.43
7	Finland	51.05	7	France	30.62	7	Canada	75.80
8	Canada	50.70	8	Singapore	30.18	8	Hong Kong SAR	74.23
9	Netherlands	50.37	9	Netherlands	28.83	9	Australia	73.17
10	Hong Kong SAR	50.32	10	Hong Kong SAR	26.40	10	Netherlands	71.90
11	Korea	50.21	11	Canada	25.61	11	Belgium	71.56
12	Japan	50.14	12	Australia	23.67	12	United States	69.87
13	Singapore	49.94	13	Italy	23.00	13	Singapore	69.70
14	Austria	49.80	14	Korea	22.98	14	Italy	69.69
15	France	48.65	15	Belgium	21.97	15	New Zealand	69.52
16	Australia	48.42	16	Denmark	21.46	16	Japan	66.72
17	Belgium	46.77	17	Sweden	20.86	17	France	66.68
18	Italy	46.35	18	Austria	19.55	18	China	65.05
19	United Kingdom	43.85	19	U.A.E.	19.18	19	Taiwan, China	64.65
20	New Zealand	41.68	20	Spain	18.43	20	Saudi Arabia	63.63
21	Taiwan, China	39.53	21	Finland	16.52	21	Germany	63.06
22	Saudi Arabia	37.62	22	Israel	14.73	22	Colombia	61.20
23	U.A.E.	37.62	23	Taiwan, China	14.42	23	Thailand	59.79

(*Continued*)

(Continued)

Demand conditions			Demand size			Demand quality		
Rank	Region	Index	Rank	Region	Index	Rank	Region	Index
24	Spain	33.93	24	New Zealand	13.85	24	Vietnam	59.45
25	India	33.75	25	India	13.42	25	Nigeria	58.91
26	Thailand	33.64	26	Mexico	12.31	26	Panama	57.36
27	Israel	33.54	27	Russia	12.15	27	United Kingdom	56.27
28	Poland	32.76	28	Saudi Arabia	11.61	28	U.A.E.	56.06
29	Russia	32.71	29	Kuwait	10.60	29	Slovenia	55.89
30	Kuwait	32.35	30	Poland	10.08	30	Poland	55.45
31	Vietnam	32.18	31	Czech Republic	9.65	31	Kuwait	54.10
32	Colombia	31.99	32	Brazil	9.29	32	India	54.09
33	Slovenia	31.91	33	Slovenia	7.92	33	Russia	53.27
34	Panama	31.03	34	Thailand	7.48	34	Turkey	52.83
35	Mexico	30.72	35	Turkey	7.42	35	Israel	52.36
36	Nigeria	30.24	36	Malaysia	7.18	36	Philippines	52.28
37	Turkey	30.13	37	Greece	7.01	37	Malaysia	51.47
38	Malaysia	29.33	38	Slovak Republic	6.99	38	Chile	51.29
39	Chile	28.57	39	Hungary	6.65	39	Indonesia	51.16
40	Indonesia	28.38	40	Chile	5.86	40	Croatia	50.68
41	Philippines	27.59	41	Indonesia	5.61	41	Spain	49.43
42	Brazil	27.54	42	Argentina	5.13	42	Mexico	49.14
43	Croatia	27.53	43	Oman	4.97	43	Greece	48.02
44	Greece	27.51	44	Vietnam	4.91	44	Sri Lanka	47.66
45	Slovak Republic	27.02	45	Panama	4.70	45	Slovak Republic	47.05
46	Czech Republic	25.42	46	Croatia	4.39	46	Bangladesh	46.54
47	Argentina	25.40	47	South Africa	3.54	47	Brazil	45.78
48	Hungary	24.44	48	Philippines	2.91	48	Argentina	45.67

(Continued)

(*Continued*)

Demand conditions			Demand size			Demand quality		
Rank	Region	Index	Rank	Region	Index	Rank	Region	Index
49	Sri Lanka	24.36	49	Colombia	2.77	49	Jordan	43.90
50	Bangladesh	23.80	50	Peru	2.66	50	Ukraine	43.54
51	Peru	22.96	51	Dominican Republic	2.28	51	Peru	43.26
52	Ukraine	22.56	52	Ukraine	1.58	52	Hungary	42.22
53	Jordan	22.46	53	Nigeria	1.58	53	Dominican Republic	42.21
54	South Africa	22.30	54	Egypt	1.50	54	Morocco	42.15
55	Dominican Republic	22.25	55	Morocco	1.31	55	Guatemala	41.38
56	Morocco	21.73	56	Guatemala	1.10	56	Czech Republic	41.19
57	Guatemala	21.24	57	Bangladesh	1.06	57	South Africa	41.06
58	Egypt	19.51	58	Sri Lanka	1.06	58	Egypt	37.51
59	Pakistan	19.05	59	Jordan	1.01	59	Pakistan	37.26
60	Kenya	11.51	60	Pakistan	0.85	60	Kenya	22.81
61	Cambodia	10.47	61	Kenya	0.21	61	Cambodia	20.86
62	Oman	7.52	62	Cambodia	0.08	62	Oman	10.08

Note: The top five countries for *Demand Conditions* are the United States, China, Switzerland, Germany, and Denmark. The United States was ranked number one in this factor due to its superior advantage in *Demand Size*. Interestingly, despite its small domestic market size, Switzerland was ranked in the top five for *Demand Conditions* due to its high ratings in purchasing power, degree of openness, and market sophistication. The sub-factor, *Demand Size*, is measured by GDP, GDP per capita, and exports and imports of goods and services. Therefore, demand size is not only determined by domestic market size but also by the degree of its openness to the international market. *Demand Quality* is measured by surveys among customers on their sensitivity to quality, design, health and environment, intellectual property rights, and new technology. Countries with strength in this sub-factor have sophisticated and demanding consumers who pressure firms to continuously innovate and improve the competitiveness of their products and services.

World Rankings: Related Industries

Related industries			Industrial infrastructure			Living infrastructure		
Rank	Region	Index	Rank	Region	Index	Rank	Region	Index
1	Denmark	65.85	1	United States	59.62	1	Denmark	79.31
2	Finland	64.15	2	Singapore	55.26	2	Finland	78.65
3	Switzerland	63.10	3	Hong Kong SAR	54.69	3	Sweden	74.18
4	Sweden	63.02	4	Switzerland	53.49	4	Austria	73.87
5	Austria	62.44	5	Denmark	52.38	5	Belgium	73.87
6	Netherlands	60.60	6	Sweden	51.86	6	Netherlands	73.33
7	Belgium	60.42	7	Austria	51.02	7	Switzerland	72.71
8	Singapore	59.96	8	Korea	50.04	8	New Zealand	70.02
9	Australia	59.30	9	Finland	49.64	9	Australia	69.97
10	New Zealand	59.25	10	U.A.E.	49.37	10	Taiwan, China	69.44
11	Taiwan, China	58.10	11	Australia	48.63	11	Spain	66.52
12	United States	57.94	12	Japan	48.58	12	Germany	65.47
13	Hong Kong SAR	57.54	13	New Zealand	48.49	13	Czech Republic	65.46
14	Germany	56.96	14	Germany	48.44	14	France	65.45
15	Japan	56.30	15	Israel	48.14	15	Slovenia	64.84
16	Korea	56.01	16	Netherlands	47.88	16	Singapore	64.67
17	U.A.E.	55.50	17	Canada	47.04	17	Japan	64.03
18	Canada	55.43	18	Belgium	46.98	18	United Kingdom	63.83
19	Czech Republic	54.89	19	Taiwan, China	46.77	19	Canada	63.82
20	France	54.63	20	Saudi Arabia	44.80	20	Korea	61.99
21	Slovenia	54.39	21	Czech Republic	44.31	21	U.A.E.	61.62
22	Israel	54.31	22	United Kingdom	44.21	22	Israel	60.49

(Continued)

(Continued)

Related industries			Industrial infrastructure			Living infrastructure		
Rank	Region	Index	Rank	Region	Index	Rank	Region	Index
23	United Kingdom	54.02	23	Hungary	44.07	23	Hong Kong SAR	60.38
24	Spain	53.83	24	Slovenia	43.94	24	Italy	58.51
25	Italy	49.90	25	France	43.80	25	Greece	58.15
26	Hungary	49.39	26	Italy	41.28	26	Poland	57.97
27	Greece	49.11	27	Spain	41.15	27	United States	56.26
28	Saudi Arabia	48.90	28	Greece	40.07	28	Slovak Republic	55.29
29	Poland	48.12	29	Malaysia	38.84	29	Croatia	55.11
30	Slovak Republic	46.48	30	Kuwait	38.79	30	Hungary	54.71
31	Croatia	45.43	31	Poland	38.27	31	Thailand	54.00
32	Kuwait	44.57	32	Slovak Republic	37.67	32	China	53.98
33	China	43.74	33	Croatia	35.74	33	Turkey	53.44
34	Thailand	43.72	34	Russia	34.51	34	Saudi Arabia	53.01
35	Malaysia	43.14	35	China	33.50	35	Argentina	52.34
36	Russia	42.30	36	Thailand	33.43	36	Chile	51.31
37	Chile	41.61	37	Oman	32.68	37	Ukraine	50.99
38	Turkey	40.66	38	Panama	32.17	38	Kuwait	50.36
39	Panama	38.78	39	Chile	31.91	39	Russia	50.10
40	Jordan	37.26	40	Morocco	29.65	40	Malaysia	47.45
41	Colombia	36.56	41	Mexico	28.39	41	Jordan	46.78
42	Ukraine	36.38	42	South Africa	28.13	42	Indonesia	46.25
43	Philippines	35.87	43	Turkey	27.88	43	Colombia	45.46
44	Dominican Republic	35.58	44	Philippines	27.85	44	Panama	45.39
45	Vietnam	35.47	45	Brazil	27.81	45	Sri Lanka	44.91
46	Argentina	35.34	46	Dominican Republic	27.74	46	Vietnam	44.73

(Continued)

(*Continued*)

Related industries			Industrial infrastructure			Living infrastructure		
Rank	Region	Index	Rank	Region	Index	Rank	Region	Index
47	Mexico	35.22	47	Jordan	27.73	47	Philippines	43.89
48	Indonesia	35.17	48	Colombia	27.66	48	Egypt	43.51
49	Brazil	34.54	49	Vietnam	26.22	49	Dominican Republic	43.42
50	Sri Lanka	34.14	50	India	25.23	50	Peru	42.21
51	Oman	33.63	51	Indonesia	24.10	51	Mexico	42.05
52	India	33.23	52	Peru	23.96	52	Brazil	41.27
53	Peru	33.08	53	Sri Lanka	23.38	53	India	41.23
54	Morocco	32.94	54	Cambodia	23.02	54	Morocco	36.22
55	Egypt	31.55	55	Guatemala	22.30	55	Oman	34.58
56	South Africa	31.24	56	Ukraine	21.77	56	South Africa	34.35
57	Kenya	27.12	57	Nigeria	21.75	57	Kenya	33.01
58	Guatemala	27.02	58	Bangladesh	21.74	58	Bangladesh	31.79
59	Bangladesh	26.76	59	Kenya	21.23	59	Guatemala	31.73
60	Nigeria	26.69	60	Egypt	19.58	60	Nigeria	31.62
61	Cambodia	24.48	61	Pakistan	18.95	61	Pakistan	29.14
62	Pakistan	24.05	62	Argentina	18.35	62	Cambodia	25.93

Note: The top five countries for *Related Industries* are Denmark, Finland, Switzerland, Sweden, and Austria. Denmark was ranked number one in this factor due to its superiority in *Living Infrastructure*. Finland was second due to its advantage in *Industrial Infrastructure* and *Living Infrastructure*. On the other hand, Sweden and Austria showed higher competitiveness in *Living and Industrial Infrastructure*. *Industrial Infrastructure* measures the infrastructure of transportation, communication, finance, and science & technology. Transportation is composed of indices such as motor vehicles, civil aviation, maritime transport, and international travel. Communication includes indices such as the number of mobile phone subscribers and internet users. Finance is composed of capital value and capital accessibility. Finally, Science & Technology is captured by the number of scientists and engineers, the quality of scientific research institutions, research and development expenditure, and international patents granted. *Living Infrastructure* is composed of indices on education, social security, and quality of life. Education is measured by public spending on education, students per teacher, secondary and tertiary enrollment rates, and international mobility of students. Quality of life is measured by the Gini index, the Human Development Index, CO_2 emissions, and the development of leisure, sports, and cultural facilities.

World Rankings: Business Context

Business context			Structure			Rivalry		
Rank	Region	Index	Rank	Region	Index	Rank	Region	Index
1	Denmark	65.85	1	United States	59.62	1	Hong Kong SAR	79.78
2	Finland	64.15	2	Singapore	55.26	2	Singapore	71.79
3	Switzerland	63.10	3	Hong Kong SAR	54.69	3	Netherlands	45.91
4	Sweden	63.02	4	Switzerland	53.49	4	U.A.E.	34.11
5	Austria	62.44	5	Denmark	52.38	5	Belgium	33.94
6	Netherlands	60.60	6	Sweden	51.86	6	Switzerland	30.46
7	Belgium	60.42	7	Austria	51.02	7	Denmark	26.68
8	Singapore	59.96	8	Korea	50.04	8	Vietnam	25.51
9	Australia	59.30	9	Finland	49.64	9	Cambodia	25.35
10	New Zealand	59.25	10	U.A.E.	49.37	10	Hungary	23.55
11	Taiwan, China	58.10	11	Australia	48.63	11	Sweden	23.13
12	United States	57.94	12	Japan	48.58	12	Slovak Republic	22.98
13	Hong Kong SAR	57.54	13	New Zealand	48.49	13	Slovenia	22.46
14	Germany	56.96	14	Germany	48.44	14	Finland	22.14
15	Japan	56.30	15	Israel	48.14	15	Austria	21.74
16	Korea	56.01	16	Netherlands	47.88	16	United Kingdom	21.24
17	U.A.E.	55.50	17	Canada	47.04	17	Czech Republic	21.17
18	Canada	55.43	18	Belgium	46.98	18	Taiwan, China	19.36
19	Czech Republic	54.89	19	Taiwan, China	46.77	19	Malaysia	18.88
20	France	54.63	20	Saudi Arabia	44.80	20	France	18.83
21	Slovenia	54.39	21	Czech Republic	44.31	21	Oman	18.61
22	Israel	54.31	22	United Kingdom	44.21	22	Thailand	18.34

(*Continued*)

(Continued)

Business context			Structure			Rivalry		
Rank	Region	Index	Rank	Region	Index	Rank	Region	Index
23	United Kingdom	54.02	23	Hungary	44.07	23	Germany	17.65
24	Spain	53.83	24	Slovenia	43.94	24	Canada	17.48
25	Italy	49.90	25	France	43.80	25	Panama	16.12
26	Hungary	49.39	26	Italy	41.28	26	Croatia	15.96
27	Greece	49.11	27	Spain	41.15	27	Spain	15.88
28	Saudi Arabia	48.90	28	Greece	40.07	28	Kuwait	15.57
29	Poland	48.12	29	Malaysia	38.84	29	Ukraine	14.92
30	Slovak Republic	46.48	30	Kuwait	38.79	30	Poland	14.47
31	Croatia	45.43	31	Poland	38.27	31	Jordan	14.41
32	Kuwait	44.57	32	Slovak Republic	37.67	32	Greece	14.37
33	China	43.74	33	Croatia	35.74	33	Israel	13.72
34	Thailand	43.72	34	Russia	34.51	34	Italy	13.14
35	Malaysia	43.14	35	China	33.50	35	Korea	12.65
36	Russia	42.30	36	Thailand	33.43	36	Morocco	12.57
37	Chile	41.61	37	Oman	32.68	37	Australia	12.55
38	Turkey	40.66	38	Panama	32.17	38	New Zealand	11.69
39	Panama	38.78	39	Chile	31.91	39	South Africa	11.51
40	Jordan	37.26	40	Morocco	29.65	40	Japan	11.42
41	Colombia	36.56	41	Mexico	28.39	41	Chile	11.16
42	Ukraine	36.38	42	South Africa	28.13	42	Mexico	10.79
43	Philippines	35.87	43	Turkey	27.88	43	Philippines	10.43
44	Dominican Republic	35.58	44	Philippines	27.85	44	Saudi Arabia	10.39
45	Vietnam	35.47	45	Brazil	27.81	45	United States	9.86

(Continued)

(Continued)

Business context			Structure			Rivalry		
Rank	Region	Index	Rank	Region	Index	Rank	Region	Index
46	Argentina	35.34	46	Dominican Republic	27.74	46	Dominican Republic	9.15
47	Mexico	35.22	47	Jordan	27.73	47	Egypt	8.80
48	Indonesia	35.17	48	Colombia	27.66	48	Peru	8.12
49	Brazil	34.54	49	Vietnam	26.22	49	Russia	7.95
50	Sri Lanka	34.14	50	India	25.23	50	Turkey	7.83
51	Oman	33.63	51	Indonesia	24.10	51	Colombia	7.73
52	India	33.23	52	Peru	23.96	52	Sri Lanka	7.67
53	Peru	33.08	53	Sri Lanka	23.38	53	India	6.54
54	Morocco	32.94	54	Cambodia	23.02	54	Indonesia	6.39
55	Egypt	31.55	55	Guatemala	22.30	55	Guatemala	6.32
56	South Africa	31.24	56	Ukraine	21.77	56	Kenya	5.71
57	Kenya	27.12	57	Nigeria	21.75	57	Brazil	5.62
58	Guatemala	27.02	58	Bangladesh	21.74	58	China	5.52
59	Bangladesh	26.76	59	Kenya	21.23	59	Argentina	5.09
60	Nigeria	26.69	60	Egypt	19.58	60	Nigeria	5.07
61	Cambodia	24.48	61	Pakistan	18.95	61	Bangladesh	4.62
62	Pakistan	24.05	62	Argentina	18.35	62	Pakistan	3.79

Note: The top five regions for the factor of *Business Context* are Hong Kong, Singapore, Netherlands, UAE, and Belgium. The top five regions were ranked in the higher places, due to their superior advantage in *Rivalry* in particular. In addition, the graphs showed higher competitiveness in the sub-factor of *Structure* among five regions. The sub-factor, *Structure*, measures the aspects of business governance and ethical practices among firms. These components were measured with survey data. Business governance includes indices such as a firm's decision process, the development of unique brands, and equal treatment. Business morality consists of indices such as social value, ethical practice, health and safety performance, and environmental concerns. *Rivalry* is composed of investment openness in terms of foreign direct investment, financial portfolio, and trade. Regions with strength in this sub-factor are more likely to have a higher degree of both domestic and international competition and are favored by multinational companies as a destination for doing international business.

World Rankings: (Unskilled) Workers

(Unskilled) workers			Quantity of workers			Quality of workers		
Rank	Region	Index	Rank	Region	Index	Rank	Region	Index
1	China	84.15	1	United States	59.62	1	Hong Kong SAR	79.78
2	Vietnam	68.15	2	Singapore	55.26	2	Singapore	71.79
3	Philippines	66.75	3	Hong Kong SAR	54.69	3	Netherlands	45.91
4	Indonesia	64.44	4	Switzerland	53.49	4	U.A.E.	34.11
5	Thailand	62.03	5	Denmark	52.38	5	Belgium	33.94
6	India	60.76	6	Sweden	51.86	6	Switzerland	30.46
7	Hong Kong SAR	60.57	7	Austria	51.02	7	Denmark	26.68
8	Panama	60.04	8	Korea	50.04	8	Vietnam	25.51
9	Colombia	59.45	9	Finland	49.64	9	Cambodia	25.35
10	Taiwan, China	59.00	10	U.A.E.	49.37	10	Hungary	23.55
11	Poland	58.63	11	Australia	48.63	11	Sweden	23.13
12	Netherlands	58.29	12	Japan	48.58	12	Slovak Republic	22.98
13	Singapore	58.07	13	New Zealand	48.49	13	Slovenia	22.46
14	Dominican Republic	58.06	14	Germany	48.44	14	Finland	22.14
15	Denmark	57.61	15	Israel	48.14	15	Austria	21.74
16	Malaysia	57.39	16	Netherlands	47.88	16	United Kingdom	21.24
17	Kuwait	57.36	17	Canada	47.04	17	Czech Republic	21.17
18	Jordan	56.99	18	Belgium	46.98	18	Taiwan, China	19.36
19	Mexico	56.80	19	Taiwan, China	46.77	19	Malaysia	18.88
20	Peru	56.65	20	Saudi Arabia	44.80	20	France	18.83

(Continued)

(Continued)

(Unskilled) workers			Quantity of workers			Quality of workers		
Rank	Region	Index	Rank	Region	Index	Rank	Region	Index
21	New Zealand	56.42	21	Czech Republic	44.31	21	Oman	18.61
22	Argentina	55.97	22	United Kingdom	44.21	22	Thailand	18.34
23	Ukraine	55.91	23	Hungary	44.07	23	Germany	17.65
24	Russia	55.88	24	Slovenia	43.94	24	Canada	17.48
25	Guatemala	55.71	25	France	43.80	25	Panama	16.12
26	Saudi Arabia	55.12	26	Italy	41.28	26	Croatia	15.96
27	Belgium	55.08	27	Spain	41.15	27	Spain	15.88
28	Bangladesh	55.04	28	Greece	40.07	28	Kuwait	15.57
29	Czech Republic	55.02	29	Malaysia	38.84	29	Ukraine	14.92
30	Chile	54.90	30	Kuwait	38.79	30	Poland	14.47
31	Sweden	54.59	31	Poland	38.27	31	Jordan	14.41
32	Italy	54.38	32	Slovak Republic	37.67	32	Greece	14.37
33	Canada	53.70	33	Croatia	35.74	33	Israel	13.72
34	Slovenia	53.57	34	Russia	34.51	34	Italy	13.14
35	Sri Lanka	52.66	35	China	33.50	35	Korea	12.65
36	Australia	52.24	36	Thailand	33.43	36	Morocco	12.57
37	Cambodia	51.67	37	Oman	32.68	37	Australia	12.55
38	Turkey	51.54	38	Panama	32.17	38	New Zealand	11.69
39	U.A.E.	51.38	39	Chile	31.91	39	South Africa	11.51
40	Japan	50.70	40	Morocco	29.65	40	Japan	11.42
41	Switzerland	50.14	41	Mexico	28.39	41	Chile	11.16
42	Brazil	49.86	42	South Africa	28.13	42	Mexico	10.79
43	Pakistan	49.81	43	Turkey	27.88	43	Philippines	10.43
44	Egypt	49.73	44	Philippines	27.85	44	Saudi Arabia	10.39

(Continued)

(Continued)

(Unskilled) workers			Quantity of workers			Quality of workers		
Rank	Region	Index	Rank	Region	Index	Rank	Region	Index
45	Greece	49.60	45	Brazil	27.81	45	United States	9.86
46	United States	49.38	46	Dominican Republic	27.74	46	Dominican Republic	9.15
47	Spain	49.32	47	Jordan	27.73	47	Egypt	8.80
48	Hungary	48.40	48	Colombia	27.66	48	Peru	8.12
49	Finland	48.37	49	Vietnam	26.22	49	Russia	7.95
50	Korea	47.96	50	India	25.23	50	Turkey	7.83
51	Austria	47.60	51	Indonesia	24.10	51	Colombia	7.73
52	Germany	45.62	52	Peru	23.96	52	Sri Lanka	7.67
53	Nigeria	45.43	53	Sri Lanka	23.38	53	India	6.54
54	United Kingdom	44.32	54	Cambodia	23.02	54	Indonesia	6.39
55	Israel	41.90	55	Guatemala	22.30	55	Guatemala	6.32
56	Kenya	41.71	56	Ukraine	21.77	56	Kenya	5.71
57	Croatia	39.66	57	Nigeria	21.75	57	Brazil	5.62
58	France	39.30	58	Bangladesh	21.74	58	China	5.52
59	Oman	38.93	59	Kenya	21.23	59	Argentina	5.09
60	Morocco	35.98	60	Egypt	19.58	60	Nigeria	5.07
61	Slovak Republic	28.56	61	Pakistan	18.95	61	Bangladesh	4.62
62	South Africa	12.10	62	Argentina	18.35	62	Pakistan	3.79

Note: The top five countries for *(Unskilled) Workers* are China, Vietnam, the Philippines, Indonesia, and Thailand. They all demonstrated strong competitiveness in this factor due to their advantage in the *Quantity of Workers*. The sub-factor, *Quantity of Workers*, is measured by the size of the labor force, employment rate, working hours, and monthly compensation for manufacturing workers. *Quality of Workers* is measured by literacy rate, attitude and motivation, education, the openness of the labor market, and the relationship between management and workers. Countries with strength in this sub-factor have a relative advantage as far as the attitude of workers and working conditions are concerned.

World Rankings: Policymakers and Administrators

Policymakers and administrators			Policymakers			Administrators		
Rank	Region	Index	Rank	Region	Index	Rank	Region	Index
1	Singapore	93.25	1	United States	59.62	1	Hong Kong SAR	79.78
2	Finland	91.80	2	Singapore	55.26	2	Singapore	71.79
3	Switzerland	89.72	3	Hong Kong SAR	54.69	3	Netherlands	45.91
4	Denmark	89.51	4	Switzerland	53.49	4	U.A.E.	34.11
5	Netherlands	89.29	5	Denmark	52.38	5	Belgium	33.94
6	Sweden	86.13	6	Sweden	51.86	6	Switzerland	30.46
7	New Zealand	84.39	7	Austria	51.02	7	Denmark	26.68
8	Australia	81.03	8	Korea	50.04	8	Vietnam	25.51
9	Canada	80.87	9	Finland	49.64	9	Cambodia	25.35
10	Germany	77.06	10	U.A.E.	49.37	10	Hungary	23.55
11	Hong Kong SAR	73.01	11	Australia	48.63	11	Sweden	23.13
12	Belgium	72.94	12	Japan	48.58	12	Slovak Republic	22.98
13	U.A.E.	71.16	13	New Zealand	48.49	13	Slovenia	22.46
14	Austria	69.18	14	Germany	48.44	14	Finland	22.14
15	France	69.01	15	Israel	48.14	15	Austria	21.74
16	Japan	68.50	16	Netherlands	47.88	16	United Kingdom	21.24
17	United States	68.07	17	Canada	47.04	17	Czech Republic	21.17
18	United Kingdom	66.60	18	Belgium	46.98	18	Taiwan, China	19.36
19	Taiwan, China	65.02	19	Taiwan, China	46.77	19	Malaysia	18.88
20	China	64.30	20	Saudi Arabia	44.80	20	France	18.83

(Continued)

(Continued)

Policymakers and administrators			Policymakers			Administrators		
Rank	Region	Index	Rank	Region	Index	Rank	Region	Index
21	Saudi Arabia	63.67	21	Czech Republic	44.31	21	Oman	18.61
22	Chile	62.07	22	United Kingdom	44.21	22	Thailand	18.34
23	Korea	60.83	23	Hungary	44.07	23	Germany	17.65
24	Israel	57.12	24	Slovenia	43.94	24	Canada	17.48
25	Italy	52.62	25	France	43.80	25	Panama	16.12
26	Greece	52.42	26	Italy	41.28	26	Croatia	15.96
27	Jordan	52.35	27	Spain	41.15	27	Spain	15.88
28	Kuwait	51.41	28	Greece	40.07	28	Kuwait	15.57
29	India	50.77	29	Malaysia	38.84	29	Ukraine	14.92
30	Czech Republic	50.56	30	Kuwait	38.79	30	Poland	14.47
31	Malaysia	48.69	31	Poland	38.27	31	Jordan	14.41
32	Slovenia	48.31	32	Slovak Republic	37.67	32	Greece	14.37
33	Vietnam	46.61	33	Croatia	35.74	33	Israel	13.72
34	Poland	46.22	34	Russia	34.51	34	Italy	13.14
35	Philippines	44.36	35	China	33.50	35	Korea	12.65
36	Panama	44.13	36	Thailand	33.43	36	Morocco	12.57
37	Indonesia	43.73	37	Oman	32.68	37	Australia	12.55
38	Hungary	43.07	38	Panama	32.17	38	New Zealand	11.69
39	Egypt	42.80	39	Chile	31.91	39	South Africa	11.51
40	Thailand	41.65	40	Morocco	29.65	40	Japan	11.42
41	Spain	40.63	41	Mexico	28.39	41	Chile	11.16
42	Oman	39.70	42	South Africa	28.13	42	Mexico	10.79
43	Russia	39.64	43	Turkey	27.88	43	Philippines	10.43
44	Turkey	38.27	44	Philippines	27.85	44	Saudi Arabia	10.39

(Continued)

(Continued)

Policymakers and administrators			Policymakers			Administrators		
Rank	Region	Index	Rank	Region	Index	Rank	Region	Index
45	Argentina	37.39	45	Brazil	27.81	45	United States	9.86
46	Pakistan	37.14	46	Dominican Republic	27.74	46	Dominican Republic	9.15
47	Colombia	36.17	47	Jordan	27.73	47	Egypt	8.80
48	Bangladesh	35.30	48	Colombia	27.66	48	Peru	8.12
49	Slovak Republic	33.69	49	Vietnam	26.22	49	Russia	7.95
50	Morocco	32.50	50	India	25.23	50	Turkey	7.83
51	Nigeria	31.83	51	Indonesia	24.10	51	Colombia	7.73
52	Dominican Republic	31.65	52	Peru	23.96	52	Sri Lanka	7.67
53	Cambodia	31.63	53	Sri Lanka	23.38	53	India	6.54
54	South Africa	27.10	54	Cambodia	23.02	54	Indonesia	6.39
55	Kenya	25.64	55	Guatemala	22.30	55	Guatemala	6.32
56	Brazil	25.42	56	Ukraine	21.77	56	Kenya	5.71
57	Ukraine	25.31	57	Nigeria	21.75	57	Brazil	5.62
58	Peru	25.31	58	Bangladesh	21.74	58	China	5.52
59	Sri Lanka	21.75	59	Kenya	21.23	59	Argentina	5.09
60	Mexico	21.57	60	Egypt	19.58	60	Nigeria	5.07
61	Guatemala	21.07	61	Pakistan	18.95	61	Bangladesh	4.62
62	Croatia	16.65	62	Argentina	18.35	62	Pakistan	3.79

Note: The top five countries for *Policymakers & Administrators* are Singapore, Finland, Switzerland, Denmark, and the Netherlands. Singapore was ranked number one in this factor due to its strength in both *Policymakers* and *Administrators*. Four of the top five countries are classified in the Small-Strong Group and the rest of one country is in the Medium-Strong Group. *Administrators* is measured by five criteria including the process of policy implementation, the results of policy implementation, ethics, education level, and the international experience of bureaucrats. Countries with strength in this sub-factor have relatively high competitiveness in morality and international experience. Comparing the top five countries for *Policymakers*, all top five countries for *Administrators* are small-strong countries.

World Rankings: Entrepreneurs

Entrepreneurs			Personal competence of entrepreneurs			Social context of entrepreneurs		
Rank	Region	Index	Rank	Region	Index	Rank	Region	Index
1	United States	82.84	1	United States	59.62	1	Hong Kong SAR	79.78
2	Sweden	82.41	2	Singapore	55.26	2	Singapore	71.79
3	Denmark	80.86	3	Hong Kong SAR	54.69	3	Netherlands	45.91
4	Finland	80.33	4	Switzerland	53.49	4	U.A.E.	34.11
5	Canada	80.11	5	Denmark	52.38	5	Belgium	33.94
6	Netherlands	80.07	6	Sweden	51.86	6	Switzerland	30.46
7	Hong Kong SAR	78.20	7	Austria	51.02	7	Denmark	26.68
8	Switzerland	76.41	8	Korea	50.04	8	Vietnam	25.51
9	Australia	73.37	9	Finland	49.64	9	Cambodia	25.35
10	Singapore	72.97	10	U.A.E.	49.37	10	Hungary	23.55
11	U.A.E.	72.08	11	Australia	48.63	11	Sweden	23.13
12	New Zealand	70.81	12	Japan	48.58	12	Slovak Republic	22.98
13	Israel	68.59	13	New Zealand	48.49	13	Slovenia	22.46
14	Belgium	68.47	14	Germany	48.44	14	Finland	22.14
15	United Kingdom	66.06	15	Israel	48.14	15	Austria	21.74
16	Austria	64.52	16	Netherlands	47.88	16	United Kingdom	21.24
17	Germany	63.72	17	Canada	47.04	17	Czech Republic	21.17
18	Taiwan, China	61.75	18	Belgium	46.98	18	Taiwan, China	19.36
19	France	58.69	19	Taiwan, China	46.77	19	Malaysia	18.88
20	Korea	58.15	20	Saudi Arabia	44.80	20	France	18.83

(Continued)

(Continued)

Entrepreneurs			Personal competence of entrepreneurs			Social context of entrepreneurs		
Rank	Region	Index	Rank	Region	Index	Rank	Region	Index
21	Saudi Arabia	57.33	21	Czech Republic	44.31	21	Oman	18.61
22	Chile	57.26	22	United Kingdom	44.21	22	Thailand	18.34
23	China	53.01	23	Hungary	44.07	23	Germany	17.65
24	Slovenia	51.39	24	Slovenia	43.94	24	Canada	17.48
25	Czech Republic	51.29	25	France	43.80	25	Panama	16.12
26	Poland	49.39	26	Italy	41.28	26	Croatia	15.96
27	Kuwait	48.81	27	Spain	41.15	27	Spain	15.88
28	Italy	48.33	28	Greece	40.07	28	Kuwait	15.57
29	Malaysia	47.78	29	Malaysia	38.84	29	Ukraine	14.92
30	Hungary	45.94	30	Kuwait	38.79	30	Poland	14.47
31	Japan	45.23	31	Poland	38.27	31	Jordan	14.41
32	Colombia	44.91	32	Slovak Republic	37.67	32	Greece	14.37
33	Dominican Republic	44.40	33	Croatia	35.74	33	Israel	13.72
34	Panama	43.69	34	Russia	34.51	34	Italy	13.14
35	Jordan	43.44	35	China	33.50	35	Korea	12.65
36	Thailand	42.55	36	Thailand	33.43	36	Morocco	12.57
37	Greece	41.77	37	Oman	32.68	37	Australia	12.55
38	Vietnam	41.08	38	Panama	32.17	38	New Zealand	11.69
39	Slovak Republic	40.74	39	Chile	31.91	39	South Africa	11.51
40	Indonesia	39.96	40	Morocco	29.65	40	Japan	11.42
41	Spain	39.93	41	Mexico	28.39	41	Chile	11.16
42	Turkey	39.57	42	South Africa	28.13	42	Mexico	10.79
43	India	39.40	43	Turkey	27.88	43	Philippines	10.43

(Continued)

(Continued)

Entrepreneurs			Personal competence of entrepreneurs			Social context of entrepreneurs		
Rank	Region	Index	Rank	Region	Index	Rank	Region	Index
44	Philippines	38.49	44	Philippines	27.85	44	Saudi Arabia	10.39
45	Mexico	37.71	45	Brazil	27.81	45	United States	9.86
46	Oman	37.17	46	Dominican Republic	27.74	46	Dominican Republic	9.15
47	Peru	37.08	47	Jordan	27.73	47	Egypt	8.80
48	Russia	35.72	48	Colombia	27.66	48	Peru	8.12
49	Egypt	35.11	49	Vietnam	26.22	49	Russia	7.95
50	South Africa	33.52	50	India	25.23	50	Turkey	7.83
51	Nigeria	33.25	51	Indonesia	24.10	51	Colombia	7.73
52	Ukraine	32.35	52	Peru	23.96	52	Sri Lanka	7.67
53	Croatia	29.72	53	Sri Lanka	23.38	53	India	6.54
54	Argentina	28.66	54	Cambodia	23.02	54	Indonesia	6.39
55	Brazil	27.56	55	Guatemala	22.30	55	Guatemala	6.32
56	Morocco	26.29	56	Ukraine	21.77	56	Kenya	5.71
57	Guatemala	25.14	57	Nigeria	21.75	57	Brazil	5.62
58	Bangladesh	22.41	58	Bangladesh	21.74	58	China	5.52
59	Kenya	21.49	59	Kenya	21.23	59	Argentina	5.09
60	Pakistan	21.06	60	Egypt	19.58	60	Nigeria	5.07
61	Cambodia	19.47	61	Pakistan	18.95	61	Bangladesh	4.62
62	Sri Lanka	17.31	62	Argentina	18.35	62	Pakistan	3.79

Note: The top five countries for *Entrepreneurs* are the United States, Sweden, Denmark, Finland, and Canada. The strength of the United States in the sub-factor *Personal Competence of Entrepreneurs*, has particularly contributed to its high competitiveness in *Entrepreneurs*. Canada was also listed in the top five, due to its strength in *Personal Competence of Entrepreneurs* despite its relative weakness in *Social Context of Entrepreneurs*. The sub-factor, *Personal Competence of Entrepreneurs*, is measured by the process of decision making, entrepreneur's core competence, education level, and international experience. *Social Context of Entrepreneurs* consists of criteria such as availability of entrepreneurs, support of the social system, openness to foreign entrepreneurs, new business development, and social status of entrepreneurs.

World Rankings: Professionals

Professionals			Personal competence of professionals			Social context of entrepreneurs		
Rank	Region	Index	Rank	Region	Index	Rank	Region	Index
1	Denmark	86.28	1	United States	59.62	1	Hong Kong SAR	79.78
2	Sweden	83.54	2	Singapore	55.26	2	Singapore	71.79
3	Netherlands	83.01	3	Hong Kong SAR	54.69	3	Netherlands	45.91
4	Switzerland	82.37	4	Switzerland	53.49	4	U.A.E.	34.11
5	Singapore	80.89	5	Denmark	52.38	5	Belgium	33.94
6	Canada	76.19	6	Sweden	51.86	6	Switzerland	30.46
7	United States	75.15	7	Austria	51.02	7	Denmark	26.68
8	Australia	75.03	8	Korea	50.04	8	Vietnam	25.51
9	Belgium	74.92	9	Finland	49.64	9	Cambodia	25.35
10	Hong Kong SAR	74.57	10	U.A.E.	49.37	10	Hungary	23.55
11	Finland	74.33	11	Australia	48.63	11	Sweden	23.13
12	China	73.23	12	Japan	48.58	12	Slovak Republic	22.98
13	New Zealand	72.91	13	New Zealand	48.49	13	Slovenia	22.46
14	India	71.42	14	Germany	48.44	14	Finland	22.14
15	Germany	67.63	15	Israel	48.14	15	Austria	21.74
16	U.A.E.	67.40	16	Netherlands	47.88	16	United Kingdom	21.24
17	Austria	67.04	17	Canada	47.04	17	Czech Republic	21.17
18	Philippines	64.91	18	Belgium	46.98	18	Taiwan, China	19.36
19	Korea	64.54	19	Taiwan, China	46.77	19	Malaysia	18.88
20	Thailand	62.47	20	Saudi Arabia	44.80	20	France	18.83

(Continued)

(*Continued*)

Professionals			Personal competence of professionals			Social context of entrepreneurs		
Rank	Region	Index	Rank	Region	Index	Rank	Region	Index
21	Taiwan, China	62.16	21	Czech Republic	44.31	21	Oman	18.61
22	Malaysia	62.01	22	United Kingdom	44.21	22	Thailand	18.34
23	Saudi Arabia	59.42	23	Hungary	44.07	23	Germany	17.65
24	Poland	58.19	24	Slovenia	43.94	24	Canada	17.48
25	Indonesia	57.95	25	France	43.80	25	Panama	16.12
26	Italy	57.06	26	Italy	41.28	26	Croatia	15.96
27	Nigeria	57.02	27	Spain	41.15	27	Spain	15.88
28	Hungary	56.32	28	Greece	40.07	28	Kuwait	15.57
29	Dominican Republic	56.10	29	Malaysia	38.84	29	Ukraine	14.92
30	Israel	55.13	30	Kuwait	38.79	30	Poland	14.47
31	Czech Republic	54.12	31	Poland	38.27	31	Jordan	14.41
32	Jordan	53.04	32	Slovak Republic	37.67	32	Greece	14.37
33	Bangladesh	52.49	33	Croatia	35.74	33	Israel	13.72
34	Vietnam	52.16	34	Russia	34.51	34	Italy	13.14
35	Greece	51.79	35	China	33.50	35	Korea	12.65
36	Colombia	51.34	36	Thailand	33.43	36	Morocco	12.57
37	United Kingdom	50.55	37	Oman	32.68	37	Australia	12.55
38	Kuwait	50.33	38	Panama	32.17	38	New Zealand	11.69
39	Turkey	48.41	39	Chile	31.91	39	South Africa	11.51
40	Panama	47.88	40	Morocco	29.65	40	Japan	11.42
41	Slovenia	47.45	41	Mexico	28.39	41	Chile	11.16
42	Russia	46.30	42	South Africa	28.13	42	Mexico	10.79

(*Continued*)

(*Continued*)

Professionals			Personal competence of professionals			Social context of entrepreneurs		
Rank	Region	Index	Rank	Region	Index	Rank	Region	Index
43	Mexico	45.95	43	Turkey	27.88	43	Philippines	10.43
44	Egypt	45.22	44	Philippines	27.85	44	Saudi Arabia	10.39
45	Japan	45.09	45	Brazil	27.81	45	United States	9.86
46	Ukraine	44.92	46	Dominican Republic	27.74	46	Dominican Republic	9.15
47	Chile	43.66	47	Jordan	27.73	47	Egypt	8.80
48	France	43.61	48	Colombia	27.66	48	Peru	8.12
49	South Africa	42.81	49	Vietnam	26.22	49	Russia	7.95
50	Slovak Republic	42.05	50	India	25.23	50	Turkey	7.83
51	Argentina	40.82	51	Indonesia	24.10	51	Colombia	7.73
52	Spain	37.68	52	Peru	23.96	52	Sri Lanka	7.67
53	Croatia	36.46	53	Sri Lanka	23.38	53	India	6.54
54	Guatemala	36.41	54	Cambodia	23.02	54	Indonesia	6.39
55	Cambodia	35.98	55	Guatemala	22.30	55	Guatemala	6.32
56	Morocco	35.62	56	Ukraine	21.77	56	Kenya	5.71
57	Brazil	34.14	57	Nigeria	21.75	57	Brazil	5.62
58	Peru	33.37	58	Bangladesh	21.74	58	China	5.52
59	Pakistan	32.23	59	Kenya	21.23	59	Argentina	5.09
60	Sri Lanka	31.56	60	Egypt	19.58	60	Nigeria	5.07
61	Kenya	19.22	61	Pakistan	18.95	61	Bangladesh	4.62
62	Oman	13.09	62	Argentina	18.35	62	Pakistan	3.79

Note: The top five countries in *Professionals* are Denmark, Sweden, the Netherlands, Switzerland, and Singapore. Each of these countries showed strengths in both sub-factors, *Personal Competence* and *Social Context of Professionals*. The sub-factor, *Personal Competence of Professionals*, is measured by the five survey criteria, including decision making among professionals, the ability to manage opportunities, core competences among professionals, education level, and international experiences. *Social Context of Professionals* is measured by five survey data, including availability, mobility, compensation, social status of professionals, and market openness to foreign professionals.

Appendix 2: List of Criteria of NCR 2021

Factor	Sub factor	Criteria
1. Factor Conditions	1.1. Natural Resources	1.1.1 Crude oil reserves
		1.1.2 Natural gas reserves
		1.1.3 Coal reserves
		1.1.4 Land area
		1.1.5 Freshwater resources
	1.2. Processed Resources	1.2.1 Oil production
		1.2.2 Natural gas production
		1.2.3 Coal production
		1.2.4 Wood production
		1.2.5 Livestock (processed)
2. Demand Conditions	2.1. Demand Size	2.1.1 GDP
		2.1.2 GDP per capita
		2.1.3a Goods and services: Export
		2.1.3b Goods and services: Import
	2.2. Demand Quality	2.2.1 Consumer sophistication: quality *
		2.2.2 Consumer sophistication: design *
		2.2.3 Consumer sophistication: health and environment issues *
		2.2.4 Consumer sophistication: international standard of IPR *
		2.2.5 Consumer sophistication: new technology *
3. Related Industries	3.1. Industrial Infrastructure	3.1.1 Vehicles
		3.1.2 Civil aviation
		3.1.3 Maritime transport
		3.1.4 International travel
		3.1.5 Mobile phone subscribers
		3.1.6 Internet users
		3.1.7 Capital value
		3.1.8 Capital accessibility
		3.1.9 Scientists & engineers
		3.1.10 Scientific research institutions *
		3.1.11 Total expenditure on R&D
		3.1.12 International patents granted

(Continued)

(Continued)

Factor	Sub factor	Criteria
	3.2. Living Infrastructure	3.2.1 Public spending on education
		3.2.2 Students per teacher (elementary)
		3.2.3 Secondary enrollment rate
		3.2.4 Tertiary enrollment rate
		3.2.5 Student international mobility
		3.2.6 Personal security
		3.2.7 Social safety net *
		3.2.8 Medical service
		3.2.9 GINI index
		3.2.10 HDI index
		3.2.11 CO_2 emissions
		3.2.12 Leisure, sports, and cultural facilities*
4. Business Context	4.1. Structure	4.1.1 Firm's decision process *
		4.1.2 Firm's decision structure *
		4.1.3 Unique brands *
		4.1.4 Equal treatment *
		4.1.5 Global standards *
		4.1.6 Shared value *
		4.1.7 Ethical and legal practices *
		4.1.8 Health, safety & environmental concerns *
	4.2. Rivalry	4.2.1 FDI openness (FDI inflows as % of GDP)
		4.2.2 Portfolio openness (Financial inflows as % of GDP)
		4.2.3 Goods openness (import as % of GDP)
		4.2.4 Services openness (import as % of GDP)
		4.2.6 Portfolio openness (Financial outflows as % of GDP)
		4.2.7 Goods openness (export as % of GDP)
		4.2.8 Services openness (export as % of GDP)

(Continued)

(*Continued*)

Factor	Sub factor	Criteria
5. (Unskilled) Workers	5.1. Quantity of Labor Force	5.1.1 Labor force
		5.1.2 Employment rate
		5.1.3 Working hours
		5.1.4 Monthly compensation for manufacturing workers
	5.2. Quality of Labor Force	5.2.1 Literacy rate
		5.2.2 Attitude & motivation *
		5.2.3 Education *
		5.2.4 The openness of labor market *
		5.2.5 Management labor relationships *
6. Politicians & Bureaucrats	6.1. Politician	6.1.1 The process of parliament/congress*
		6.1.2 The result of legislation*
		6.1.3 Ethics (e.g., bribery & corruption) *
		6.1.4 Education level *
		6.1.5 International experience *
	6.2. Bureaucrats	6.2.1 The process of government
		6.2.2 The result of policy implementation
		6.2.3 Ethics (Bribery & corruption)
		6.2.4 Education level *
		6.2.5 International experience *
7. Entrepreneurs	7.1. Personal Competence	7.1.1 The process of decision making *
		7.1.2 The result of decision making (e.g., the ability to seize opportunities)
		7.1.3 Entrepreneur's core competence
		7.1.4 Entrepreneur's education level
		7.1.5 Entrepreneur's international experience
	7.2. Social Context	7.2.1 Availability of entrepreneurs *
		7.2.2 New business
		7.2.3 Support of the social system *
		7.2.4 Social status of entrepreneurs
		7.2.5 Openness to foreign entrepreneurs *

(*Continued*)

(*Continued*)

Factor	Sub factor	Criteria
8. Professionals	8.1. Personal Competence	8.1.1 The process of decision making *
		8.1.2 The ability to manage opportunities *
		8.1.3 The professional's core competences *
		8.1.4 The professional's education level *
		8.1.5 The professional's international experience *
	8.2. Social Context	8.2.1 Availability of professionals *
		8.2.2 The mobility of professionals *
		8.2.3 Professional's compensation *
		8.2.4 Social status of professionals *
		8.2.5 Openness to foreign professionals *

Note: * Survey data.

350 *The Competitiveness of Nations 1*

Appendix 3: Sources and Notes

Factor conditions	

1.1.1   Crude oil reserves
U.S. Energy Information Administration
https://www.eia.gov/international/data/world
World Development Indicators
The World Bank Group, https://databank.worldbank.org/reports.
    aspx?source=world-development-indicators

1.1.2   Natural gas reserves
U.S. Energy Information Administration
https://www.eia.gov/international/data/world
World Development Indicators
The World Bank Group, https://databank.worldbank.org/reports.
    aspx?source=world-development-indicators

1.1.3   Coal reserves
U.S. Energy Information Administration
https://www.eia.gov/international/data/world
World Development Indicators
The World Bank Group, https://databank.worldbank.org/reports.
    aspx?source=world-development-indicators

1.1.4   Land area
World Development Indicators
The World Bank Group, https://databank.worldbank.org/reports.
    aspx?source=world-development-indicators
Taiwan Statistical Data Book 2019, National Development Council,
    Republic of China (Taiwan), https://www.ndc.gov.tw/en/News.aspx?n=
    607ED34345641980&sms=B8A915763E3684AC

1.1.5   Freshwater resources
World Development Indicators
The World Bank Group, https://databank.worldbank.org/reports.
    aspx?source=world-development-indicators
FAO AQUASTAT
Food and Agriculture Organization of the United Nations, http://www.
    fao.org/aquastat/en/

1.2.1   Oil production
World Oil Review 2020
https://www.eni.com/assets/documents/eng/scenari-energetici/WORLD-
    OIL-REVIEW-2020-vol1.pdf
Global Energy Statistical Yearbook 2020
https://yearbook.enerdata.net/crude-oil/world-production-statitistics.html

(Continued)

1.2.2	Natural gas production U.S. Energy Information Administration https://www.eia.gov/international/data/world World Gas and Renewables Review 2020 https://www.eni.com/assets/documents/eng/scenari-energetici/WORLD-GAS-AND-RENEWABLES-REVIEW-2020-vol2.pdf
1.2.3	Coal production U.S. Energy Information Administration https://www.eia.gov/international/data/world
1.2.4	Wood production FAOSTAT Database Food and Agriculture Organization of the United Nations, http://www.fao.org * It is the sum of roundwood and sawnwood production in cubic meters.
1.2.5	Livestock FAOSTAT Database Food and Agriculture Organization of the United Nations, http://www.fao.org * The livestock includes butter and ghee, sheep milk butter, buffalo milk butter, cow milk butter, goat milk cheese, buffalo milk cheese, goat milk cheese, sheep milk cheese, skimmed cow milk cheese, whole cow milk cream fresh ghee, buffalo milk ghee, butteroil of cow milk lard milk, dry buttermilk milk, skimmed condensed milk, skimmed cow milk, skimmed dried milk, skimmed evaporated milk, whole condensed milk, whole dried milk, whole evaporated silk, raw tallow whey, condensed whey, dry yoghurt.

Demand conditions

2.1.1	GDP World Development Indicators The World Bank Group, https://databank.worldbank.org/reports.aspx?source=world-development-indicators Taiwan Statistical Data Book 2019, National Development Council, Republic of China (Taiwan), https://www.ndc.gov.tw/en/News.aspx?n=607ED34345641980&sms=B8A915763E3684AC National Statistics, Republic of China (Taiwan) https://eng.stat.gov.tw/mp.asp?mp=5
2.1.2	GDP per capita World Development Indicators

(Continued)

	The World Bank Group, https://databank.worldbank.org/reports.aspx?source=world-development-indicators Taiwan Statistical Data Book 2019, National Development Council, Republic of China (Taiwan), https://www.ndc.gov.tw/en/News.aspx?n=607ED34345641980&sms=B8A915763E3684AC National Statistics, Republic of China (Taiwan) https://eng.stat.gov.tw/mp.asp?mp=5
2.1.3	Goods and services: Export World Development Indicators The World Bank Group, https://databank.worldbank.org/reports.aspx?source=world-development-indicators Taiwan Statistical Data Book 2019, National Development Council, Republic of China (Taiwan), https://www.ndc.gov.tw/en/News.aspx?n=607ED34345641980&sms=B8A915763E3684AC National Statistics, Republic of China (Taiwan) https://eng.stat.gov.tw/mp.asp?mp=5
2.1.4	Goods and services: Import World Development Indicators The World Bank Group, https://databank.worldbank.org/reports.aspx?source=world-development-indicators Taiwan Statistical Data Book 2019, National Development Council, Republic of China (Taiwan), https://www.ndc.gov.tw/en/News.aspx?n=607ED34345641980&sms=B8A915763E3684AC National Statistics, Republic of China (Taiwan) https://eng.stat.gov.tw/mp.asp?mp=5

Related industries

3.1.1	Vehicles International Organization of Motor Vehicle Manufacturers http://www.oica.net/category/vehicles-in-use/ The European Automobile Manufacturers' Association (ACEA) https://www.acea.be/statistics/tag/category/vehicles-per-capita-by-country
3.1.2	Civil aviation World Development Indicators The World Bank Group, https://databank.worldbank.org/reports.aspx?source=world-development-indicators Statistical Yearbook of the Republic of China 2019, National Statistics Republic of China (Taiwan) https://eng.stat.gov.tw/lp.asp?CtNode=6340&CtUnit=1072&BaseDSD=36&mp=5

(Continued)

(Continued)

3.1.3	Maritime transport
	World Development Indicators
	The World Bank Group, https://databank.worldbank.org/reports. aspx?source=world-development-indicators
3.1.4	International travel
	World Development Indicators
	The World Bank Group, https://databank.worldbank.org/reports. aspx?source=world-development-indicators
	Statistical Yearbook of the Republic of China 2019, National Statistics Republic of China (Taiwan)
	https://eng.stat.gov.tw/lp.asp?CtNode=6340&CtUnit=1072&BaseDSD=3 6&mp=5
	* International travel includes the number of both arrivals and departures.
3.1.5	Mobile phone subscribers
	World Development Indicators
	The World Bank Group, https://databank.worldbank.org/reports. aspx?source=world-development-indicators
	Statistical Yearbook of the Republic of China 2019, National Statistics Republic of China (Taiwan)
	https://eng.stat.gov.tw/lp.asp?CtNode=6340&CtUnit=1072&BaseDSD=3 6&mp=5
3.1.6	Internet users
	World Development Indicators
	The World Bank Group, https://databank.worldbank.org/reports. aspx?source=world-development-indicators
	Statistical Yearbook of the Republic of China 2019, National Statistics Republic of China (Taiwan)
	https://eng.stat.gov.tw/lp.asp?CtNode=6340&CtUnit=1072&BaseDSD=3 6&mp=5
3.1.7	Capital value
	World Development Indicators
	The World Bank Group, https://databank.worldbank.org/reports. aspx?source=world-development-indicators
	Taiwan Statistical Data Book 2019, National Development Council, Republic of China (Taiwan), https://www.ndc.gov.tw/en/News.aspx?n= 607ED34345641980&sms=B8A915763E3684AC
3.1.8	Capital accessibility
	World Development Indicators

(Continued)

(Continued)

	The World Bank Group, https://databank.worldbank.org/reports.aspx?source=world-development-indicators https://data.imf.org/regular.aspx?key=61545855 Statistical Yearbook of the Republic of China 2019, National Statistics Republic of China (Taiwan) https://eng.stat.gov.tw/lp.asp?CtNode=6340&CtUnit=1072&BaseDSD=36&mp=5
3.1.9	Scientists & engineers Statistics of Science & Technology Institute for Statistics, UNESCO, http://stats.uis.unesco.org Taiwan Statistical Data Book 2019, National Development Council, Republic of China (Taiwan), https://www.ndc.gov.tw/en/News.aspx?n=607ED34345641980&sms=B8A915763E3684AC
3.1.11	Total expenditure on R&D Statistics of Science & Technology Institute for Statistics, UNESCO, http://stats.uis.unesco.org Statistical Yearbook of the Republic of China 2019, National Statistics Republic of China (Taiwan) https://eng.stat.gov.tw/lp.asp?CtNode=6340&CtUnit=1072&BaseDSD=36&mp=5
3.1.12	International patents granted Patents issued by the United States to residents of foreign countries FY 2019 USPTO performance and Accountability Report, https://www.uspto.gov/sites/default/files/documents/USPTOFY19PAR.pdf
3.2.1	Public spending on education Statistics of Education Institute for Statistics, UNESCO, http://stats.uis.unesco.org Taiwan Statistical Data Book 2019, National Development Council, Republic of China (Taiwan), https://www.ndc.gov.tw/en/News.aspx?n=607ED34345641980&sms=B8A915763E3684AC
3.2.2	Students per teacher (elementary) Statistics of Education Institute for Statistics, UNESCO, http://stats.uis.unesco.org Taiwan Statistical Data Book 2019, National Development Council, Republic of China (Taiwan), https://www.ndc.gov.tw/en/News.aspx?n=607ED34345641980&sms=B8A915763E3684AC

(Continued)

(Continued)

3.2.3	Secondary enrollment rate
	Statistics of Education
	Institute for Statistics, UNESCO, http://stats.uis.unesco.org
	Taiwan Statistical Data Book 2019, National Development Council, Republic of China (Taiwan), https://www.ndc.gov.tw/en/News.aspx?n=607ED34345641980&sms=B8A915763E3684AC
3.2.4	Tertiary enrollment rate
	Statistics of Education
	Institute for Statistics, UNESCO, http://stats.uis.unesco.org
	Taiwan Statistical Data Book 2019, National Development Council, Republic of China (Taiwan), https://www.ndc.gov.tw/en/News.aspx?n=607ED34345641980&sms=B8A915763E3684AC
3.2.5	Student international mobility
	Statistics of Education
	Institute for Statistics, UNESCO, http://stats.uis.unesco.org
	* It is average of inbound and outbound tertiary students as % of tertiary enrollment.
3.2.6	Personal security
	NUMBEO Quality of Life Index, https://www.numbeo.com/quality-of-life/rankings_by_country.jsp?title=2020
3.2.8	Medical service
	NUMBEO Quality of Life Index, https://www.numbeo.com/quality-of-life/rankings_by_country.jsp?title=2020
3.2.9	Gini index
	World Development Indicators
	The World Bank Group, https://databank.worldbank.org/reports.aspx?source=world-development-indicators
	Organization for Economic Co-operation and Development (OECD) Statistic
	https://stats.oecd.org/index.aspx?Datasetcode=IDD
	CIA Factbook
	https://www.cia.gov/library/publications/the-world-factbook/
	Statistical Yearbook of the Republic of China 2019, National Statistics Republic of China (Taiwan)
	https://eng.stat.gov.tw/lp.asp?CtNode=6340&CtUnit=1072&BaseDSD=36&mp=5

(Continued)

(*Continued*)

3.2.10	HDI index UNDP Human Development Reports http://hdr.undp.org/en/data http://hdr.undp.org/sites/default/files/hdr2020.pdf
3.2.11	CO_2 emission International Energy Agency https://www.iea.org/subscribe-to-data-services/co2-emissions-statistics

Business context

4.2.1 FDI inflows (% of GDP)
UNCTAD Foreign Direct Investment database
http://stats.unctad.org/FDI/

4.2.2 Financial inflows (% of GDP)
International Monetary Fund (IMF) Statistics, http://data.imf.org/regular.
   aspx?key=62805744

4.2.3 Goods import (% of GDP)
World Development Indicators
The World Bank Group, https://databank.worldbank.org/reports.
   aspx?source=world-development-indicators
Taiwan Statistical Data Book 2019, National Development Council, Republic of
   China (Taiwan), https://www.ndc.gov.tw/en/News.aspx?n=607ED3434564198
   0&sms=B8A915763E3684AC

4.2.4 Services import (% of GDP)
World Development Indicators
The World Bank Group, https://databank.worldbank.org/reports.
   aspx?source=world-development-indicators
Taiwan Statistical Data Book 2019, National Development Council, Republic of
   China (Taiwan), https://www.ndc.gov.tw/en/News.aspx?n=607ED3434564198
   0&sms=B8A915763E3684AC

4.2.5 FDI outflows (% of GDP)
UNCTAD Foreign Direct Investment database
http://stats.unctad.org/FDI/

4.2.6 Financial outflows (% of GDP)
International Monetary Fund (IMF) Statistics, http://data.imf.org/regular.
   aspx?key=62805744

(*Continued*)

(Continued)

4.2.7   Goods export (% of GDP)
World Development Indicators
The World Bank Group, https://databank.worldbank.org/reports.
   aspx?source=world-development-indicators
Taiwan Statistical Data Book 2019, National Development Council, Republic of
   China (Taiwan), https://www.ndc.gov.tw/en/News.aspx?n=607ED3434564198
   0&sms=B8A915763E3684AC

4.2.8   Services export (% of GDP)
World Development Indicators
The World Bank Group, https://databank.worldbank.org/reports.
   aspx?source=world-development-indicators
Taiwan Statistical Data Book 2019, National Development Council, Republic of
   China (Taiwan), https://www.ndc.gov.tw/en/News.aspx?n=607ED3434564198
   0&sms=B8A915763E3684AC

Workers

5.1.1   Labor force
World Development Indicators
The World Bank Group, https://databank.worldbank.org/reports.
   aspx?source=world-development-indicators
Taiwan Statistical Data Book 2019, National Development Council, Republic of
   China (Taiwan), https://www.ndc.gov.tw/en/News.aspx?n=607ED3434564198
   0&sms=B8A915763E3684AC

5.1.2   Employment rate
World Development Indicators
The World Bank Group, https://databank.worldbank.org/reports.
   aspx?source=world-development-indicators
Taiwan Statistical Data Book 2019, National Development Council, Republic of
   China (Taiwan), https://www.ndc.gov.tw/en/News.aspx?n=607ED3434564198
   0&sms=B8A915763E3684AC

5.1.3   Working hours
LABORSTA
International Labor Organization, http://laborsta.ilo.org
OECD Data,
https://data.oecd.org/emp/hours-worked.htm

5.1.4   Monthly compensation for manufacturing workers
LABORSTA
International Labor Organization, http://laborsta.ilo.org

(Continued)

(*Continued*)

5.2.1	Literacy rate
	World Development Indicators
	The World Bank Group, https://databank.worldbank.org/reports.
	aspx?source=world-development-indicators
	Macrotrends, https://www.macrotrends.net/

Policymakers & Administrators

6.2.1	The process of government: Government effectiveness
	Worldwide Governance Indicators
	World Bank, https://info.worldbank.org/governance/wgi/
6.2.2	The result of policy implementation: Regulatory quality
	Worldwide Governance Indicators
	World Bank, https://info.worldbank.org/governance/wgi/
6.2.3	Ethics (Bribery & corruption)
	Worldwide Governance Indicators
	World Bank, https://info.worldbank.org/governance/wgi/

Entrepreneurs

7.1.2	The result of decision making: Opportunity perception
	Global Entrepreneurship Index Data
	https://thegedi.org/2019-global-entrepreneurship-index/
7.1.3	Entrepreneur's core competence: Networking
	Global Entrepreneurship Index Data
	https://thegedi.org/2019-global-entrepreneurship-index/
7.1.4	Entrepreneur's education level: Human capital
	Global Entrepreneurship Index Data
	https://thegedi.org/2019-global-entrepreneurship-index/
7.1.5	Entrepreneur's international experience: Internationalization
	Global Entrepreneurship Index Data
	https://thegedi.org/2019-global-entrepreneurship-index/
7.2.2	New business: Ease of Doing Business
	World Bank, https://www.doingbusiness.org/en/rankings
7.2.4	Social status of entrepreneurs: Cultural support
	Global Entrepreneurship Index Data
	https://thegedi.org/2019-global-entrepreneurship-index/

Index

Printed in the United States
by Baker & Taylor Publisher Services